A TEACHER'S
GUIDE TO MANAGEMENT OF
PHYSICALLY HANDICAPPED STUDENTS

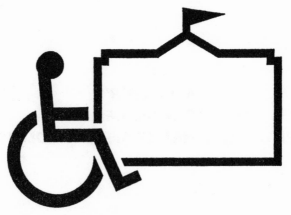

The international sign indicating accessibility to wheelchairs, and a sign for school.

A Teacher's Guide to Management of Physically Handicapped Students

By

JUNE B. MULLINS, Ph.D.

Associate Professor
School of Education
Division of Specialized Professional Development
Program in Special Education
University of Pittsburgh
Pittsburgh, Pennsylvania

CHARLES C THOMAS · PUBLISHER
Springfield · Illinois · U.S.A.

Published and Distributed Throughout the World by
CHARLES C THOMAS • PUBLISHER
Bannerstone House
301-327 East Lawrence Avenue, Springfield, Illinois, U.S.A.

© *1979, by* CHARLES C THOMAS • PUBLISHER
ISBN 0-398-03818-X
Library of Congress Catalog Card Number: 78-9629

With THOMAS BOOKS careful attention is given to all details of manufacturing and design. It is the Publisher's desire to present books that are satisfactory as to their physical qualities and artistic possibilities and appropriate for their particular use. THOMAS BOOKS will be true to those laws of quality that assure a good name and good will.

Library of Congress Cataloging in Publication Data

Mullins, June.
A teacher's guide to management of physically
handicapped students.

Bibliography: p.
Includes index.
1. Physically handicapped children—Education—
Handbooks, manuals, etc. I. Title.
LC4515.M84   371.9'1   78-9629
ISBN 0-398-03818-X

Printed in the United States of America
C-1

ACKNOWLEDGMENTS

THE FIRST DRAFT of the book was written while I was in Australia on sabbatical leave from the University of Pittsburgh. I am most indebted to the School of Education of the University of Pittsburgh for enabling me to have this fine opportunity.

The book is organized with an introductory section, and later sections and chapters dealing with commonly understood categories of diseases and disorders. Doctor Godfrey Stevens contributed to precision in the terminology of the title and headings.

Aspects of normal development and functioning are explained briefly in the appropriate chapters and related to the specific diseases and impairments covered. This was done in the belief that teachers need to have knowledge and understanding of the etiology of physical handicaps and rationale for treatment procedures. Then they will be less frightened and dismayed about these problems, some of which are surrounded by myths and misconceptions.

The various chapters were sent for peer review to colleagues who had particular interest and knowledge in the different areas. I am most grateful to these people who gave very thoughtful and critical input on specific chapters. These experts are listed below and credited with the chapters they so kindly reviewed:

Lee Bass, M.D.	Children's Hospital Pittsburgh, Pa.	Chapter 13
Barbara Bazron, Ph.D.	Dir., Special Education Region 5, New Jersey	Chapter 22
Milton Bilder, M.D.	Shady Side Hospital Pittsburgh, Pa.	Chapter 6
Becky Carson, M.Ed.	Allegheny County Intermediate Unit Pittsburgh, Pa.	Chapter 17
Robert Chubon, M.Ed.	Rehabilitation Counseling University of Pittsburgh	Chapter 10
Dvenna Duncan, Ph.D.	Special Education University of Pittsburgh	Chapter 24

Alex J. Ducanis, D.Ed.	Division of Specialized Professional Development University of Pittsburgh	Chapter 3
Lynda Katz Garris, Ph.D.	Western Psychiatric Institute Pittsburgh, Pa.	Chapter 14
Kenneth Garver, M.D., Ph.D.	Magee-Women's Hospital Pittsburgh, Pa.	Chapter 4
Doris Hamilton, M.S., P.T.	United Cerebral Palsy Pittsburgh, Pa.	Chapters 11 & 12
Lonnie Jenkins, M.D.	Decatur, Georgia	Chapter 22
Sharon Maloney, R.N., M.S.	Boston, Mass.	Chapter 18
Betty Jane McWilliams, Ph.D.	Cleft Palate Center University of Pittsburgh	Chapter 7
William W. Mullins, Jr., M.D.	University of Minnesota Minneapolis, Minn.	Chapters 8, 15, 16, & 23
Joseph Novak, M.D.	St. Francis Hospital Pittsburgh, Pa.	Chapter 5
Ralph Peabody, Ed.D.	Special Education University of Pittsburgh	Chapter 25
Marie Renvers, R.N., M.Ed.	Children's Hospital Pittsburgh, Pa.	Chapter 9
John B. Reinhart, M.D.	Division of Behavioral Sciences Children's Hospital Pittsburgh, Pa.	Chapters 19 & 20
Betsy Sacks, M.S.W.	Children's Hospital Pittsburgh, Pa.	Chapter 21
Earl B. Young, Ph.D.	Special Education University of Pittsburgh	Chapter 14
Sydney Wolff, Ph.D.	Special Education University of Pittsburgh	Chapter 26

Students and staff at the Home for Crippled Children, The Regional Comprehensive Rehabilitation Center for Children and Youth, Pittsburgh, Pennsylvania, were helpful as consultants and models for the illustrations. Miriam Bisdee and I are very appreciative of their input. Also, my many experiences in this agency have contributed much to knowledge and insights contained in the text. Of particular assistance were the following staff members of the Home:

William R. Bauer, M.Ed.	Director of Education
Anna J. Chorazy, M.D.	Chief, Medical Staff
Helen C. Paytok, R.N., R.P.T.	Senior Program Coordinator for cerebral palsied children
Mary E. Petruska	Secretary
Mary G. Reisler, M.S.	Senior Program Coordinator for children with physical disabilities
Leo A. Urbanowicz, B.A.	Director of Public Relations
Beate Vogl, M.Ed.	Senior Program Coordinator for children with learning disabilities

The typing of this manuscript was a large task. Dale Drummond of Melbourne, Australia nobly struggled with the handwritten first draft. Later preparation was shared by Nancy Blatnica, Felicia Belles, Evelyn Curry, Irene Petrovich, and Margie Vargo. I am most grateful to them for their fine efforts. Also, I am indebted to David H. Elder for the cover symbol and various figures, charts, and schematic drawings that appear throughout the book.

I owe special thanks to Miriam Bisdee for her sensitive drawings, particularly those of actual children. These drawings underscore the purpose of the book: to address the physical and health care needs, in an educational context, of growing, developing, young people who happen to have a physical handicap.

My husband, William Wilson Mullins, has my deep gratitude for his good advice and constant encouragement.

My baby has not lived in vain—
this life has been to him what it is to all
of us, education and development.

SAMUEL TAYLOR COLERIDGE
Letter to Thomas Poole
April, 1799

CONTENTS

A TEACHER'S
GUIDE TO MANAGEMENT OF
PHYSICALLY HANDICAPPED STUDENTS

Section I

ORIENTATION

In mainstream and special education there is renewed interest in placing physically or health handicapped students in educational settings on the basis of learning needs rather than on the basis of disabilities or diseases. Therefore, more teachers can expect to have students in their classes who have special medical and physical management requirements. This book is designed to fill a perceived gap between the excellent texts concerned with educational assessment, prescription, clinical teaching, and behaviour management and those equally fine, medically oriented texts that describe disease entities. Here, physical handicapping conditions and health problems are discussed from the viewpoint of the school. Special conditions are described so that the teacher can understand the problems that confront the student and the management strategies that are implied in the classroom setting. Considerable attention is paid to the psychological environment as well as the physical environment that the teacher and classmates provide. Teaching techniques, as opposed to management techniques, are discussed only when they seem to relate rather uniquely to physically and health handicapped pupils. An extensive appendix furnishes some very specific information that might be helpful to the school staff, parents, and students.

3

Chapter 1

A PHILOSOPHICAL FRAMEWORK

All nature is but art, unknown to thee
All chance, direction which thou canst not see
All discord, harmony not understood
                                        Alexander Pope

   The whiteness of a man's teeth primarily
   belongs not to him, but to them.
                                        St. Thomas Aquinas

FOR THOSE TEACHERS who plan to include handicapped pupils
in their regular classes, as well as those who have chosen to
work in special settings with exceptional children, a number of
helpful concepts have grown out of work in many areas of study
and from a number of theoretical viewpoints. It is hoped that the
following discussion will give the reader a helpful philosophical
framework in which to think about problems and issues concerning handicapped people.

THE CONCEPT OF NORMALITY

   The concepts of normality and health are not absolute and precise as they are generally used in society. Whether an individual
is considered to be normal or average can only be decided with
immediate reference to such variables as age, sex, population
group, race, and culture. For example, the complete helplessness
of the newborn baby and infirmity of the very old are not considered abnormal, but the same conditions in a young adult are
deemed to be severely incapacitating. We expect different physical attributes and some different physical abilities between males
and females. When the normal physical or behavioral attributes
of one sex are displayed markedly in the other sex, the individual

5

may well be considered to some degree abnormal. Rather common examples of this are the condition of developed breasts on a man, or an extremely tall woman.

Again, population group or racial differences are marked, and variations that might be far from average for one group might be normal for another. For example, an individual who might seem very short by Anglo-American standards might be quite average by standards of a Spanish-American group. Finally, cultural and ethical considerations greatly influence what human variations, natural or created, are considered normal.

Physical variations are also socially valued, or devalued, and often are given a moral or religious connotation. For example, in some tribal cultures the tallest men are given leadership roles. In some New Guinea societies obesity is considered beautiful. In America there are fashions in standards of beauty and behavior. An idolized movie star with a very distinctive profile creates a new ideal, whereas previously someone in her situation might have had a "nose job."

Culturally determined physical alterations or maiming have been practiced throughout the world. In recent history of the western world, boys were castrated to preserve their high voices (castrada) or to be eunuchs serving in women's quarters. Dickens describes the crippling of children to serve as beggars. The Chinese have only in the present generation abandoned the practice of foot binding of girls.

The culturally sanctioned alterations most widely observed in America are the practices of circumcision (a religious rite in Judaism), ear piercing, and tattooing. These practices are here termed cultural to distinguish them from common, more therapeutic interventions such as straightening of teeth, removal of skin blemishes, or operating on crossed eyes.

Even standards of health change. If a woman today "swooned" as often as did Victorian or ante bellum heroines, as described in literature, we would probably consider her quite sickly. In the same vein, a generation ago a middle-class American woman might be confined to bed in a hospital for two weeks after the normal delivery of a baby. Current medical practice reduces this time to a few days.

In sum, when we talk about physical normality and health, we should remember that expectations are influenced by a person's age, sex, population or racial group, and culture. Standards and values pertaining to physical differences, whether caused naturally or deliberately, vary enormously among ethnic, religious, and cultural groups. Thus the physical attributes of any person will be seen by that individual and persons surrounding him or her in terms of these relative expectations and values.

THE STATISTICAL MEANING OF AVERAGE

For the statistician there is a rather precise definition of the *average,* which is sometimes very useful to the educator, psychologist, or physician. The statistician is always concerned with measurement of physical attribute, characteristic, or behavior that can be systematically observed in a number of cases (or subjects) or in one case measured through time. The various values in these observations can be measured along some numbered continuum. The statistician will make a large enough number of observations to ensure that there is a representative sample from which to make comparisons and generalizations.

Any set of measured values of a selected attribute or behavior can be graphically arranged in a frequency plot or histogram as shown in Figure 1A.

In this plot the continuous range of possible values of the attribute is divided into a number of suitably chosen equal intervals, represented by the horizontal widths of the bars; the number of cases of individuals with attributes falling in the range of a given bar is then indicated by the height of that bar. For example, Figure 1A, which plots the heights of a representative number of students in a certain school, shows that there are more students in the interval of 5 feet 7 inches to 5 feet 8 inches than in any other interval.

For many purposes, the entire set of data can be satisfactorily represented by two numbers mathematically calculated from the measured values or individual attributes or behaviors to obtain (1) the average or *mean* value, which essentially locates a center of the distribution, and (2) the *standard deviation,* which is a measure of the spread or variability of the distribution from the average. In Figure 1A, the average is 5 feet 7½ inches, shown as a dotted vertical line, and the standard deviation is 3 inches, indicated by the horizontal double arrow. It is clear that nearly all values of the distribution are within a few standard deviations of the average.

A further simplification in the description of a set of data (attribute values) occurs in many practical cases in which the shape of the histogram plot is satisfactorily described by the so-called *normal curve* or normal distribution; this curve is shown in Figure 1B superimposed on the corresponding histogram. Qualitatively, normal distribution shows that most values lie in the central hump, with a few values in the wings or extremes deviating markedly up or down from the mean or average. The hypothetical normal curve is shown in Figure 1C.

If a distribution is essentially normal, very precise statements can be made about frequencies of various attribute values from a knowledge of the average and the standard deviation alone. Thus the relative proportions of the frequencies in each standard deviation interval from the average are expected and therefore can be predicted. The extremes in variability of any measured attribute or behavior are natural because they will almost always occur and occur with a predictable frequency. The hypothetical example can be made more realistic. Suppose the carpenter in a junior college has been asked to build a deep, covered shelf above a counter in the art room in which the students can keep their supplies. The carpenter wants to know where the shelf should be placed for convenient access to most of the students. He might decide to check the height of a sample of the students to determine how high the shelf should be to allow the students to see materials in the back and comfortably reach them. He will plan to place the shelf at the eye level corresponding to the average height of the students. To decide the height of the shelf, he could call in a random sample of students from the college to see how tall they are on the average. He would be sure to include both males and females. If the college had several very different population groups, he might need to assure representatives from all of these so that his sample would not be biased.

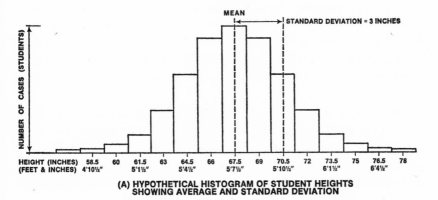

(A) HYPOTHETICAL HISTOGRAM OF STUDENT HEIGHTS SHOWING AVERAGE AND STANDARD DEVIATION

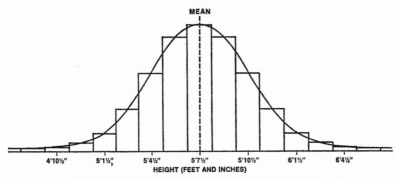

(B) THE SAME HISTOGRAM FITTED TO THE NORMAL CURVE

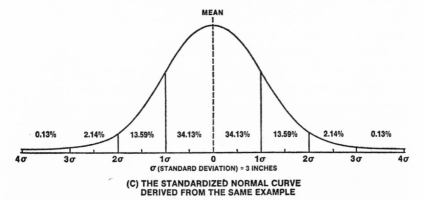

(C) THE STANDARDIZED NORMAL CURVE DERIVED FROM THE SAME EXAMPLE

Figure 1. Hypothetical example plotting the heights of a sample of junior college students.

Now the carpenter would probably choose a height for the cupboards that "most" people found convenient. If he had recorded the height of the students, he could have plotted a histogram like the one in Figure 1A. Then he could have computed the statistical mean, or average, and the standard deviation of his sample.

Suppose the mean or average height of his group was 5 feet 7½ inches with a standard deviation of 3 inches as in Figure 1A. We will assume that the shelf was convenient for students of the average height (5'7½") and for those students as much as 3 inches shorter (5'4½") or up to 3 inches taller (5'10½"). These students have a height *typical* of junior college students.

Now what about the students who are between 1 and 2 standard deviations out from the curve (that is the short ones from 5'1½" to 5'4½" and the tall ones from 5'10½" to 6'½")? The somewhat tall might have to bend or stoop to see in the back of the shelf. These students, whose eye level would measure between 1 and 2 standard deviations above the mean or average, comprise about 13.6 percent of the college group. Also, what about the comparable group of 13.6 percent on the other side of the average who are somewhat short and must stand on tip toes, or strain to see and reach to the back of the shelf? This *marginally* atypical group of "sort of" tall and "sort of" short students, about 27 percent in all, will probably just make do, as they have had to do in the rest of the world where most things have not been made quite with their dimensions in mind.

Now let us consider the very few (about 4.6%) students at the two extremes or wings of the curve; that is, those whose eye level is above or below 2 standard deviations from the mean or average, who each comprise a group of about 2.3 percent at each end, or at the *extremes* of the normal curve.

These are students whose height as young adults is below 5 feet 1½ inches or above 6 feet ½ inch. These people are probably perceived as being somewhat abnormal with respect to height. As children, they may have been taken to the physician to ascertain if their deviant height had been related to a correctable condition. Their teachers may have had to placate parents and handle questions about physical differences in class. Teachers may have found it necessary to discourage taunts from other children. The individual, being very short or very tall, will have an exceptionality, which is an abnormal height. Extremely short or extremely tall persons may be medically defined as showing dwarfism or giantism.

The problem with statistical classifications, and even consequent medical classifications, is that they are of only limited use in real life. If the teacher knows simply that a dwarf will be entering the class, that fact is not very helpful. Nothing can be assumed about learning ability, personality adjustment, athletic prowess, or family adjustment, any one of which might be of much more importance to the pupil and school than the fact of dwarfism.

Even the physical environment cannot be arranged ahead on the basis of this classification. Some dwarfs are taller than others; one might prefer to put up with inconvenience, rather than have special equipment. Another might be so advanced academically that he will be another teacher's concern next week.

Persons do not fit on the normal curve. Only types of measured characteristics and behaviors of individuals can be compared with similar measurable characteristics and behaviors of others in a statistical way. Furthermore, the meaning of one's measurement or "score" for a characteristic is a personal one. At face value one might think that on any so-called intelligence test (all of which measure some kind of behavior related to cognition) the most desirable score would be the very highest. In some cases, that is so, but the fact of deviating intellectually so far above the norm, or mean, has proved a terrible burden for some children. They are "exceptional"; they are exceptions in a statistical sense, and they are therefore a concern to the Council for Exceptional Children.

Some children show marked deviations in more than one dimension and are thus multiply handicapped. It is an unfortunate medical fact that when a person has one physical aberration there are more likely to be others. Hence, more children with cerebral palsy also have mental deficiencies and sensory problems than a comparable group without cerebral palsy. More children who are mentally deficient will have physical anomalies than a comparable group of non-mentally deficient children.

A pitfall encountered when assigning labels on the basis of a statistical or medical classification is stereotyping, or making unfounded generalizations on the basis of the one label. A severely cerebral palsied person with great difficulty in speaking, eating, and walking, who drools and grimaces, may be (and has more chance of being) more mentally deficient than his or her nonhandicapped peers. However, in the particular case, as for example the case of the Irish writer and painter Christy Brown, the individual may be very gifted. That is one reason the teacher has very little knowledge when told that a "CP" (person with cerebral palsy) will be entering the class. The fact of the impairment will make a difference in the classroom, but so will all the other attributes, measurable and unmeasurable, that the students and teachers bring to their classes.

Statistical comparisons can only be made on the basis of objective, measurable attributes. The "essence" of a person can be missed if the description of the person is reduced to numbers. It is almost impossible to measure personality characteristics such as warmth, curiosity, and creativity.

Because of unavoidable errors of measurement, standardization and sampling, and extraneous influences on the particular testing or measurement situation, relatively small differences between persons' scores or measurements are not of statistical significance and should not be considered important. However, it may be of great interest to the teacher to know that a student is fairly typical (within plus or minus one standard deviation of the mean and like 68% of his peers) or marginal in a positive or negative direction, or very extreme in such measurable skills as math achievement, time for running the 100-yard dash, or ability to read the figures on the blackboard from across the room.

THE CONCEPT OF DEVIANCY

Sociologists, anthropologists, and psychologists have been interested in cultural definitions of deviancy and consequent social management of persons who are considered "deviants." Deviants, of course, are persons who have one or more significant characteristics, physical or behavioral, that are far from or deviate widely from the accepted or idealized norm or average for that characteristic.

The idealized norm or average gives us a social image of what things should be like and sometimes ignores realities. It is given to society through the mass media, school, and other social and religious institutions. When disparities become too great, or ignored and denigrated groups become articulate, social ideals and mores have to change to redefine the collective ideal or norm.

It appears as if American society has passed through a period where the ideal cultural norms were narrowly defined, therefore prohibiting even relatively large groups such as black Americans or the aged to feel as if they "belonged." Such groups have often felt like "second-class citizens."

The following are the words of sociologist Irving Goffman, written in 1963, before the height of the civil rights movement, before the "women's lib" movement, and certainly before "gay lib," "old power," "deaf power," "single parents," and other advocacy groups, which have since emerged:

> For example, in an important sense, there is only one complete unblushing male in America: a young, married, white, urban, northern, heterosexual, Protestant, father, of college education, fully employed, of good complexion, weight, and height, and a recent record in sports. Every American male tends to look out upon the world from this perspective, this constituting one sense in which one can speak of a common value system in America.[1]

CULTURE CHANGE AND THE HANDICAPPED

American society is now in a time of great culture change. Since Goffman's statement of 1963, there have been Catholic and Southern presidents. Women (not even mentioned by Goffman) and blacks have achieved high office. Native and Japanese Americans have been the objects of retributive legislation. The right to treatment, to information, to privacy, consent, and redress are increasingly spelled out by the courts. Textbooks, for the first time, include fair representation of population minorities such as Spanish Americans and inner-city children. Publishers have attempted to remove sex bias by destereotyping child caring, housekeeping, cooking, and careers. Educators have attempted to provide a wider range of children with equal access to appropriate role

1. Irving Goffman, *Stigma: Notes on the Management of a Spoiled Identity* (Englewood Cliffs, Prentice-Hall, 1963), p. 123.

models. The whole concept of normal has therefore been broadened in American society.

Even though there is now a liberalized definition of what is normal, average, or "O.K.," there are still physical and behavioral deviants–those persons differing widely, in some important manner, from "most" people. All societies have deviants and in some manner must cope with them. In some societies special functions and roles give deviance its place, that then permit the deviant to "belong." For example, in present day Korea, blind persons are enjoined to become masseurs or fortune tellers. Many superstitions surround the condition of blindness (the blind may not ride street cars, for example), but the blind person is not an outcast.

Our culture has shown a relative inability to integrate its deviants. Hence, persons such as the profoundly handicapped, very elderly, and mentally disturbed have been committed or "warehoused," often in cruel and inhumane conditions. Marginally handicapped or marginally different persons, such as those in wheelchairs, the so-called educable mentally retarded, migrant workers, homosexuals, orphans, unwed mothers, and the urban poor, have been ignored or consigned to a kind of cultural limbo, which will ensure that they cannot improve their condition.

The handicapped comprise a disadvantaged group that has received increased attention by society. Recently legislation, court decisions, and constitutional amendments (such as the 14th) have been extended to include the rights of handicapped persons and have granted new services and privileges to them.

The most important educational legislation for handicapped children was signed into law November 29, 1975 by President Ford. Public Law 94-142, The Education of All Handicapped Children Act, requires that states accepting the substantial attached moneys provide an appropriate individualized education for *all* handicapped children. Due process procedures are included to assure compliance. This federal law was antedated by the Right to Education Consent Agreement in Pennsylvania, which then became the first state in the union to provide education for all handicapped children–no matter how involved, whether in institutions or in homes. Thousands of families had access to educational services for their children for the first time. These children have often made important gains in school, even after years of educational neglect. Public Law 94-142, as the Right to Education Consent Agreement before it, stipulates that the appropriate individualized education should occur in the "least restrictive environment." The assumption is made that the best environment for any child is the regular classroom in a neighborhood public school where the child will go from a home environment.

Children who have previously been excluded from special education because they were too "special" will now have the right to education that other children have. The appropriateness of the educational experience implies a cascade system of special educational services, which are diagramed in Figure 2. The regular classroom in a public school is assumed to be the best placement for any child who can be supported in such an environment. Therefore, some children who have been excluded from regular education on the basis of impairments and disabilities can be expected to reenter the educational mainstream. Further, young handicapped children may not ever experience the exclusion and segregation that have frequently been the situation of their older counterparts. It must be stressed that supportive services will be brought to the regular education setting. If children with special needs are simply "thrown" into a regular setting without a support system for the students, teachers, and parents, we would be back to the situation that motivated the whole development of special education. In other words, special education and services will be brought to as normalized an educational environment as is possible, given the specific circumstances.

In reality the opportunities for placement do not necessarily depend on any one factor, such as the nature or severity of the handicapping condition. For example, a deaf or blind child in a relatively large city may be able to attend the community school and have the services of a resource room or itinerant teacher of the hearing or visually impaired. That same deaf or blind child living in a rural, less populated area might have to attend a residential school in order to receive appropriate special education services these handicaps require. Again, a child in a wheelchair

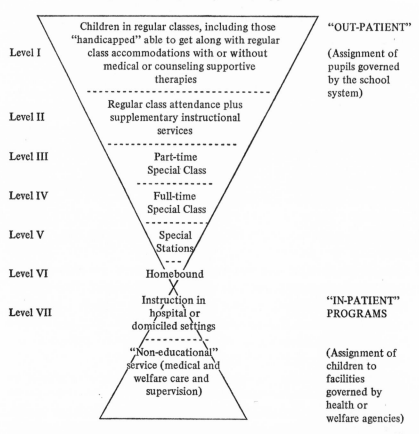

Level I	Children in regular classes, including those "handicapped" able to get along with regular class accommodations with or without medical or counseling supportive therapies	"OUT-PATIENT" (Assignment of pupils governed by the school system)
Level II	Regular class attendance plus supplementary instructional services	
Level III	Part-time Special Class	
Level IV	Full-time Special Class	
Level V	Special Stations	
Level VI	Homebound	
Level VII	Instruction in hospital or domiciled settings	"IN-PATIENT" PROGRAMS
	"Non-educational" service (medical and welfare care and supervision)	(Assignment of children to facilities governed by health or welfare agencies)

Figure 2. Cascade system of special education services. From Evelyn Deno, Special Education as Developmental Capital, *Exceptional Children, 37(3):* 229-237, November, 1970, Courtesy of the Council for Exceptional Children.

in the inner city might not be able to negotiate the stairs in an old, elevatorless school that was built before the present laws, which mandate the elimination of architectural barriers. Therefore, that child might be bused to a newer school on one floor, or one with elevators and ramps, that would be the neighborhood school for the crippled child in that area.

A child with no family, or an abused child, handicapped or not, may have to be institutionalized if a foster home cannot be found. However, it is increasingly the practice to send even institutionalized children to schools in surrounding communities for all or part of the day.

The trend toward integration and normalization of deviant members of society has broad and real consequences for the school, both in regular and special education. Marginally different children will no longer be given pejorative labels and segregated on the basis of their differences. Children with significant handicaps will have the opportunity to work and learn with nonhandicapped peers. These new standards of tolerance and practice will have to extend to the adults in the school community as well and eventually into the entire community.

Another highly significant event for handicapped persons was President Carter's signing of a regulation implementing Section 504 of the Rehabilitation Act of 1973. Section 504 prohibits discrimination solely on the basis of handicap against otherwise qualified handicapped individuals in programs receiving federal financial assistance.

The 504 regulation is a landmark in the quest of handicapped citizens for equal treatment, and it will be a fundamental guidepost to the new era of civil rights for the handicapped. It calls for the following changes in the actions and attitudes of institutions and individuals who are recipients of funds from the Department of Health, Education and Welfare:

> All new facilities must be barrier-free, i.e., readily accessible to and usable by handicapped individuals.

Barrier-free design for the physically handicapped as stated in the first paragraph from the above excerpt include the following:

1. At least one building entrance at ground level.
2. Doors 32″ wide that open easily.
3. Level thresholds to buildings and rooms.
4. Sloping ramps instead of stairs (ratio 1′ to 12′).
5. Safe parking for the handicapped at least 12′ wide and close to entrance.
6. Sidewalks 4′ wide with ramps at all crosswalks.
7. Elevators in multi-floored buildings with low controls.
8. Restrooms with wide stalls, 32″ wide doors and grab bars.

9. Handrails on all stairways extending 18″ beyond top and bottom steps.
10. Lower drinking fountains and public telephones.

Programs or activities in existing facilities must be made accessible to the handicapped within 60 days, and, if not, other alternatives—such as reassignment of classes or home visits—will achieve program accessibility, structural changes in the facilities must be made within three years. No exceptions to the program accessibility requirement will be allowed.

Employers may not refuse to hire handicapped persons, if reasonable accommodations can be made by them to an individual's handicap and if the handicap does not impair the ability of the applicant or employer to do the specific job.

Employers may not require pre-employment physical examinations and may not make a pre-employment inquiry about whether a person is handicapped, or the nature or severity of a handicap, although employers may make a pre-employment inquiry into an applicant's ability to perform job-related functions.

Every handicapped child will be entitled to free public education appropriate to his or her individual needs, regardless of the nature or severity of the handicap. In those unusual cases where placement in a special residential setting is necessary, public authorities will be financially responsible for tuition, room and board.

Handicapped children must not be segregated in the public schools, but must be educated with the non-handicapped in regular classrooms to the maximum extent possible.

Educational institutions and other social service programs must provide auxiliary aids, such as readers in school libraries or interpreters for the deaf, to ensure full participation of handicapped persons.

All recipients of HEW funds must complete within one year of self-evaluation process, in consultation with handicapped individuals and organizations, to determine which of their policies and practices need to be changed to assure equal opportunity for handicapped Americans.[2]

This book is addressed to management problems that confront teachers who are integrating children with physical handicaps and

2. Remarks of HEW Secretary Joseph A. Califano, Jr. at the White House Conference on Handicapped Individuals, May 23, 1977.

health problems in the classroom and in the school community. To the teacher or administrator who has lacked exposure in this area, these problems may seem to be very difficult. Actually, special educators know that physical problems such as paralysis, seizures, and blindness are relatively easy to surmount. The learning problems encountered in such groups as the prelingually deaf, aphasic, or the severely mentally deficient are a far more difficult challenge than the physical management problems. However, teachers cannot begin to teach physically different children until they have been satisfactorily provided for in the school environment. It is difficult to teach a child who cannot get in the door!

For successful integration of exceptional children, attitudes should be congruent with legislated practice. In schools where the community, administrators, and teachers share the same spirit, even severely and multiply handicapped children have found a place in the regular public school community. In a pluristic society the school can be the milieu where boys and girls learn self-respect, mutual tolerance, and appreciation of the myriad ways in which human beings develop their unique potentials. In such a social and educational environment the ideals of cooperation and contribution, rather than competition and contention, will prevail. In such schools and classrooms, there is a place for the handicapped child, the eccentric child, and for the "funny-looking kid" (known as the FLK in special education parlance).

Review Guide

After reading Chapter 1 the reader should be able to define the following terms:

normal	extreme
statistical average	exceptionality
mean	deviancy
standard deviation	idealized norm
typical	deviant
marginal	

After reading Chapter 1 the reader should be able to do the following:

1. Give two types of human characteristics that can be measured statistically.

2. Give four important factors that influence decisions on an individual's normality and health.

3. Name ten groups of people who have sometimes been treated as second-class citizens in the United States.

4. List three factors that might adversely affect placing the handicapped child in the best educational environment.

5. Give the main purposes of Public Law 94-142.

6. Specify the preferential order of educational placement for handicapped children.

Chapter 2

AN ECOLOGICAL DISCUSSION OF HANDICAP

The human condition is such that pain and effort are not just symptoms which can be removed without changing life itself; they are rather the modes in which life itself, together with the necessity to which it is bound, makes itself felt. For mortals, the "easy life of the gods" would be a lifeless life.

Hannah Arendt

| WEE PALS - kid power ® by Morrie Turner |

Courtesy of © King Features Syndicate, Inc., 1977.

I N CHAPTER 1, we have discussed how relative and sometimes even arbitrary are the definitions of *normality, average, exceptional,* and *deviancy.* With these concepts in mind, we will go on to explore some other terms used in special education and rehabilitation so they can clarify our thinking and be more useful in communication. They are called ecological terms to stress the interdependence of the individual with the total environment. Ecology, or bionomics, is the science of the relationship of organisms and their environments.

IMPAIRMENT[1]

An impairment is a physical deviation from what could be considered physically normal. It could be a defective structure, such

1. The author is indebted for the essence of the definitions below to Godfrey Stevens, *Taxonomy in Special Education for Children with Body Disorders.* Department of Special Education & Rehabilitation, University of Pittsburgh, 1962.

as a cleft lip or palate. It could be a defective function such as
that occurring in a pancreas, thereby causing diabetes. It could be
a defective physical organization, such as in the case when some
bones grow too rapidly in relation to other bones. An impairment
could be a defect in development, such as is the case when the
embryonic bony structure of the spine does not close, causing
spina bifida. An impairment may affect most of the body, as in the
case of metabolic disorders such as cystic fibrosis. It may affect
one or more of the sense organs such as the eyes or ears. It may
affect a system such as the digestive system. It may be confined to
one member of the body, for example, a club foot.

Impairments may be very minor, such as the condition of having six fingers on one hand. Small skin blemishes might be considered very mild impairments if at all. Freckles would not be considered by most to be an impairment. A red birth mark (called a
port-wine stain) on the buttocks might be considered a minor impairment. The same blemish on the face would cause more concern. Thus, while impairments are physically measurable and objective, it is still difficult to separate subjective values from them.

Impairments may or may not be genetic or inherited; causes of
many are unknown. About 5 percent of newborn babies have significant birth defects. Some inborn errors are apparent at birth,
such as congenital amputations, and some will be manifest later,
such as muscular dystrophy. Other impairments will be acquired
at some later time, most often through accidents (trauma).

In the discussion of the concept of normality, it was mentioned
that unusual physical attributes are sometimes highly valued in
some cultures.

> Among the Palaung, an Eastern Clan, "it is lucky to have extra
> fingers or toes, and extremely lucky to be born with a hare-lip."
> Among the Dahomeans of West Africa, children born with anoma-
> lous physical characteristics are held to be under the guardianship
> of special supernatural agents. Some of these children are destined
> to bring good luck, and the fate of others must be determined by
> signs from the supernatural.[2]

In American culture, facial moles may be valued as "beauty

2. Human Relations Area Files at Yale University Appendix 1953.

marks." Social and ritual maimings are the culturally acceptable, deliberate impairing of individuals.

Notwithstanding interesting examples of positive evaluations attributed to certain impairments, probably most persons, including most impaired individuals themselves, would agree with Beatrice Wright's assessment:

> Although one could add hundreds of examples showing differences among cultures in evaluation of physical characteristics, one wonders if there is not a core of physical attributes essential to the perception of "body whole" and "body beautiful" in all societies. Is there any culture, for example, in which the absence of legs at birth is considered beautiful, or does not destroy the intactness of the body?[3]

Thus, impairments can be considered unfortunate realities of life with which people have to live. As we will see in Chapter 4, some are inevitable consequences of the evolutionary process itself.

DISABILITY

While educators are inclined to use the words *exceptional, special,* or *handicapped,* rehabilitation personnel are apt to speak of the *disabled.* Some precision added to the term *disability* will be useful for both kinds of professionals.

A disability is a functional limitation experienced by the individual because of an impairment. It refers to what the individual cannot do (in the expected way) because of a physical problem. Hence, the person with paralysed legs cannot walk. The person born without eyes cannot see. A person with diabetes cannot digest sugars. A dwarf cannot easily drive a large car.

Not all impairments cause disability. Consider the port-wine stain birth mark: it does not impede function, any more than do pierced ears or tattoos.

While impairments are measurable and objective, the disabilities they engender are more subjective. Think about the condition of missing a finger. Some forms of work are very hazardous to fingers, and the missing digit is not particularly disabling to

---

3. Beatrice A. Wright, *Physical Disability—A Psychological Approach* (New York, Harper & Bros., 1960), p. 255.

most. What if a pianist or violinist loses a finger, where excellent dexterity is the basis of a life's work? Such misfortunes have occurred. Both Richard Straus and Maurice Ravel wrote piano concertos for the left hand for a performer whose right hand had been seriously injured. Again, ability to walk is not a skill necessary to be President of the United States, as Franklin Roosevelt demonstrated. However, two strong legs are mandatory in a dancer and helpful for a mail carrier.

The disability imposed by many impairments can be compensated and contained much more effectively than many people realise. Persons with physical impairments can be fantastically resourceful in managing their life situations.

It should be obvious that a person in a wheelchair is as able to marry as anyone else. It might surprise some to learn that a crippled woman is black belt in karate, or that a paraplegic man flies a plane and sails a boat. It is very important that we as teachers open options and encourage ingenuity rather than decide what another adult or child can do on the meagre basis of what *we* could do (or think we could do), given the same dilemma.

HANDICAP

The words *disabled* and *handicapped* are often used interchangeably, but here they will be distinguished in order to highlight some important concerns.

A handicap is the disadvantage imposed by impairment or disability, which the person experiences in his particular environment. The handicap depends on the physical and psychological characteristics of the person, on the culture, and specific circumstances in place and time, in which the handicapped person finds himself.

Handicap, then, is not objective and measurable. It does not exist in the abstract. It is not a physical thing, like an impairment, or even the relatively observable curtailment of function or behaviour that comprises a disability. A handicap is an experience. The action and reaction of the handicapped person's mind and body to the impairment and disability are part of that experience. The action and reaction of others in the environment are part of the experience.

Can one have an impairment without a disability? Yes, a birth mark, or complete hairlessness are examples.

Would a large facial port-wine stain be a handicap? Quite likely, but a noted scholar, so blemished, became president of Harvard University some years ago. Whether it was a significant handicap to him might depend in the first instance on parental attitude and later on a host of actions and reactions to environmental situations. Physicians who do cosmetic surgery are frequently sought by individuals who feel their whole lives have been ruined by noses, breasts, wrinkles, etc. that would often not seem out of the ordinary to others.

Can one have a disability without an impairment? Probably not, in the sense the terms are used here. Can one have an impairment and disability that are not a handicap? Since handicap is a subjective experience, a general answer to this question cannot be given. Some diabetic persons are so in control of their disease and have such satisfactory lives that probably they consider their management problems a minor inconvenience rather than a handicap. This is probably true for many people with artificial limbs, well-controlled seizures, and mild hemophilia as well. Here the impairment is relatively minor when compared with that of others who have the same medical diagnosis, and the disability is well contained.

Can one have an impairment that is enhancing? Some examples were given in the case of some tribal societies and in the social practices of circumcision, ear piercing, and tattooing in American society. "Beauty marks" were also mentioned. None of these impairments are disabling.

Can one have an impairment and disability that are enhancing? The following are two somewhat bizarre examples:

Some years ago the Aga Kahn was motivated to enormous obesity, since he collected his people's yearly taxes as his weight in gold. Extreme obesity certainly limits physical function and is most disabling from the standpoint of health and longevity, but it was valued in this instance.

A case is known to the writer of an adolescent girl of the Chinese upper class who missed having her feet bound for the accustomed period because of a Japanese invasion. She escaped her village and lived with a missionary until the hostilities were over. She went back to her village on two normal feet and was literally outcast by the society because she did not have the small crippled feet appropriate to young women of her class. She was subsequently adopted by the missionary, from whom the story came. She must at least have felt ambivalent about the desirability of this impairment and disability.

Lastly, can one have a handicap without the possession of an impairment or disability? For the purposes of this book, the answer is no. When handicapped persons are discussed, it is assumed that they are impaired and will usually have some degree of disability. Still, their handicap will be relative to their perceptions and their environments, and they may be socially handicapped more than is necessary.

By conservative estimate, 10 percent of all school children have significant impairments and disabilities in one or a combination of physical, cognitive, and behavioural areas, and therefore have consequent handicaps. They are children in the extremes of the normal curve. The extremely gifted are not included in this percentage unless they also have another exceptionality.

From this group of obviously exceptional children, we move to a grey area of children sometimes referred to as mildly handicapped. These would include the "funny-looking kid," the "educable mentally retarded," the "learning disabled," and the "socially maladjusted," who are marginal in their deviancy from the norm. With these children, much of the handicap may be a socially imposed one.

Lastly, since handicap is a perceived experience, the term can certainly, in other contexts, be used legitimately to describe normal persons and groups who are assigned to a devalued position and therefore feel socially handicapped.

Women as a group have felt socially handicapped. Indeed, for a time at least, Freud thought that women were physically imperfect and therefore could never fully achieve psychosexual maturity possible to their ideal male counterparts.

Members of racial, religious, and ethnic minority groups can feel handicap. Malcolm X was told by his eighth grade English teacher that it was not legitimate for a black youth to aspire to anything but manual work, although he was exceptionally academically able. He should choose a nonacademic career and stifle his hopes. His reaction to this treatment, as he perceived it himself, was the turning point in the struggle that carried him to a position of high leadership. If he had not been the victim of this prejudice and injustice, he felt he would have only become another "fat cat" (quotes mine) in his local community.[4]

Older people can be targets for devaluation. In an economy with high unemployment, a job seeker over forty or fifty years of age may feel handicapped and face discrimination.

The environmental mechanisms that act upon stigmatised groups to make them feel handicapped are exactly the same responses that further handicap an impaired and disabled person beyond the handicap imposed by impairment and disability.

Physically handicapped persons can recount over and over experiences similar to that of young Malcolm X. "You can't go to your local school, swim, be an engineer, marry, have children, etc., etc., etc., because you can't walk, see, hear, are just plain ugly, etc., etc., etc."

Job restrictions and laws are often punitively restrictive for whole classes of handicapped persons. *De facto* segregation is promulgated by such things as architectural barriers, lack of translating services, and thoughtlessness.

What is so challenging and hopeful for teachers is the real possibility of reducing the handicap of pupils who have impairments and disabilities. The first step is, of course, to include these children in the regular school community itself rather than segregating them. However, the teacher who does not know what the physical problem is doing to the child and how the child is reacting to the problem is hard pressed to provide an appropriate environment for the pupil, much less educate him in academics. The teacher who is sensitive to the meaning of the physical or health problems to his handicapped student (as well as to others in the school environment) is in a strong position to facilitate learning.

---

4. Alex Haley, *The Autobiography of Malcolm X* (New York, Grove Press, Inc., 1964), pp. 36-38.

SOMATOPSYCHOLOGICAL GUIDELINES

The relationship of physique to social and psychological factors is a domain explored in a branch of psychology termed *somatopsychology* (*somato* is body; *psychology* is the science of mental processes and behaviour). Somatopsychologists have made important contributions to the understanding of the psychology of disability.

Somatopsychology is concerned with the impact one's particular body characteristics have on one's life space, as a stimulus to others, and as a stimulus to one's own self. These psychologists analyse coping mechanisms that are used by individuals and groups of individuals who share some valued or devalued characteristics. They have formulated guidelines to healthy attitudes toward disablement and approaches to environmental accommodation, stressing emotional barriers to adjustment of the handicapped.[5]

The guidelines are general principles that enable the disabled person and those around the disabled person to be aware of and reduce the external or social contribution to the handicap imposed on the person who is impaired and disabled. These can be very useful to the teacher.

The first guideline involves *enlarging the scope of values*. This refers to a person's extending his view (and that of those around him) beyond the limitation of his disability to those many things he *can* do. In rehabilitating parlance, it is taking the *dis* out of disability.

An individual can be viewed primarily in terms of negative or tragic aspects (succumbing aspects) or in terms of constructive possibilities (coping aspects).

Unfortunately, even those in the helping professions frequently are guilty of emphasising the negative aspects of handicap for purportedly good reasons. Wright discusses the Pulitzer award poster portraying a boy on crutches wistfully watching from the

---

5. Beatrice A. Wright. "Issues in Overcoming Emotional Barriers to Adjustment in the Handicapped," *Rehabilitation Counseling Bulletin XI Special*, Fall 1967, p. 53-59.

sidelines while other children play football. The poster is an inducement for inoculations against polio.

> This cartoon may arouse maudlin sentiments, pity, and perhaps guilt, but what is being questioned is whether it contributes to the development of adjustive attitudes and constructive action. . . . Are we lying when we tell parents that the child with crippled legs can participate in sports, can have happy times, even though he will know the suffering of frustration and rejection? (P.57)

A public service message was recently sponsored by a local agency concerned with birth defects. Its purpose was to encourage pregnant women to have prenatal checkups and maintain a proper diet. It ended with a picture of a beautiful young mother holding an equally beautiful infant, saying "I'm glad *I* was *good* to *my* child." Again, we must weigh the obviously sincere purpose behind this message with its implications. Does it not suggest that the mother of a handicapped child was *not* "good" to her child, was in some way to blame for her handicapped child? Does not the approach inspire fear and pose the *threat* of a handicapped child to pregnant women?

Here is another example of the mixed messages in the mass media. A colleague had a four-year-old daughter who went to one of an agency's preschools for developmentally delayed children. A photograph of the child's very beautiful face covered the entire front of an elaborate fund-raising magazine the agency printed. The only caption across the picture was "This is Jamie, she is retarded." Now Jamie was certainly educationally retarded. It happens to be true also that Jamie had been very slow to talk but was progressing very rapidly. It was also the case that Jamie was lame. For a while her doctors thought she would never walk, but she was walking fairly well without crutches or canes. The point is that an attractive little girl with a droll, sensitive, and determined personality, who was making fine progress, was reduced to one negative designation or succumbing aspect, bleak in its implications. In fairness it should be said that the same agency will decry labels, talk about educating the whole child, thereby upholding the coping aspects in the school situation.

The second guideline has been called *subordinating physique,* and this simply means that other values should assume greater potency in a person's life than his physical makeup. It might seem obvious that if one has a physical limitation that cannot be remedied one should be encouraged to work around the physical problem and use strengths in mind and personality rather than focus on weaknesses of body.

The Adlerian idea of compensation and overcompensation for physical inferiorities is an intriguing one. One wonders if Helen Keller would have become a scholar and writer if she had not been deaf and blind. Would Marcel Proust have become a famous writer if he had not been an invalid? Would Henry Viscardi, born without legs, have become a successful entrepreneur if he had been a physically normal immigrant's son? For some very unusual handicapped persons and some parents of handicapped children, the suffering seems the crucible in which the personality is purified and strengthened. These cases are extraordinary rather than usual. Most persons are not made better by being handicapped or sick, any more than they are by being poor or old.

The third guideline is known as *containing the disability* so that it does not spread to affect what is healthy and normal about a person.

There is an unfortunate tendency to stereotype persons on the basis of a diagnostic label. For linguistic simplicity, teachers will sometimes say they have a "CP" or "hemi" or "MD" in the class. This is certainly not the case, and this way of talking is to be discouraged. Rather, teachers have a particular child in the class who, along with many other attributes, has a special impairment and disability such as cerebral palsy, hemiplegia, or muscular dystrophy. Physical and medical problems do not occur and are not handled in the abstract. Any disease or disability will manifest itself uniquely in each individual. The other attributes possessed by the individual are also unique and varied. These other attributes cannot, in most cases, be predicted on the basis of a diagnostic label. Unfortunately, there are many children who are discouraged from succeeding because of preconceived notions about a diagnostic label.

There is today a professor in a large university who can be labeled "legally blind" and who was educated in a residential school for the blind, where he learned Braille. It was not until his adolescence that he realized that he had enough vision to read book print, which he learned to do and has done ever since.

For another example, there is a very vital, energetic, married career woman in a wheelchair who was educated in a residential school for crippled children. She remembers vividly the time when she expressed the wish to be a housewife. She was told by her teacher to get that idea out of her head because she could never marry.

Combatting stereotypes is a never ending struggle for handicapped persons. If special educators so easily fall prey to these mistakes, what can we expect of other persons, presumably less knowledgeable in this area.

"Classic" cases are found most often in textbooks rather than in persons and are only general descriptions. Every person will respond both physically and psychologically in a unique way to an imposed physical problem. When developing management strategies to facilitate the integration of handicapped children, the teacher must be aware that the particular child in his or her environment will act and react in a unique fashion to the needs of the situation as that child perceives the situation. Obviously, generalizations must be made, and principles will be recommended; however, we are admonished to remember that for any diseases and disabilities, suggested management strategies for coping with these problems must be tailored to the specific child with his or her especial problem, at a particular point in time, with special attention to that child's strengths and assets and the teacher's skills as well.

The fourth guideline is *upholding asset evaluation.* Here emphasis is not only given to what a person can do, but evaluation takes place in terms of the requirements of the situation rather than an unattainable "normal" standard. The handicapped person is allowed to feel that it is all right to be different, to do things in different ways, or not to be able to do them at all. He or she is allowed to have self-respect and self-fulfillment in the avenues that are open, despite the handicap.

We mentioned earlier the desirability of a classroom atmosphere where the spirit is one of cooperation rather than competition. That does not mean that students are discouraged from doing their very best and receiving recognition for high quality. It does imply more emphasis on self-fulfillment for its own sake rather than for the sake of invidious comparisons with others.

Even very young children are able to identify with others and applaud a feat that is easy for them but is a triumph for a friend. Mutual respect and kindness can be nurtured and, in fact, are often more prevalent in children than in their prejudiced elders. It is suggested that the so-called "cruelty of children" only comes about when it is implicitly condoned and encouraged or at least expected by those in charge.

Attention to assets rather than deficiencies can be given far more often than might be imagined, even in the area of disability itself. For example, first let us free our own minds from a preconceived idea that the only way to get from class to class is walking on two feet. Actually, that distance *can* be independently traversed by crawling (as a pretoddler knows), on a tricycle, in a walker, on crutches, or in a wheelchair by a crippled child or teacher. When the normal children or teachers try to use some of these alternate methods, such as manipulating crutches or a wheelchair, they find that successful negotiation takes strength and skill. The crippled person has developed these attributes to a greater degree than others and can be admired for them. Similarly, blind persons have trained themselves to heightened awareness (that the layman mistakenly attributes to a "sixth sense"), which is phenomenal. Persons who use hooks for hands develop a high degree of dexterity, marvelous to the rest of us. The lipreading of some deaf persons seems almost unbelievable. Naturally it would be patronizing, particularly with older children and adults, to be pointed in praise of these disability-related assets; but pupils will pick up the implicit respect if it is there, just as they pick up implicit denigration.

In summary, the teacher should be careful to distinguish the realities of physical impairments and disabilities from handicaps imposed by unknowledgeable persons or an insensitive society. Attention to the four guidelines above will help the teacher to establish a facilitating rather than handicapping classroom environment.

Review Guide

After reading Chapter 2 the reader should be able to define the following terms:

Ecology

Somatopsychology

After reading Chapter 2 the reader should be able to answer the following questions:

1. What is the distinction between impairment, disability, and handicap?
2. What are the four somatopsychological guidelines for dealing with handicapped persons?

Chapter 3

THE TEACHER AS A MEMBER OF THE
REHABILITATION TEAM

Men polish each other as diamonds do.
Mathias Theodor Mommsen

THE THREE STAGES OF HEALTH CARE

THE FIRST STAGE of health care is *prevention* of disease and disorder. The medical professions have been increasingly concerned with preventative medical procedures and practices such as well baby clinics, mass inoculations, and patient education. Also, educators and persons in social services contribute to prevention of problems through public information programs and provision of services in many special areas. It will be emphasized in the chapters ahead that the classroom is an ideal place to teach and practice safe and healthy ways of living.

The second stage of health care is concerned with the *treatment* and arrest of health problems. It is the time during which a patient is diagnosed as sick, is treated, and recuperates. The patient is chiefly under the care of medical and other health care personnel.

When students are patients, the school staff can do little but act in a supportive role to the parents and sick child and to the often anxious classmates. However, early diagnosis and intervention in problems can frequently prevent complications and be of crucial importance to the course of treatment. In an important sense, teachers can be careful observers of conditions that require medical attention. A teacher can observe, for example, that a child's eyes water or that he rubs his eyes and squints when attending to close work. It is *not* within the teacher's ability to decide that such a child needs glasses. It *is* legitimate for the teacher to recommend, through the best channel of communication he has established, that the child have his eyes checked by a specialist.

Whenever some behavior or physical idiosyncrasy which is uncharacteristic of the child is observed, it is always best to recommend an examination by a competent professional. Physical problems, rather than psychological or learning problems, may account for erratic behaviors. The teacher may notice that the child is not attending to what is said in the classroom. Rather than assuming a psychological cause, it would be better to have the child's ears checked. Sudden changes in energy level, behavior, or distractibility may have a physical cause, which is relatively easy to ascertain.

There is the case of the teacher who decided her pupil had a visual-perceptual problem. Months later, a medical exam showed the child to be almost blind. On the other hand, the teacher, in close and day-to-day observation of a child, may pick up behaviors that were missed by the physician. There is the case of the preschool child who was diagnosed as totally blind after one ophthalmological examination. Her teacher noticed that she was trying to use her eyes, and today, although she is visually handicapped, she reads book print. Thus, while the teacher does not have the skill to make definitive diagnoses such as "brain damage" or other medical judgments, the teacher has great skill in detecting atypical appearance and behavior and drawing it to the attention of other professional colleagues.

The third stage of health care is said to be *rehabilitation*–the support system that follows the patient after the treatment phase is over–that is after the operations are over and the stitches are out, or the disease has run its course, or long-term treatment has been prescribed.

Many persons with the impairments discussed in this book require habilitation or rehabilitation services during most of the course of their lives. Early medical intervention will prevent much secondary physical and psychological damage. Delivery of the proper therapies at the appropriate periods will give the child and adult the best possible chance for a good life.

Therapies may be delivered through the hospital or clinic. However, they may be successfully managed in the context of the school. Indeed, the pupil personnel services in the school may be the major ones utilized at some times in the child's life, particularly in a school that can maintain a broad spectrum of supportive staff. At other times treatment and therapies may be received from other institutions and agencies.

During the course of the school years, the teacher should be a pivotal member of the rehabilitation team. The value of the teacher in this capacity has not always been appreciated, but increasingly other professionals are relying on the teacher (as they are also on parents), and teachers are developing a new sense of their own professionalism.

Teachers are in a position to contribute in some ways better than any other of the support personnel dealing with their pupils: they can often establish a closer rapport with parents and the child than can other professionals. By the fact of being teachers, they know how to speak in layman's language, and in very simple language, to persons who are often confused by professional jargon. Further, they share with the child and parents many positive, enjoyable experiences that leave a residue of goodwill impossible for the professional who only sees the child in a context of pain, sickness, or anxiety.

Teachers are in the most advantageous position to observe a child objectively over a good part of the day and over a long period of time, in relation to the child's peers. Thus they can distinguish normal swings of good days and bad days from real progress and real decline. They observe behavior that is inacted in a familiar and trusted environment, rather than in an unknown institution or with a strange therapist. They know what milestones of development are to be expected of most children of a given age and can compare these in a natural setting.

When a child has a chronic illness, the teacher, as an active agent in the rehabilitation team, will be particularly alert for danger signs. What might have been the result of a late night or a "bad day" for a normal child could be the onset of diabetic coma for that more fragile child, for example. Further, the school, like the home, is the setting in which the student will use knowledge, techniques, and equipment acquired in various treatments and therapies.

CHANNELS OF COMMUNICATION

It is important for teachers to learn how to utilize other professionals, to communicate with them, and to define their own roles as educators in order to create a rehabilitative atmosphere in the school.

When the teacher interacts with other professionals, either school personnel or others, or with the family or agencies, some attention must be paid to the chain and channel of communication that are established. The teacher should give prior thought to this, with regard to the particular situation. For example, one parent might be most receptive to a very informal phone call from a teacher saying, about a child whose illness requires close attention, "Johnny was a little listless today and said he was very tired. I just thought you should know." Another parent might overreact to the statement; another would only respond if such a comment came from the school nurse. Again, if an epileptic child has a seizure, who is to be notified? Do the parents or caretakers work? Who should be called in an emergency?

Preferences, and even idiosyncrasies of colleagues, should be considered. For example, does the school counsellor or social worker wish to make all agency referrals, such as a contact with the Bureau of Vocational Rehabilitation? What is school policy with regard to information about genetic counseling or birth control? Can the teacher comfortably talk directly to the pupil or parents? Attention to the chain of communication is important both for safety's sake and so as not to "step on anyone's toes." Whenever a teacher is uncertain about intervening in a matter that is not strictly educational in nature, it is best for him or her to seek advice from others in the school–the principal, the school nurse, the psychologist, school social worker, speech therapist, and other teachers, as seems appropriate. Further advice may be solicited from the family physician or therapists working with the handicapped child. Interdisciplinary cooperation requires a great deal of tact and respect for role function. Of course, the handicapped student and family deserve the first consideration and must also be members of the team.

MEDICAL AND REHABILITATION SPECIALTIES

It is assumed that teachers are familiar with the professionals who routinely serve in pupil personnel capacities. However, in dealing with physically handicapped students, the support system may involve medical and rehabilitation specialists whose roles are not as familiar. These are therefore listed below for reference.* These professionals will be working in many different contexts; some will be staff or adjuncts to the school, others will be in various agencies, institutions, or private practice.

Physically handicapped children often are served by a medical team. Surgery and hospitalizations are sometimes a way of life, and rehabilitation may be lifelong.

Fewer than half of those practicing medicine are generalists, that is general practitioners. Within the medical specialties, the official instruments for certification are the various specialty boards in the following fields grouped in relevant categories:

The Surgical Specialties

Surgery–The general surgeon is a specialist who undertakes the diagnosis and treatment of certain bodily disorders by means of a wide range of operative procedures. A surgeon also understands the medical aspects of the injury or disease he or she is treating surgically. A number of surgical specialties are recognized by separate specialty boards. Those who practice these specialties may utilize, on occasion, nonsurgical therapy in caring for their patients, but they are qualified to perform surgical procedures. Among the surgical specialties are the following:

NEUROSURGERY: Surgery of the brain, spinal cord, and the peripheral and the autonomic nervous systems.

---

* The author is indebted to the following references for these descriptions:
Perkins, D. C., Lewin, M. and Felton, J. S.: *A Survey of Medicine and Medical Practice for the Rehabilitation Counselor.* Washington, Vocational Rehab. Administration, 1966.

American Hospital Association: *Job Descriptions and Organizational Analysis for Hospitals and Related Health Services.* Washington, U.S. Dept. of Labor, U.S. Govt. Print. Office, 1970.

ORTHOPEDIC SURGERY: The preservation and restoration of bony structures, joints, and related structures. Further specialization within this field is encountered in hip surgery, hand surgery, correction of congenital deformities, or muscle transplants, for example. The orthopedic surgeon also undertakes many nonsurgical tasks, such as the prescribing of corrective devices such as braces, working with a physiatrist in the formulation of a rehabilitation plan, serving as an expert witness in medicolegal cases, or evaluating disabilities of orthopedic origin.

THORACIC SURGERY: Surgery that is limited to the chest or thorax and includes operative procedures on the lungs, heart, or other chest structures.

PROCTOLOGY: Surgery that is limited to treatment of diseases of the anus and rectum, but in some instances this specialty extends to surgery of the lower intestinal tract. (Proctology is also a medical specialty.)

PLASTIC SURGERY: The surgical repair of soft tissue. It is frequently identified as reconstructive surgery, and the goals may be either functional or cosmetic restoration, or both.

UROLOGY: The study of diseases of the genitourinary or GU system, which includes the kidneys, ureters, bladder, and related organs and structures. Surgical procedures are only one segment of this specialty, which includes treatment of congenital anomalies, injuries, infections, neoplasms, and metabolic disturbances of the GU system.

In addition to the discrete surgical specialties discussed, some surgeons select certain areas of the body or groups of patients for specialized study. Thus, there are specialists in pediatric surgery or pediatric neurology. The line of demarcation between the physician and the surgeon is not always a sharp one.

Other Medical Specialties

ANESTHESIOLOGY: One of the newer specialties, whose practitioners not only administer local and general anesthetics, but participate in patient care before and after the surgical operation, as well as during the procedure itself.

OBSTETRICS AND GYNECOLOGY: Obstetrics is the management

of childbirth, including care before and after delivery, while gynecology includes the diagnosis and treatment of disorders of the female reproductive system. Comprising this system are the uterus, fallopian tubes, ovaries, vaginal tract, and related structures. This combined specialty is both medical and surgical, and urology and endocrinology are important components.

DERMATOLOGY: The study of diseases of the skin. This specialty was formerly identified as dermatology and syphilology, and although the latter part of the designation has been dropped, the venereal diseases, exclusive of gonorrhea, are still within its scope. Many systemic or generalized diseases with cutaneous manifestations, such as lupus erythematosus, sarcoidosis, and porphyria, are first seen by the dermatologist. The specialty is also known as cutaneous medicine.

OTOLARYNGOLOGY: The specialty that concerns itself with diseases of the ear, nose, and throat. The totality of the specialty is more accurately conveyed by the term *otorhinolaryngology*. More informally, it is often called ENT (ear, nose and throat). A generation or two ago, the treatment of disorders of the eye was grouped with the organs covered by this specialty, but it has since branched off into a separate specialty. Otolaryngology is both a medical and a surgical specialty and embraces such subspecialties as otology, laryngology, rhinology, bronchoesophagology, and maxillofacial surgery. In some hospitals this specialty is subsumed under head and neck surgery.

OPHTHALMOLOGY: The specialty that is concerned with treatment of disorders of the eye and is a surgical as well as a medical specialty. Like the dermatologist, the ophthalmologist often makes the first tentative diagnosis of systemic diseases that manifest themselves by characteristic ocular changes. The term *oculist,* though still in popular usage, is considered an obsolete term for this specialist; he is an ophthalmologist. The older designation persists because of this specialist's concern with the measurement of visual skills and the prescribing of lenses to correct refractive errors.

PHYSICAL MEDICINE: A medical specialty that uses physical energies or means to diagnose and treat diseases involving muscles, the nerves that innervate them, ligaments, tendons, and joints. The physical modalities include heat, cold, light, electricity, water, ultrasound, manipulation, massage, exercise, and mechanical devices. The physician who practices this specialty is a physiatrist, and he often functions as a key member of the rehabilitation team. The term *physiatry* is not in common parlance.

ONCOLOGY: The study of tumors or new growths. The specialty embraces the diagnosis of tumors and their treatment, surgically, radiologically, and medically.

PEDIATRICS: The specialty that embraces the total medical care of children from the neonatal period through adolescence. It concerns itself with the physical, psychologic, and social problems that bear on growth and development. More recently there have been suggestions that adolescent medicine should be established as a related field.

NEUROLOGY: The study of diseases of the nervous system. This is sometimes considered a subspecialty under internal medicine. However, within the specialty fields, it comes under the jurisdiction of a joint board that also covers psychiatry. Relatively few diplomates of this board hold certification in both specialties, and the present trend is to view neurology as an independent specialty. It is relevant, in this respect, that within the National Institutes of Health there are both a National Institute of Neurological Diseases and Blindness and a National Institute of Mental Health. Frequently, following study of a neurologic disorder, the patient will be referred to a neurosurgeon for surgical care.

PSYCHIATRY: The science of diagnosing and treating disorders of the mind, both organic and functional. Though this is a medical specialty, it is closely linked to the social sciences in its inquiry into human behaviour. The specialty includes treatment of the neurotic, the psychotic, and the mentally retarded. Psychoanalysis is one of the treatment techniques employed in psychiatry. Others include the use of individual or group therapy, electroconvulsive therapy, and the administration of tranquilizing or energizing medications.

PATHOLOGY: The science that deals with the nature of disease on the basis of the gross or microscopic examination of diseased tissue. Practitioners of this specialty may function either as surgical pathologists who examine the tissues of surgically removed specimens or as clinical pathologists who are skilled in the performance and interpretation of diagnostic laboratory tests.

RADIOLOGY: The diagnosis and treatment of disease by means of X-ray, radium, and other radioactive materials or sources.

PREVENTIVE MEDICINE: This specialty concerns itself with programs of prophylaxis against disease, whether communicable or not; the focus is not so much on the resistance of the individual organism to disease as on the environmental conditions conducive to good health or to disease. It includes four major subdivisions:

General Preventive Medicine, in which the specialist usually devotes himself primarily to teaching and research in this field in the medical school setting.

Occupational Medicine, which is concerned with the health, productivity, and adjustment of the worker in industry and other places of employment. In a sense, this specialty serves as a link between medicine and changing economic, social, and political trends.

Public Health, which assumes responsibility for the protection of groups of people against disease and for the promotion of maximum health through broad scale programs at the community level. Its programs may include communicable disease control, maternal and child health, environmental health, venereal disease control, nutrition, community mental health, alcoholism rehabilitation, epidemiology, and vital statistics.

Aviation Medicine, which places special emphasis on health evaluation of flight personnel for flight in standard (commercial or private) aircraft and on the environmental and health problems occasioned by man's probing of outer space. The specialty, in its more sophisticated form, is termed aerospace medicine, or space medicine.

Internal Medicine and Its Subspecialties

Internal Medicine is perhaps the specialty with the broadest scope and the one whose jurisdiction is most difficult to define.

The internist is sometimes identified as the physician who treats all disorders not requiring surgery, often termed a general practitioner with the benefit of extensive additional education. It is true that he or she resembles the general practitioner to the extent of having a more continuous relationship with the patient than do physicians in the other specialties and dealing with illnesses that involve more than one body system. The range of the specialty of internal medicine can best be grasped by identifying major subspecialties that it includes.

ALLERGY: The identification and treatment of hypersensitive responses to specific irritating substances.

CARDIOLOGY: The study of diseases of the heart. This usually includes disorders of the blood vessels, the two systems being termed jointly the cardiovascular system. Often the kidneys are involved, the entire organ system being known as the cardiovascular-renal system.

ENDOCRINOLOGY: The study of the endocrine glands (the glands of internal secretion, the ductless glands), which secrete hormones into the blood stream. These glands include the thyroid gland, the pituitary gland, the pancreas, the adrenal glands, and the gonads or sex glands.

GASTROENTEROLOGY: The study of diseases of the stomach and the intestinal tract (gastrointestinal or GI system), and the liver and gall bladder (hepatic system).

HEMATOLOGY: The study of the diseases of the formed elements of the blood and the blood-forming organs.

CHEST DISEASES: This rather generically named specialty is concerned with diseases of the lungs (pulmonary diseases). The physician who practices this specialty sometimes has been called a phthisiologist, particularly so when the major emphasis was on the diagnosis and treatment of tuberculosis, but is known more commonly as a chest physician.

GERIATRICS: The study of the diseases of old age and of the health problems that appear or become more severe in the aged.

RHEUMATOLOGY: The study of disorders of the joints. Since the term *rheumatism* is not medically precise, it is often applied by the layman to pain in the muscles, tendons, or bones. The diagnosis and treatment of arthritis come within the scope of the rheumatologist.

DENTISTRY: That department of medicine concerned with the prevention, diagnosis, and treatment of diseases of the teeth and adjacent tissues, and the restoration of missing dental and oral structures.

Aesthetic dentistry, the preservation, repair, and restoration of the teeth and adjacent tissues, performed so that the work has natural and pleasing appearance.

Operative dentistry, the branch of dentistry concerned with actual operations upon the natural teeth or the soft tissues of the oral cavity, as distinguished from those operations performed in the dental laboratory.

Prosthetic dentistry, that branch of dentistry dealing with the replacement of missing teeth or oral tissues by artificial means.

Confusion exists concerning some practitioners, such as chiropractors and osteopaths. The chiropractor adheres to a therapeutic system based on the theory that disease is caused by an interference with nerve function and that normal conditions are restored by adjusting the body structures, particularly by manipulating the vertebrae. Manipulation also at one time figured importantly in the repertoire of the osteopath, but the concept of osteopathy is a much broader one: That the normal body, when in correct adjustment, is a vital machine capable of producing its own remedies against infection and other toxic conditions. The osteopath searches for and removes, if possible, any condition in the joints, tissues, diet, or environment that is a factor in destroying natural resistance. The scientific training required of osteopaths is substantial, and as it expands, the differences between osteopaths and doctors of medicine tend to diminish.

Within the medical sciences there are also a number of highly specialized functions not directly involved in medical practice but performed by highly trained persons who may or may not be physicians. Among these are virology, immunology, epidemiology, toxicology, and biostatics. The teacher is unlikely to have occasion for direct contact with these personnel.

In the course of participating in the rehabilitation of the handicapped child, the teacher may interact with or communicate with professionally trained persons in the health sciences other than physicians. Some are familiar to everyone–dentists, pharmacists, and nurses, for instance. Some health care specialists work closely with physicians, and they often carry out the long-range therapies, which have been selected in consultation with physicians. Frequently it is these specialists who will work most closely with the teacher as well as with the child.

Health Care Professionals Most Frequently Interacting With Teachers and Physically Handicapped Students

ANAPLASTOLOGIST: constructs artificial portions of the body to replace what has been removed or destroyed. The substitute parts are fashioned from moulds (moulages) and fabricated in plastics.

AUDIOLOGIST: assesses the extent of hearing loss, evaluates the effect the loss will have on the communications facility of the patient, and participates in rehabilitation programs.

DENTAL HYGIENIST: works under the direction of a dentist, doing prophylactic cleaning of teeth and otherwise promoting preventive dental health.

DIETICIAN: has responsibility of providing persons (particularly in hospitals and other institutions) with food that is nutritionally adequate in terms of their individual needs.

OCCUPATIONAL THERAPIST: carries out a program of creative, educational, and recreational activities with two objectives: To accelerate physical and mental recovery, and to develop skills that will be useful after recovery. These include functional prevocational and homemaking skills and activities of daily living, and sensorimotor educational, recreational, and social activities.

OPTOMETRIST: examines and refracts eyes without the use of medicines, and prescribes lenses and visual training (orthoptics) when needed.

ORTHODONTIST: a dental specialist concerned with the realinement of malformed teeth and the correction of malocclusion.

OPTICIAN: interprets the prescription of the ophthalmologist or the optometrist and prepares eyeglasses in accordance with it.

NURSE: Registered Nurse–one skilled in the care of the sick, who has been graduated from a nursing school and passes a state board examination to qualify for the title R.N. A school nurse sees children in school, and a visiting nurse assists persons at home.

Licensed Practical (Vocational) Nurse–cares for chronic disease and convalescent patients, the aged, maternity patients, and well babies, under the supervision of a physician or a professional nurse, and may work in a hospital.

PATIENT EDUCATOR: instructs patients in prescribed academic subjects to prevent mental decondition, improve mental and physical condition, and aid in attainment of knowledge and skills that will meet patients' vocational activities. Prepares reports of patients' emotional reactions to and progress in individual and group training situations, to provide clinical data for evaluation by the rehabilitation team.

PHYSICAL THERAPIST: helps patients overcome neuromuscular disability through the application of a range of therapeutic modalities, including exercise, massage, heat, water, light, and electricity and conducts medically prescribed exercise to prevent complications due to disability following disease or injury. Helps the patient reach maximum performance and assume a place in society while learning to live with the limits of his capabilities.

PODIATRIST: treats diseases and disorders of the feet, such as corns, calluses, bunions, and skin infections. He is permitted to perform surgery within the scope of his training. Formerly the podiatrist was known as a chiropodist.

PROSTHETIST: makes artificial arms and legs (prostheses) and adjusts them to fit the amputee.

PSYCHOMETRIST: administers standardized tests that measure intelligence and various personality factors; works under the supervision of a clinical psychologist.

PSYCHIATRIC AIDE: provides care (other than those tasks requiring a registered nurse) for patients in a mental hospital.

REHABILITATION COUNSELLOR: provides psychological and vocational evaluation and counseling for handicapped individuals.

SPEECH THERAPIST: identifies patients with speech problems, tests, evaluates, treats, and gives guidance and counseling regarding these problems.

SOCIAL WORKER: contributes to diagnosis and treatment through an understanding of the social elements of patients' lives in relation to disability, illness, or problem. The social worker assists the patient and his family in handling financial, social, and emotional problems that result from a severe or prolonged illness or disability.

Other Health Care Specialties

MEDICAL RECORDS ADMINISTRATOR AND TECHNICIAN: has the responsibility of maintaining complete records of hospital patients, both inpatients and outpatients. These records include the results of physical examinations, laboratory tests and X-ray examinations, operative procedure data, reports of pathologic examinations, orders of attending physicians, progress notes, pertinent correspondence, and copies of outgoing summaries or reports.

MEDICAL TECHNOLOGIST: performs a variety of laboratory procedures required for diagnostic purposes. These might include complete blood counts (hemoglobin level, number of red cells, number and types of white cells, number of platelets), serologic tests, blood chemistry determinations, urinalyses, and electrocardiograms. In some instances, the technologist is also trained to do electroencephalograms.

X-RAY TECHNOLOGIST: positions patients, makes X-ray examinations, develops and processes exposed film, and keeps records of the examinations and the interpretations by the radiologist. He does not administer X-ray or other energies therapeutically.

Many of the above specialties require licensing by the State. In most cases, these personnel are organized into national professional associations. Since requirements for membership in these associations are not uniform, such membership does not necessarily attest to the qualifications of a specific practitioner, although it is evidence of sustained interest in and identification with the profession.

TEAMING FOR INDIVIDUALIZED EDUCATIONAL PROGRAMMING

When physically handicapped children have been segregated from their normal peers for school, it has usually been done for other than educational reasons. One reason has been that architectural barriers in the form of curbs, steps, and narrow doorways have prevented many students from physical attendance in schools. The new national standards for accessibility in buildings and facilities in public buildings have begun to decrease this obstacle.

The other reason frequently articulated in favor of segregation of physically handicapped students is their need for therapies: physical and occupational therapies, speech therapy and mobility training. Educators might question why time should be spent in the school day on therapies. In most cases, the therapies should not take precedence over education, although they will undoubtedly do so in hospital schools. Most students will not need and will not receive daily therapy. It would seem advantageous to employ itinerant therapists, who would work with the student in the community school and, better still, work with the classroom teacher, just as teachers of the blind have done for many years. Teachers, then, can apply techniques of positioning, self-help devices, and word practice on a daily basis, working closely with their rehabilitation counterparts.

Public Law 94-142 mandates that school districts develop and implement an *Individual Education Program* (IEP) in order to provide appropriate services to children who have been identified as exceptional. In some states "exceptional" will include gifted and talented children as well as those who have traditionally been considered handicapped. The IEP is required to insure the provision of appropriate services for children with special needs.

Planning the IEP with input and consent of the parent(s) is an important responsibility of the classroom teacher. The pupil personal services of the school will usually be vital to the formulation of IEPs of all handicapped children. The school counselor, psychologist, home school visitor and others will team with teachers both in mainstream and special education settings.

There are some unique aspects of the IEP for children with physical impairments and disabilities. In order to make assessments, determine short- and long-term educational objectives, and to create alternative strategies for meeting these objectives, the medical and paramedical personnel may give essential input at some times. They may be involved in the continuing assessment of some students. Strategies of teaming may differ greatly depending on the setting. Teachers in a hospital school or those delivering homebound instruction, for example, will obviously have differing channels of communication with other team members from teachers in regular or other special educational settings. It is worth the effort to open avenues of communication. The IEP goals, objectives, instructional plan, and ongoing evaluation will be much enhanced by interdisciplinary cooperation, both in formulating instructional and management concerns. Specific interdisciplinary teaming will be suggested in the following chapters relative to discrete disorders and their implications for physical management of students in educational settings.

Review Guide

After reading Chapter 3 the reader should be able to define the following terms:

audiologist	rehabilitation counsellor
occupational therapist	speech therapist
patient educator	social worker
physical therapist	surgeon
psychometrician	orthopedist
IEP	

After reading Chapter 3 the reader should be able to answer the following questions:

1. What are the three stages of health care?
2. What role does the school play in each of the three stages?
3. In what sense is a teacher a diagnostician of health problems?
4. What is the difference between an ophthalmologist and an optometrist?

5. What professionals are usually involved in pupil personal services in schools?
6. Who contributes to the formulation of an IEP?
7. Name two therapies commonly conducted in special schools.

Chapter 4

GENETIC MECHANISMS AND DEVELOPMENTAL DISABILITIES

For want of a nail the shoe was lost
For want of a shoe the horse was lost
For want of a horse the rider was lost
For want of a rider the battle was lost
For want of a battle the kingdom was lost
And all for the want of a horseshoe nail
Old Nursery Rhyme

I N UNDERDEVELOPED COUNTRIES in the world, the threats of starvation and infectious diseases are still major problems as they were in pioneer days in America. Now, because of highly developed technology and tremendous advances in knowledge and medical practice in the United States, malnutrition and infections can be controlled and are in general, diminishing greatly as causes of handicaps in children. Concomitantly, improvement in health care and sophisticated medical techniques have enabled babies to survive who would have died of their defects under more primitive conditions and have allowed people who have debilitating medical problems to live longer lives. In one ironic sense, then, it could be said that modern medicine has led to an increased prevalence of human afflictions. It has certainly changed the proportion of categories of illness and handicapping conditions and has increased vastly the average life span in general and among handicapped persons. So, while the figure "one in ten" seems to hold for school children who will possess a significant handicap, the nature and proportion of the handicaps have varied even in recent years.

51

RELEVANCE OF GENETIC KNOWLEDGE FOR TEACHERS

At this time, conditions present at birth account for over 5 percent, or half, of the handicapping conditions affecting school children. Some of these are hereditary, involving genes and chromosomes; some are new mutations. Others are errors in early development, whose cause may or may not be known. The teacher may ask about the relevance of an understanding of mechanisms of heredity and development to the classroom situation. Are not the present needs and problems of the child the main concern, or perhaps the only concern?

The first reason the teacher should become informed is the important contribution he or she can make toward prevention of defects, first as a citizen and second as an educator, particularly of nubile youth. The importance of prenatal care, the availability of services for counseling and medical help, and well-known facts about specific disorders can be made available through the school to all students.

Secondly, physically handicapped students in school or students who have handicapped persons in their families will want information about disorders. (The teacher must be very cautious here and may often defer to other professionals.) Here again, the informed teacher knows where to turn; he or she knows about genetic and family counseling, of services and aids provided by agencies, and the legal rights of disabled students and their families. Thirdly, the teacher can, through knowledge and understanding, contribute to a healthier attitude toward disabilities and parental and social responsibilities.

THE BEGINNING OF LIFE

Below, a very brief description of the mechanisms of heredity and development is given in order to provide a background for later discussion.*

Cells are the basic unit of all living things from the very simplest, one-celled organisms to humans with trillions of specialized cells packaged together in unique combinations in each individual.

---

* For a more detailed discussion, the reader is referred to Apgar and Beck's book, *Is My Baby All Right?* (1973) (see Appendix).

Cells in human beings are found in many shapes and sizes. Some individual nerve cells extend all the way from the brain to the toe. Some cells, such as those of the hair or skin, have a short life and reproduce themselves over and over by a process of cell division (mitosis). Other cells, such as brain cells, do not reproduce, so when brain cells are destroyed they do not regenerate.

The cell is distinguished by an outer membrane that permits transfer of food, wastes, and cell products. Within the cell is a nucleus that controls its functioning. Each nucleus in an individual also contains the hereditary blueprint for that individual: whether the individual was to be a plant, insect, or human, for instance, and what unique combination of attributes that particular being will possess.

This blueprint, or set of instructions, is written in what is called a genetic code. Recently understood are the mechanisms by which the directions for the development of an entire individual are transmitted in one cell at conception.* This information is contained on small, threadlike structures called *chromosomes,* which can actually be stained and observed microscopically in certain stages of cell development. The number of chromosomes found in cells of different types of organisms varies. Some types have as few as four to a cell, others have as many as 500.

Normal human beings have forty-six chromosomes in each cell, two of which carry directions for sex characteristics (as well as other characteristics) and are therefore called the sex chromosomes. The other forty-four chromosomes direct the development of the rest of the individual. Hence chromosomes control the operation of the cell itself, the entire living being, and also provide directions for producing a new living organism of the type of the reproducing ones.

The most important component of a chromosome is deoxyribonucleic acid (DNA), which is a ladderlike structure, or double helix, made up of four bases, abbreviated as A,T,C, and G. These

---

* For a more detailed discussion, the reader is referred to the following:
James Watson, *A Personal Account of the Discovery of the Structures of DNA* (New York, Atheneum, 1968).
Isaac Asimov, *The Genetic Code* (New York, Clarkson N. Potter, Inc., 1962).

protein compounds always pair, A with T, and C with G, to make the rungs of the ladderlike threads. Attached to these compounds are a sugar and a phosphate molecule, which make up the sides of the ladder. In the DNA ladder or helix in a chromosome, there are up to tens of millions of rungs following each other in a particular order. The order of the combinations of the four compounds specifies the heredity of the individual. The smallest information units are triplets of the paired compounds. For example, a segment of the ladder might read: CG, AT, AT; GC, TA, GC; and so forth, for about 6 billion chemical rungs for a human being.

A section of the DNA ladder that prints the code for some particular piece of genetic information, such as the segment that is involved in producing a particular protein essential to life, is called a *gene*. A gene may consist of roughly 500 to 2000 rungs on the DNA ladder. Little is known about where specific genes for particular traits are located on human chromosomes, but some gene mapping studies are being done.

The forty-six chromosomes occur in pairs, each pair of which is somewhat different in shape. One set of twenty-three chromosomes is transmitted to an offspring from the mother, the other set of twenty-three from the father at the time of conception, through the process of cell division and reduction called *miosis*.

During miosis, sections of matched chromosomes *cross over,* so the genes are "reshuffled" before each partner contributes one chromosome from each pair to the offspring. In this way possibilities for new gene combinations from each partner are multiplied.

The chromosomes are arranged in pairs. The non-sex chromosomes each consist of hundreds to thousands of genes arranged linearly and matched with a similar gene in the other member of the chromosome pair. Therefore, there are two genes for a given trait.

Chromosomal aberrations, either hereditary or those that occur in the process of development, can cause pathological conditions. The most common of these is Down's syndrome, which will be discussed later.

The sex chromosomes are somewhat different. The X chromosome is shaped like an *X* and carries genes. The Y chromosome, very small and shaped like a *V* (conventionally drawn upside down), is now known to have some active genes and also acts as a partner with the X chromosome. The genetic composition of males and females is distinguished *only* by the sex chromosomes. Normal females possess two X chromosomes with all the pairs of genes that occur on these two chromosomes. Thus femaleness is due to a double dose of X. Normal males possess an X chromosome, with genes on it, and a Y chromosome. Thus the Y chromosome dictates maleness.

We have said that each parent only gives twenty-three chromosomes to the new being, or one gene in each pair. (If this were not true the new individual would have 92 chromosomes.) Therefore, the mother will contribute one of her two X chromosomes to the new offspring, with a 50-50 chance that it will be one or the other chromosome. Likewise, the father will contribute one of his two sex chromosomes, the X or the Y, to the new offspring, with a 50-50 change that it will be one or the other chromosome. If the father contributed an X, the offspring has two X chromosomes and is a girl. If the father contributed a Y, the offspring is a boy. It can be seen then that the genetic determination of a baby's sex is made by the father. Since it is a chance occurrence which chromosome he contributes, 50 percent of the offspring will be boys and 50 percent will be girls.

Of all the mistakes in the number of chromosomes that are possible, those involving the sex chromosomes are the most frequent but seem to do less damage than errors in other chromosomes. Occasionally a girl has only one X chromosome (Turner's syndrome). Two Xs are necessary for a woman to be able to bear children. A female may have more than two X chromosomes, and a male may also. A male with an XXY condition (Klinefelter's syndrome) generally has immature sexuality, infertility, and the possibility of mental retardation. Some males have XYY, but there are only controversial studies about the effect of the XYY syndrome on behavioral or physical patterns.

While some of the genes on the X chromosome are specifically related to the different sex characteristics, there are others that regulate other characteristics that do not pertain to sex differences. One of these gene loci, for instance, regulates whether or not adults lose the hair on their heads. These genes are called *sex-linked* genes because they occur on the X chromosome. A male then, will have only one gene for a sex-linked characteristic, since his Y chromosome does not carry some genes. A female will have two genes for a sex-linked characteristic, one on each X chromosome.

The matching genes in a pair of autosomal chromosomes have the same basic function, such as determining blood type or eye color. On the gene loci for blood type, there can be the characteristics A or B, or lack of the characteristics, O. Therefore, pair combinations that are possible are AA and AO (Type A); BB and BO (Type B); AB (Type AB); and OO (Type O).

Often, however, genes do not act with equal power. When one gene of a pair carries directions that take precedence over those coded by the matching gene, the gene is said to be *dominant* (Fig. 3). The other gene is *recessive* for that characteristic and will be masked by the dominant gene, if it is present (Fig. 4). If both genes in a pair are recessive, the recessive characteristic will show.

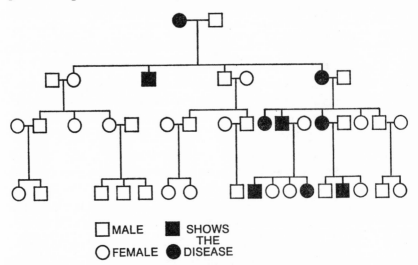

Figure 3. Autosomal dominant inheritance. The mechanism in Huntington's disease, osteogenesis imperfecta, Marfan's syndrome, and Waardenburg's syndrome.

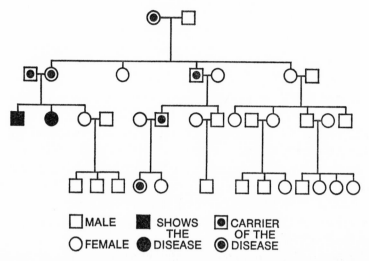

Figure 4. Autosomal recessive inheritance. The mechanism in Cooley's anemia, cystic fibrosis, muscular dystrophies (some), PKU, sickle cell disease, and Tay-Sachs disease.

The dominant characteristic will show in two cases: when both genes are dominant or when one gene is dominant and one recessive.

The characteristic brown in eye color is dominant over the characteristic blue, which is recessive. A blue-eyed person has two recessives for blue eyes (let us label this gene pair bb). A brown-eyed person could have a double dominant (labeled BB) for brown eyes, or have one dominant gene that masks the recessive gene (Bb). Two blue-eyed parents would not produce a brown-eyed child. Two brown-eyed parents could produce a blue-eyed child because each could have been Bb and given the recessive trait to their child. In fact, the chances are one in four (Fig. 4).

Actually, interaction among the genes is more complicated than these illustrative examples suggest. For instance, recent studies have revealed a gene that represses the gene for brown eye color. Therefore, one of the parents could actually be Bb but have blue eyes because of this repressor gene. The child could inherit B, but not the repressor gene, and have brown eyes.

When the gene for a trait is located on the sex chromosome, the situation is different. A female will have two genes for the trait, while males will often only have one gene for that trait. Therefore, males have a 50-50 chance of inheriting and showing the recessive trait from a mother who is a carrier of the trait but does not show it. A boy will have no contribution from his father for a sex-linked trait. Girls, on the other hand, will not show the recessive trait and one-half will be carriers, as shown in Figure 5.

The reason for explaining the transmission of recessive genes in detail is that a number of inherited pathological conditions are due to recessive genes, which are inherited in this very definitive way, either on autosomal or sex-linked chromosomes. That is why parents who look perfectly normal can transmit deleterious genes to offspring, so that their children either continue to be carriers or show the condition.

The fact is that the human population, or *gene pool* of the human population, contains many "bad" genes. Almost 2,000 inborn errors of metabolism have been identified to date, most of which are inherited in an autosomal recessive pattern.

Most genes that cause very serious problems are recessive. Otherwise, the conditions they cause would kill all persons carrying

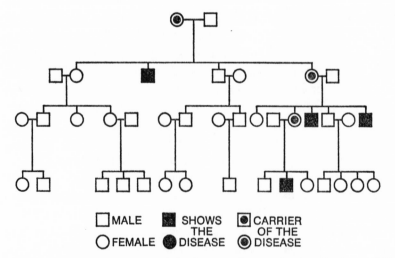

Figure 5. Sex-linked recessive inheritance. The mechanism in hemophilia and muscular dystrophy (Duchenne).

them before child-bearing age or would prevent reproduction. If they were dominant, they would soon die out because they could not be transmitted. As recessives, they can be carried for many generations before the chance occurrence of two similar recessives brings the condition to light. An interesting, if tragic, case of a dominant gene transmission is Huntington's disease (Fig. 3), which strikes persons between thirty and forty-five after their usual child-bearing age. It causes a progressive, fatal deterioration of the brain and nervous system. (The well-known musician Woody Guthrie died of this disease, and his children have a 50-50 chance of inheriting it. Apparently, his son Arlo shows signs of it at the time of this writing.)

The closer one person is in heredity to another, the more likely it is that both share the same recessives. That is why groups that intermarry frequently may have a larger percentage of some kinds of problems in their gene pool. That is also a reason why marriages between close relatives are discouraged. One-eighth of the genes of first cousins, for example, are similar. Human eugenics is quite different from animal and plant eugenics where, with possibilities for experiment and control, offspring are often bred very closely.

Often it is not just a single pair of genes that is responsible for a characteristic, but rather a combination of genes. In the case of skin color, for example, at least eight different pairs of genes are involved, so intermediate shadings are possible.

Many disease conditions, as well as normal conditions, seem to be a result of a combination of genetic factors (the predisposition) and developmental and environmental factors (precipitating and perpetuating factors) acting together to create multifactorial causes of an individual's physical condition and behaviour. Diseases of this kind "run in families" but are not as predictable (and probably are more preventable) as those with a simple chromosomal or genetic inheritance. Conditions such as this are cancer and heart disease.

In the course of time since life began, there has been the gradual evolution of organisms from very simple one-celled beings to the many species and subspecies of plants and animals that are

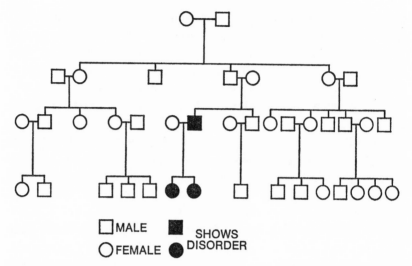

Figure 6. Sporadic due to dominant mutation. The mechanism in achondro-plasia and some osteogenesis imperfecta.

present today. This process depends on inheritable alterations called mutations. Mutations are changes in genetic material, which can occur in any cell. When they occur in the reproductive cells and the offspring lives, the mutation can be passed on to succeeding generations. Mutations are necessary for the evolution of the species, and they are valuable in helping organisms adjust to new environmental situations that demand new inherited characteristics.

Spontaneous mutations occur constantly and seem to result from background radiation and chemicals. Mutations can be experimentally induced in the laboratory and have been accidentally increased through use of medical X-rays. The effects of radiation from bombs in war, in laboratories, and in hydrogen bomb tests have apparently accelerated mutations.

When a mutation and consequent new characteristic is advantageous, the "mutant" is more likely to procreate. The new variety, being more successful, thus drives out or at least competes with the old variety. Most mutations are harmful; most will be so deleterious that a viable organism will not be created. Less harmful mutations cause many of the conditions described in this text. Some, as we shall see, are of advantage in one environmental situation and a disadvantage in another. The appearance of a mutation is shown in Figure 6.

MEDICAL ADVANCES WITH GENETIC KNOWLEDGE

In the past twenty years many advances have been made in the science of genetics concerning the relationship of chromosomal and genetic aberrations to developmental and metabolic anomalies. The very real benefits deriving from the advances in genetic research are highlighted by the history of the understanding of metabolic disease, phenylketonuria or PKU. This problem originates in the liver, the largest organ of the body, which has, as one function, the breakdown of the proteins of foods into amino acids, the building blocks of metabolism. PKU is an error of metabolism in which there is the absence of an enzyme that is necessary for the liver to convert one amino acid, phenylalanine, into another amino acid, tyrosine.

Since the mother of the PKU child has normal metabolism, the baby is somewhat protected prior to birth. However, as soon as the newborn child with PKU begins to drink milk, the phenylalanine becomes absorbed. The blockage in the metabolic process builds the phenylalanine level, and it spills over into the urine, where it can be detected. Usually, this condition interferes with the growth of the brain, and untreated individuals will become severely mentally retarded and hyperactive. Tyrosine is important in the production of body pigments, so even PKU children from dark parents will be inclined toward light skin and blue eyes.

PKU is one of the very few types of mental retardation amenable to medical treatment in the following way. Phenylalanine is a compound that forms about 5 percent of the protein an individual normally eats. By careful and very early control of diet, before the overload of phenylalanine and substances derived from it can damage the brain, the mental retardation can be prevented, or at least substantially reduced. The diet can apparently be discontinued later in childhood, and the child will remain free of symptoms.

Because PKU often involved more than one child in a family, researchers recognized it as a familial disorder. Studies with involved families indicated that approximately one in four children in the families has PKU. From this it was concluded that PKU was inherited and caused by a single recessive autosomal gene.

Among well-baby populations the diagnosis of PKU, prior to mass mandatory screening, usually came after PKU was discovered in a defective older sibling. Unfortunately, this meant that one person in a family had to be sacrificed in order to discover the disease. In the mid 1960s routine screening of all newborn infants became mandatory in hospitals throughout the United States. In this manner a child from a previously unidentified family could derive maximum benefit from early identification and immediate treatment procedures. Chemical tests are now available to discover if a person is a carrier of PKU. One person in seventy carries this recessive gene, but the disease is rare, affecting one child in 10,000 (Fig. 4).

It is now realized that many of the inborn errors of metabolism occur in a single, specific step in chemical functioning of the body, which is in turn controlled by a single gene. The defect may be in the production of an enzyme (as in PKU) or several enzymes, which make other chemical actions work incorrectly. It may be an error in the precise order of the amino acids determined by genetic directions contained in the DNA (as in sickle cell disease). Therefore, the concept of inborn errors of metabolism includes all birth defects that are caused by abnormal genes.

GENETIC COUNSELING*

Medical technology has advanced markedly in the areas of contraception, abortion, artificial insemination, and *in utero* identification and treatment of certain abnormal conditions. The law is reflecting concerns of society regarding the right to life, the right to abort, the right to die, and the rights of natural parents. Predictions for future developments are heard regarding test-tube

---

* The following remarks are based on a presentation entitled, Parents Have a Right to Information About Heredity, included in *Proceedings,* 80th Annual Convention, APA, 1972.

babies, direct intervention for genetic abnormalities, mandatory birth control, and eugenic planning.

On the clinical and counseling level, however, professionals have not often enough interpreted research findings and explained options open to lay persons who have problems and concerns in these areas. Their reluctance does not apparently stem primarily from religious convictions, but rather from having developed no clear guidelines concerning their various responsibilities to their patients, clients, and students.

Recently, the money-raising campaign of the Muscular Dystrophy Association included the repeated plea in the news media –"Help medical science find the cause of this disease." Now in one sense of the word, the cause of the Duchenne type of muscular dystrophy is known. It is a genetic aberration that is transmitted as a sex-linked recessive (Fig. 5). Families with as many as five brothers afflicted with muscular dystrophy have been identified in some instances. Sometimes parents of these children do not seem to understand the hereditary component of the condition, or the chances of their future offspring developing it.

It would be completely presumptuous for anyone to assume that these parents would have done otherwise had they known the odds for their children. The beauty and meaning of life are not measured by the number of its days. Suffering and sacrifice can lead to deepening love and final serenity for afflicted persons and those around them. To choose an extraordinarily difficult life of caring for an exceptional child is a highly moral and courageous decision. However, to undertake the same life from ignorance of alternatives is to have been deceived.

Genetic information concerning the hereditary component of many disorders including hemophilia, galactosemia, diabetes, sickle cell anemia, cystic fibrosis, phenylketonuria, Down's syndrome, and Tay-Sachs disease, while well known to specialists, is not always available to the general public and seldom taught in school. Facts about hereditary causes may even be somewhat suppressed by professionals responsible for education and health care. Why have people been seemingly reluctant to acknowledge the hereditary component of many disorders? Probably many professionals have wanted to spare the feelings of parents who already have the burden of an afflicted child. For example, it is naturally not pleasant to make clear to the mother of a hemophiliac son that she has transmitted a deleterious gene to him and that her daughters have a 50 percent chance of being carriers also (Fig. 5). She could be made to feel as if she has a "bad seed" and could become guilt ridden and ashamed.

If the facts about heredity are examined squarely, however, it may be that parents of afflicted children and the children themselves can have a healthier view of "why this had to happen to me." The facts are that the human species transmits a very high proportion of deleterious genes from generation to generation. Exact percentages of these vary in the gene pools of various racial and geographic groups, but no group is immune and no person is immune from these probabilities. The chance outcropping of hereditary disorders is inevitable and is the price to be paid by humanity for the development of the human race. Genetic disorders are a part of the biological scheme of existence just as is death itself, and in this sense they might be considered God's will. Enlightened parents and their afflicted offspring can be freed from irrational guilt and self-recrimination by understanding these biological facts of heredity.

It follows reasonably that the total human community has the obligation to share the responsibility for individuals who require extraordinary medical and educational care and attention. It can be predicted how many individuals will be born disabled by genetic aberrations. Usually, it is not known specifically who will bear them. It is unjust to ask an individual family to sacrifice all its funds and all its resources on a defective child because they were the ones chosen on Nature's roulette wheel.

Some individuals contend that any human control over procreation is blasphemous. People differ in good conscience regarding sexual abstinence, contraception, abortion, sterilization, artificial insemination, and any other practice leading to eugenics or population control. Free society upholds the right of individuals to their convictions, but such convictions cannot be arrived at with integrity unless all options are known and all consequences considered. Free society does not uphold the right of one group to decide on the mores of other groups or the right to suppress information just because it is inimical to one group's point of view or because the truth is not pleasant.

Knowledge of the advances in medical science should be available to all prospective parents. Parents' organizations and money-raising and service organizations for disability groups should share responsibility with the helping professions in providing information about incidence of hereditary disorders, probabilities based upon known situations, location of genetic clinics and other appropriate facilities, and the options open to parents with regard to bearing disabled offspring.

New developments in contraceptive and abortion techniques, sterilization, artificial insemination, and new advances in genetics and embryology have vastly increased the options of parents concerning procreation. For example, a woman over forty years old who has a relative with Down's syndrome may have a one out of six chance of carrying a child with Down's syndrome. She can be advised of this probability and also that Down's syndrome can be detected *in utero.* She has then a choice whether to conceive a child at all, conceive a child and abort a defective fetus, or accept her possibly defective offspring for whom she has prepared herself psychologically. All these factors have to be carefully weighed in view of the need for perpetual care of most Down's syndrome individuals and the fact that the older mother is halfway through her life span. Spina bifida, also, can be detected in utero.

A woman from a family carrying known sex-linked recessives such as muscular dystrophy or hemophilia has a right to know that sex can be determined *in utero.* She can decide whether or not to bear children, to have only girl children and chance aborting a normal boy, or take her chances with a defective child.

If a couple is relatively sure they are both carriers of Tay-Sachs disease (Fig. 4), they might decide not to risk having their own children. The husband might undergo voluntary sterilization, or the wife might undergo the more complicated procedure of a tubal ligation. They might decide on artificial insemination. (In 1957, it was estimated that 100,000 babies had already been born by this means.) On the other hand, they might take their chances on the possibility of a diseased baby who will have a difficult and relatively short life.

A member of the Sickle Cell Anemia Society has aptly pointed out that screening procedures for the disease can accomplish little at the present state of medical knowledge unless identification of the carriers of the sickle cell is followed by counselling in family planning (Fig. 4).

If knowledge is available and options are considered, all parents should have a more realistic and positive attitude toward the disabled child they may produce. The diabetic parent who has chosen in knowledge to have a child who may develop diabetes has decided that this handicap can be lived with, and he or she has a positive attitude toward the disabled child produced. How different this is from the frequent case, where the uninformed parent is shocked and dismayed that he has transmitted a defect, and he is therefore disappointed in his offspring.

If all prospective parents realize that the possibility of producing a defective child is a real one, and if school and society are supportive of such children and their parents, the children numbering in the 10 percent who are exceptional (from heredity or other causes) will not have the added burden of guilt-ridden, shocked, or unprepared parents with whom they must begin to make their lives.

In the short run, it may be easier not to face the realities. In the long run, all parents and children will profit from a forthright and honest assessment of hereditary probabilities and other risks inherent in parenthood.

Review Guide

After reading Chapter 4 the reader should be able to define the following terms:

cell nucleus	gene
chromosomes	gene pool
genetic code	sex-linked gene
sex chromosomes	mutation
DNA	PKU

After reading Chapter 4 the reader should be able to answer the following questions:

1. What are three reasons teachers need to know about the mechanisms of heredity and development?
2. What are three conditions in modern times that have changed the proportions of handicapping conditions?
3. What percentage of school-age children will possess a significant handicap?
4. What is the percentage of children showing handicapping conditions at birth?
5. How many chromosomes are in each cell nucleus of a human being?
6. What sex chromosomes are possessed by a female?
7. What is the function of the Y chromosome?
8. Why can normal parents transmit abnormalities to their children?
9. What are the two main benefits of mutations?
10. Why are most deleterious (bad) genes recessive?
11. How are the bad effects of PKU prevented or reduced?
12. What are the benefits of genetic counselling–give at least three reasons.

Section II

ABNORMALITIES OF THE BONES AND MUSCLES

After a momentary silence spake
Some Vessel of a more ungainly Make;
"They sneer at me for learning all awry:
What! did the Hand then of the Potter shake?"
Omar Khayyan

From the standpoint of learning, abnormalities of the bones and muscles should not be a deterrent. Usually students with these problems are healthy and should be expected to show the normal range of intelligence. Attention to physical modifications may be necessary, and temporary special educational arrangements may be needed. Of major concern is a happy psychological environment in the school and home.

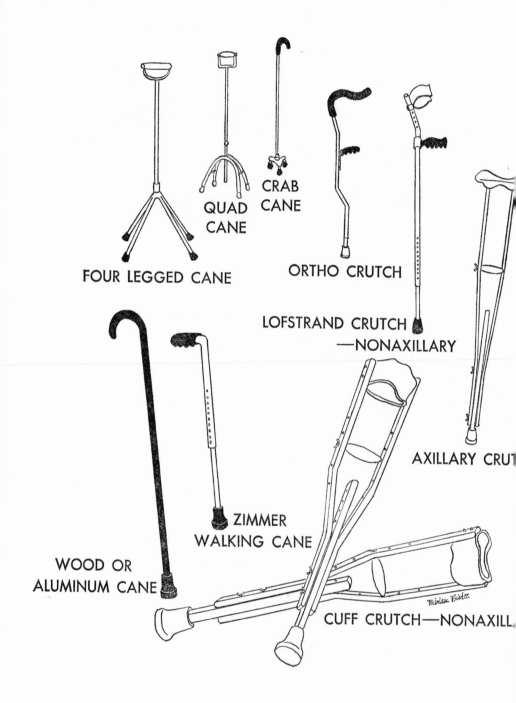

FOUR LEGGED CANE

QUAD CANE

CRAB CANE

ORTHO CRUTCH

LOFSTRAND CRUTCH
—NONAXILLARY

AXILLARY CRUT

WOOD OR ALUMINUM CANE

ZIMMER WALKING CANE

CUFF CRUTCH—NONAXILL

Chapter 5

AMPUTATIONS

Does it matter—losing your legs
For people will always be kind
And you need not show that you mind
When the others come in after hunting
To gobble their muffins and eggs.
Siegfried Sassoon

A<small>N AMPUTATION</small> is an impairment that can occur any time during a life span. An infant can be born a congenital amputee, with an incomplete extremity or extremities. At the other extreme, therapeutic amputations are done on very elderly persons in order to add months or years to their lives, and on children for the same reason. The care and treatment of a child born with a missing limb are very different from management of an older child or youth who has had an acquired amputation, either traumatic, as the result of an accident, or elective, as a therapeutic procedure. In amputees below the age of sixteen, about 75 percent of the impairments are congenital, affecting boys and girls equally.

Amputations can be unilateral, that is only one limb is affected. Eighty-five percent of all amputations in children are unilateral rather than affecting both corresponding limbs (bilateral). Among children, there are twice as many upper extremity as lower extremity amputees. Among adults, conversely, there are over ten to twenty times as many lower extremity amputees as upper extremity amputees.

CONGENITAL AMPUTATIONS

In normal fetal development, the tiny embryo exhibits arm buds on the twenty-sixth day of life. Within forty-eight hours, the buds

71

form into an upper and lower arm. Within the next three days, each arm begins to grow the beginnings of a hand. Several days after the arm buds erupt, at about the end of the first month of development, buds for legs will appear and develop in the same manner.

There are genetic causes of a number of the congenital defects. These defects include lack of fingers and toes, or too many fingers and toes; partial amputations, where the affected limb seems to have been pinched or strangled; and a condition where there is an absence of most of the arm and forearm bone with the hands developing right out of the shoulders, or a comparable or imperfect development of the thighs and legs, with feet present (*phocomelia:* phoco = seal; melia = limb). Parents with such defects can frequently learn their odds for transmitting them from genetic counsellors.

Many congenital amputations are of unknown cause. With others, viruses, chemicals, and radiation may be suspected or known causes. A notable example of a specific cause of birth defects (teratogen) was the drug thalidomide, which was a popular tranquilizer in Germany and England, put on the market in 1957. While this drug was harmless for most children and adults, it finally was proved to have an arresting effect on the fetal developmental process for an unknown reason, when taken within the thirty-eighth to fifty-fifth day after pregnancy had begun. Half of the babies affected had malformations that were severe enough to cause death, but in Germany alone 3,000 survived infancy. They have lived with various deformities associated with the time of drug ingestion, ranging from absence of ears, complete absence of limbs, phocomelia, and internal abnormalities. About one-fourth are severely disabled, but most are of normal intelligence. The United States was spared the epidemic because thalidomide was never allowed to be manufactured in this country.

Other drugs such as quinine and aminopterin (used in high doses to promote abortions) and Myleran® (a treatment for leukemia) seem to contribute to birth defects when taken in early pregnancy. Chemicals such as mercury are also known to contribute toward birth defects. In current thinking it is postulated that inherited disposition makes some fetuses particularly vulnerable to some teratogens. So, for example, only half of the fetuses exposed to rubella virus within the first trimester of their mother's pregnancy actually were malformed at birth.

The facts about heredity and teratogens need to be promulgated in biology and health courses and in those programs designed to prepare young persons for marriage and parenthood. Many foundations and agencies are also helpful sources of information and public education for the prevention of birth defects.

ACQUIRED AMPUTATIONS

Among older persons, the most frequent cause of elective amputations is vascular complications resulting from long-term diabetes or cardiovascular conditions. These complications usually involve the lower extremities. Therapeutic amputations in young adults and children are more often needed to prevent the spread of bone cancer.

The most common cause of death in the United States today is accidents, which, in the age group five to fourteen, account for almost twenty times as many deaths as any illness, and in the age group one to four, account for five times as many deaths as any illness. Significant numbers of children also survive car, snowmobile, and farm equipment accidents and the like with resulting loss of limbs in the birth to sixteen age range, with boys and girls equally affected. Among young to middle-aged adults accidents and war injuries necessitate amputation in three times as many men as women.

PHYSICAL ADAPTATIONS

The treatment and management of an amputation will vary enormously depending on all the factors that have been discussed: whether it is congenital or acquired; how many and which limbs are affected; how extensive is the amputation; how old is the amputee.

There are four main thrusts of possible treatment: (1) surgery, (2) physical therapy, (3) prosthesis (substitution of an artificial part), and (4) re-education to acquire efficient use of the prosthesis and self-help devices (orthotics). The teacher's concern will probably be primarily with the last thrust, where there may be some useful coordination between the physical or occupational therapist, nurse, or physician to assure that the student is making the most therapeutic or efficient use of his limbs in the course of the school day.

In general, it can be said that a bilateral amputation is more than twice as incapacitating as a unilateral amputation. The higher the amputation, the more serious it is, in terms of residual function and the success of a prosthesis.

With very young amputees most experts feel that therapy should follow the natural development of the child. Tailor-made prostheses are constructed for these children as early in life as possible. Some sort of support should be provided for those with leg problems at an age when the child would normally begin to stand and walk. Artificial arms of a simple type may be provided at about five months of age. Children with no arms can begin to operate a hook by age two. In the meantime, babies begin with a rubber baby mitt and progress to a passive hook that can be opened so it can hold a lollipop or rattle. Thus the child will grow up feeling the prosthesis is part of him. After being fitted for artificial limbs, he learns that small movements of a muscle can trigger the hook fingers of the artificial arm. He learns how to use it to reach rattles that hang on the crib. Gradually, dexterity improves, and he is able to pick up objects and pull himself upright in his crib. Those with deformed feet can be taught to walk on prosthetic legs at an early age.

Children are not as sensitive to the cosmetic appearance of an appliance, so utility rather than cosmetic considerations is most important in fitting a prosthesis. The loss of one hand or partial arm may or may not necessitate an artificial limb. Or, a prosthesis may be used in some instances and discarded in others, such as sports. A cosmetic hand can replace the hook for some occasions.

With bilateral absence of upper limbs, usually the child will wear two hooks operated mechanically by intact limb or shoulder muscles. With a complete lack of arms, rather than using prostheses, some persons become remarkably adept at using their toes, feet, and legs to write, eat, and drive. These persons are usually congenital amputees, whose compensatory limbs have been trained for a lifetime, rather than recent amputees.

Artificially powered limbs are useful in some, but not all cases. The Heidelberg arm presently is the best prosthesis for children whose torso muscles are extremely underdeveloped. It is a gas-operated machine that allows the wearers to rotate their artificial wrists through 180°, to bend their elbows, swing their arms at the shoulder, and to grasp utensils and pencils with hooks. It is powered by carbon dioxide, which is contained in an unobtrusive 8-inch aluminium cylinder worn at the child's back and refilled every few days. The wearer releases the gas to power the arm movement by moving the muscles in the shoulder or arm stump against highly sensitive control valves in the Heidelberg arm's shoulder and chest. Although it was originally designed for adults, it is easily adapted to children with phocomelia because the finger-like protrusions from shoulders or elbows make it easier for them to manipulate control valves. If a child with phocomelia has long enough arms so the hands can touch, they are quite functional, so that prostheses are usually not recommended. Other "power arms" are coming into use and simulate living limbs. One of these uses a braided nylon tube that swells and shortens when inflated with carbon dioxide. A new prosthesis, which must be fitted very soon after an amputation, is controlled by nerve impulses from the remaining stump.

Modern artificial lower limbs can look so natural and work so well that they are difficult to detect. It is far easier to walk if the amputation is below the knee even if the amputation is bilateral. Unilateral above the knee amputees also walk quite well, but those with bilateral injury may sometimes or always use a wheelchair, crutches, or canes.

For severely handicapped children, more adaptations are necessary to prepare the child to be as independent as possible. Most orthopedic clinics have developed a variety of these, among which are: a zipper on the neck of a shirt; a loop on the trousers, underclothes, and dresses; slits in the socks; Velcro® adhesive tape beneath buttons for fastening; wall hooks and rubber mattresses with adhesive surface to aid the child in wriggling into and out of clothing; wheelchairs with tank treads for going up stairs; steel-top desks with magnetized attachments that can be raised or lowered depending upon the child's use of his hands or feet.

A child who has grown up with an amputation has probably acquired skill in compensating and adapting to the situation. Therefore, when the teacher is unsure if the pupil can execute some physical task, probably the person to ask about it is the child himself.

Because children with amputations can be expected to be intelligent and alert, they can be helpful in figuring out classroom modifications that they might need. They might also require some assistance going to the toilet. This can be planned with them.

In the area of physical activity, they should be encouraged to do as much as they are able. Swimming is an excellent sport for most physically handicapped children. Bilateral leg amputees have become swimming champions. Some unilateral leg amputees are fine skiers.

Tricycles and even bicycles can be powered with one leg or modified to allow for body steering. Oversize tricycles are available for older children and adults, and they can give the amputee an added measure of freedom at school and at home.

Management of the prosthesis may result in some temporary problems. With rapidly growing and very active children, there may be a temporary "grounding," when the child must do without a prosthesis while it is being repaired or replaced. Certainly it is better to encourage the normal vigorous exercise of children than to try to save wear and tear on an artificial limb.

The child may experience occasional pain, necessitating an adjustment of the prosthesis. The child may need to be excused from class for a medical appointment or physical therapy. Routine absences, however, should always be discouraged in favor of rescheduling therapies so they do not interfere with important school activities.

With younger children particularly, a prosthesis, brace, crutch, or wheelchair can present a safety problem. A hook can be a dangerous weapon, for example. One preschool teacher solved this problem by removing the artificial arm for the foreseeable future until the child was to mature. This is somewhat akin to chopping off a child's arm or tying him up for misbehaving and is certainly not the best remedy. The child with "hardware," needs to learn self-control just as the very strong child learns not to misuse strength. Students with hooks can avoid being bullied or pushed around when the troublemakers realize that the amputee does have a formidable weapon if necessary.

The person who has been even temporarily on crutches, due to a sprained or broken leg, knows that the use of crutches takes energy and a surprising amount of skill. With a brace or a cast on also, it is even difficult to maneuver into a small car. The back seat of a four-door car is easier for the disabled person to negotiate. Bus and stair steps may be managed best going up backward.

The teacher can survey the physical environment of the class to see what modifications would be helpful to the crutch walker, and parents may need some suggestions for home management. Traffic patterns between pieces of furniture may need to be altered. For example, manipulating crutches to get to a chair behind a desk may present some difficulties. Small scatter rugs should be eliminated; they may contribute to slipping on crutches. It is well to work out convenient places for crutches when the student is not using them: sometimes they may be placed flat on the floor and out of the traffic pattern; at other times they may rest upright against a counter top or table.

The physiotherapist will have instructed the patient in the use of crutches on the stairs; a handrail is an important asset. At first it is reassuring to have someone between the crutch walker and the bottom of the stairs to give assistance. It is sometimes easier to maneuver the stairway using a handrail and one crutch; in this case the person needs to develop the facility to get the second crutch to the end of the stairway. When starting at the top of the stairway, the second crutch can be pushed down the stairs ahead. When starting at the bottom of the stairs, the second crutch may be placed alongside the other or moved ahead on the stairs as the walker goes up.

A simple solution to carrying things while moving about on

crutches is a tote bag; this is fine for small objects such as books, facial tissues, a sandwich. The shop or laboratory may call for simplification of work tasks. When hands are full of crutches it is difficult to carry equipment. With a table on rollers one can move many things. Rearrangement of storage areas may make it easier to reach objects without losing balance. It is convenient to have long tongs to reach small objects.

Independence for the amputee will be a gradual thing . . . it is obviously related to the physical strength and motivation of the person. It may not proceed smoothly; on some days the student is able to do more than on others. The teacher can help by being sensitive to his needs and openly discussing them to find solutions.

Many have stressed the importance of the psychological factor in predicting how well an amputee will adjust both physically and educationally. Studies of child amputees have pointed to the importance of parental acceptance in the ultimate good adjustment of the child with an amputation. This seems to be a more important variable than the time the defect was acquired or even the severity of the defect. Teachers can assuage the anxieties of parents, who are often far more conscious of a defect than teachers or schoolmates will be. In most cases a student with an amputation should present very few problems to the school, and it is hoped that the school will not present problems to the student!

Review Guide

After reading Chapter 5 the reader should be able to define the following terms:

congenital amputation	bilateral amputation
therapeutic amputation	phocomelia
acquired amputation	teratogen

After reading Chapter 5 the reader should be able to answer the following questions:

1. What are six common adaptive aids to help amputees with daily activities?
2. What are three important causes of amputations?
3. What is the usual relationship between ability to learn and amputations?

4. When are prostheses usually first fitted on the individual with an amputation? Why?
5. What is the most important variable in psychological adjustment of children with amputations?

Chapter 6

ARTHRITIS

Arthritis walked the earth with the dinosaurs: it has been found in the skeletal remains of reptiles that lived more than one hundred million years ago. It has been observed in horse, mouse, whale, dolphin and bird, affecting animals that walk, swim or fly.

Grand Rounds
Presbyterian University Hospital
Pittsburgh, Pennsylvania

THE TERMS *arthritis* and *rheumatism* do not refer to a specific disease entity, but represent an all-inclusive descriptive title for a large group of acute and chronic inflammatory pathological conditions that principally affect the joints and supporting structures. The bones, the connective tissues, blood vessels, cartilage, muscles, and nerves can be involved in varying degrees. The disturbances are characterized by swelling of the joints and related supporting tissues, which results in pain and stiffness, and later by deformities.

Human beings rely on the skeleton for support and the joints for movement. The skeletal bones are linked together in various ways, and joints are classified into three types, based on the kind of tissue found between the bone surfaces. Fibrous joints contain dense fibrous tissue that provides stability where tight union is achieved, such as between the bones of the skull. Junctures containing connecting material made of cartilage permit a limited degree of motion, as in the intervertebral discs of the spinal column. The most common type of joint in the body, the synovial joint, allows the greatest degree of movement. Such joints are the chief articulators of the extremities: the finger, wrist, elbow, shoulder, toe, ankle, knee, and hip. These joints are the sites of the most

80

frequent forms of arthritis. In the synovial joint, the touching surfaces of the bone are covered with articular cartilage, and the articular cavity is lined by a smooth membrane (the synovium). This tissue lies on connective tissue (subsynovium) that has few blood vessels and cells. The smooth surfaces of the bone are lubricated by fluid.

OSTEOARTHRITIS

Osteoarthritis is due to wear and tear on the joints; it is therefore generally associated with the middle and later years of life and is part of the normal process of aging. However, it may occur at any age, especially with joints that undergo unusually hard usage. It is therefore a danger with children who have some orthopedic imbalance, poor posture, overweight, injury, another joint disease, or must compensate for a weakness or loss by straining a limb. In these cases, osteoarthritis develops as a condition secondary to the original problem.

Normally, smooth cartilage coats the bone ends so that they may move smoothly against each other. In early primary osteoarthritis, this cartilage, because of a biochemical abnormality, begins splintering and disintegrating so the underlying bone is exposed, and movement causes pain. The gliding surfaces of smooth normal cartilage are gradually replaced by hardened bone. This degeneration frequently leads to bony outgrowths at the joint edges (spurs that are seen on X-ray) and in the tendons, the fibrous tissue at the end of the muscle, which attaches to bone. The bony projections may also be found on the ligaments, the tough connective tissue that connects the articular ends of the bones. It may occur in any joints, including those of the spine. Thus, after some years, there can be limitation of motion of the joints due both to the pain, if they are moved, and to the mechanical destruction of the joint contour.

Three common congenital abnormalities are usually of little concern if they have medical intervention, but they may lead to serious osteoarthritis by middle years if left untreated. One of these is congenital dislocation of the ball and socket joint of the hip, where the head of the thigh bone (femur) is not placed in the socket of the hip (acetabulum). When treatment for this disorder has been recommended, the child may be casted and immobilized, usually in infancy. This condition affects six times as many girls as boys. A second common problem involving the hip joint is Legg-Perthes disease. This describes a condition of no known cause where there is a loss of blood supply to the growth center of the thigh bone at the hip joint. The bone in the growth center dies, and the growth plate is replaced by new bone. The healing goes on for a period of about two years, during which time it is very important to protect the hip bone so that the new head of bone will not form into a flat, irregular shape (coxa plana), which will lead to early degenerative arthritis of the hip. Children, usually boys, develop this problem between the ages of four and eight, so they will be a concern of the school while recuperating from this disease.

A variety of deformities of the foot involve muscular imbalance (talipes). The most common is club foot. Early medical procedures such as exercise, bracing, or surgery relieve the imbalance so that the child can walk properly. Many secondary arthritic deformities in crippled children can be prevented or lessened if attention is paid to proper positioning, splinting, exercise, and diet control. Even in a school where routine physical therapy is given, most of the crippled child's time is spent in the classroom, so the teacher needs to learn techniques of physical management. Also, the teacher may be the first to notice a slight limp, imbalance, or expression of pain, which might initially indicate the need for medical intervention.

SPONDYLITIS OF ADOLESCENCE

This type of arthritis is systemic; that is, it affects the entire body rather than pertaining to isolated joints, like osteoarthritis. This is primarily a disease of adolescence and early adult years, occurring much more often in males than females. It is characterized by pain in the back and legs. It may progress to severe painfulness in the entire back. There is a strong familial tendency toward this disease, which can be severely crippling.

RHEUMATOID ARTHRITIS

Rheumatoid arthritis is a biochemical systemic abnormality that is most usually manifest in adults, with the highest incidence in the fourth and fifth decades and with three times as many women as men having the condition. However, it can occur in infancy, and cases appear in about 3 in 100,000 children each year. It occurs in girls more often than boys and begins particularly between the ages of one to four, or between nine to fourteen years. Spontaneous remissions occur in 10 to 20 percent of cases.

The causes of rheumatoid arthritis are not fully understood. A virus or a microbe (bacteria) may be the initiating factor. But unlike that which happens ordinarily when the body is invaded and calls forth the defense system (antigen-antibody reaction), the patient with rheumatoid arthritis has a unique response. The whole pathologic process is complicated and deals with many reactions. Some of these pertain to the protecting mechanism of the body. For reasons not well understood, these substances react upon the synovium and ultimately lead to chronic changes.

Hence the defense mechanisms in the patient with rheumatoid arthritis do not fulfill the role of defender but actually enter the pathologic process as an instigator creating further trouble. The antibody (rheumatoid factor) produced by the white cells at the site of the injured synovium combines with the initiating substance and forms an immune complex. Substances are liberated that try to neutralize or destroy the complex, but they also attack the structures of the joint cavity.

Juvenile rheumatoid arthritis begins before the age of sixteen. The pattern of joint inflammation is similar to that in adults. The symptoms may wax and wane for several years. The joint involvement may be sudden or begin gradually. There is joint stiffness and limited motion. The joints may be hot, swollen, and very painful. When only one or two joints, such as the weight-bearing joints of the knee or ankle, are affected, recovery is likely to occur sooner. More diffuse involvement of joints may last longer and lead to residual joint complications. When the disease flares up, children may have fever and poor appetite. The most serious consequences of juvenile rheumatoid arthritis relate to possible inflammation of the eye. This requires careful treatment because it could cause blindness.

There are no cures for juvenile arthritis, but spontaneous remissions can occur in practically all patients. Even with some residual damage, most of these children will eventually lead active lives. Medical management includes reducing pain and disability. Aspirin is the medicine most frequently prescribed, in large doses, to control the inflammation of the joints and reduce pain. A side effect of the aspirin may be a high tone hearing loss, which will disappear when medication is reduced or discontinued. A number of new drugs are available. The use of drugs must be carefully evaluated because their side effects can sometimes be worse than the underlying disease, such as anemia and internal bleeding. There may be a need for surgery on the involved joint. The role of surgery is the reconstruction of joints. A special diet is not necessary but good nutrition is very important. Anemia may be corrected by iron supplements.

Basic to all patients is the need for rest. Daytime rest periods are important. Splints may be used to immobilize a painful joint, and the child may use a wheelchair or crutches. An exercise program is initiated to maintain joint motion and to prevent muscle atrophy. Physical measures are designed to increase activity from a passive exercise plan to a more active program. Exercise of the joint, up to the level of tolerance for the pain, is important to prevent muscle weakness and to preserve the normal range of motion of the joints. The child may exercise the joints and is encouraged to do so (active exercise). A physical therapist may put the child through range of motion exercises (passive exercise), sometimes in conjunction with heat therapy or even anesthesia.

ADAPTATIONS IN SCHOOL

The student with arthritis needs help in planning a school day to conserve energy. Wasteful movements, such as several trips up and down stairs, can be eliminated. Permission should be granted if the student needs to get up and walk during class or if extended time is needed to get from place to place. The physical education program will have to be modified for the arthritic students because they must avoid severe twisting or jarring, such as that encountered in body contact sports. Exercises in warm water and eventually swimming are recommended.

There are some personality characteristics that are frequently found among arthritic children. Among these are anger, depression, and mood swings. It would seem natural that a child suffering pain, helplessness, and uncertainty about the condition would feel angry and depressed. Further, arthritic children have few ways to vent their anger and fear. They may be resentful of medical persons and parents who seem powerless to cure their disease, but on whom they are so dependent. They may be angry at their own bodies, which seem so treacherous. They cannot "let off steam" by kicking a ball or having a fist fight.

It has been sometimes observed that arthritic children seem inhibited and uncommunicative. The disease itself seems to teach passivity. To sit very still in a flexed position eases pain. Immobility leads to further immobility and increased dependency and to further cause for anger and depression.

The arthritic child then, should be given the opportunity to talk out deep, negative feelings. Psychotherapy has even seemed useful in influencing the course of the disease in some cases. Some formal counseling at school or even rap sessions with the teacher may be helpful. The child might have been told at home that it is not ladylike to swear, but she really has something to swear about. A happy outlet for strong feelings may be through art productions or story writing. Here the emphasis should be on self-expression rather than on a finished product and on truth rather than beauty or nicety.

A number of researchers have suggested that the physical predisposition to arthritis, coupled with certain psychological influences, can precipitate the disease. Some studies have associated oversolicitous, compulsive mothering with the condition. Overprotectiveness, however, could easily be a reaction of parents to a child in such pain and consequent physical dependency. It is certainly true that psychological and physical stress can exacerbate the symptoms of arthritis. Children are urged to avoid fatigue and stress, even when they seem to be in complete remission. While permanent remissions in rheumatoid arthritis only occur in about 20 percent of all adults, the childhood form has a far better prognosis (prediction of outcome). Sixty to seventy percent of children will be free of active disease after a period of ten years, and with excellent care, there is a good chance that there will not be a residual associated handicap.

Teachers often report that arthritic students are among their best students academically. They are often forced to be sedentary and seem to derive pleasure from doing excellent seatwork. They expect their condition to improve, and they can prepare themselves for full productive lives ahead.

Review Guide

After reading Chapter 6 the reader should be able to define the following terms:

    congenital dislocation of the hip
    Legg-Perthes disease
    club foot
    spondylitis of adolescence
    systemic
    rheumatoid arthritis
    rheumatoid factor

After reading Chapter 6 the reader should be able to answer the following questions:

1. In what type of joint is arthritis apt to develop?
2. What are the two main disabling consequences of osteoarthritis?
3. What are the three physical symptoms during an acute attack of juvenile arthritis?
4. What might be the possible causes of negativism in the arthritic child?
5. What are two modifications in school that will ease the physical problems of the arthritic child?
6. How can teachers help the arthritic child with negative feelings?
7. What can the arthritic student expect of his future physical condition?

Chapter 7

CLEFT

Call nothing ugly, my friend
save the fear of a soul
in the presence of its own memories.
Kahlil Gibran

ONE OF THE MOST FREQUENT defects that a teacher is likely to encounter is cleft lip and/or cleft palate. These are developmental abnormalities that are manifest in early fetal development, resulting in an incomplete union of the lip and/or the incomplete closure of the lateral halves of the roof of the mouth, the soft palate and the uvula, the roof of the mouth (the hard palate), or all together (Fig. 7). The cleft may or may not extend through the jaw.

About one in 500 to 750 children is born with some degree of this impairment. The percentage of affected boys is higher than that of girls. Black Americans have an incidence of probably less than half that of whites. American Indians have more cleft abnormalities than white persons. The Japanese have the highest incidence of cleft lip and cleft palate of all races. They are twice as likely as whites to have the disorder.

There is evidence that heredity plays a major role in clefting. In most cases, there is probably a hereditary predisposition to the defects, with environment also having an influence. The hereditary influences on cleft lip and cleft palate operate independently. They are genetically two independent malformations. In identical twins, where the genetic inheritance is the same, cleft lip occurs in both children in only 40 percent of the cases. Therefore, some intrauterine environmental factor must have influence also.

87

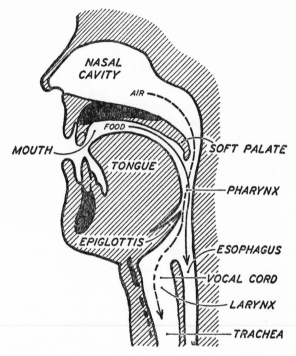

Figure 7. Relationship of passageways for food and air.

Cleft lip and palate are associated with other birth defects in about 16 percent of the cases. In these cases, the impairment may be secondary to a far more serious problem, such as a congenital heart defect, digital deformities, or one of the major craniofacial syndromes, which often include clefts.

CLEFT LIP

Persons with cleft lip were even drawn on monuments in ancient Egypt. The cleft lip impairment starts to develop after the face begins to form, about four weeks after conception. Normally, two horseshoe-shaped swellings begin to emerge, one on each side of the midline of the face, and progress slowly together to form the nostrils. Other bulges of tissue just below come toward the midline to join the tips of the nasal swellings and will eventually result in the completed upper lip (Fig. 8). The gap between these lumps of tissue is still present at six weeks after conception but will fuse soon after in normal development. When a part of the fusion process does not occur, some degree of cleft lip is present. It is sometimes erroneously referred to as harelip. The cleft can be very small, or it may extend all the way to the nostril. It may occur only on one side (unilateral cleft), or on both sides (bilateral cleft), with a large gap extending to the nose existing where the upper lip should be. The cleft may extend through the upper jaw into the palate, so the defect is both cleft lip and cleft palate.

From a cosmetic point of view, cleft lip is more serious than cleft palate, because it is obvious. The baby looks shocking and may have feeding problems, although these are less severe than in the baby with cleft palate.

Surgery for cleft lip is performed at an early age. This depends on the baby's condition, growth, and the preference of the surgeon. However, the operation is most often done at about three months after birth. Fortunately, techniques of cosmetic surgery have advanced far, and surgery can achieve what seems to the layman as miraculous results. However, all surgery produces scarring. Even when it is the most successful, surgery does not completely restore the face to normal. Nevertheless, the repaired cleft, particularly when it was not severe in the first place, may be a very minor blemish. Surprisingly, it is often the nose that is more disfiguring than is the lip.

Psychologically, the first impact of the baby with cleft lip on the

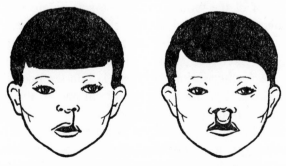

Figure 8. Unilateral and bilateral cleft lip.

parents varies a great deal. Grief is the most frequently experienced reaction, and that must be resolved. On the other hand, the medical team can be far more hopeful about this defect than about many others. Therefore, there is a tendency on the part of parents to say, "Take the baby away and fix it up." Some surgeons feel that if the surgery is done very early, the parents will always be critical of what cannot help but be an imperfect lip. If, however, parents have time to learn to love and accept their impaired baby as it is, they will have a more realistic perspective and appreciate the tremendous improvement effected by the surgical repair. Cleft lip is a relatively minor disorder with modern surgical intervention and does not have mechanical implications for speech.

CLEFT PALATE

Among white children who have clefts, about one-third have isolated cleft palates without cleft lips and two-thirds have both. When a mild degree of cleft palate exists without cleft lip, it can actually go undetected at birth.

Just as the tissue of the lip might have failed to unite early in the fetal developmental process, so the solid, hard palate and tissue of the roof of the mouth can fail to unite, creating a gap that may involve progressively the uvula, the soft palate, and the roof of the mouth (the hard palate, Fig. 7). It may also involve the front of the upper gum and tooth formation. This latter defect is often referred to as a prepalatal cleft and is embryologically associated with cleft lip. Again from a cosmetic point of view, the involvement of the teeth is the most notable. Actually, though, the cleft in the roof of the mouth and in the soft palate is a far more serious problem. The normal palate separates the mouth from the nasal cavity. When the closure has not taken place, sucking and swallowing are interfered with, and fluid tends to come out the baby's nose. A further serious problem is interference with speech production. The soft palate is the functional part of the palate, and its damage affects both speech and swallowing.

In the case of cleft palate, surgery is usually not done during the first year. An appliance may sometimes be fashioned that fits in the roof of the mouth of the infant to aid the feeding process, but this is not usually necessary. Feeding the baby may be a difficult and unhappy procedure. However, properly instructed parents seem to do well, and elaborate feeding devices are no longer encouraged routinely. The pediatrician is very essential in this area.

The age of surgery for cleft palate varies. It may be undertaken in rare instances as early as three months but sometimes is delayed until age six or seven. The usual age for repair of the palate is sometimes in the second year of life. The surgical closure of the palate is possible unless the child's health is poor. There was for many years a continuing debate between those who believed in prosthetic management of clefts and those who advocated surgical repairs. Today, it is very rare to have the cleft palate "team" elect to handle the conditions prosthetically except in special cases. Sometimes prosthetic treatment will be utilized as an initial method of restoration as was mentioned, then in combination with surgical intervention. Some children will always wear a palatal or dental appliance. The management team will, therefore, include dental specialists such as prosthodontists. The orthodontist is also essential because cleft children have problems with both maxifacial growth and malaligned teeth.

All infants with cleft palates have middle ear disease accompanied by hearing loss. About half of these clear up after palatal surgery, and about half persist. Ear care is vital from birth on, so the otolaryngologist is a vital member of the team as is the audiologist.

The development of normal speech may be hindered by cleft palate. The child with cleft palate does not experience the normal basic coordinations for sucking and swallowing in infancy and for the early stages of speech development. Articulation problems can arise from malformed gums and jaws and misplaced or missing teeth. Incomplete closure of the nasal cavity from the mouth can give the voice a nasal quality, so the child "talks through his nose." This windy speech is called hypernasal speech. A hearing loss may also slow speech acquisition and precision.

The high incidence of potential speech disorders makes the speech pathologist an important member of the treatment team. It is quite important to know that, with proper management, close to normal speech has become the expected result rather than the exception with cleft children.

It is important to distinguish *speech* from *language*. "Language is to be interpreted as a symbolic system which encompasses all aspects of communication, both expressive and receptive. Speech is the oral expression of those symbols."[1] Therefore, a person may have very poor speech for one reason or another and still have developed good language with which to think or write. Occasionally also, a person may have very good speech production but lack the language development to say anything of much meaning.

Children with clefts may have rather slow language development as well as speech problems. Nursery school is frequently recommended for children with clefts, particularly for the inherent stimulation of language afforded, as well as for the very important aspects of socialization.

THE LEARNER WITH CLEFT

The child with cleft should present few management problems of a physical or psychological kind. Unfortunately, some problems may be created for the child by misinformed or thoughtless persons.

The personality and the parent-child relationship of the child with cleft are not in some sense unique because of the handicap. It may be true that the parents had an initial terrible shock, and the child has had repeated hospitalizations, pain, and earaches, but children are very resilient. Many children with cleft have healthy personalities and good relationships with their parents. Some have very serious problems, including trouble with peer relationships.

The student with a cleft lip must come to terms with the reality of looking different from others even though the repair is a very successful one. The point of view taken in this book is that it is not inherently tragic to have a facial blemish or slightly different speech. Of course, if you tell people something often enough, they may believe it, so there is a self-fulfilling prophecy possible. As always, a teacher's respectful acceptance of any student, with appreciation of abilities and realistic management of problems, will foster an atmosphere in the class where others will follow suit.

---

1. Betty Jane McWilliams, "Psychosocial Development and Modification," *ASHA Reports,* No. 5, 1970.

The teacher may be the first to realize that this student (and perhaps the teacher and parents also) needs the support system of other pupil personal services. The psychologist or school social worker, as well as the speech pathologist, may be of great help. Community resources can be investigated. Some cleft palate clinics have group sessions where young persons with the same problem can talk out their feelings and frustrations, for example.

Some persons feel that if a student with a speech problem prefers to write, rather than speak, or let others volunteer answers and comments, his preference should be honored. Others feel that a student who does not communicate as the others do has been implicitly, at least, allowed to fail. The teacher should make every effort to have all of the class members respect everyone's speech. The teacher's own example of a relaxed and patient attitude toward the speaker who has problems will probably be the most important factor in creating an accepting classroom atmosphere.

The student with cleft may have a hearing problem that should be treated as are hearing problems from other causes. These are discussed in Chapter 26. If the student has a weak voice, or articulation that is difficult to understand, the teacher might be able to suggest a most advantageous position for desk or chair for some class activities. This student may have to be excused from class for speech therapy. An effort should be made to schedule therapy sessions in free periods so that the child is not further handicapped by missing instruction. In addition, since speech therapy can be inappropriately administered, this aspect of the program should be coordinated with the treatment team.

Finally, as with any speakers whose speech calls attention to itself (as with persons who stutter, have athetosis, or laryngectomies), the speaker's feelings should be considered with regard to recitation. Ideally, the students will feel comfortable in the classroom and be happy to communicate.

Children with cleft are in general within the average limits of intelligence. They are also, of course, distributed through the total range of abilities on various intelligence tests. Therefore, it should not be assumed that the child with cleft has intellectual retardation. This misapprehension is frequent, particularly if the student has an accompanying speech defect. Obviously, it is a great disservice to a child to miscalculate his learning ability, and to do it a priori is most unfair.

Since persons with cleft can expect to have the same school performance as others, it would seem to follow that they should have the same vocational success and ultimate social adjustment as most persons. Unfortunately, vocational success does not always come easily, perhaps because of the prejudices of others rather than any fault in the person with the cleft. Therefore, the school staff may suggest that the student ask for the services of the Bureau of Vocational Rehabilitation (BVR). When the student is sixteen, BVR counselling and school counselling can be coordinated, to plan ahead for the student. Financial assistance may be provided for vocational training or higher education. It is a personal impression that quite a few persons with clefts find their way into rehabilitation and special education fields, as if their experiences have made them very sensitive to the needs of others.

Review Guide

After reading Chapter 7 the reader should understand and be able to define the following terms:

cleft lip	hard palate
cleft palate	soft palate
hare lip	hypernasal speech
unilateral cleft	language
bilateral cleft	speech

After reading Chapter 7 the reader should be able to answer the following questions:

1. What are the two main speech problems that a student with cleft palate may have?
2. Give three ways the teacher can help to minimize these problems in the classroom.
3. Why is it important to distinguish speech skills and language development in students with cleft?
4. What is the most serious problem for the otherwise normal person with a repaired cleft?
5. Give two ways the teacher can help with this problem when planning for the student's future.

Chapter 8

UNDERSIZED PERSONS

How glorious it is—and also how painful—to be an exception.
de Musset

THE LITTLE ELF

I met a little Elf man, once,
   Down where the lilies blow.
I asked him why he was so small,
   And why he did not grow.
He slightly frowned, and with his eye
   He looked me through and through.
"I'm quite as big for me," said he,
   "As you are big for you."
John Kendrick Bangs

THE GROWTH of an individual depends on many different processes, which are affected by certain specific genes, and on environmental factors such as nutrition. There are a number of disorders in which unusually short stature is a major characteristic. Deformity, fragility, and arrested sexual development accompany some of the specific diagnostic entities. Persons with short stature may be referred to as midgets or dwarfs. In common parlance, midget refers to an extremely small person who is otherwise normally proportioned. A dwarf is a small person who is abnormally proportioned. Persons of short stature have sometimes designated themselves "Little People."* At least fifty-two types of short stature have been identified. Some of the most common ones will be described in detail.

---

* See the organization, Little People of America, listed in the Appendix.

NORMAL BONE GROWTH

The human skeleton is the bony framework supporting and protecting the soft parts of the body. Bones are the individual members of the skeleton.

The composition of the bone is as follows: (1) The outer layer of living tissue is dense, semirigid, porous, calcified, connective tissue. The connective tissue contains an insoluble protein matrix of collagen fibers. This matrix is arranged in a linear fashion to hold the bone salts of calcium and phosphorous, which in turn lend hardness to the bone. Collagen is also present in joint ligaments, the skin, and the white of the eye. (When collagen is boiled, it is converted into gelatin.) Each pair of abutting bones forms a joint at their junction. At the joint the bones are each covered by a moulded cover of noncalcified connective tissue, the cartilage, which allows the bones to move smoothly against each other.

The outer covering of the bone joining the smooth cartilage at the joint area is a fibrous membrane. Bones grow in width because this membrane lays down new layers of bone. The bone has a rich supply of blood vessels to sustain the life and growth of its cells. A shutting off of blood vessels or an infection can cause death of a part of a bone.

(2) The inner layer of the bone is less dense and contains the bone marrow, where blood cells are formed.

(3) Near each end of the growing bone is a line of cartilage (epiphysis) from which the bone grows in length in a child. In the mature person, growth ceases, and the cartilage at the epiphysis becomes obliterated as the bone above and below fuses.

The bone growth is usually completed in late adolescence. At that time the cartilage at the growing line is gradually replaced with bone, under the influence of the hormones that cause sexual maturity. When this cartilage has completely turned to bone, no more growth will take place.

The regulation of tissue growth depends on *hormones.* Hormones are proteins that are manufactured in one part of the body and transported to other parts of the body where they exert their effect. Seven types of hormones are known to be secreted by the front part of the *pituitary gland,* a tiny, egg-shaped organ connect-

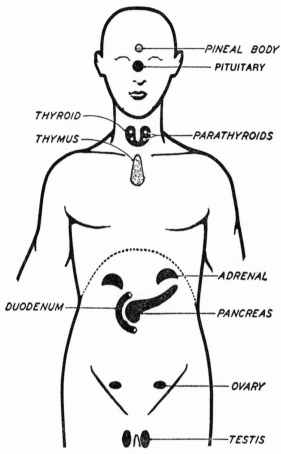

Figure 9. Locations of the glands of internal secretion. The liver and the stomach are not shown.

ed to the hypothalamus in the floor of the brain (Fig. 9). One of these hormones is called the *human growth hormone* (HGH). HGH is a protein substance made up of 188 amino acids linked in a precise way into a single chain. The other pituitary hormones carry instructions to various internal organs, including the gonads (ovary and testis), which are in turn then stimulated to secrete their own hormones that govern our secondary sexual characteristics and influence sexual behaviour.

ACHONDROPLASTIC DWARFISM

Achondroplasia is the most common form of dwarfism. Students with this condition are seen rather often in school, since it occurs in one in 10,000 births. The cause of the condition is a failure or retardation in the cartilaginous portions of the growing line of the long bones (epiphysis), which results in depressed lengthwise growth of bone. While the head and trunk will be of normal size, there is a characteristic shortening of the arms and legs. The arms and legs may be bowed, and the legs may be stumpy looking. Spinal curvatures are frequent, and the dwarf may have swayback. The head may be large, with characteristic facial features; the forehead is wide, and the bridge of the nose is flattened and depressed. Achondroplasia begins long before birth and is usually obvious at birth.

Death is fairly common the first twelve months, but the children who live can be expected to have normal intelligence and normal physical fitness. Their fertility is thought to be normal. Until the development of cesarean birth, it was not safe for affected women to have children.

There is no treatment for the growth defect itself. Sometimes accompanying hydrocephalus or club foot will require medical intervention. Bracing and surgery may be needed to correct spinal curvatures or alleviate pain and to lessen the bowing of the limbs.

Even among relics of prehistoric culture, there is evidence of dwarfs. Statues showing persons with achondroplasia were carved by the ancient Egyptians. Dwarfs often lived in the royal households of Europe and were often the court jesters. Their intelligence and agility have been utilized in the circus and, recently, films and television. It has even been fancifully suggested that their condition includes a "happiness hormone," optimism, and confidence.

The transmission of achondroplasia is of interest because it is usually the result of gene mutation (Figure 6). The gene is a dominant autosomal trait, so it can be transmitted to offspring of a parent with the condition. If a person with the condition has offspring with a normal person, the couple has a fifty-fifty chance of producing a dwarf in each pregnancy. If two achondroplastic dwarfs mate, they have a twenty-five percent chance of producing a normal child since both carry one recessive, normal gene. Usually, however, children with achondroplasia are born to parents of normal size who do not have another child with the condition.

Since this mutation is such a common one, the incidence of achondroplasia is being monitored in the United States to determine whether it is more common in areas that have received more radioactive fallout due to thermonuclear reactions of bomb testing.

HYPOPITUITARISM

Persons with this condition are sometimes referred to as pituitary dwarfs because their stunted growth is due to a lack of normal functioning of the hormones of the pituitary gland (Fig. 9). Under this broad classification are several different medical entities, with specific treatment needs, and various causes.

The child who will show these conditions looks normal at birth, since the pituitary hormones do not seem to be crucial for normal fetal development. In the first year of life, however, growth will proceed more slowly than average.

The most serious situation results from a lack of all seven of the pituitary hormones, including of course, the human growth hormone (HGH) and the two hormones regulating secondary sexual characteristics in adolescence. Persons with this defect have *panhypopituitarism* (pan = all; hypo = below). They show a childish face, a thin voice, and slender limbs. Their parts are all proportioned smaller, giving the impression of an adult in miniature. Their sexual development will not reach maturity. They cannot reproduce but they can have sexual intercourse. Since the hormones that produce sexual maturity are missing, the line of growing cartilage (epiphysis) does not turn to bone, so they may continue to grow into adulthood. They can be expected to be of normal intelligence. The cause of panhypopituitarism is generally unknown. It can be secondary to a tumor on the pituitary gland, and in some rare cases it is due to a genetic defect.

Another form of dwarfism is caused by the lack of only one of the seven pituitary hormones, the human growth hormone (HGH). These persons also are normally proportioned, but very small. Their skin tends to be soft and wrinkled, and their faces are somewhat doll-like. There is a characteristic high pitched tone to their voices. They develop sexually and are able to bear children. This form of hypopituitarism is generally inherited as an autosomal recessive trait. Parents who have produced a dwarf offspring are both carriers of the trait and have one chance in four of producing another dwarf (Fig. 4). If two dwarfs with this trait marry, all their children will be dwarfs, since they only possess recessive genes.

In recent years treatment of hypopituitary dwarfism has been very successful in some cases, so that dwarfed infants have had a chance of reaching average adult height. Human growth hormone, given to the dwarfs, must be obtained from the fresh pituitary glands of a human corpse. The pituitary glands of other animals are not effective, and as yet the hormone has not been synthesized. This treatment produces best results when begun in early life. At first the treated child will show a big growth spurt and then decrease to a slower pace. If the treatment is terminated, growth reverts to the initial abnormal level.

In the United States, as abroad, there is an exceedingly short supply of the human growth hormone. Therefore, it is not available to all who might profit from it, among the five to ten thousand children estimated to have hypopituitarism.

OSTEOGENESIS IMPERFECTA

Osteogenesis Imperfecta (OI), the "Swiss cheese disease," means imperfect bone formation. It is also referred to as brittle bones. Its characteristic symptoms are brittle bones, which fracture easily, a bluish coloration in the white of the eye, a thin skin, and eventual serious hearing loss. While it may develop in a mild form later in life, it is often congenital. Babies are born with short, deformed limbs, broken bones, and a soft skull.

The basic defect appears to be in the protein matrix of collagen fibers in the bone. In the normal bone the fibers are in a linear arrangement. In OI they are in a feltlike mesh, similar to that observed in the developing fetus. Because the protein matrix is deficient, it does not hold the normal amounts of calcium and phosphorous bone salts, so bones are weak and brittle. The bones of the middle ear are affected. The immature collagen in tissue results in greater elasticity of joint ligaments and skin. The collagen of the white of the eye is thin, so the underlayer of the eye shows through as a blue coloration.

This condition had been noted as early as the seventeenth century and was observed in three generations of families in the eighteenth century. One-half of the cases are sporadic (Fig. 6). The remainder are usually due to the inheritance of a single dominant gene, but the effect of that gene can be moderated or influenced by other genes of the chromosomes. Therefore, the symptoms can vary greatly from one individual to another, even though the gene for the trait has been passed down equally. (This phenomenon is known as *variable expression.*)

About one person in 40,000 develops osteogenesis imperfecta. Screening tests are now available for parents and relatives in families where it has occurred. It can also be detected *in utero,* so the option of abortion of the defective child is open.

Some infants with OI die at birth or live only a short time. Children with OI are very fragile and subject to many fractures. Their frequent and long hospitalizations may preclude regular school for some time. The surgical treatment of OI is to put metal rods down the bone canal, between the end of the long bone, to strengthen and straighten them. The rods must be surgically adjusted as the youngster grows. Braces, canes, crutches, and wheelchairs may be necessary. Since the possible hearing loss is conductive, a hearing aid may be of value.

Teachers have found these children to be quick, fun loving, and social. Since they are often very small, they are not difficult to lift and move in a classroom situation. By adolescence, when the bones stop growing, they tend to become stronger. Medical intervention may have been very helpful. While these individuals are physically stunted and deformed, many lead very productive lives.*

---

* An excellent account of the maturing of a girl with OI is written by her mother, Beverly Plummer, in the book *Give Every Day a Chance* (New York, Putnam, 1970).

Obviously, the OI student will have to focus on rather sedentary pursuits. An electric typewriter can be used to great advantage, but most students have good enough hand function to use a pencil, paint brush, or hold a musical instrument. Some have enough fitness for swimming, and some have even enjoyed being hoisted on a shoulder for mountain climbing!

PSYCHOLOGICAL DWARFISM

There is a system of medicine concerned with the interdependence of mental processes (psyche) and physical functions (somatic), which is termed psychosomatic.[1]

The main emphasis in this area is to study the effect that mental and emotional states and thoughts can have on physical states. While the whole notion of separation of mind and body is an artificial one made for the sake of convenience in thought and discussion, everyone knows that some functions and behaviours are more essentially "mental" or "emotional" while others are more essentially "physical." Concomitantly different diseases or illnesses are associated in varying degrees with mental or emotional states.

A rare condition, but one that dramatically illustrates the psychosomatic relationship, is that of psychological dwarfism. A study at Johns Hopkins Children's Medical and Surgical Center concerned thirteen children who were thought to be dwarfs.[2] The children were distinguished from others with short stature by bizarre behaviour and intellectual retardation, which seemed to occur in association with emotional deprivation. To support their contention that psychological factors influenced growth, the researchers pointed out that when the children were removed to an environment where they received tender care, they began to grow at spectacular rates, even enough to catch up with normal children. Another striking fact produced by the study was one child's failure to grow and his weight loss when he was returned home to his socially dislocated family. The mechanism retarding growth in

1. Normand L. Hoerr and Arthur Osol, *Blakiston's Illustrated Pocket Medical Dictionary*, 2nd ed. (New York, McGraw-Hill Book Co., 1966).

2. Robert M. Blizzard, JoAnne Brasel, and Gerald F. Powel, Study Reported in News Publication, Johns Hopkins University, Jan.-Feb., 1967.

such a manner is not understood. Further, it is a puzzle why only one child in a family would react in this way.

UNDERSIZED PERSONS AT SCHOOL

Diminutive size should not be much of a physical management problem in the elementary grades since furniture, lavoratories, and equipment are child size. In high school, vocational, and college settings some adaptations may have to be planned with the student. Some architectual modifications that are convenient for persons in wheelchairs also benefit very small adults, not to mention children. These include lowered telephones, washbowls, drinking fountains, and elevator buttons. Parents and older students will need advice on where to buy clothes and where to get specialized equipment and obtain genetic information. Little People of America is a valuable resource in these areas.

Psychological concerns may be far more serious than physical concerns. It has been observed that human beings have an automatic, unthinking tendency to orient themselves toward others on the basis of stature being the index of age and mental maturity. It is very difficult not to react to a mature small person on the basis of the silhouette of physical appearance and, hence, influence that person's self-image and options for response. Even though parents and teachers are intellectually aware of the inappropriateness of babying and patronizing, it is very easy to fall prey to this behaviour.

It is hard not to think it cute and laughable when a thirteen-year-old boy, with brittle bones and weighing 35 pounds, types letters dictated by his favorite cerebral palsied girlfriend in class, who weighs four times as much. Surely, there would be a less condescending reaction if the youngsters were both normal. Again, when speaking to a mature, well-formed teenager you would not want to say, "Hop up in the chair, Bud," but you might catch yourself doing so if he were a 3½ foot tall achondroplastic dwarf.

The coping reactions of dwarfs to such widespread babying may be of several types; these are attempts on the part of the child and adult to preserve integrity and identity in the face of a true dilemma. One response is to accept the babying and become a sort of Peter Pan, who does not grow up. Actually, this is a response of many handicapped persons who have had to be physically dependent because of their impairment. This infantile stance becomes harder and harder to maintain, and being babied on all sides may lead to unbearable stress with adolescence and maturity. A second response is to resist the babying and fight for respect and equality. To do this, the dwarf will need to develop some social sophistication and maturity to make up for a lack of physical power. It is important that teachers and classmates support rather than infantize the student at school, to present a healthy example to parents and others.

Some dwarfs of good physique and learning ability have ended up in special education because they could not take the social pressures of regular school life. Social isolation is an unfortunate solution for students who will be expected to compete equally in adult life.

A common response of handicapped persons is a compensatory denial of any problems at all. This is very comfortable for non-handicapped persons because it relieves the anxiety of the listener and others of any responsibility. A sensitive teacher will "listen with the third ear" and examine closely how the student's situation might be improved. Visits to the school counsellor or psychologist might be very helpful.

A compromise role that some develop is mascotism, or the Tom Thumb reaction. The mascot capitalizes on small size and uniqueness. Although he or she may resent being small, there is not resentment of other persons noticing it and responding to it. The mascot then defines a role in the social structure on which to capitalize and in which to function in sports and other group activities.

There are cases of dwarfed children who, having had the benefit of hormone treatments relatively late in childhood, had already come to terms with the social problems of short stature. They find the "readjustment syndrome" so severe that an occasional child will wish to terminate treatment. As de Musset's quotation says, uniqueness has two sides.

An expert in this area has emphasised the importance of

helping small persons develop assertive personalities and a repertoire of bold, humerous, and even sarcastic rejoinders to the fawning, taunting, and personal remarks of thoughtless persons.[3] Thus in a clothing store or restaurant the child may initially declare his age and request appropriate treatment. If nicknames such as Shrimp, Small Fry, and Midget are too offensively used, nasty names are suggested in retaliation, such as Oneball (to insinuate a genital defect).

Dialogues of counter attack are given:

Q: Are you a midget?
A: Is your father a horse?
Q: Why are you so short?
A: For the same reason you were born so stupid.

Or, in a situation were less flippancy might be more effective, "Lady, where I come from we don't ask such personal questions about medical things."

Money also stresses the importance of age-appropriate clothing in all instances and of make-up for adolescent girls.

Education concerning human sexuality is a controversial issue in some regions and schools. It may be even more so when the students involved are handicapped. It is often very difficult for parents to relinquish the dependency relationship with a handicapped adolescent and to acknowledge that their offspring is becoming a mature sexual adult, even though impaired, disabled, or different. Unfortunately, the support system in the helping professions often reinforces this dependency and denial as well.

Teachers are cautioned to consult with administrators and others on the school staff with respect to sex education so that the school's programs and policies are understood and can be explained and developed with input by parents and even the youngsters themselves. Of course, if some parents do not want their children to participate in classes where such subjects as human reproduction, genetic counseling, and sexual practices are discussed, their wishes must be honored. However, the ideas and attitudes

---

3. John Money. "Dwarfism, Questions and Answers in Counseling," *Rehabilitation Literature, 28(5):*134-138, May, 1967.

of parents can change as they think about these problems with respect to their growing children, so it is important to keep an open, noncensorious dialogue with them on these issues.

The very short person faces some unique problems as a teenager and young adult with regard to sex life and marriage. All dwarfs are capable of having sexual intercourse and a regular sex life, but it may be difficult to find a partner of suitable height. In hereditary forms of dwarfism, a decision will have to be made on the advisability of producing more dwarfs. Some persons have suggested that to continue the strain would lead to an advantageous subvariety of the human race. Literature has also chronicled, however, the problems of dwarf parents who have produced normal children. Of course, these are personal decisions, which outsiders cannot make for any couple. A possible rule of thumb in transmitting one's characteristics might be offered, "If my partner and I have been reasonably happy and productive as we are, I don't mind giving our children the same traits and characteristics that we have."

Review Guide

After reading Chapter 8 the reader should be able to define the following terms:

growing line (epiphysis)	achondroplasia
hormone	hypopituitarism
pituitary gland	panhypopituitarism
human growth hormone	osteogenesis imperfecta (OI)
secondary sex characteristics	psychological dwarfism

After reading Chapter 8 the reader should be able to answer the following questions:

1. What stops normal bone growth in adolescence?
2. How is achondroplasia transmitted?
3. How can hypopituitary dwarfism be medically treated?
4. Why is this treatment difficult to obtain?
5. What are four typical responses of small persons as social coping reactions?
6. What sensory disorder is likely to develop in individuals who have OI?

Chapter 9

SPINAL CURVATURES

I, that are curtail'd of this fair proportion
Cheated of feature by dissembling nature,
Deformed, unfinished, sent before my time
Into this breathing world, scarce half made up,
And that so lamely and unfashionable,
That dogs bark at me as I halt by them.
Shakespeare
Richard the Third

THE ELEMENTS of the musculoskeletal system form a complexly engineered structure which allows mobility, dexterity, and strength.

Defect involving the bony column of the spine may be a primary problem or a result of another condition or disease. The effect will be a spinal curvature, which in turn may have serious repercussions on subsequent body functioning.

This is because the parts of the musculoskeletal system are so interdependent that injury to one small segment can be very incapacitating, sometimes irreversibly so. On the other hand, bones and muscles have great recuperative power, and medical intervention can be highly successful.

STRUCTURE OF THE SPINAL COLUMN

The spinal column or backbone consists of thirty-three bones, which were formed embryonically on either side of the neural tube from which the brain, brain stem, and spinal cord arise. The vertebrae (backbones) grow to encase the spinal column and protect the delicate tissue of the spinal cord inside. The base of the skull has an opening in the bone for the spinal nerves to proceed

107

from the spinal column to the brain. Between the bones of the column are hard but flexible fibrous discs of cartilage, which cushion the bones. If these discs slip or rupture, they cause the nerves radiating from the vertebrae to be pinched. Ligaments (bands of flexible, tough, connective tissue) support the vertebrae in their upright position and also allow movement in some parts of the spine (Fig. 10).

Thirty-one spinal nerves, connected to the spinal cord, exit between the bones of the vertebrae. Seven *cervical* vertebrae are in the neck area, numbered from the first at the base of the brain stem to the seventh at the shoulder. The cervical vertebrae can

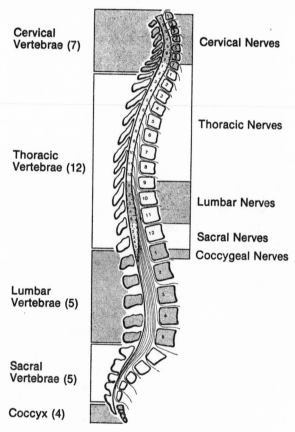

Cervical Vertebrae (7)

Cervical Nerves

Thoracic Nerves

Thoracic Vertebrae (12)

Lumbar Nerves

Sacral Nerves

Coccygeal Nerves

Lumbar Vertebrae (5)

Sacral Vertebrae (5)

Coccyx (4)

Figure 10. Spinal column and spinal cord.

bend and twist. Next are the twelve *thoracic* vertebrae to which the ribs are attached. The ribs are the twenty-four flat, curved bones that protect the inner organs of the upper body. There are five vertebrae that make up the small of the back in the region called the loins. This is the *lumbar* area of the spine. Below, five *sacral* vertebrae are fused into a curved triangular bone, which is the keystone of the pelvis (a ring of bone, including the hip bone, that rests on the lower limbs). Finally, there are the four fused, rudimentary vertebrae of the *coccyx*, or "tail bone."

TYPES OF SPINAL CURVATURES

Specific regions of the spine will reflect different disorders and will show characteristic curvatures.

Neck Imbalance

Wryneck (torticollis) is usually a temporary disorder of pre-school children related to a throat infection. Because of infection, the structures in back of the throat that are in front of the spine become swollen, leading to a stretching of the ligaments supporting the vertebrae in the cervical region. The children will have head twisted to one side and chin rotated to the opposite shoulder. A neck collar, heat, and muscle relaxants are the usual treatment. Sometimes the joints will dislocate, and traction will be needed. Twisting injuries to the neck can also cause torticollis.

There is a congenital torticollis due to a false tumor or scar tissue forming in the muscle tissue on the side of the neck. This will usually be medically corrected before school age. A congenital malformation of the vertebrae (Klippel-Fiel syndrome) causes a shortened neck, mimicking the appearance of torticollis. Sprengel's deformity is also congenital. Here one shoulder blade is high riding, and the arm on that side may not have full range of motion. Surgery is usually performed before a child is ten to improve appearance and enhance function of the arm.

Hunchback

Hunchback (kyphosis) refers to a rounding of the back in the thoracic region. It may be a congenital condition, sometimes associated with another disorder such as dwarfism. It may be acquired, either because of a temporary softening of the bone or because of weak muscles. Children with partial paralysis of back muscles due to polio or spina bifida may develop marked kyphosis. Juvenile kyphosis is symptomatic for one or two years usually in the age group of eleven to sixteen. It is controlled by the use of a Milwaukee back brace and curtailment of strenuous physical activity if the youngster experiences pain.

Hunchback is not only psychologically distressing, as the words of Richard III attest, but it can also cause bone and muscle stress and cramping of the internal organs. The teacher may expect some physical fragility and discomfort of students with this condition.

Swayback or Lordosis

Lordosis is a swayback in the lumbar area of the spine. It accompanies some other conditions, such as some dwarfism and an adult form of muscular dystrophy. When muscles are weak or imbalanced, an individual may have to compensate with swayback in order to be able to walk, as is the case with some persons with cerebral palsy. Therefore, it often is not corrected because worse problems would result from a spinal immobilization.

A rather common condition, called Spondylolisthesis, usually occurs between the last lumbar vertebra and the sacral area. It is a slipping forward of one vertebra on another, due to a defect in a portion of the vertebra. It causes pain and may require surgery and a three to four month period at home.

In school-aged children, there are rarely problems with the intervertebral discs. Occasionally, a child will have a ruptured disc, and this may require surgery for its removal. It may be six to eight weeks before the child can return to full activity.

Scoliosis

Scoliosis refers to a lateral curvature of the spine, usually in the thoracic area of the spine. Therefore, one side of the body will be higher than the other. If the scoliosis is *functional,* it can be corrected at will by the child. This might be the case with poor posture or a short leg. The most serious consequence of this type of scoliosis is the possibility of a secondary osteoarthritis, due to the abnormal wearing of the vertebral joint, and consequent pain.

A far more serious type of scoliosis is *structural;* the child cannot voluntarily straighten the spine. Structural scoliosis may be congenital. A child may be born with a lateral dislocation of the spine when there has been an improper formation or segmentation of the bones of the spine. Such a condition may be helped by early bracing or corrective surgery.

Scoliosis may accompany another congenital abnormality of the joints and muscles. It is a frequent concomitant of arthrogryposis multiplex congenita, a condition of unknown cause in which otherwise normal children are born with stiff, stuffed-sausage-like limbs and weak muscles. While splints, casts, braces, and surgery are only of limited usefulness on the extremities of these children, the spinal curvature can be managed by early surgical correction and spinal fusion. Scoliosis may be due to a neuromuscular imbalance caused by cerebral palsy, paralytic disorders, muscular dystrophy, or spina bifida. Frequently, medical intervention is not helpful in these cases.

The most commonly seen scoliosis is developmental and of unknown cause. It typically develops in the age group twelve to sixteen, just as the adolescent enters a growth spurt before skeletal maturity is reached. Girls are eight times as likely to develop the condition as boys. The first signs to be detected may be a slight unevenness of height of the shoulders or pelvis or a slight hunchback. X-rays can verify the diagnosis of curvature. Scoliosis does not progress after the growth period is over, but persons who were not treated may be very deformed in adulthood. They may suffer considerable osteoarthritis and consequent joint pain by middle age.

When the scoliosis is mild, treatment may be restricted to exercises to keep the back strong and supple. A more severe case may require the use of a Milwaukee brace for all or part of the time day and night for a period of two to four years. The brace is cumbersome, consisting of a plastic pelvic mould with rigid projections front and back to a high metal collar that fits at the base of the skull and high under the chin. In this manner the spine is held rigidly upright for the remainder of the growth period. The youngster will be taught exercises to do both while wearing the brace and when it is removed. Physical activities while wearing the brace are strongly encouraged. The brace is certainly not what the young adolescent girl or boy would like to wear to school and social functions. Every effort should be made to make them feel O.K. about this temporary accoutrement, because if it is not faithfully worn, more drastic medical intervention will be necessary. The fact that it is a temporary inconvenience and will lead to a healthy spine should make the situation more bearable.

If the curvature progresses with conservative treatment or was severe in progression in the first place, surgery will be done. Before surgery, the child will be put in a body cast from the pelvis to high under the chin. Then, stainless steel rods will be inserted to straighten and strengthen the spinal column. The spine is fused by using bone transplants from another part of the body. Traditionally, the child is returned to a body cast, which may extend like a space suit from the top of the head, with a hole for the face, all the way to the pelvis. This is worn for six to twelve months and usually necessitates the patient being prone on a bed or cart.

There are several more recent treatments of scoliosis. One corrects the curvature with a cable device and another, used in serious cases, accomplishes traction by pelvic pins and a metal "halo" implanted in the skull bone during the course of treatment.

INSTRUCTIONAL MODIFICATIONS

The child with surgery for scoliosis or other orthopedic problems may spend considerable time in a children's hospital. Many children with frequent or prolonged hospitalizations can take their schoolbooks and keep up with their classes. Some hospitals have schoolrooms, where beds can be wheeled, and others have bedside teachers. The most educationally progressive hospitals may have a relationship with the community school in the area, where children can attend regular classes, even in carts and wheelchairs.

Children with scoliosis come into the hospital feeling well. As time progresses they begin to undergo medical procedures and begin to miss their homes and usual routines. They may need special help to cope with the situation. The hospital teacher may put aside the planned lesson just to listen. Hospitalized children benefit as well from talking over their experiences and anxieties with others with similar problems. If there are a number of patients in various stages of treatment, it is encouraging to the new child to see the progress of peers. Further, children understand hospital procedures better when they can see them demonstrated rather than hear an abstract explanation.

Children struggling with an unfamiliar environment, discomfort, and anxiety are not in the best situation to do schoolwork. The teacher may simplify tasks so that they are not so physically taxing. For example, the student could be asked to underline a correct word, rather than to write it.

Hospitalized and homebound children can take advantage of the services of the Library for the Blind and Physically Handicapped, which is a branch of the Library of Congress (see Appendix). The use of talking books, rather than reading, is often easier for a weak or bedridden student. Page turners and optical aids make visual reading easier from a prone position. Some interesting schoolwork or good literature can be a welcome change from the continuous drone of inane television programs, which so often pervade children's hospital wards. The body-casted child will keep a hand mirror available to see what is going on to the side and back in the school and ward.

When the child with scoliosis returns home, there may have to be some temporary modifications in living arrangements with which the social worker or physician may help. The youngster's bed may be moved to the first floor, for example. A visiting nurse may be engaged to help with periodic bathing. Arrangements can be made for homebound instruction in many school districts. This instruction usually comes under special education services, and the teachers are particularly knowledgeable in the area of physical handicaps. Students with scoliosis are usually a joy to teach. They are reconciled to the treatment and anxious to keep up their schoolwork. Since they feel good and are energetic they welcome academics as an alternative to long, unoccupied hours of confinement.

A helpful arrangement made available for homebound students is a school to home telephone service. This is not seen as a replacement of the home teacher but as a supplement, perhaps necessitating fewer home visits. This system is a two-way communication between the regular classroom and home or hospital, providing a sick or handicapped student with actual participation in the work of the class. Using a microphone and loud speaker at both ends, the telephone circuit enables the shut-in to hear classroom discussion and participate in recitation. The school equipment is portable and can be carried from one classroom to another. School to home service is available from the telephone company. The cost is frequently reimbursed completely or in part by State Departments of Education or underwritten by interested local civic organizations.

This service seems particularly valuable for students who are absent from school for six weeks or more but only temporarily removed from their class. However, it has been used by some very incapacitated students who have never been to school, but are "adopted" by classmates who then learn to know their peer through the system, correspondence, and home visits. It seems to be a more helpful technique for children who are nine and over and at least of low average academic ability. The latter have often improved their school performance with this help.

There will be close cooperation between the regular teacher and the homebound or hospital teacher in maximizing the effectiveness of this aid. Parents and nurses also may be very helpful, and of course, the physician will give input on physical tolerances and other health concerns.

Homebound instruction is a valuable aid in minimizing the effort of transition from a sheltered, noneducational environment back to the school community. Nevertheless, the student who has just returned to school may require some understanding and leeway while catching up, academically, physically, and socially.

Review Guide

After reading Chapter 9 the reader should be able to define the following terms:

vertebrae	hunchback
spinal column	neck imbalance
swayback	scoliosis

After reading Chapter 9 the reader should be able to answer the following questions:

1. What are the five sections of the spinal column?
2. What are the four types of abnormal curvatures likely to occur in the spinal column?
3. In what places is a student recuperating from scoliosis likely to be educated?
4. What facilities from the Library of Congress are helpful to the student bedridden with scoliosis?
5. What is school to home telephone service?

PROBLEMS OF THE CENTRAL NERVOUS SYSTEM

Blessed are Thou O Lord our God,
King of the universe,
Who varies the form of Thy creatures.
Circa 500-200 BC A blessing
said by Jews upon meeting
a handicapped person.

In this section, disorders are discussed that have in common some kind of problem affecting the central nervous system (CNS). This system includes the entire nervous apparatus of the body, including the brain, brain stem, spinal cord, the cranial and peripheral nerves, and the groups of nerve cell bodies, the ganglia.

The nervous system transmits and processes information from the environment and exercises control over the skeletal muscles. It exerts a regulating influence over the involuntary muscles, glands, and viscera. Disorders involving the brain may result in cognitive and behavior deficits of far more educational consequence than the physical management problems discussed here. However, some of the physical problems are formidable, and they require a cooperative and knowledgeable school staff to lessen the handicapping aspects of the resulting disabilities.

117

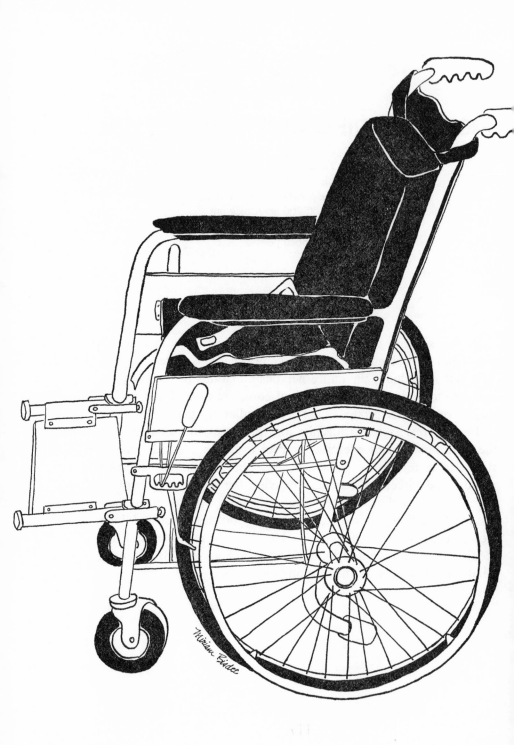

Chapter 10

SPINAL CORD DAMAGE

Deformities and imperfections of our bodies,
as lameness, crookedness, deafness, blindness,
be they innate or accidental, torture many men,
yet this may comfort them that those
imperfections of the body do not a whit
blemish the soul, or hinder the operation of it,
but rather help and much increase it.
                    Robert Burton
                    Anatomy of Melancholy

WHEN THE SPINAL CORD is injured, there is interruption of the nerves and pathways going to and from the various parts of the body to and from the brain. Spinal cord pathways that have been completely severed will not regain function. Therefore, some paralysis and lack of sensation will result. The amount of function lost will depend on the completeness of the severance and the level of the spine at which the injury occurred.

ETIOLOGY OF IMPAIRMENT

Formerly, poliomyelitis was a common crippler of children and adults. In the past most special schools and classes for physically handicapped children primarily served postpolio patients. Polio is a viral infection of the motor cells in the spinal cord. The affected cells control muscle movement. If the infection has caused only a swelling of the cells and their supporting tissues, the affected person will recover completely. If the cells are destroyed by the virus, there will be resulting paralysis of the regions controlled by the affected cells. Postpolio patients can have all degrees of paralysis and very spotty damage. The polio vaccine has caused a dramatic drop in polio incidence.

119

Most special schools and classes for physically handicapped children now have a preponderance of children with cerebral palsy, spina bifida, muscular dystrophy and multiple handicaps, and few postpolio cases. Every now and then a child who never was given the vaccine contracts polio. This has sometimes led to rather severe emotional problems for the patient and family, which have extended to the school.

An abnormality of unknown cause, arthrogryposis, is also a result of disease of spinal cord cells that control muscle movement. This problem begins early in fetal life when muscle development and contractions are begun. There is an early lack of movement in the developing fetus, and it is conjectured that this contributes to the congenital stiffness and deformities of the affected infants. Such children have some correctable deformities, but they will always be stiff with limited motion. They will be functional in a wheelchair but will have some upper extremity involvement. They can be expected to be normal learners.

Another disease of progressive deteriorization of the motor nerve cells of the spinal cord and motor nucleus of the cranial nerves is called spinal muscular atrophy. This disorder of unknown origin may lead to death in infancy, or proceed more slowly so that the afflicted person can have a minimum disabling weakness. The involvement of the cranial nerves, outside the spinal cord, may cause more difficulty than the spinal cord injury. Other diseases may affect the spinal cord. Tuberculosis is a bacillus that may lodge in the spine. Spinal tumors can cause damage.

Multiple sclerosis (MS) is a chronic disability usually manifest in young adults, but occasionally seen in children under the age of ten. It and other similar diseases involve a loss of the white, fatty substance forming the covering myelin sheath of some nerve fibers. These demyelinizing diseases distort or block the nerve impulses. In MS there is disappearance of myelin in irregular patches with replacement by scar tissue at scattered spots in the spinal cord but not in the peripheral nerves, or in the brain. The condition may include long periods of remission during which normal life can be resumed. The average duration of the disease is twenty-seven years. In the later phases of the disease, the scar tissue penetrates the surface sheaths of myelin, affecting the nerve fibers themselves and causing loss of function and sensations in the particular limbs and organs served by the fibers.

Presently, the most common causes of spinal cord injury are accidents (which are also the greatest causes of death in children). It is a tragic fact that many of these could be prevented by more careful driving and wearing seat belts, care in testing water depth before swimming, keeping guns unloaded, and other safety measures. (Accidents on the trampoline and diving board have been reduced by the use of spotter belts. The belt, purchased from athletic equipment firms, has leads to two persons on opposite sides, who can assist the student to achieve proper rhythm and balance before he tries stunts on his own.) It is also a tragic fact that some of these injuries are self-inflicted. Childhood attempted suicides and violent behavior are on the rise in the United States. Hospitals and rehabilitation agencies are well acquainted with young persons whose backs or necks were broken in violent encounters.

ANATOMY OF THE SPINAL CORD (FIG. 10)

The brain stem connects with the spinal cord, which averages about 18 inches in length and ¾ inch in diameter. The spinal cord is a cable consisting of grey nerve cells with their white tails that relay information to and from the brain and the limbs, trunk, bladder, rectum, joints, bones, and skin. The spinal cord is arranged in segments corresponding to the vertebrae, the spinal bones that encase and protect the delicate nerve tissue. The spinal cord ends at the second of the lumbar vertebrae, because the vertebrae grow faster and for a longer period than the spinal cord, so the vertebral column outgrows the cord. The cord segments are designated by their corresponding vertebrae levels: cervical, thoracic, lumbar, sacral, and coccygeal. Two grooves running the length of the spinal column carry thirty-one pairs of nerves. Each spinal vertebra forms two openings between itself and the next vertebra. Through these pass the pairs of nerve bunches, one sensory, the other motor.

These nerves to the limb and trunk muscles are the peripheral nerves. The nerve roots toward the back of the column transmit messages from the sensory cells of skin, muscles, joints and bones *to* the brain. Through them the brain will interpret sensations of pain, temperature, pressure, and position. The nerve roots toward the front transmit messages *from* the brain to the muscles.

The nerve roots evolving into the major nerves of the arms leave from the third cervical vertebra down to the third thoracic vertebra. The nerve roots evolving into the major nerves of the legs emerge from the lower lumbar and sacral areas.

DISABILITIES FROM SPINAL CORD INJURY

Roughly speaking, damage to the spinal cord will cause both lack of sensation and paralysis below the area of spinal injury. Therefore, the higher the injury to the spinal cord, the greater the disability.

Injury of the spinal cord at the small of the back is frequent because the lumbar region is flexible. Any sudden and violent flexion or extension of the vertebral column can sever or damage the cord. This causes paralysis of the lower extremities, or paraplegia. The paraplegic will not be capable of movement below the site of the lesion and will not be conscious of sensation below the site, provided the cord has been completely transected. Usually people with paraplegia will use a self-propelled wheelchair, although they may stand and walk with short or full leg braces (again depending on site of lesion). Ambulation is generally only practical for those with injuries below the T12 (twelfth thoracic) vertebra.

The region of cervical spine between the fifth and sixth vertebrae (C5 and C6) is a flexible area of the neck very prone to injury. Severe whiplash or going through the windshield in an auto accident can sever the cord. Diving in a shallow pool or a fall from horseback can break the neck. Trampoline, ski, and football injuries also cause this damage. When the lesion is in the cervical area, all four extremities will be paralysed; by definition this is quadriplegia.

Typically, quadriplegics will use a motorized wheelchair, if they can afford this very expensive item. Some have found a less expensive golf cart to be very satisfactory. Many will have enough hand function to use a pencil and spoon, but they may use an orthotic hand device. A few will master self-transfer to wheelchair, car, and bed, and even to drive a car with hand controls. Motivation seems to be the vital element in achieving mastery of these tasks.

In most cases quadriplegics will have difficulty breathing. Poliomyelitis can even spread to the brain stem and affect the muscles of respiration. Quadriplegics must resort to diaphragmatic breathing since they do not have the function of their chest muscles. During their acute stage of recovery they may have had assisted ventilation through a tracheotomy. When the injuries occur above the C4 (fourth cervical vertebra), the nerve that controls the diaphragm is frequently damaged. These persons with severe respiration problems may have to spend a portion of the day in a mechanical lung, or on a rocking bed, or use a portable respirator to help them breathe. Respiratory problems are frequent for many quadriplegics, and in fact, respiratory complications are a frequent cause of their death.

The temperature control mechanism of the body is also disrupted below the level of the lesion so that the ability to perspire is lost. The loss of the body's cooling capacity in a high level injured person results in an intolerance to prolonged exposure to high temperature. As the environmental temperature rises above 85° (F), the body temperature rises and can reach 104 or 105° (F). Unless a treatment is applied, such as ice packs or cold baths, all the complication of a high fever can occur.

Quadriplegics, like most paraplegics, will lack bowel and bladder control. They will usually require more help in self-care management than persons with a lower lesion. While bladder and bowel control are usually lost, automatic reflexes will empty the bladder and rectum when they are filled. Bladder and bowel management programs are crucial to the medical and psychosocial well-being of the spinal cord damaged person. Problems are frequent, and renal failures are a major cause of death among the spinal cord injured. Some problems will require the attention of the teacher, or at least special consideration.

An internal catheter may be fitted to males and females. It is a small rubber tube inserted through the tube, the urethra, that carries urine from the bladder to the outside of the body. A catheter may be inserted permanently or, with females, inserted intermittently. A female can be taught to catheterize herself by inserting a small tube into the bladder and draining her bladder into the toilet every two to four hours. Females are more difficult to catheterize than males, and those with only partial urinary control may have to use disposable diapers and plastic pants. Infections are often a troublesome result of catheterization.

For the male, a soft rubber tube or condom is placed over the penis. The tube is attached to an external urinary collection bag attached to the leg, and suspended from a waist band. It is not visible under clothing. It is easily emptied periodically by a person with good hand and arm function.

Many females and some males may elect a surgical procedure to help with urinary management. Urinary diversions that are surgically performed are of two kinds. In the ileal loop or conduit, the tubes that normally carry urine from the kidneys to the bladder are implanted in a segment of bowel tissue, which is brought out through an opening on the surface of the abdomen. The urine passes into a watertight collection appliance that is worn on the skin over the opening. In a ureterostomy the ureters are brought to the surface through one or two openings at waist level, and an appropriate appliance is worn. With a carefully planned high protein diet and suppositories, satisfactory elimination of the bowel can usually be achieved without surgery.

Curtailment of sexual function is a concern of many teenagers and adults with spinal cord injury.[1] This realization has recently come to rehabilitation therapists, who had formerly focused their efforts on mobility problems and frequently ignored sexuality. However, it may be that this issue is being overplayed by some overzealous persons. It is relatively certain that men with paraplegia or quadriplegia cannot ejaculate and thereby impregnate a woman. Some spinal cord injured males do produce viable sperm. Therefore, artificial insemination for those spinal cord injured males who want children may be possible, but the procedure is

---

1. R. W. Hanson and M. Franklin. "Sexual Loss in Relation to Other Functional Losses for Spinal Cord Injured Males," *Archives of Physical Medicine and Rehabilitation,* 57:291-293, June, 1976.

difficult and generally not available. Women with cord injuries can bear children.

It is felt that the estimates of percentage of men able to perform the sex act and of those men and women who can experience orgasm have been too low. Curiously, it is easier for a quadriplegic man to have an erection than one with paraplegia. This is because a very high lesion allows a lower automatic reflex arc to become dominant and more effective in maintaining an erection than when some higher center control is only partially present.

The entire body is innervated by the spine, but the head has twelve pairs of nerves, the cranial nerves, which are concerned with sensations of sight, sound, smell and taste, and hearing. These nerves also control sensorimotor functions for the face, head, neck, tongue, heart, and a small portion of the viscera. These cranial nerves are radiated directly from the brain's underside, so they are still intact even in a person with a high spinal cord injury.

Therefore, while a person with spinal cord injury will not have control and sensation below the site of lesion, a number of important functions are left of crucial importance to the child or adult who is going to surmount the disability. Eye function and hearing will be normal. Speech will be intelligible, although it might be weak because of shallow breathing in quadriplegics. Facial muscles and therefore facial expression are unimpaired. The person's brain is as keen as ever.

REHABILITATION*

Until a few years ago, a person who was paralyzed did not live very long. If born paralyzed, he or she usually died in infancy. If the paralysis was caused by an accident or disease, he or she died soon after it began. Of the 400 Americans with spinal paralysis carried off the battlefields of World War I, 90 percent were dead within a year of receiving their wounds. Quadriplegia almost always ended in death.

---

* The reader who wishes a detailed text in this area is referred to D. C. Burke and D. D. Murray, *Handbook of Spinal Cord Medicine* (New York, Raven Press, 1975).

It is a grim reality that persons who have suffered a spinal cord injury are often additionally traumatized by well-meaning persons who attempt to help them at the site of the accident. The injured person should not be lifted or carried in a position that will bend the spine, nor should he or she stand, sit up, or lift the head before medical help is present.

Intense medical treatment of the spinal cord injury will be necessary for months in the hospital and possibly in rehabilitation centers. The patient will be under the care of an orthopedic specialist at first. Surgery may be necessary. When the acute medical problems have been brought under control, a program of intensive physical rehabilitation will be instituted. The patient may be under the care of an orthopedist or physiatrist who will work closely with the nursing staff and physical therapy department. Several areas in the country now have regional spinal cord injury centers to help assure optimal care.

Patients will soon be strapped in a standing position on a tilt board to prevent vascular and urinary problems. Pressure sores (decubital ulcers), popularly known as bed sores, are a very serious complication in persons who are immobile, and particularly with those with spinal cord lesions. Unless measures are taken for their prevention and early care, the tissue breakdown can be thoroughly incapacitating and even life threatening. In fact, next to renal and respiratory failures, complications from decubital ulcers are a leading cause of death among the spinal cord injured. The patient will use a pressure distributing mattress, first in the hospital, then at home. A wheelchair cushion will always be used at home and school.

In school, students in wheelchairs tend to be immobile for prolonged periods. If the physician or physical therapist has recommended a change to a prone or standing position for part of the day, it is very important for the teacher to follow through on this. Such positions can be assumed even for instructional periods, perhaps by use of a wedge cushion under the chest to prop up the student lying prone, or a standing table.

As injured persons progress to the wheelchair, they will learn to shift position and learn routine self-examination with a mirror, because skin care will be a life-long problem. With young paralysed students, the school staff including teachers and aides should be alert to the beginning of skin breakdown.

Paraplegics will undergo a rigorous training to strengthen the muscles of the upper body, which will be used for transfer from bed to wheelchair and eventually to crutches if the injury is below the twelfth vertebra in the thorax (T12) (see Fig. 10).

A program for self-care will involve activities of daily living training (ADL). A bowel and bladder management program will be instituted. The patient will learn eating, dressing, and transfer techniques. Orthotic devices such as hand splints and braces will be fitted when needed. Progressive hospitals have professionals to counsel adult patients and their partners on the subject of sexuality. Alternative methods of obtaining sexual satisfaction will be explored and sometimes taught. Special techniques may be experimented with in order to determine what areas of the body are sensitive to sexual stimulation. In short, the long hospital experience will be used to restore the injured person to the fullest degree of physical and health function possible.

Ideally, with persons sixteen and over, the rehabilitation counsellors from the hospital cooperate early with the State Bureau of Vocational Rehabilitation (BVR) as to the future of the injured person subsequent to leaving the hospital. A decision may be made to send the client from the hospital to a rehabilitation agency for further ADL (activities of daily living) training and in job-related skills. A youth may learn typing as a prelude to returning to school or for a job, for example. Client evaluation will determine the best vocational plan for the future. BVR may finance further training in a postsecondary or college course. They might finance a job evaluation and job training program in an agency, and they will help with eventual job placement.

The younger patients with cord injury will anticipate return to home and school. It is unfortunate that they sometimes do not have access to school programs during the long physical rehabilitation process. The teacher may need to contact the school system about hospital instruction or phone to classroom service. Tutoring can usually be arranged. Hospital education should definitely be encouraged both for its educational and psychological advantage. Visits from classmates and even volunteer readers can lessen the boredom and depression of the hospitalized child.

The loss experienced in spinal cord injury is psychologically shattering. Accidents are most frequently experienced by vigorous young persons. They may go through stages of mourning from denial to eventual acceptance, which are described in Chapter 21. Reactive depression is common and understandable. The school staff has a responsibility to engage early and actively on the rehabilitation team with an educational input that will help the child and family see the possibilities for a productive, happy future. The anticipation of a return to the classroom and assurance of a warm reception will do much to alleviate depression and make the slow process of rehabilitation more bearable.

THE WHEELCHAIR AS A MOBILITY AID

Students who spend most of their waking moments in a wheelchair are susceptible to postural problems, muscle atrophy, and pressure sores. Physical therapy may be continued after a child's return to school. Any possible mobility should be encouraged even though it may be more time-consuming. The wheelchair is the last resort for people who cannot possibly ambulate in any other manner.

For many persons, the wheelchair is their only means of transportation. The wheelchair is more than just a means of transportation. It becomes a vehicle in its own right, a functional aid to its user, and an extension of his body. For many persons, a wheelchair prevents their disability from becoming a confining handicap. This is especially true for children who are naturally very active. There are advantages of the wheelchair for a chronically handicapped child, even a very young one. It allows the child to assume responsibility for his activities of daily living, such as eating and cleanliness; it encourages the child to become involved with recreational activities and a vocational program. It helps reduce the adverse psychological effects of being completely immobile, especially if the child can operate the chair himself. Also, it alleviates the pathologic consequences of immobility by helping to prevent such things as kidney stones and muscle atrophy of the functional part of the body.

The selection of a wheelchair is based upon a careful examination of the youth, including ability to move, endurance, and general physical condition. Other factors that must be considered include the physical environment in which the chair will be used, the individual's age, weight, and height, and the cost of the wheelchair. The cost may run into hundreds of dollars. To aid in the trial of different chairs, or in cases of temporary disability, a chair can be rented from a supply house.

The ideal wheelchair should be easy to propel and maneuver, versatile, adaptable to various situations, and allow for addition of accessories. In some cases, certain parts may have to be excluded for more important ones. For the person whose wheelchair has come to be like a part of his body, the chair's appearance is an important consideration.

The most common type of wheelchair is constructed of chrome-plated metal tubing. The seat and back are made of leatherette or plastic that collapses for easy folding. It has two large and two small wheels with handrims for self-propulsion, and it also contains armrests, footrests, and handbrakes. This type of wheelchair comes in four basic sizes: adult, junior, large child, and small child. The small child chair is considered for the two to six year old, although it is probably easiest to use a regular baby carriage or stroller until the child can self-propel. The large child chair is for the six to twelve year old, and it has adjustable features that allow for growth. The junior and adult sizes are very similar, thus the names actually apply more to weight and dimensions than to chronological age. Since the amount of space a wheelchair occupies is a prime consideration, a small adult might find a junior chair more appropriate because of its reduced overall measurements. The most frequent type of wheelchair is the rear wheel drive chair. It has two small wheels in front and two large wheels in the back. The rear wheels have concentric handrims, which are turned for self-propulsion. For those individuals who cannot manage to propel themselves, there are push handles to be used by an attendant. This type of chair also has a tipping lever to be used to tilt the chair for curbs and steps. Pneumatic tires are an asset for wheeling on rough or semihard terrain.

Motorized wheelchairs are driven by a battery. When the battery is fully charged, the chair can travel for a distance of 2 to 10 miles on level ground at a speed of about 4 miles per hour. Since the battery adds an additional weight of approximately 30 to 70 pounds, the chair must be of heavy-duty construction. This chair is controlled by push button with only one finger, or even by a head control. It should certainly be considered for people who have no motion, who have to strictly limit their activity, or who have to travel long distances and conserve energy. Propelling a wheelchair requires up to five times the energy expenditure of walking. Because of fatigue, many wheelchair-bound persons have had to limit their life space to essentials. Having a motorized wheelchair can permit them to engage in much more extensive activities and put more enjoyment in their lives.

The major parts of chairs include: tires; brakes, which lock the large wheels in place; an adjustable seat; a backrest with optional headrest; armrests that are either stationary or removable; and footrests that adjust to fit each individual properly. With regard to footrests, no child should ever be left with legs dangling in space. Footrests should be used, or blocks under the feet if feet do not reach the ground.

Depending on the condition and needs of the disabled individual, a number of accessories are available. Some of these include a wheelchair narrower that reduces its width by 3 to 5 inches, a commode attachment, crutch and cane holders, an antitipping device, a sliding board to aid in transfer from the wheelchair to another surface, and a hydraulic seat for lifting persons from the wheelchair to another surface. For the person who is confined to a wheelchair for most of the waking hours, there are numerous additional useful accessories such as pockets, luggage boxes, racks, ashtrays, nameplates for identification, trays for eating and writing, and a safety belt.

The physical or occupational therapist will help the disabled student to master necessary abilities for use of the chair. These are learning the use of handbrakes, handrims, and footrests; forward and backward propulsion; turning; travel over rugs, doorsills, ramps, stair, soft ground, and pavement; and transfer from wheelchair to bed, chair, car, toilet, and crutches. If the student is properly trained, minor architectural barriers will not become frustrating obstacles. Proper training will prevent incorrect wheelchair use, poor posture, and unnecessary accidents.

Accidents in wheelchairs are caused primarily by runaway chairs and by chairs that are pushed too rapidly by other children. If the teacher institutes two simple rules, the majority of wheelchair accidents can be prevented. The rules are: *no speeding with wheelchairs;* and *lock the brakes on all stationary wheelchairs.* Bruised legs seem to be an occupational hazard of teachers who have young students on wheels.

Some architectural installations and modifications are necessary to accommodate "wheelers" in the schools. Ramps should be installed so wheelchair users will have access to the entire building. The ramps should have no more than 5° slope, or persons in wheelchairs will have a difficult time propelling themselves from level to level. One of the prime dangers with wheelchairs is that of gathering too much speed, especially on long ramps. To prevent the danger of runaway chairs, long ramps should have an occasional levelling, or landing. Ideally, the ramps and corridors in the school should be wide enough for two wheelchairs to pass, but this is not always a possible situation. Corridors 5 feet wide are the recommended standard. Ramps can be made of wood, so they are relatively inexpensive to install. Schools should also have elevators that are accessible to students and others who are handicapped. Elevators equipped with delayed action doors and lowered control buttons are ideal.

Doorways to classrooms and facilities should be built wide enough for wheelchairs to pass through. Narrow doors can be easily widened by removing the door frame. The aisle between desks should be large enough for a wheelchair to pass between (2½ feet), and a desk or table used as a desk should be high enough to accommodate the wheelchair (2½ feet). Designers of new buildings can assure that there are lowered public phones and water fountains for wheelers.

It should not be assumed that the person in a wheelchair is always a spectator or the scorekeeper. Physical educators have developed many adaptive techniques to include handicapped students in sports programs. The first organized wheelchair sports came about after World War II. Since that time, children and adults have been actively participating in sports such as basketball and adapted track and field events. The popularity of football has spread to wheelchair sports in the form of touch football with a shortened field and five players. The most severely disabled wheelchair user can bowl. Special equipment that permits severely disabled individuals to participate in bowling include a bowling stick (a long, fork-shaped stick that aims and releases the bowling ball) and elevated metal ramps (tubular ramps from which bowling ball is pushed). The regular bowling rules apply. The sport of swimming is becoming more and more popular. Special pools with handrails descending into the water are being constructed across the country. Many of the pools have ramps for wheelchairs. Dancing, especially square dancing, has become an enjoyable means of socialization for many wheelchair users.

Although wheelchair users have been actively participating in organized sports for a relatively short period of time, they have reached a high degree of sophistication. The Paralympics (Olympic games for disabled athletes) have been in existence since 1960, and larger numbers of individuals are participating in them each time they are held.

INSTRUCTIONAL MODIFICATIONS

Since students with spinal cord injuries may be expected to be normal learners and they must make the most of their mental abilities, it is extremely important to give them the very best academic and vocational opportunities. In some cases only very mild modifications will be necessary in terms of educational arrangements. Each student must be assessed individually with the help of the rehabilitation team. If it is determined that the student cannot function adequately, one of two steps may be taken: The student may be admitted to the activity after certain modifications in its structure have made it possible for him to compete successfully and to acquire the desired learning; or the school may waive a particular requirement and, after careful consideration, prescribe another that is considered an adequate substitute. In effect, the school takes responsibility for reducing barriers to the students that are inherent in its regular curriculum. Ideally, these modifications do not result in a lowering of standards. They are essentially ways of circumventing a barrier, to allow the student to achieve mastery of a subject matter area through slightly different means.

Some modifications in writing techniques may be necessary for quadriplegics. Typing may be far easier than handwriting or writing with a mouth- or headpiece. If a limitation in the use of the shoulders, arms, hands, and fingers prevents a student from taking notes, as required in the class, another student can make a duplicate set of notes for him. If a student cannot physically take a test, the manner of administering it should be changed. With the help of a person who can write what the student says or use of an electric typewriter and flexible time limits, virtually any disabled student can manage the physical aspects of a test. For example, a student with severe hand limitations who cannot write or type can dictate his essay test responses to a person who will write what he or she says. This will naturally require more time than if he himself typed or wrote the answer, but he will have completed the test.

If papers or reports are required, a manually handicapped person could possibly type his own or dictate his work for a typist later to transcribe. In a lab situation the instructor and student together can assess the physical requirements of the laboratory experiments. Those that are within the student's capacities are retained intact in the program, and those that go beyond his physical resources are modified, by, for example, teamwork with other students or substitution of certain experiments for others.

The physically handicapped student has the right to free services of the Library of Congress, Division of Blind and Physically Handicapped (see Appendix). Tape recorders, talking books, and automatic page turners that this organization can provide can make academic life much easier.

The use of selected reading material for the therapeutic effect on the handicapped student may be very beneficial. This use is referred to as bibliotherapy. The writer James Baldwin beautifully describes the effect of reading on his understanding as an under-privileged black child.

> I was looking in books for a bigger world than the world in which I lived. In some blind and instinctive way I knew what was happening in those books was also happening all around me. And I was trying to make a connection between the books and the life I saw and the life I lived.
>
> You think your pain and your heartbreak are unprecedented in the history of the world, but then you read. It was books that taught me that the things that tormented me the most were the very things that connected me with all the people who were alive, or who had ever been alive.[2]

In professional publications, there are numerous articles detailing the use of literature to aid persons who are in some way in need of help.[3] Many severely handicapped persons with constricted life space have described their situations and their reconciliation with life, often writing in iron lungs, by pen in mouth, or a left foot. The injured athlete may get much more help from reading Jill Kinmont's story of life after her ski accident than from kind but un-understanding sympathy from able-bodied persons. Further, if the whole class reads good literature about a handicapped person, their appreciation of their injured classmate will be enhanced. Parents also can profit from this literature and books by parents of handicapped children (see Mullins & Wolfe, Appendix 2).

Students with extreme life problems need encouragement and opportunity to work them through. Teachers can be encouraged to use creative writing classes for such a purpose, as well as other art forms. It is quite possible that artistic outlets learned in school will become the basis of future vocation. There are many artists who paint by mouth, and musicians and authors in beds and wheelchairs.

Architectural modifications in the home, such as lowered sinks

---

2. Remarks made in the program "My Childhood," presented over Channel 5, WNEW-TV, New York, May 31, 1964.

3. June Mullins. *Bibliotherapy for People in Quandaries.* American Psychological Association, Annual Meeting, August, 1974, New Orleans.

and cupboards, electric lifts on stairs, widened doors, and accessible bathrooms have helped paralyzed persons with successful homemaking. The ability to housekeep may make the difference between independent or institutional living for adults. It may also free a partner in a marriage or other housemates to take jobs outside the home. Group homes in residential communities are a very happy arrangement for handicapped persons who have special needs. By pooling their resources, which may well include hiring or inviting in able-bodied persons as well, they manage very successfully. Many handicapped persons eventually prefer to move out of such living centers, which they perceive as transitional living facilities and to fully join the mainstream of society.

In vocational planning, a problem is often not being able to work, but getting *to* work. The person in a wheelchair has difficulty with public transportation because trains and buses usually do not have hydraulic lift steps or a free place for the chair to stand inside. Taxis may be inordinately expensive and consume job earnings. Some, but not many, organizations provide transportation for the handicapped. If a person can drive, often with a hand-controlled car, there must be a parking space close to the work site and an accessible path to the job. In the work setting, there must be accessibility to toilet facilities, and the work station must be adjusted to the dimensions of the wheelchair.

Paraplegic and quadriplegic persons have been successful in many vocational pursuits, but they have often found architectural barriers and prejudicial attitudes more handicapping than their disability. Therefore, they have often banded together to solve their common problems, either through such groups as are listed in the Appendix, or privately. One law office, for example, is completely run by men and women lawyers in wheelchairs.

Vocational success among the spinal cord injured correlates much higher with general educational level of an individual than it does in relation to the severity of the injury. This fact should be taken very seriously by school personnel.

When architectural planning is done before the construction of homes, schools, and places of business, accessibility is not expensive or difficult. Fortunately, lawmakers, architects, rehabilitation personnel, educators, and consumers have contributed in recent years to the removal of architectural barriers in public buildings and in new buildings. Physical plant modifications required by law are being included in plans for new secondary and postsecondary vocational buildings, and some of the older postsecondary vocational buildings are being remodeled to make them physically accessible. (The Appendix lists references relevant to architectural standards.)

The symbol on the jacket of this book is the international sign indicating accessibility to wheelchairs. These signs are appearing with increasing frequency on public buildings, in the washrooms of airports, highway stops, and schools. Do not be put off by the "Wheelchairs Only" sign. Go in and check out the facilities. Disabled persons need the support and understanding of the citizens to remove handicapping architectural barriers.

Review Guide

After reading Chapter 10 the reader should be able to define the following terms:

spinal cord	multiple sclerosis
spinal column	paraplegic
spinal nerves	quadriplegic
cranial nerves	T12 injury
poliomyelitis	C6 injury
arthrogryposis	pressure sores
spinal muscular atrophy	bibliotherapy

After reading Chapter 10 the reader should be able to answer the following questions:

1. What are five common causes of spinal cord injury?
2. What are the three most frequent complications that cause death of spinal cord injured persons?
3. What should a teacher's policy be with regard to footrests for children in wheelchairs?
4. What is the most important factor in successful rehabilitation of the spinal cord injured person?
5. What are two rules to prevent wheelchair accidents?
6. What are five important functions left to a quadriplegic?

7. What are five specific examples of instructional modifications that can ease the integration of a spinal cord injured student in the classroom?

8. What is a high correlate of vocational success among the spinal cord injured?

Chapter 11

SPINA BIFIDA

In nature there's no blemish but the mind;
None can be called deformed but the unkind;
Virtue is beauty, but the beauteous evil
Are empty trunks, o'erflourished by the devil
Shakespeare
Twelfth Night

S PINA BIFIDA (open spine), in its severe form, is one of the most serious birth defects. The cause is considered to be the result of a combination of genetic factors and prenatal influences acting together in some little understood way. There is also evidence that teratogens such as lead poisoning of the mother can result in this condition. Its incidence in the United States is three times higher than for the world population.

By the thirtieth day of pregnancy, the neural tube from which the brain, brain stem, and spinal cord are formed is completely closed in normal development of an embryo. When, for unknown reasons, the neural tube fails to develop completely and to close, the embryo will have the condition spina bifida, to greater or lesser degree.

CLASSIFICATION OF SPINA BIFIDA

Spina bifida is classified on the basis of degree of severity of the condition: that is, whether there is only a defect in the back arches of the backbone (vertebrae), whether there is a defect in the backbone and also of the protective coverings of the spinal cord (the myelomeninges), or, in the most serious case, there is involvement of all three; the backbone, the covering of the spinal cord, and the spinal cord itself. The defect can occur anywhere along the spinal column from the neck area (cervical vertebrae) down to the "tailbone" (coccyx) (Fig. 10).

Spina Bifida Occulta
(spina = spine; bifida = separate in two parts; occulta = hidden)

This is an extremely common condition that affects about one in ten persons, but we are not aware of it unless the condition should be discovered on a back X-ray. In spina bifida occulta, one or more of the vertebrae that make up the backbone, or spinal column, are not completely formed. This condition does not often require treatment. There may be a small dimple, a patch of hair, or a birthmark over this slight impairment.

Spina Bifida Meningocele
(meninges = coverings of the spinal cord; cele = sac)

When the bony opening in the backbone is more pronounced, the covering of the spinal cord begins to protrude through the opening, forming an outpouching or mass on the infant's back under the skin. Since the spinal cord is not involved, the nerve pathways below the defect are not affected. A child may have surgery to remove the sac, or cyst, because it is vulnerable to injury. Meningocele occurs in fewer than one in 1,000 births.

Spina Bifida Myelomeningocele
(myelo = cord)

This is the most severe form of spina bifida where the abnormality of the bone is large enough that the spinal cord and nerve roots also have protruded out from the spinal column. They form a sac, which at birth is more or less covered with a transparent membrane with spinal fluid oozing through it. This very serious error in early development is the most common cause of spontaneous abortions (that is, naturally occurring abortions), which can be expected in one out of four conceptions. About three infants in 1,000 live births will be born with myelomeningocele; many die in infancy or early life. However, the life expectancy is continuing to increase with improved medical care.

The sac on the newborn baby is of variable size from that of a fist to a small basketball. Since the nerves within the sac are of almost no use, surgery is usually done quite soon after birth to repair it. There will be paralysis and lack of sensation in the parts of the body that should have been supplied with the nerves that were in the sac.

A serious deformity associated with spina bifida myelomeningocele is hydrocephalus, which occurs in an estimated 60 to 80 percent of the cases. Cerebrospinal fluid should flow freely through the fluid cavities (ventricles) of the brain and around the spinal cord, supplying nourishment. In hydrocephalus (water brain), which can also occur by itself as a defect, the spinal fluid circulation is blocked in the brain. Because the fluid cannot get out of the brain cavities (ventricles) where it is formed, the cavities swell to compress brain cells and nerve fibers, which progressively causes brain damage. At the same time, the skull bones are also subject to pressure so that if hydrocephalus is unchecked, the head can expand to several times its normal size. By such time the brain is severely damaged.

When the infant shows signs of hydrocephalus, it is treated promptly by a surgical procedure. Various drainage shunts have been devised, which are plastic tubes with a valve inside that opens in response to a certain fluid pressure. The tube is placed in the ventricle and led out behind the ear and under the skin to the lymph system, atrium of the heart, or abdomen, where excess spinal fluid is drained to remove pressure on the brain. If all goes well, the shunt system is only replaced every few years as the child grows. There is the possibility of mortality from complications in the shunt operation. However, more children would possibly die if shunt surgery is not done.

Some children who have had shunt operations will still be mentally handicapped. Undoubtedly, the degree of mental retardation in those children was reduced by the operation. Furthermore, some children with spina bifida who show a small degree of hydrocephalus (sometimes unavoidable even with the shunt) are of normal intelligence.

PHYSICAL PROBLEMS AND MEDICAL TREATMENT
WITH MYELOMENINGOCELE

At present there is professional controversy concerning the desirability of taking extraordinary measures to save the lives of these children, who will face many hardships and will require enormous commitments of care and money on the part of their families. The decision whether or not to intervene must be made very early in the infant's life, and it is ultimately up to the parents. There are some rather clear-cut cases where medical intervention would not be recommended by physicians: when the sac is a large and open wound without healthy skin around it; when the infant has already contracted meningitis (inflammation of the membranes of the cord or brain); when the infant already has much hydrocephalus (increase of the volume of cerebral spinal fluid within the skull); or other defects that are life threatening. There are other cases where early medical intervention would be strongly recommended; when the myelomeningocele is very low on the spine, for example.

Whenever the spinal cord is injured or defective, there will be more paralysis and disability the higher the injury or defect is located along the back. This is because the nerves supplying the lower parts of the body grow out from correspondingly lower parts of the spinal column. Therefore, a child with a myelomeningocele in the lower back (or sacral area) may have some weakness in the feet or legs and the possibility of some foot deformities in later life, but the disability will be mild.

Usually, the myelomeningocele occurs in the small of the back (in the lumbar region). The following discussion will assume that the myelomeningocele is in this area, but the reader should remember that the condition may be higher on the spine, causing greater disability, or lower on the spine, causing less.

Typically, the child with myelomeningocele will be paraplegic, receiving no sensation and being paralyzed and flaccid in legs, ankles, and feet. The parents will be advised to prop their baby in a sitting position when a normal baby should sit. Frequently, the infant of crawling age is fitted by a physical therapist with a sort of extended skateboard to which he is strapped, belly down, and which he can propel with his arms. By this method, he can satisfactorily explore the home and school environment as a normal crawler does. As soon as babies are of toddler age, they usually are fitted with long leg braces and eventually with short crutches.

Some boys will continue to walk with long leg braces and crutches into adulthood. Some boys and most girls will have to use a wheelchair, at least for extended travel, by high school age. Crutch walkers with paraplegia swing all their weight with their arms and hands. There is some concern that constant weight bearing can break down the hands so that dexterity can be lost by adulthood. Therefore, the child should not be pushed to walk to excess. Short crutches are usually prescribed for young spina bifida children. This is done to prevent them from carrying their weight on the armpit (axilla), because the axillary nerve tends to be damaged by repeated pressure.

Several common orthopedic complications found with spina bifida are dislocation of the hip, club feet, contractures, and spinal deformities. Careful bracing, positioning, and exercise may alleviate these conditions, and surgery may be required. Due to a lack of active muscles, there is a decreased blood supply to the bones. Therefore, the bones are prone to the condition osteoporosis. In this condition, calcium is leached from the bones, and they become weak and brittle. Some babies are born with fractures, and half of those that occur later in children with spina bifida seem to happen spontaneously, without trauma. This condition is far more common in children who are immobile. Therefore, it is very important to provide opportunities for the child with spina bifida to have exercise and to have periods of weight bearing. For the latter, a standing table with a desk is very helpful in class.

Skin without sensation to pressure, temperature, and pain is particularly prone to breakdown. Clothing, braces, and irritation from urine can cause blisters, sores, ulcers, and infections. The older child with paralysis will learn self-inspection of the skin, using a mirror on the parts that cannot be seen directly.

The bowel is not subject to voluntary control in myelomeningocele. However, bowel problems can usually be managed quite satisfactorily. The child's diet may be somewhat controlled; laxatives and suppositories may be used, and with conditioning, bowel control is established by school age. Therefore, it is seldom a problem in school.

Because the myelomeningocele is almost always above the level in the cord where the major nerve should come out to supply the bladder, the child will also lack bladder control. Further, the bladder is spastic and unable to void completely. It is inclined to distend, overflow in a dribble, and accumulate wastes. Kidney failures and infections are a source of great distress to persons with myelomeningocele. Daily medication is necessary to resist bladder infections, and medicines frequently must be switched. The urinary system must be watched with great care by the urologist.

Urinary tract complications are the major cause of death in children with spina bifida who have survived the dangers of hydrocephalus and meningitis in the early months of life. They continue to be the greatest hazard to adults with spina bifida. There is the constant danger of urinary infections.

Credé's method (named for the gynecologist Credé, who developed the technique) is a manual elimination of the bladder achieved by applying pressure down the lower abdomen to force the urine out. The technique is taught to the parents and begun in infancy and used until at least two years of age. A diaper is placed below the child to catch the urine. Eventually, the child may be able to sit on the toilet for Credé's method, and when he or she has achieved enough growth and strength in the arms, may perform the procedure him- or herself.

If the use of Credé's method proves a satisfactory solution, it will probably be the method of choice. It is satisfactory in the long run for about 5 percent of children with myelomeningocele. Often Credé's method does not result in the child being dry for two hours. Rather than diapering the child, which can result in skin breakdown on paralyzed skin, as well as odors and dampness, a catheter may be used every four hours if the bladder is not spastic, or constantly if the child dribbles constantly. The catheter is a hollow tube of metal, glass, hard or soft rubber, or rubberized silk, which is introduced into the bladder through the discharge canal (urethra) to pass urine, which will be collected in an external bag. For males, urinary collecting devices are usually satisfactory, although they must be designed so as not to interfere with braces. Catheterization is much more complicated for females.

Some physicians favor a urinary diversion operation, sometimes called an ileo-loop. (The ileum is the lower portion of the small intestine.) In this surgery, the tubes (ureters) that carry urine from the kidneys are detached and routed into a segment of the small intestine. The piece of intestine is brought through the wall of the body to make an opening (stoma) about the size of a quarter in the lower part of the abdomen. A plastic bag is fitted over the opening to collect urine, which empties out every few minutes as it would have done into the bladder. The collection bag is emptied or disposed of periodically in the toilet.

Sometimes an intestinal diversion is also done, and a child may have two openings in his abdomen. The collection bags are undetectable under clothing. Medical practice differs concerning the optimal time for such surgery. Some doctors feel that it is psychologically better to wait until the child is mature enough to understand fully the alternatives available, and then to request one. Girls, in particular, may find the diversion easier to manage than other procedures.

Some adults with spina bifida can have normal sex activity. Some women with spina bifida have delivered normal babies.

The foregoing discussion should have made it clear that the medical management of spina bifida is complex and ongoing. The surgical and therapeutic interventions and surveillance imply an investment of time and money by the family, particularly in the early years of life, that is exorbitant. The youngster with the problem is confronted with pain, inconvenience, and periods of hospitalization. However, it can be expected that medical techniques for treatment will continue to improve.

As was mentioned, controversy surrounds the subject of medical intervention with infants having spina bifida. The permission for early surgery, which is necessary to give the child the best chance for the best life the impairment will allow, rests with the parents. Their alternative is to refuse the special medical procedures and hope for an early and merciful natural death for their child. It is they who must examine and weigh ethical and medical realities in light of their own resources. It would be completely inappropriate for others to question their judgment or be anything less than supportive of them in their agonizing final decision.

There are several ways educators can be of service on this issue. They can alert youth to the kinds of problems they can expect to encounter, medical resources, and sources of help that they may need to utilize as future parents. If they know ahead of time of probabilities and options with respect to birth defects, they will be better prepared for the sometimes awesome responsibilities of parenthood.

Further, young people should become aware of the support systems available to parents who can anticipate heavy, disability-related expenses. Parents in need may not be aware of possible financial aid for which they may be eligible. They can be referred to the Crippled Children's Program of their state and to the Social Security Supplementary Program for possible assistance.

MANAGEMENT IN THE SCHOOL

Some but not all children with spina bifida will have learning problems. When children with spina bifida are retarded, there is a good chance that they are brain damaged by the hydrocephalus. Thus, some will also have sensory problems such as blindness or hearing impairment. They may have perceptual problems, as distinguished from cognitive problems. It has been observed that their verbal and social abilities are usually relatively high, sometimes giving an overoptimistic impression of their general learning ability. On the other hand, it is possible that perceptual motor development has been stifled in those children who did not have the opportunity to explore their environment physically in the early years.

Those children with spina bifida who do not have signs of hydrocephalus are in the normal range of intelligence. Therefore, some of them are academically superior. By now a number of persons with spina bifida have grown to adulthood and are living full and useful lives.

The school problems caused by limited mobility, incontinence, and shunt care require close communication and cooperation of school personnel with the medical team and parents. Accommodations may need to be made for therapy sessions, transportation arrangements, assistance for toileting, special furniture, and frequent absences. The teachers who work with these children know that these management modifications are well worth the effort.

The school will need to make some accommodations to the mobility problems of the child with spina bifida. Depending on the level of lesion and functional ability, preschool children may learn a swing to crutch gait where both legs swing together, which is slow and very difficult for stair-walking. The school-aged child may be able to learn the four point crutch gait, which alternates the legs as in normal walking but is not as good for the hips. Children with spina bifida, having normal bodies above the site of lesion, develop strong arms and upper torso muscles and become incredibly agile. Those who must travel from class to class in wheelchairs may have enough mobility to walk to and get into the bus themselves. Therefore, they may want to leave a wheelchair at school, rather than transport it every day.

A child with some difficulty in sitting on a regular chair or at a regular desk may be positioned more satisfactorily in a table that surrounds the chair on three sides and a chair with straps. The physician may have prescribed a number of hours a day for the child to stand, locked in leg braces. A standing table, in which the child is safely strapped and able to do desk work, can be easily constructed. Both sitting and standing tables can be put on wheels, as was the rolling sled so the child can be moved without being repositioned. The teacher is cautioned to be sure the furniture is either adjustable or changed to fit the child's growth and that the student does not sit for prolonged periods, because pressure sores (decubital ulcers) may develop.

Exercise should be encouraged whenever possible. When leg braces are removed for floor games or a swimming program, great caution must be exercised in putting them on again. Every preschool teacher knows how easy it is to stuff a foot, toes down in the shoe. The normal child will respond in pain and limping to this mistake. The paralyzed child cannot feel the misplacement. Also, the bones in the paralyzed area are weak and prone to break.

Shunt management may take the cooperation of the teacher. It is not infrequent that the shunt slips or the valve blocks. In some types of shunt, the teacher can feel the little valve of the shunt behind the child's ear. The teacher should be alert to the displacement of the shunt. If a child seems drowsy and irritable in class or complains of headaches, sometimes this could be an indication that the shunt system needs medical attention.

Bladder management may prove to be the most difficult problem that the child with spina bifida presents in school. It might be somewhat facetiously remarked that for many years the toilet was the educational measure of school readiness. When a child was presented for nursery school, the first question was not, "Is it boy, girl, smart, strong, good?" but rather, "Is it toilet trained?" Now that early childhood education has been extended down to infants, regular educators have found that youngsters *can* learn in diapers! Since special education has been extended to profoundly handicapped children, special educators are now more inclined to expect that a certain number of their pupils will be incontinent, and "operation potty" will be routine in many of their classes. Incontinence is not a legitimate basis for exclusion from the otherwise appropriate educational environment, any more than are other physical attributes that are irrelevant to a child's learning and social ability. It must certainly be granted, however, that it is very hard on a student to have to wear diapers in school, and it may be also distressing to others who must be around that pupil. Above were described some of the different methods by which kidney and bladder problems are handled in spina bifida. None is completely satisfactory. Different doctors prefer different ones, and medical practice differs in different localities. The teacher needs to be a willing partner here on the rehabilitation team, but he or she should not become involved in any way with choosing the best method. That ultimately must be a decision between the medical team, parents, and child, considering each child's unique situation.

In some cases students with spina bifida will continue to need manual elimination of the bladder by Credé's method. A nurse or physical therapist can teach this technique to older siblings, teacher aides, and student teachers. Since it does not have to be done more often than every two hours, a parent may be willing to come to school to help with this task.

Some cautions are in order about this technique: it should be learned from a medically oriented professional who demonstrated on the particular child who is to use the method. Every person's bladder is situated a little differently. Great care must be taken not to apply too much pressure, or the bladder will rupture. Further, initial pressure must be applied at the uppermost part of the bladder. Otherwise, the pressure can force the urine back up the

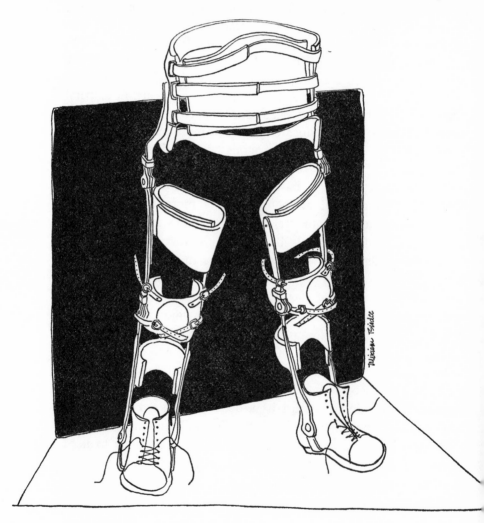

tubes (ureters) that drain the kidneys, thus contributing to the destruction of kidney tissue.

Catheterization of young females might be taught to school personnel by a nurse or physical therapist. They will be cautioned to be very careful to insure cleanliness as a precaution against infections. Older girls will take care of this procedure themselves.

If the collection device proves to be satisfactory, the school child should be able to care for it himself in school, and it should not present a problem except in the rare instances when the bag bursts or becomes disconnected. Ileal-loop surgery, particularly with girls, makes urinary management easier in school. The intelligent child can change the bag without aid from the teacher.

Rapidly improving medical care allows an optimistic view of the physical development of the child with spina bifida. The improving support system in rehabilitation including the Bureau of Vocational Rehabilitation will help the family of the student with spina bifida and help this student realize a full potential in school and beyond.

Review Guide

After reading Chapter 11 the reader should be able to define the following terms:

spina bifida occulta
spina bifida meningocele
spina bifida myelomeningocele
hydrocephalus
Credé's method

After reading Chapter 11 the reader should be able to answer the following questions:

1. What are the usual methods of ambulation for the spina bifida boy or girl?
2. What are three alternative methods of bladder management in spina bifida myelomeningocele?
3. What is a possible symptom of shunt slippage?
4. What can the teacher expect in academic ability in children with spina bifida?
5. Why must special care be taken when putting on a spina bifida child's shoes?

Chapter 12

CEREBRAL PALSY

*Handicapped Children Swimming**

A measure of freedom. Mike, floating,
would not manage so without
the red life-jacket but would sink,

messy as weed; but with it
lies, weak, like a shirt,
and the eyes, and the tongue

uncontrolled, extended, show
the delight it is to be
horizontal on water, strapped there

by nothing but sunlight. Connie,
who otherwise moves with crutches
and stiff braces, is strong

through water. Becky, seeing always
badly, lies washed by the sense
of her own fragility, liking

the help of warm hands. Gregg
rides and plucks at the water
while Danny makes his own music

in his mind as he lilts
completely quiet. Mike's delight
opens like a flower as he floats.

He doesn't know he is floating
now in this poem. I have
nothing in fact to sustain him

and I know he will never stand
up alone. But whatever sustains
the children here is important;

inflamed with the success
of water, released, they mingle
and soften there, as wax

on wetness, limp as wet bread
on water's kindness. Those fingers
can grasp as competently at air

and water as mine. Their bodies
are milky and do not need
cleansing, except from deformity.

Water cannot wash their
awkwardness from them, water is
simple, and defects difficult;

but they float for a while, never
as free as the times they fly
in dreams, over the cliffs

harvesting in the sea, the bats
exquisite with radar, but
something, a measure of freedom.

And Mike is lucid on water,
still physically cryptic, physically
glinting, but Mike has grace

for a while, this is his best
floating since before birth,
where he lay bunched like any

other unformed—encircled, contained,
his mother not knowing the
uncontrol of those limbs that

threshed and kicked at her
from out of the orchard of water.
Light queues to be present

as these imperfect children
float, perched rolling on
the foliage of water, shredded,

thick as May, shifting to new
flowerings of face, though their
limbs are weeds. Sunlight

strolls among them, padding,
healthy, firm, as our hurt
weak fleet gently disturbs the

soft clock of water. The shock
comes when you see the muscular
men who played with them

in the pool carry them
in huddles from the pool, sunlight
spreading its crime on them.

Michael Dennis Browne

DEFINITION OF CEREBRAL PALSY

CEREBRAL (BRAIN) PALSY (PARALYSIS) is a term referring to a nonprogressive but not unchanging neuromuscular involvement due to brain damage suffered during development. To elaborate that definition, cerebral palsy describes a group of symptoms (a syndrome) of motor dysfunction due to lesions or developmental defects in the brain, which have occurred at any point in a person's development, before or after birth and before maturity. The condition is nonprogressive in the sense that the original damage does not worsen. However, the responses and reactions of the body to the condition will be different at different stages of development.

Cerebral palsy (CP) is one of the most common crippling disorders of childhood, affecting 3 to 6 in 1,000 births. Here is one of the few cases in which one can legitimately infer presence of brain damage. If a child has been diagnosed medically as having cerebral palsy, that child, by definition, has brain damage. However, the simple information that a child has brain injury is of very little use to the teacher. The actual behaviours and feelings of a child are of far more relevance to the classroom situation than a diagnosis of an actual or presumed organic basis for these.

CAUSES OF CEREBRAL PALSY

The word *cause* must be used in a very particular way here. The causes discussed below are conditions and situations that are associated with the syndrome of cerebral palsy to a greater degree than they would be associated with a randomly selected group. For example, consider the relatively sizable group of children who have been breech births; that is, their feet preceded their heads through the birth canal, rather than the other way around. Breech birth does not automatically cause cerebral palsy. However, more children of breech births will have cerebral palsy than a random sample will. Also, there will be a higher percentage of breech births within the cerebral palsied population than in a randomly selected group. This, then, is the sense in which the word *cause* is used in this discussion.

The causes of cerebral palsy are important to know because some of them can be prevented. In most cases, perhaps 95 percent, cerebral palsy is not hereditary. Therefore, persons who have it do not have to worry about transmitting it to their offspring. However, some of the causes are related to hereditary factors. A particular kind of cerebral palsy is associated with Rh blood factor incompatibility between parents. Maternal diabetes also increases its likelihood.

Any kinds of complications in pregnancy and delivery increase the chances for cerebral palsy: placental bleeding, placenta previa, premature or delayed birth, multiple births, breech birth, forceps delivery, cesarean section. A common problem in many of these situations is that the baby's vulnerable brain tissue is deprived of oxygen. Good obstetrical care paradoxically both decreases cerebral palsy from such causes and yet saves cerebral palsied babies who would have died without such care.

Maternal infections can cause cerebral palsy. Most notable is maternal rubella (or German measles) when contracted during the first trimester of pregnancy. Rubella is associated with infant mortality and many serious and multiple birth defects including hearing and vision loss, heart malformations, cataracts, and severe mental retardation. Some babies with these conditions have been found to have rubella virus in their tissues, even though some of their mothers did not know that they had had the disease. A rubella vaccine has been developed that can eliminate this cause of birth defects. The vaccine contains live German measles viruses, weakened so they do not cause a full-blown infection but which will still trigger the body to manufacture antibodies that will protect against future exposure to the disease. To make sure that the vaccine is not inadvertently given to anyone who might be pregnant, it is given to girls under twelve. It should be emphasized that no woman should get pregnant unless she is sure she has had rubella or has been immunized against it. Fortunately, free mass programs of inoculations are becoming routine in the United States.

The general condition of the mother is also a factor. More cerebral palsy is associated with malnutrition, with mothers who are over forty, and with mothers who are teenagers, than in the general population.

Toxins are a cause of birth defects that can contribute to a higher incidence of cerebral palsy. That includes the excessive use of medicines and other drugs, including alcohol.

Chemical and mechanical means of attempting abortion cause cerebral palsy. It can be hoped that with medical services increasingly legally available, there will be fewer cases of self-abortion attempts.

Before the harmful effects of X-ray were understood, they contributed to the incidence of cerebral palsy. Now the use of radiation on pregnant women is curtailed whenever possible.

Brain damage acquired after birth, while the child is still developing, can result in cerebral palsy. Tragically, cerebral palsy is high among children who have suffered child abuse. Accidents kill and maim more children than all the diseases put together, and many result in serious head injuries or poisonings, as well as burnings.

Diseases that damage the brain, such as encephalitis and meningitis, tumors and blood clotting tumors in the arteries can also lead to cerebral palsy. When brain damage is acquired after the developmental period, that is in a mature adult, it will not be called cerebral palsy. However, strokes, for example, are brain damage that can cause much the same kind of neuromuscular involvement as that found in cerebral palsied children.

School curriculum in subjects such as health, science, family, and sexuality can focus on the prevention of cerebral palsy. Safety precautions with regard to traffic, toxic substances, and fire can be taught to all children in school. As they come closer to parenthood, these concerns and principles of good diet, health care, family planning, and child care be emphasized with all students.

CLASSIFICATIONS OF CEREBRAL PALSY

Cerebral palsy can be classified on the basis of its severity. It can be very mild–so that with borderline cases it is not productive to try to distinguish the child from the "clumsy child" or "klutz," who is so well known to teachers. On the other hand, cerebral palsy can be totally incapacitating. It is frequently classified as *mild, moderate,* and *severe.*

Cerebral palsy is also classified on the basis of limb involvement (which again can be more or less involvement). *Hemiplegia* describes an involvement of the upper and lower limbs on the same side. *Paraplegia* is involvement in the lower limbs only. *Diplegia* means major involvement in the lower limbs and minor involvement in the upper limbs. *Quadriplegia* means involvement of all the limbs.

Cerebral palsy is most frequently classified on the basis of the kind of neuromuscular involvement the person has, and this is based on the locus of the brain damage. Lesions in different parts of the brain produce different symptoms of motor dysfunction. Since a person can have lesions in more than one area, he may show a mixture of symptoms.

The cerebrum is the largest part of the brain. It is divided into lobes (frontal, parietal, temporal, and occipital; see Fig. 11). These lobes have various functions in reasoning, memory, interpretation of sensations, voluntary acts, and control of certain reflexes. Motor ability is approximately localized on the rear portion of the frontal lobe. Speech is localized on parts of the frontal, temporal and parietal lobes, while writing ability is situated more on the temporal lobe. Bodily sensations are located on the parietal lobe. The surface area of the brain is called the cerebral *cortex*. The *sensory* cortex first receives sensation from the body; the *motor* cortex transforms the brain's commands into bodily movement. The motor cortex and the sensory cortex just behind it are like two arches across the top of the brain. The area on the right controls the left side of the body; the area on the left controls the right side.

Spastic cerebral palsy refers to symptoms caused by damage to the motor area of the cerebral cortex (Figs. 11 and 12). It is the most common form of cerebral palsy. Because of the damage to specific brain nerve cells and their nerve fibers, the affected limb or limbs will not have the smooth reciprocating action of opposing muscles that marks normal movement. Some muscles will be too strong and tight, while opposing ones will be too loose and weak. Muscles can be so tight that they pull limbs into deformity and can literally pull the hip bone out of its socket. When an attempt is made to move the muscle, it contracts too strongly (increased

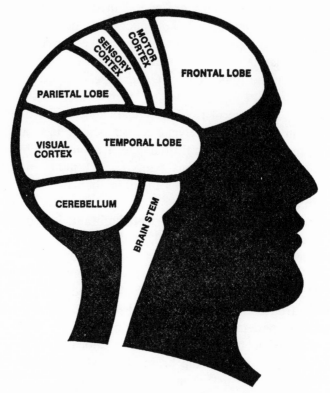

Figure 11. The brain.

stretch reflex) so movement will be jerky; sometimes muscles continue to contract repeatedly. Children who have spasticity have increased deep tendon reflexes. Usually the muscles show hypertonicity and stiffness, but some spastics are "floppy" and have low tone.

Since the spasticity is related to injury in the higher centers of the brain, the brain damage may also extend to centers of perception, reasoning, hearing, vision, and speech. Many children with spasticity have sensory and cognitive problems that are of far more educational consequence than their motor problems.

Beneath the cerebrum are the subcortical centers of the brain stem, which regulate the flow of information coming to the brain and control automatic movements and body posture. Damage in this area can result in *athetoid* cerebral palsy, the second most frequent form.

In athetosis the limbs show involuntary and contorted movements. The individual may have normal muscle tone but have contorted, flailing, or jerking motions; he may have very tense muscles, which block contorted motions. One can distinguish athetoid from spastic tension by exercising a rapid repetitive movement of a limb joint. In the athetosis the muscles will become soft, while in spasticity they become tighter and resistant. The involuntary movements of athetosis halt with sleep. Involuntary movement of the face, tongue, and smooth muscles of the throat seriously interferes with swallowing and results in characteristic "athetoid speech," which is slow, dysrhythmic, and distorted.

In unmixed athetoid cerebral palsy, the brain damage is far from the centers of higher learning, and reasoning is not affected. There are many instances of persons with this affliction making substantial contributions in literature, science, art, and medicine.

Another part of the brain, the cerebellum, takes up about 20 percent of the cranial cavity. It rests below and to the rear of the

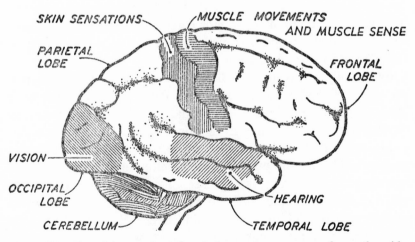

Figure 12. The right cerebral hemisphere of man, seen from the side. Shown are the four lobes and the localized areas concerned with special functions. Association areas are unshaded. "Skin sensations" lie in the parietal lobe; "muscle movements" lie in the frontal lobe.

cerebrum. It is in no way involved with conscious life. Rather, it is a timing and coordination mechanism for muscle movements. It allows for subtle and fine coordination as well as equilibrium. The cerebellum has a damping function–it collects information about moving parts while they are moving and sends feedback signals to the outer cortex. Messages from the cortex initiate appropriate breaking contractions of opposing muscles so movement slows and stops at the desired point. A lack of this damping function is called *ataxia*. *Ataxic cerebral palsy* is a result of lesions in the cerebellum. Persons with this condition walk in an uncoordinated manner, like sailors on a rolling ship, or as if they were intoxicated. In fact, there are instances of people with ataxia being arrested for drunkenness!

There is a very specific type of ataxia that is a rare, inherited disease called *Friedreich's ataxia*. This disease is not cerebral palsy because it is progressive, leading to death in around twenty or thirty years. The balance problems encountered by youth with this condition as it progresses will be much the same as those with cerebral palsy.

The final two types of cerebral palsy are given for completeness, but they are rare and probably will be infrequently seen in a regular classroom situation. In *tremor* cerebral palsy there is a shakiness of the limb involved. It may only occur when there is an attempt to use it. *Rigid* cerebral palsy is a very severe form of spasticity, usually involving the whole body (quadriplegia). The person is in total and constant tension, so that this is sometimes called "Lead Pipe" cerebral palsy. It is usually accompanied by lack of development and severe mental retardation.

Many cerebral palsied persons are seizure prone, and the more severe the CP, the more likely the possibility of seizures. It can be assumed that the brain damage accounts for the seizures, which are therefore *traumatic epilepsy*. Medication is usually given for seizure control. An unfortunate side effect of some medication may be a deteriorating effect on the gums, which may then affect the teeth.

THERAPEUTIC SERVICES

In the definition of cerebral palsy, it was stressed that the brain injury must have occurred within the developmental period, before maturity. Brain injury in a young child will affect the entire development of the organism in a far different way from comparable injury in a mature adult. This is to some extent due to the plasticity of the young brain. In the developing brain, some functions can be taken over by other portions, for example. On the other hand, the mature adult will have established normal patterns, acquired knowledge and stored memories that may be intact after an injury that would have precluded normal development in the young child. Therefore, the kind of rehabilitative therapies that have been developed with brain injured children are very different from those used with adults who have sustained traumatic brain injuries or suffered paralytic strokes. The main professionals on the rehabilitation team have been the surgeon, the physical therapist (PT), the occupational therapist (OT), and the speech therapist or pathologist. Each of these specialties represents a certified profession, but there is often overlap in their philosophies and practice and ideally close cooperation among them in planning the ongoing rehabilitation program.

There are serious controversies regarding the most acceptable philosophies and modes of treatment within each of these professional groups. Some professionals are strict adherents of one or another philosophy or method, while others are more eclectic in their point of view and practice. All of the legitimate therapists will have to take into account the impact of cerebral palsy on growth and development. They will be most helpful to the teacher and other school staff in planning day to day for the cerebral palsied child. The teacher who has in class a child with a significant degree of cerebral palsy should definitely ask to see the physical therapist or physician handling the child for reassurance and for specific techniques.

As in any profession, some individuals are more ethical than others, with respect to the risks they are willing to take, the money they demand, and the cures they promise. Desperate parents may shop around and invest themselves in terms of time, money, and effort in therapies and treatments that are useless or even detrimental. The informed teacher will want to know something about different practices and points of view, of course. However, these controversies are not in the sphere of education, so it would be very unwise for the teacher or other educational personnel to become involved in decisions concerning surgical interventions or rehabilitative techniques, as opposed to educational decisions. It *is* legitimate for a teacher to recommend a person from the appropriate profession for a "second opinion."

The teacher of brain-injured children may be exposed to the philosophy and practice known as the Doman-Delacato method. This therapy enters the province of education because its advocates advance a methodology with which to improve learning ability and teach children more effectively.[1]

Briefly, the technique is based on the resemblances between the course of development of an individual (ontogeny) with the evolutionary development of the species (phylogeny). In the early stages of embryonic development, the human embryo does resemble those of lower forms and will briefly have body hair, a tail, and so forth, so that the statement is made, "Ontogeny recapitulates phylogeny." Some advocates of this theory have extended this concept to apply to neuromuscular patterns and to cognitive learning.

The practice, then, is to train or retrain children in basic patterns of movement according to evolution from fish, to amphibian, to reptile, and to anthropoid. Thus, initial treatment would be patterning exercises, starting with swimming motions (neonates can swim instinctively), progressing onward to cross-pattern creeping and crawling. Progression through later developmental milestones, in a perceptual-motor training program, say the advocates, will lead to correcting the dysfunctions of the higher brain centers and allow for successful academic learning even in very impaired children. A very rigidly prescribed schedule of patterning must be strictly followed or all efforts will be in vain. Patterning may either necessitate the services of at least two or three adults at a session (one for each set of limbs and one at the head) or the purchase of a costly machine that can pattern automatically, in the many hours of exercise required. Other techniques may include swinging the child upside down, shining a light periodically in the

---

1. C. H. Delacato. *A New Start for the Child with Reading Problems* (New York, David McKay, 1970).

eyes night and day, and tying down limbs. Music is systematically excluded from the child's experience in some cases. Claims of successes have been made for this method. The interested reader is urged to study the subject further, being sure that readings include other authors than the inventors of the method.

However, the teacher is urged not to become embroiled in a controversy over this method with parents or students. It is not necessary to use these techniques in the classroom setting. If they are suggested the teacher can affirm that such training is more in the province of the physical therapist than the educator.

MANAGEMENT IN THE SCHOOL

It always has been emphasized in this book that impairments and diseases do not exist in the abstract but in individuals, so that each person has a unique manifestation of a condition. This is an overriding truth in the management of the child with cerebral palsy. The severity, type of condition, and its other complications must be considered in relation to all the child's assets and abilities. Even the problem of initial assessment may be a difficult one and require cooperation of student personnel services and the medical team if the cerebral palsy is severely disabling. The teacher may be working closely with the psychologist, speech therapist, aides, physical therapist, and dietician to manage the activities of daily living (ADL) in the school and to make necessary educational adjustments in the academic situation.

Areas that might require adjustment and modification are discussed below, but first a word to those teachers who have not had exposure to cerebral palsied people. It might be shocking to a teacher to learn that a student who cannot feed himself, or drools, or has unintelligible speech is going to join nonhandicapped peers in school. Also, while little children are almost always attractive, cerebral palsy often tends to make grotesque the looks and behavior of maturing people. When distorted mouths and bodies and bizarre motions are added to the ordinary plaints of adolescence, such as pimples, weight problems, scraggly beards, and awkwardness, the teacher might find the cerebral palsied student repulsive on first appearance. Fortunately, experience has shown over and over that when a successful encounter is possible, people soon get over the initial repugnance to almost any impairment or disability and begin to see the beauty of the person inside, rather than the shell. Armed with that attitude, the school staff can create an atmosphere where young persons also will be accepting. Remember, students are usually more flexible and open than the school establishment!

It is no longer a question of *whether* severely handicapped persons will be educated, but *where* and *how* they will be educated. The law specifies education in the least restrictive environment. A responsive school can "unrestrict" the environment even for students with such a complicated condition as cerebral palsy.

The cerebral palsied student may be confined to a wheelchair. Even here there are levels of independence that must be assessed. Can the student transfer alone in and out of the car, to the toilet, and desk? Some students will have enough strength and coordination to propel their own chairs. Others must use a motorized chair, which is very heavy and considerably less portable in a car or bus. As we have said before, modifications for wheelchairs are not difficult. Ramps, high tables, door frames removed are relatively inexpensive.

The cerebral palsied child may be heavily braced, even if the braces do not enable walking. Braces are used to prevent contractures of strong spastic muscles that would eventually cause bone deformities and further limit mobility. Children may even be braced at night. Cerebral palsied children may also wear hand splints and weights to prevent contractures and reduce extraneous motion. Teachers who do much lifting of heavy children must use proper techniques or they will end up with bad backs. The physical therapist can help the teacher to learn to anticipate the reflex patterns that will follow certain positioning so that he or she can avoid eliciting pathological reflex patterns and can encourage the normal ones.

For example, when the very involved cerebral palsied person is tilted back, he may go into extension–that is, the head goes back and the arms and legs shoot out, making transfer difficult. If the child is grasped behind at chest level, however, his head will bend forward and limbs will not be resistant to transfer from chair to desk, etc.

Proper positioning of a cerebral palsied child is very important in order to prevent contractures, to save the teacher from unnecessary effort, and to place the child in the very best attitude for learning. Techniques will be worked out in consultation with an orthopedist, who may be doing surgery on the child, and the physical therapist who is an invaluable aid to the teacher. The PT can demonstrate, for example, how to tie the child in the wheelchair, or regular chair (usually at hip height). The child may have a hard wedge placed high between the thighs to prevent hip dislocation and increase the base of sitting support. Special equipment might be ordered, such as an adjustable standing table, or a prone board on wheels that the child propels, belly down. The handling of splints and braces may be necessary, particularly with younger children.

An inventive school carpenter or parent may become involved in designing a supportive wedge-shape prone cushion of hard foam rubber for the child on which he has support up to the chest, with arms free and head down to manipulate materials on the floor. Cerebral palsied children are much easier handled on their "bellies" than on their backs, where they frequently have the tendency to go into extension. For transfer, feeding, or putting on wraps, they can often be better manipulated from behind for the same reason. The PT or perhaps the occupational therapist may help the teacher adapt educational materials for the student. An extreme case (but one very satisfactory for some writers and artists) is a head device or a porcelain mouth piece to hold a pen, paint brush, or pusher for a typewriter for persons with no use of their hands.

Bowel and bladder control are not usually difficult for cerebral palsied children even though they may be paraplegic (involved in the lower limbs). They do not have the more complete paralysis, caused by spinal cord injuries, such as spina bifida. With mobility limitations, there might be need for help with clothing, hygiene, and transfer to and from the toilet. Some simple modifications such as an arm bar or removable raised toilet seat might be all that is required to allow a person in a wheelchair complete independence at the toilet. That is providing, of course, that the wheelchair can fit through the door!

Some cerebral palsied students will need help in eating. Older students or peers might be enlisted to rotate this task. Actually, it could be far cheaper for a school system to pay an aide to attend to special physical requirements of physically handicapped students than to pay for their transportation and education elsewhere.

The importance of positioning for eating is stressed. It is not good practice to tilt a youngster back and "bird feed." (The reader can determine why by attempting to chew and swallow while tilting back the head.) Sometimes a youngster's arms must be tied so they do not flail and spill food and dishes. Whenever possible, the handicapped child should be encouraged to self-feed. Granted, this might be a slow and somewhat messy proposition. The social benefit of eating with everyone else is invaluable, however. Also, independence in self-help skills is of tremendous importance for the future life of the handicapped person and may be the most important achievement of the school years.

There are a number of feeding aids for the handicapped (see Appendix). There is a swivel spoon for those who lack wrist rotation. Plates with suction cups, frequently used for infants, will not be knocked off by extraneous movements. Dishes with high sides make food piling easier. A piece of Saran Wrap® fastened to a placemat makes a nonskid surface. Some cerebral palsied persons cannot drink from a cup. Straws are easily substituted. Naturally, special aids should be discarded when they are no longer needed. The teacher may be in charge of the younger child's equipment. Older students may always carry a swivel spoon or a straw in purse or pocket. The teacher should talk over any special needs with the student.

There are some special dietary needs of many cerebral palsied persons that may be of some concern to the teacher. Some CP individuals, particularly those with athetosis, are in constant motion and, hence, burn up a great deal of energy. They are often underweight for their height and age. Their caloric requirements may be three times those of a normal counterpart. The student should be allowed enough time to complete lunch, even if he or she sits through two periods. On the other hand, some children with spastic CP incline toward obesity. This may be a result of their forced inaction, or eating may be a compensation for other pleasures not enjoyed, or it may be forced on the child by over-solicitous parents. The teacher can involve others in solving these problems. The dietician can plan with the parents for healthful packed lunches, or with the school cafeteria with regard to food selection.

Educational assessment is influenced by the palsied condition. The deliberate motions of the cerebral palsied person are very slow, since limbs do not respond smoothly to the commands of the brain, but jerk, overshoot, and spasm often with concomitant extraneous movement from other parts of the body. Therefore, movements such as those required for writing or speaking can be slow and laborious. These difficulties will make timed tests for psychological and educational assessment both unfair and inaccurate. At least in day-to-day testing the teacher is usually more concerned with mastery than in normative testing, so time can be extended and modifications in administration can include oral testing and use of the tape recorder for example.

The psychologist will have to select tests tailored to the physical abilities of the handicapped student. For example, as an assessment instrument for general level of intellectual functioning, the Peabody Picture Vocabulary Test might be appropriate *if* the person can point or in any way indicate yes and no, *if* he can hear and understand speech, and *if* he has good enough vision and perception to interpret pictures. The test is untimed and does not require speech or any movement save eye blinks or tongue movement.

One of the most heart-rending situations is to encounter a person with a great deal to say and no way in which to communicate. The problem of indistinct speech is very frequent with cerebral palsied persons. Their muscle involvement often makes it difficult for them to take in enough breath for speech, and incoordination makes the formulation of words difficult. This is true even for some persons who have very good language. Tongue thrust, a reflex present at birth that aids the nursing process, disappears during infancy in normal individuals. Cerebral palsied persons may retain this reflex, even in an exaggerated pattern, and it, too, can interfere with clear speech as well as with eating. (It is interesting to note that some tongue thrust and a primitive swallowing pattern are also quite frequent in children labeled Straus syndrome, hyperkinetic, or learning disabled.)

The characteristic athetoid speech was mentioned. It is very difficult for persons not accustomed to this speech to understand it. It is embarrassing for the listener and frustrating for the speaker to have to have unsatisfactory communication, even when remarks are repeated. It is sometimes easier to understand a person with athetoid speech if one turns an attentive ear rather than looking at the distracting grimaces, drooling, and spasmodic head turnings that accompany efforts to speak.

It has been noted by some physicians that adults with athetosis seem to speak better with alcohol consumption. It has been a moot point with the author whether the handicapped person's speech actually improves, or whether the drinking partner's tolerance and patience improve, to make the encounter more successful. At any rate, the teacher should not endorse social drinking, at least not for minors and certainly not at school.

A particular type of athetosis is associated with children from Rh incompatible parents. The neuromuscular manifestation may be so mild that only a small "spillover" of extraneous movement is observed and may be scarcely significant in itself. However, it can be accompanied by a far more educationally relevant language problem. Some experts think the problem is due to *deafness* (the inability to receive auditory information). Others are inclined to consider the condition *receptive auditory aphasia* (the inability to interpret and process auditory information, which has been received). This type of child will need speech and language therapy, and the teacher will have to work closely with the therapist on a coordinated program.

Handwriting is frequently mentioned as a difficult skill for children with CP to master. It is worth the effort for the student to at least learn a legible script for times in the student's later life that it *must* be used, even if it is not used for school work. Of course, writing is even more important for persons who cannot use the spoken word. Printing, or a simplified cursive script—whatever is easiest for the student—should be permitted. The point of writing is communication, not art. Large pencils and pens or an implement put through a rubber ball may make grasp easier. Pencils can be tied to the desk so they can be easily retrieved when knocked off. Paper can be taped on the desk.

The typewriter, and particularly the electric typewriter, is a boon to persons with limited dexterity and weak hands. Sleeves for the typing keys can be ordered from the manufacturer so that the wrong key is not hit inadvertently during random motion. Typing can be accomplished by means of pencils attached upside down to hand clasps, or by a head or mouth gear, as mentioned. Typewriters can be used by very little children. Again, the school's investment in a typewriter is very small when compared with the cost of transportation out of a district or to a private school.

On an experimental basis, electronic equipment has been made for communication of extremely handicapped people. Teachers will find commercial teaching machines and other "hardware" very helpful with the cerebral palsied student.

For children with limited speech, either the very young child or the older student who is not yet ready for reading and writing, the communication board (or talking board) is very effective (Fig. 13). It consists of representations (such as pictures) or symbols (such as words), which are printed or manipulated on a flat surface. The speaker points to the symbol in sequence using a finger, or pointer. It can be easily made by the teacher or in cooperation with the speech therapist or occupational therapist. A very simple talking board could have pictures, or even small toys, representing "water," "toilet," "outside," "lunch," so the child can communicate simple needs. Talking boards can become more and more complex, next utilizing words with the pictures, then sight words, the alphabet, and symbol signs, such as question marks. They can also be devised for special subjects. For example, a child might indicate what song he would like from pictures representing those he knows.

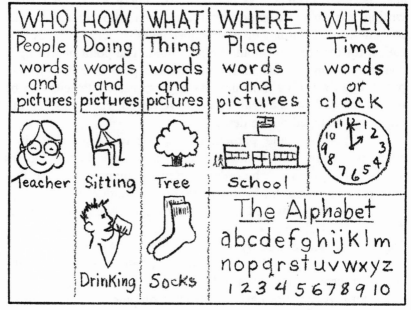

LANGUAGE SHEET: FROM A LANGUAGE BOARD

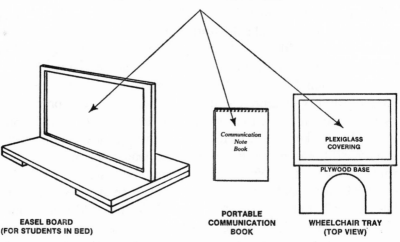

Figure 13. Language board and communication book.

A specialized symbol system, the Bliss system, has been found successful by some teachers. It was developed by an Australian immigrant who based it on principles of pictographs and universal sign languages of multilingual tribes. American Sign Language (ASL), the manual communication system used by the deaf, is not too successful for nonverbal cerebral palsied children since they lack the needed manual coordination. However, some schools are simplifying ASL to one-handed signing for cerebral palsied students.

The use of concrete objects, such as cuisinère blocks and wooden numbers, which can be selected and manipulated, may be helpful in arithmetic with nonverbal and speaking children alike. Real things, as opposed to representation of symbols of things, are often very effective with children who may be stimulus deprived because of their limited mobility.

A word is necessary about cerebral palsied students when they leave school. With new opportunities for appropriate education, even more will meld into society and, from a societal point of view, will be like everyone else. Others, even very able people, may need some degree of ongoing help as adults, whether in community homes or institutional settings. Some may become fully employed; some work in sheltered workshops. Some (men and women) can be homemakers for families and some may be just able to maintain themselves in a home situation. Others, of course, will live with parents or in institutions as wards of the state. There is nothing inherently tragic in any of these situations. What *is* tragic is potential left undeveloped, opportunities denied, respect withheld, and treatment unkind.

Review Guide

After reading Chapter 12 the reader should be able to define the following terms:

diplegia	motor cortex
paraplegia	spastic cerebral palsy
hemiplegia	athetoid cerebral palsy
sensory cortex	ataxia

After reading Chapter 12 the reader should be able to answer the following questions:

1. What are the four characteristics necessary for a definition of cerebral palsy?

2. Name six conditions associated with or causing cerebral palsy.
3. Why is the effect of brain injury in a child different from comparable brain injury in an adult?
4. Why do some persons with spastic cerebral palsy also have cognitive, perceptive, and sensory problems?
5. Why do athetoids frequently have very high academic ability?
6. What is the meaning of "ontogeny recapitulates phylogeny"?
7. What are three reasons why proper positioning of the cerebral palsied child is important?
8. What are some alternatives to standardized tests in assessment of cerebral palsied students?
9. Name five adaptive materials or devices the cerebral palsied student might use in school.

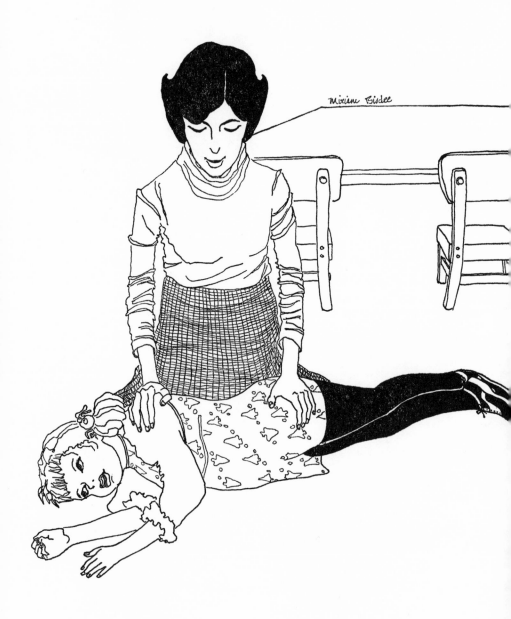

Maxine Bidee

Chapter 13

EPILEPSY

Then suddenly something seemed torn asunder before him; his soul was flooded with intense inner light. The moment lasted perhaps half a second, yet he clearly and consciously remembered the beginning, the first sound of the fearful scream which broke of itself from his breast and which he could not have checked by any effort. Then his consciousness was instantly extinguished and complete darkness followed.

It was an epileptic fit, the first he had had for a long time. It is well known that epileptic fits come on quite suddenly. At the moment the face is horribly distorted, especially the eyes. The whole body and the features of the face work with convulsive jerks and contortions. A terrible, indescribable scream that is unlike anything else breaks from the sufferer. In that scream everything human seems obliterated and it is impossible, or very difficult, for an observer to realise and admit that it is the man himself screaming. It seems indeed as though it were someone else screaming from within the man. That is how many people at least have described their impression.

Feodor Dostoievsky
The Idiot

THE TERM *epilepsy* (or convulsion, seizures, or fits) is used to describe a wide variety of abnormalities of brain function due to many causes. Seizures are associated with abnormal discharges of the electrical impulses of the brain. These spontaneous alterations in brain function are electrochemical and can be measured by a machine, the electroencephalograph. This instrument records a graphic record (EEG) from wired electrodes which are glued to the surface of the scalp in various locations over the brain.

CLASSIFICATION OF EPILEPSY

Seizures can be classified as generalized, which involve the brain pervasively, or as focal, which may be pinpointed to a specific

173

portion of it. Seizures may be associated with brain injury, such as that caused by tumors or accidents (traumatic epilepsy), or are a primary disease of spontaneous, or unknown origin (idiopathic epilepsy) in about two-thirds of the cases.

The person with persistent epilepsy, then, is often one with no identifiable pathology, but rather a person with a low seizure threshold. To elaborate, every neuron in the cerebral cortex has an excitation threshold. A signal coming to the neuron from another nerve cell must be of the threshold level or greater strength, or the neuron will not fire. Normal threshold level prevents misfiring. It is thought that certain neurons in epileptics are especially sensitive, having a threshold far below normal. Instead of a normal sequence of nerve-to-nerve information, large groups of nerves fire at the same time, and instead of stopping after the data is transmitted, they continue to fire. General, uncontrolled firing in the motor areas causes the severe muscular movements of grand mal epilepsy, described above.

Since there are always minute changes in electric potential associated with the mental functioning of the cerebral cortex, seizures are sometimes viewed as brain activity at one extreme of a continuum. At a less extreme distance on the continuum would be placed the sudden, spontaneous, and vehement mentation associated with the creative process, popularly called a "brain storm." Epilepsies, then, are more severe "storms," or paroxysmal alterations of brain functions that begin and end spontaneously. It is assumed that everyone is capable of experiencing a seizure, and about 17 in 100 persons will experience an isolated experience of this type at some point, precipitated by factors such as emotional stress or fatigue. Another 20 percent of seizure-free persons have abnormal EEG patterns.

Five young adults in 1,000 are seizure prone, that is, they have a tendency to recurring seizures. The term *seizure free* is applied to those who, either with or without medication, have not experienced a seizure for a minimum of six months to two years.

There are many types of seizures described and variously classified. The more common ones, and those of greater significance to the teacher, are described here.

Febrile Convulsions

In an estimated 2 percent of normal children under five years, convulsions have resulted from high fever. These children may require prompt medical attention at the time, but they can be expected to grow out of the tendency toward convulsions. This group is to be distinguished from another estimated 1 percent whose early seizures are associated with brain injury, cerebral palsy, and severe mental retardation.

Psychomotor Seizures

These result as an abnormal electrochemical discharge in a localized group of neurons in the brain. Such seizures are sometimes called focal epilepsy. They are usually caused by irritation of the focus. A blow or wound that destroys tissue, vascular abnormalities, infection, fever, or tumor may cause a focus. The constant irritation lowers neuron threshold.

There is a brief period of automatic behavior in which the child may make chewing or swallowing motions, finger objects, or wander aimlessly around. The attacks last only a moment or two, after which normal activities are resumed. They may occur several times a week with one child and only once a month with another. About one-fifth of school-aged children with epilepsy show this kind or other miscellaneous episodes.

These attacks could easily be misinterpreted as bad and willful behavior in school. Also, the pupil may miss the continuity of directions or instruction, which will have impact on learning. Otherwise, these seizures do not usually present much of a problem to the school.

Petit Mal

Petit mal (small illness), sometimes referred to as absence attacks, is seen in children from about five to ten years old. Petit mal is characterized by a momentary lapse of consciousness for perhaps five to twenty seconds or lack of contact with reality, but the child does not usually fall. Among school-aged children with epilepsy, about one-fourth have petit mal.

The indication of a petit mal seizure may be very subtle. The child might only appear to be staring, or might flutter the eyes or show small eye movements. Less usual forms of petit mal are a single muscle jerk or a simple fall. Petit mal attacks may recur several times a day, but they usually disappear before adulthood. Medication is sometimes given for petit mal seizures. It is possible that the petit mal attacks progress to grand mal seizures.

Petit mal seizures may be misinterpreted as the child's daydreaming or as a sign of disinterest. A watchful teacher may be the first to recognize the problem for what it actually is. These losses of attention may seriously interfere with learning, because the child may miss a part of the instruction or sequence during the attack. The child is not aware of the momentary loss. His consequent confusion could be taken as stupidity or willful lack of concentration by the unknowing parent or teacher.

Grand Mal

Grand mal (large illness) is the most serious of the kinds of epilepsy, which about one-half of school-aged epileptics will have, either alone or in combination with another type. It is characterized by loss of consciousness and convulsions. The onset of epilepsy can be at any age. However, a single attack is rather common at the onset of adolescence, and three-fourths of all cases begin before twenty years of age.

While the general or "classic" pattern of the grand mal seizure will be described, it is important to emphasize again that disorders do not exist in the abstract. A particular person will react and respond physically as well as psychologically in a unique way. Therefore, it is more important to look to the student and his or her parents and doctor rather than the book when devising management strategies. The particular pattern of reactions that an individual has in a grand mal seizure tends not to vary through the years. Therefore, when the teacher has worked out some guidelines for the management of a given child, these are likely to remain valid for subsequent episodes.

In about half of the cases, people have a warning (aura) that the seizure is coming. This may be experienced as a strange odor, a headache, or odd feeling, such as Dostoievsky, himself epileptic, describes in the opening quotation. This is very helpful to the child with epilepsy, who then can plan a safe position; there is little time to get off the stairs or sit down before consciousness is lost. The teacher can discuss this with even a young student. A simple plan might be, "When you feel funny, just slip out of your seat to the floor." A child with frequent seizures may wear a football helmet to protect against head injury. It should be mentioned that attacks are less apt to take place in school, where the pupil is mentally and physically active, than when the child is idle or asleep.

The convulsion begins with a sudden loss of consciousness. As muscles contract, air may be forced from the lungs so the person may cry out, while falling to the ground. The eyes may roll up, and breathing may cease momentarily. During this stiff (tonic) stage, there may be loss of bladder or bowel control, but this is rare. Rigidity of the muscles usually gives way to jerking of the arms and legs (clonic phase). The jaws may clench and the teeth gnash. Because of inefficient swallowing of saliva, there may be foaming of the mouth. Usually within fewer than two minutes the individual becomes more relaxed and enters the last stage (the postictal state), where there may be some confusion and a wish for deep sleep for some minutes to hours. The person has no memory of the seizure itself.

A seizure looks terrible, but it is not an extremely serious event. Children do not die of seizures, so everyone can be reassured on that concern. There is a rare complication when the child who is seizuring goes into repetitive seizures without regaining consciousness (status epilepticus). This is a medical emergency and requires hospitalization. The real problem is impaired circulation following the attack. This can be determined if the child shows a blue pallor (cyanosis). If it is present, then effort should be made to breathe for the child or get air in before medical help can be obtained.

MEDICAL TREATMENT

Medical intervention is advised in the event of a first seizure.

The seizure could indicate some ongoing pathology or be due to a metabolic abnormality, and this must be checked out. If there is not a physical problem, it is still very important to initiate treatment quickly. With seizure control it is better to "nip it in the bud," rather than allow more seizures to occur. This is not necessarily because having a seizure causes damage in itself (there are opinions on both sides of that issue). Rather there is a tendency on the part of the body to react to seizures with more seizures, or to few seizures with fewer seizures.

From 60 to 80 percent of seizures can be well controlled with medication, which will be taken daily, even up to three or four years after control is achieved. Dilantin®, phenobarbital, and the bromides lessen the severity and frequency of seizures. These drugs are, in general, not habit forming. In recent years many new anticonvulsant drugs have been made available for difficult cases. An important consideration in the classroom is the possibility that the medication will cause side effects of drowsiness, headaches, or nausea. The teacher should report what seem to be undue side effects, and be understanding when the medicated child is somewhat less alert than other students.

The predisposition to epilepsy makes a child more susceptible to physical and psychological strain. Excessive fatigue and emotional stress can precipitate a seizure. General physical health should be maintained at a high level, and students should avoid irregularities in routine. Persons with epilepsy are advised not to use alcohol.

In general, the school can assume that the student with epilepsy is a normal learner who can partake of the usual school activities. Some physicians advise against participation in highly competitive sports such as inter-high school football, where a vulnerable youth would not feel like pulling out when feeling overexertion. Many physicians recommend swimming programs and other vigorous athletics. However, prior assumptions cannot be made, for each student will present a unique case.

It has been emphasized before that persons are not well identified by a medical or health problem. Therefore, a person who has seizures or epilepsy should never be referred to as an epileptic, rather referred to and thought of as a person who has that particular problem.

GUIDELINES FOR MANAGING SEIZURES

The following guides will aid the teacher in handling the seizure:

1. Utilize the aura for positioning when possible.
2. When the start of a seizure is evident, ease the child to the floor, away from hard objects such as the wall or chair legs that can be struck during the convulsion.
3. Loosen tight-fitting clothes at the neck to facilitate breathing.
4. Use a coat or rug to raise the head slightly, and turn the head to the side to release saliva and to allow the tongue to fall forward rather than roll back to block the throat.
5. Execute the strategy developed in advance with regard to tongue biting.

There is much professional disagreement on preferred procedure here. The teacher cannot get the best answer from a book but will have to exercise his or her own judgment. It is the pattern of some seizures that the tongue is inclined to protrude while the teeth gnash together, so there is a very real danger that the tongue will be badly bitten. Therefore, the suggestion sometimes was made that an object be placed between the teeth so that the teeth would be prevented from biting the tongue. Well-intentioned persons committed the following serious errors, which would be laughable if they were not tragic: Some put their fingers in the person's mouth. The tongue was not bitten off, but the finger was. Others put lead pencils in the person's mouth, which were bitten in pieces and were inclined to choke the seizuring child. Others, seeing the teeth clenched closed, were determined to get a hard object in the mouth and broke teeth attempting to do so. At this point some professionals just advised, "leave well enough alone." However, some persons with epilepsy know that they have a pattern of tongue biting. Find out if this is so with your student from himself or parents; if so, prepare in advance what article you would use to prevent tongue biting. It is very handy to use a large, twisted man's handkerchief, which is soft but bulky and keeps hands out of danger. Another possibility is a wooden tongue depressor, wound with adhesive tape. The school nurse or physician may be helpful in making a selection.

6. After the seizure is over, let the child rest comfortably in a safe place, covered by a coat or blanket for warmth.

7. If this is a first attack, or if consciousness is not regained quickly, notify medical personnel and the parents, immediately.

If the students in the class are not familiar with seizures, the teacher will have to handle their anxieties over the strange behavior of their classmate. With younger children in particular, this might be done as soon as the grand mal is over and the child is resting comfortably. Children need to be assured that the seizure did not hurt, even though the cry or convulsions may have seemed to express pain. They need to know that their classmate will be fine after waking. It can be emphasized that this sickness is not contagious. It is just a particular behavior that some persons have, and in general we do not know why.

It might also be well to anticipate with the class how the classmate will feel about the episode if it is not a frequent occurrence. The teacher can lead the students toward the conclusion that this is not something to laugh about or taunt over, because it would hurt the classmate's feelings. Again, a calm, matter-of-fact attitude rather than one laden with emotion will reassure the class and minimize the social effect of the seizure.

The affected person will have no recollection of the seizure itself. Therefore, it is important in a first seizure for the teacher to take the student aside at a propitious time and briefly explain what happened: that he fell unconscious, jerked, and went to sleep. If a device was used to part the teeth, that should be explained. The teacher can also simply state that the parents, or school nurse, etc. will be informed so the child will be sure to have the best care. Also, he can be told that the rest of the class talked awhile about the seizures and they understand what happened. An open, non-secretive approach should allay or forestall any shame or embarrassment that the child might feel with regard to the seizure. This attitude carries over to the parents of the student with epilepsy, and the other classmates will also help to keep the problem in perspective.

CHANGING PUBLIC ATTITUDE

The word *epilepsy* is Greek for *seizure*. Patients with "falling sickness" were described by Hippocrates (460-377 BC) in a monograph titled, *On the Sacred Disease*. Julius Caesar and Othello were described by Shakespeare as having epilepsy. The great Russian author Feodor Dostoievsky had epilepsy and well illustrated the disease in his book *The Idiot*.

For some reason, social stigma has accompanied this disorder in an apparent deep-rooted emotional response. In the United States, restrictive legislation regarding right to entry, right to marry, to drive a car, carry insurance, and compulsory sterilization have penalized and stigmatized adults who have epilepsy. Such strictures have often been counterproductive, since they have discouraged persons from getting medical help because then they would be labeled and, in some situations, registered with the state.

Fortunately, laws are being liberalized and, increasingly, handicapped persons are able to obtain redress under civil rights legislation. Employment programs are being sponsored for adults with epilepsy, some who had been institutionalized or who never had had the opportunity to work.

The school is a powerful change agent. If the students can feel all right about their problems, and staff feel the same, then parents will not need to feel fearful and secretive about this disorder. The tremendous social handicap will be lessened, and children with epilepsy, also, will be allowed to become the best they are able.

Review Guide

After reading Chapter 13 the reader should be able to define the following terms:

generalized epilepsy petit mal
focal epilepsy idiopathic
febrile convulsions aura
psychomotor seizures grand mal

After reading Chapter 13 the reader should be able to answer the following questions:

1. Why are psychomotor seizures sometimes misinterpreted as bad behavior?
2. In what way might petit mal seizures interfere with a child's learning?
3. Why is the aura helpful to the student with epilepsy?
4. What are possible side effects of medication for epilepsy?
5. What are seven important guidelines for managing grand mal seizures?
6. What societal prohibitions have sometimes prevented persons with epilepsy from fulfilling their potential?

Section IV

SYSTEMIC DISORDERS

We learn as much from sorrow as from joy,
as much from illness as from health,
from handicap as from advantage—
and indeed perhaps more.

Pearl Buck
Harold Ober Association, Inc.
1959

The disorders discussed in this section affect the body as a whole. They are very common and have probably been encountered by the reader among friends and relatives, if not in the classroom. All of these metabolic and organic problems can cause death or can shorten life. However, with modern medical and health care advances, they are more likely to be impairments and disabilities with which people live and still have fulfilled lives. Each kind of disorder will present some rather specific problems and special needs for educational management.

Chapter 14

DOWN'S SYNDROME

"Whose talent is more or less is not the point: the validity is."
Marya Mannes
Out of My Time

D OWN'S SYNDROME was named for Langdon Down, who gave a description of the condition in 1866. (It is also known as Mongolism due to a superficial resemblance of the eyes of those with Down's syndrome to the eyes of Oriental people.) Due to chromosomal abnormalities, a number of physical characteristics may be present. The cluster of a number of these characteristics warrants the diagnosis of Down's syndrome. Chromosomal studies provide the most accurate way of diagnosing it without doubt. It is present in about one in 600 births with no differences according to race.

In most cases of Down's syndrome, the cells of the body have forty-seven chromosomes instead of the normal number, forty-six. The extra genetic material is an extra twenty-first (or possibly 20th) chromosome (trisomy 21, or primary trisomy).

The hereditary form of Down's syndrome is also a chromosomal aberration where the chromosomal material of the twenty-first chromosome is stuck onto another chromosome, usually chromosome number fifteen (translocation).

A last, rare form of Down's syndrome is mosaicism, in which only some cells show the abnormal chromosome count, and the person or the parents may only show some characteristics of Down's syndrome. It is a mutation or elimination of chromosomes.

185

CHARACTERISTICS

More than sixty-five characteristics have been associated with Down's syndrome, and no one person will have all of them. Usually all of the cells in the body will have the abnormal number of chromosomes, and the entire body will be affected. The Down's syndrome child is sometimes called "the unfinished child," with a correlation between the number of physical stigmas and degree of mental subnormality in some cases. Down's syndrome is almost always associated with some degree of mental subnormality. Down's syndrome is the most common cause of mental retardation.

Typically, the head of the affected person is flat and broad, and the hair is coarse and stringy. An increased epicanthic fold in the inner corners of the eye contributes to the almond-shaped eyes. The tongue is fissured and frequently does not fit in the oral cavity. It frequently protrudes while the facial features are at rest or during speech. The shape of the oral cavity may be abnormal. The skin is rough, dry, and prone to blemish. The fingers are stumpy, and there is a characteristic single horizontal crease in the palm of the hand. Stature is relatively short.

From a medical point of view, the concomitant health problems are the most serious characteristics of this disorder. There are frequently congenital heart defects and birth defects such as cleft palate. Children with Down's syndrome are prone to upper respiratory infections. They frequently have hearing problems. Many Down's syndrome children will develop cataracts in their eyes during their childhood. The development of surgical techniques and the use of antibiotics have contributed to increasing the life expectancy of the Down's syndrome child and to lessening the amount of illness experienced.

Physical development is affected, also. Muscles are flabby, and consequent obesity is often seen. Large muscle functioning is often poor, and eye-hand coordination is difficult. In adult males, the sex organs are underdeveloped, so these adults will rarely have offspring. Girls do ovulate and menstruate. There are a few cases reported where they have given birth to children, some of whom were normal.

MECHANISM OF TRANSMISSION

The transmission of Down's syndrome is important to understand because it is so prevalent, and because there are some options open toward its prevention. It is estimated that over 50 percent of Down's syndrome is not hereditary. Rather, its frequency is associated with the mother's age. Whereas a mother aged twenty-five to thirty-four has a $\frac{1}{1000}$ chance of bearing a Down's syndrome child, the risk goes to $\frac{1}{280}$ from ages thirty-five to forty, to 1 in 80 if she is forty to forty-four and 1 in 40 if she is over forty-four. An explanation for this phenomenon seems to relate to the age of the mother's eggs. Unlike sperm, which are constantly being produced, the oocytes, which will mature into fully developed eggs, are present in the mother before she is born and may remain in this arrested state for forty-five or more years. It is conjectured that overage affects the cell division process, which then results in trisomy. Half the babies born with Down's syndrome were born to older mothers. Trisomy, then, is not hereditary, but could be diminished if older women chose not to bear children, or to abort fetuses with Down's syndrome.

The junction of chromosomal material with another chromosome is called a translocation. When Down's syndrome occurs more than once in a family, particularly with young mothers, this type of inherited Down's syndrome is suspected. The parents of the child who has Down's syndrome due to a translocation are both usually normal. However, one of them, usually the mother, has the twenty-first chromosome attached to another chromosome. The mother is normal because she has the proper amount of chromosomal material in her body. If she gives a normal twenty-first chromosome to her baby and the fifteenth chromosome with the extra twenty-first chromosome, those two twenty-first chromosomes will be added to another from the father. The child will have three twenty-first chromosomes, and Down's syndrome will result.

The mosaic form of Down's syndrome is due to a mutation or elimination of chromosomes in fewer or more cells of the body. It is a rare form of the disorder.

It is possible to identify Down's syndrome in the fetus by the twelfth or thirteenth week of pregnancy, because some of the cells of the baby slough off into the amniotic fluid of the womb. A hollow needle can be inserted into the uterus, with little risk, to obtain a sample, which can then be analyzed microscopically through a process called amniocentesis. If the cells contain extra genetic material, the mother can elect an abortion. This course might more frequently be chosen by older parents, who might see problems in caring for a handicapped child in later years. Genetic counseling is recommended both for older mothers and for couples who have had a Down's syndrome child. Health insurance contributes to this screening.

Down's syndrome is the most common of chromosomal abnormalities. Many abnormalities are incompatible with life, so are never seen in living beings. A rare syndrome, cri du chat (cry of the cat), which causes extreme mental deficiency, shortened life, and a characteristic voice, is due to a part of chromosome number five being missing. Geneticists stress that if it were possible to eradicate all cases of genetic abnormality, valuable genetic variability might be lost. The variation that is abnormal and undesirable now might in the future, under slightly different environmental conditions, be advantageous and even life saving. These biological facts might give comfort to parents who have produced children with genetic defects.

It should be stressed that children with Down's syndrome can give much comfort to their parents. Pearl Buck, whose only child was so affected, implies this in the quote that opened this section of the book.

EDUCATIONAL PLANNING

Mental retardation is a concept describing subaverage intellectual, hence, cognitive and social functioning. Since it is used as a label to describe behavior, it is more arbitrary and subjective than labels denoting a physical impairment, such as amputations, or hearing deficit. When we look at individuals at the bottom end of the continuum of the normal curve with respect to any tests of intellectual functioning, it is obvious that those who are barely life sustained (LSMR) or those who have never developed language (prelingual mentally retarded, PLMR) are definitely mentally deficient. If we looked the gray area of minus one to minus two or so standard deviations out (IQ 85 down to 70 or 65), it often becomes a very subjective and even biased judgment whether or not these individuals are different enough to be labeled retarded. Traditionally, the schools label at least some students with these IQ numbers as educable mentally retarded (EMR). These EMR classes frequently have an overrepresentation of male, poor, and minority children. Persons who have been in such classes all through their school days often graduate and meld into the regular community, supporting themselves, having families, and living in a manner indistinguishable from the rest of the community.

A classification of mentally retarded persons, all of whom will always need a special support system (unlike many so-called educable mentally retarded persons), is discussed here and summarized in Figure 14.

It must be emphasized that categorization of mentally retarded individuals should be tentative; it cannot be made with great assurance until the developmental period is over. Little is known about the developmental growth curves of exceptional children. In some cases, such as children with delayed speech, atypical growth patterns transpire to be the only exceptionality. (Even among normal children, patterns of maturation vary enormously.) Educators should always be willing to reassess and reprogram for children who have not progressed according to their predictions. (Indeed one of the greatest pitfalls in special education is that of forcing children to fulfill the educator's prophecy, either in terms of over- or underachievement.)

It has been observed by special education teachers that there is an upward progression of individuals through categories as they receive educational attention. Thus, persons considered life sustained mentally retarded may be weaned from tube feeding or learn to sit or walk. Persons considered prelingual mentally re-

Life sustained mentally retarded	LSMR
Prelingual mentally retarded	PMR
Severely mentally retarded	SMR
Trainable mentally retarded	TMR

Figure 14. Classification of mental retardation.

190 Management of Physically Handicapped Students

tarded may show understanding of language through eye blinks, taps, gestures, or words when given the opportunity. The severely mentally retarded are transferred to trainable mentally retarded (TMR) classes, and TMRs learn to read. Thus, the categories suggested below should be regarded more as developmental check points than labels.

Life Sustained Mentally Retarded (LSMR)

These children are required to have a specific therapeutic environment because of physical needs (actually without reference to level of learning ability). An educational program is secondary to life sustaining procedures. Such a child may be attached to a machine such as a respirator, to feeding devices, or be too fragile or weak to be moved from bed, or need a peculiar temperature or atmosphere. (Therefore, a normally learning child might also be in such an environment. However, most will be profoundly mentally retarded as well.)

There are several educational implications and foci for teacher competencies when dealing with these students: the educational program must be in the therapeutic environment. Particular attention must be paid to the possibilities and limitations in positioning and other health care activities. Since the therapeutic environment is by necessity abnormal and understimulating, a program of stimulation through all available sensory avenues should be considered. Since independence is so severely limited, any potential for movement and expression should be utilized and explored for organization, feedback, and communication in the educational experience. Eye contact, eye blink, smiling, pointing, touch, and rhythmic movements may be utilized. Opportunities for human contact and communication should be a large part of the program. Since learning experiences are inherent in many therapeutic and daily living activities, educators need to work closely in team effort with physical therapists, occupational therapists, nurses, house parents, and so forth to increase the human and learning potential of every activity.

Prelingual Mentally Retarded (PLMR)

These children usually have physical problems but have sufficient health and mobility to be transported to a specifically educational environment for a daily program. These children will not have developed a linguistic system (either verbal or gesture) by school age. Developmentally these children are approximately at a one or one and one-half year level maximum in communication skills.

Here too are specific educational implications and foci for teacher competencies. Educational goals will include the attempt to teach a very simple linguistic system, either verbal or gestural as appropriate. The management of the classroom routine and systematic teaching will utilize nonlinguistic techniques, such as use of concrete and primary reinforcers, cues, signs, and feedback, paired with simple symbols and frequent prompts.

Internal physical and cognitive insufficiencies and social restrictions have probably led to reduced stimulation in both the human and physical spheres for these children. Therefore, as with LSMR children, the school environment can compensate by offering a highly stimulating program specifically directed to the available sensory avenues.

Training emphasis will be on basic self-care techniques such as toileting, feeding, and dressing, on maximizing mobility skills, and on simple receptive and expressive language development. Repetition and practice can be made meaningful and enjoyable by use of highly stimulating simple materials and concrete experiences.

Severely Mentally Retarded (SMR)

These children are on the interface of the PLMR (prelingual mentally retarded) population and the TMR (trainable mentally retarded) population. Again, there are special implications for teaching that arise from the mental potential of these students. The severely mentally retarded interface group can develop a simple communication system, either verbal or gestural, by school age. Among the latter systems one of the best organized and codified is American Sign Language (ASL), long utilized by deaf persons. There is increasing interest in the use of ASL with hearing individuals who have not developed verbal language, e.g. aphasic, autistic, and trainable children.

A classroom organized on the basis of a linguistic system allows the use of verbal-gestural cues and feedback, secondary reinforcers, and group instruction. Long-range goals can include the possibility of rudimentary academic learning; recognizing words such as one's name, *stop* or *men,* for example.

Trainable Mentally Retarded (TMR)

In the past the labeling of children was part of a process of exclusion. Educable mentally retarded meant a student on an academic track, but not in the mainstream. The TMR label acknowledged some ability to master language, and to learn very simple academics and some vocational skills. Increasingly, these students have been included in public planning in ways designated by state departments or departments of welfare and education.

Most people on the TMR level will appear physically a little different from normal people. Most will continue to be dependent on a special economic and social support system for all of their lives.

With the young, still-maturing person of any of these levels, consideration of critical periods for optimum progress through developmental stages will be paramount. With all the developmentally young, the techniques of play will prove most fruitful: that is organization of instruction through imitation, simple drill games, and dramatic play.

It should be noted that even a curriculum based at the one- to two-year-old developmental cognitive level can be made surprisingly age appropriate for older, severely mentally retarded individuals through careful selection or creation of materials. Vocabulary, puzzles, lotto pieces, picture books, and dramatic play can as easily reflect adult interests as those of children.

With older individuals new units will have to be added to the curriculum also. Self-care activities, for example, must include the management of menstruation and of sexuality. Acknowledgment of the adult status of even the most limited person should be pervasive in the teaching process.

In special education and in all the helping professions we are plagued by the vestiges of an old charity model: we do *for* and *to* our pupils and clients (with the best of intentions) rather than doing *with* or even allowing *them* to assume the activist role (a threatening situation for some professionals).

This last activity is most difficult to achieve with the severely retarded and prelingual populations because the hallmark of such persons is extreme dependency. The prelingual population, shocking to most of us, includes individuals who may be incapable of moving a muscle save an eyelid, or a sound save grunt, or a smile save a reflex. Those severely retarded individuals capable of the simple communication of the emerging infant are a world ahead in communicating their needs in relation to our ends as educators. The ability to indicate yes or no, in gesture or word, is the essential foundation of feedback,* the most basic requirement for any learning except for association† itself.

Specific competencies for the teacher of highly dependent persons will include therefore, the ability to recognize and foster any degree of autonomy and independence in dependent individuals congruent with their communication abilities, and the ability to recognize, encourage, and respond to any communications that the individual may indicate through body signs, eye contact, gesture, or language.

Individuals in the SMR population often have physical stigmata, such as physical and sensory defects that accompany their aberrant behavioural and cognitive characteristics. To many, these are frightening, even abhorrent mistakes of nature. Society, which as a whole has hidden these persons from sight and thought, now demands that our teachers redress the sins of the past and create a new educational system that will allow our most variant human beings to become full members of society. What is surprising is that so many young teachers have risen to the occasion and worked creatively and constructively with these persons, as their few counterparts inside the walls of the institutions have all the time.

---

* *"Feedback:* (3) A direct perceptual report of the result of one's behavior upon other persons; e.g. the perception of the return smile that greets ones own. (cp. knowledge of results)." English and English, *Comprehensive Dictionary of Psychological and Psychoanalytical Terms: A Guide to Usage,* 1958.

† *"Association:* A functional relationship between psychological phenomena established in the course of individual experience and of such nature that the presence of one tends to evoke the other; or the process whereby the relationship is established." English and English, *Comprehensive Dictionary of Psychological and Psychoanalytic Terms: A Guide to Usage,* 1958.

The distinguishing competencies necessary for such work seem to lie in the realm of personality and affective variables. Attributes of patience, tolerance, humor, respect, maturity, warmth, and creativity come to mind. These are manifest in such divergent talents as ability to teach on the floor, encouragement of physical closeness and touching, converting dull drills into enjoyable games, and tolerance for smells, excretions, deformities, and prostheses.

The problem of tolerance for variability should lessen as society as a whole becomes more tolerant and inclusive. Concerted efforts on the part of educators can hasten that day.

MAINSTREAMING THE STUDENT WITH DOWN'S SYNDROME

Persons with Down's syndrome have traditionally formed a sizeable proportion of the population of residential institutions for the retarded. Until rather recently, parents were advised at birth to commit these children immediately to lifetime residential care. These large, often understaffed, facilities may have contributed to a decrease in intellectual functioning of their residents, as well as to a decrease in level of physical well-being. It can be assumed that individuals with Down's syndrome have often not realized their full potential when isolated and segregated from the normal family and society. Now, supportive services, including early childhood education and therapy, are increasingly available to parents and foster parents who choose to raise their handicapped children themselves, rather than commit them to institutions.

Teachers can expect some degree of mental retardation in Down's syndrome children, but the range of intellectual functioning can vary enormously, from a severe subnormality to a near average or low average level. Very early intervention with the child and parents will be helpful in raising the child to the highest possible level of functioning.

It has sometimes been observed that the physical development of the young Down's syndrome child outpaces intellectual growth, often giving the preschool child an overoptimistic prognosis for later achievement level. However, teachers are seeing these students learn some academic work and interact successfully with their normal peers in more and more cases. They may be placed with children younger than themselves and may progress more slowly. Whatever the potential of the individual child, all can learn to a degree academically, socially, and vocationally, and they will often do so better in the regular classroom (where there is curriculum flexibility) than in a segregated, isolated setting. It has been observed that there is a tendency to infantalize children with Down's syndrome. Indeed they have often been reported passive and compliant, overweight, perhaps from overfeeding. On the other hand, hyperactivity has been reported. The possibility of normal role models for these children may have a very beneficial normalizing effect on their behavior.

Classmates will probably notice the different learning pattern of their Down's syndrome peer. In handling their concern, the label "retarded," which is a relative and somewhat subjective judgment, probably ought to be avoided in favor of saying a student "learns more slowly" or "needs more help with a subject."

The retarded student needs a more repetitive, concrete, and structured curriculum than the average learner. If such a child is mainstreamed, an individualized program of instruction is essential.

The language level of the person with Down's syndrome will naturally reflect the level of cognitive functioning. The mechanism of speech may also be affected because of the abnormally large tongue and peculiarly shaped oral cavity. The communication handicap can be a problem both in the instructional program and in socialization. Higher functioning children can be taught to keep their tongues in their mouths. This will improve their appearance.

The teacher may actually find the academic modifications less difficult than coping with some social adjustment challenges due to the odd appearance of the student with Down's syndrome. The appearance may not seem so disparate in the very young child, but becomes more prominent as the child grows older. The physical characteristics of Down's syndrome are as objective and obvious as any other physical impairments. The physical fact of difference is obvious to the handicapped child as well as to his peers. However, children have great resilience and flexibility in reckoning with their differences and those of others. Whether their attitudes mature to those of fear and distaste or to those of acceptance and respect will to a great extent depend on the cue of the teacher.

Even nursery school children may comment on some of these characteristics of their Down's syndrome peer, but questions and remarks are probably inspired more by curiosity than as derogatory attitudes. Therefore, they can be dealt with in a straightforward way: "Yes, that's the way Mary is made. We are all different." The older children can be told that their classmate has Down's syndrome, which gives him or her a special look, just as one's sex or race does.

Down's syndrome children often lack muscle tone. Further, they may be understimulated physically as well as mentally because of their differences. They can profit from a vigorous physical education program. If the student does better in athletics with children younger than his or her chronological age, a younger class would probably work out well, particularly since these children are generally small for their ages.

ADOLESCENCE AND ADULTHOOD

Developing sexuality is often a worry for parents of youth whose limited intellectual capacity might lead others to take advantage of them. For this reason, handicapped adolescents are sometimes kept from engaging in what would be matter-of-course heterosexual contacts and social activities for the normal teenager. Rather than proceeding this way, it is suggested here that the home and school cooperate to include even retarded youth in programs, courses, and counselling having to do with human sexuality, preparation for family living, and child care. There is good material on various aspects of hygiene, developed in simple language with illustrations, which may well serve the normal youth as well as the retarded. Counsellors find that even comparatively intellectually limited youth can understand concepts such as menstruation, contraception, conception, sterilization, family planning, responsibilities of child rearing, and venereal disease, if they are presented appropriately. Even young persons who are destined always to remain in a relatively sheltered environment are sexual beings. Denial of sexuality has not prevented its materialization (as many parents and caretakers know to their woe). Rather than further handicap disabled youth, is it not incumbent on educators to share the knowledge and wisdom concerning life planning that are the right of normal youth? Agencies such as Planned Parenthood and educators such as Sol Gordon (see Appendix) have contributed practical information for retarded youth and their families to help them cope with their immerging sexuality.

Persons with Down's syndrome need provision in educational, vocational, and community living programs as they mature. Some few of these individuals may be expected to achieve economic self-sufficiency. They can profit from work study programs in high school. If they have the level of potential for competitive employment, they can receive the benefits of the Bureau of Vocational Rehabilitation, and they may enter training programs in such job careers as maintenance or food service. They may become members of community homes, where they will be among the most physically able when compared with others with physical disabilities.

Many persons with Down's syndrome are born to older parents who may be anxious about their prodigy who may outlive them. Almost all of them will probably require a support system throughout their lives. As was mentioned, lifetime commitment to a state school and hospital has been a traditional solution to the problem of caring for such persons, particularly if they have a significant degree of mental retardation.

Now there is a trend toward community centers for exceptional persons who need continuing protection and special programs in their adult lives. The Department of Labor licenses three levels of vocational facilities:

The highest level is the Sheltered Workshop. In such a setting, a person will do competitive work, but in a sheltered environment. Disabled persons who are intellectually normal may need this type of center. Some persons with Down's syndrome may also function well in such a setting.

The next level is the Work Activities Center. Here the setting will offer contract employment, and individuals can earn some money, but they are not expected to be competitive with regular work settings. Probably a greater number of adults with Down's syndrome will be found here.

The last level is the Therapeutic Activities Center. In this type of setting there is emphasis on Activities of Daily Living (ADL) skills and on recreational activities that are commensurate with quite limited physical and intellectual ability. A good proportion of adults with Down's syndrome will be found in this population. Some agencies will be licensed on more than one level. Clients can move to a higher level when they show ability.

Review Guide

After reading Chapter 14 the reader should be able to define the following terms:

    syndrome
    trisomy
    translocation
    life sustained mentally retarded
    prelingual mentally retarded
    severe mental retardation
    trainable mental retardation
    educable mental retardation

After reading Chapter 14 the reader should be able to answer the following questions:

1. What is the chief cognitive symptom associated with Down's syndrome?
2. What are five physical symptoms that may be visible in a person with Down's syndrome?
3. What are three health problems that may accompany Down's syndrome?
4. About what percentage of Down's syndrome is hereditary?
5. With what is the nonhereditary form associated?
6. Name three options open to a mother over the age of forty, with respect to pregnancy.
7. What are two common communication problems of a student with Down's syndrome?

8. What can be said about the intellectual level of students with Down's syndrome?
9. What is the probable effect of early institutionalization on the intellectual development of a Down's syndrome child?
10. What is an important social reason for mainstreaming a Down's syndrome child?
11. How should a teacher handle students' questions concerning the peculiarities of Down's syndrome?
12. Is individualized instruction necessary if Down's syndrome students are mainstreamed?
13. What are three vocational programs that might accommodate the adult with Down's syndrome?

Chapter 15

HEART PROBLEMS

The term "heart" carries a heavier super cargo of symbolic mean-
ing than any other organ of the body. We use it to describe more than
function—to identify character and personality in such terms as light-
hearted or heartless. We speak of "the heart of the matter," and being
"broken hearted." In short, we identify heart with the very essence of
our being.

Jean Spencer Felton
Dorothy Cantrell Perkins
Molly Lewin

OF THE CHILDREN BORN with heart disease, almost a third will die in their first year. Congenital heart defects can be hereditary or developmental. They can be the only problem or occur in connection with other disorders such as Down's syndrome. They may be related to infections such as maternal rubella. Common defects will be openings in walls that separate the heart's four chambers, valve problems, or constriction of channels or arteries. These defects originate during the first one to three months of embryonic development, at the time the heart is being formed. Acquired heart damage can occur because of infections, hardening of the arteries, and hypertension. A common cause of heart damage among school-aged children is rheumatic fever.

THE FUNCTION OF THE HEART

The heart is a hollow organ centered a little to the left of the narrow flat bone in the front of the chest (sternum). It is slightly larger than a closed fist and weighs under a pound. It is a muscular pump controlled by the tenth cranial nerve (vagus nerve) in addition to a number of sympathetic nerves. The heart is divided into four chambers. Blood is pumped through these chambers,

200

aided by a series of valves that open and close to allow the progress of blood.

The excursion of blood through the heart begins with dark venous blood, which returns to the heart through the veins after having delivered its oxygen and other nutrients to tissues throughout the body (Fig. 15). It enters the right upper chamber (right atrium), then empties into the right lower chamber (right ventricle) through a three-leafed valve (tricuspid valve). The right ventricle drives the blood under low pressure through the pulmonary valves and pulmonary artery to the lungs, where the blood then circulates through the lungs. As it passes over countless minute air sacs, a gaseous exchange takes place as the blood disposes of its carbon dioxide (the end product of cell metabolism)

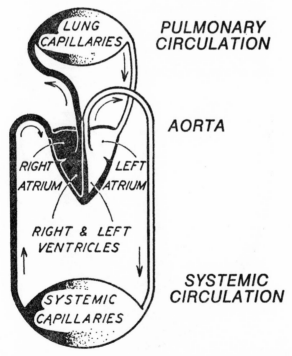

Figure 15. The conduction system of the heart. The beat originates at the sinus node (or primary pacemaker) and spreads through auricular muscle (black arrows). In this spread, the A-V node is activated and transmits an impulse to the ventricles along the A-V bundle and its branches.

and acquires a fresh supply of oxygen. After the blood is oxygenated, its appearance is bright red.

This oxygenated blood now returns to the upper left chamber of the heart (left atrium) through the four pulmonary veins (Fig. 16). The left atrium pumps the blood through the mitral valve to the left ventricle, which pumps the oxygenated blood out a valve into the major artery of the body (the aorta). The pressure in the left ventricle is high, and equal to the individual's blood pressure. The oxygenated blood is distributed throughout the arterial system. This system is connected through the capillaries to the venous system, which again returns the blood to the heart.

The system of distribution of blood to and through the lungs

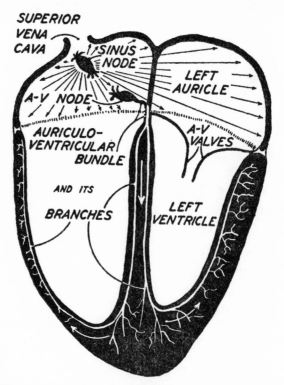

Figure 16. The structure of the heart. The complete separation of the heart into two halves makes possible the pumping of unmixed aerated blood to the systemic capillaries under high pressure. Arrows indicate the direction of blood flow.

and, after oxygenation, back to the heart is called the pulmonary (lung) circulation. The system carrying the blood through the rest of the body is called the systemic circulation.

The heart is located within a sac (the pericardium; peri = around; cardium = heart). The wall of the heart is made up of three layers: a thin membranous inner layer, a thin outer layer, and a thick muscular middle layer (myocardium), which is responsible for the strong pumping action of the heart.

The heartbeat originates in the form of a minute electrical impulse generated at a node sometimes called the pacemaker. This impulse sets in motion another electrical wave, which results in an atrial contraction, then a ventricular contraction. These electrical impulses of the heartbeat are the basis for electrocardiograph readings (ECG) important in diagnosis of irregular function of the heart.

The pumping action occurs in two phases: A phase of vigorous muscular contraction when the blood leaves both ventricles (systole), and a filling phase when the blood enters the heart (diastole). When the physician listens to the normal heart, a low, prolonged sound signifies the closing of the tricuspid and mitral valves, followed by a shorter, high pitched sound signifying the closing of the pulmonic and aortic valves as the blood proceeds simultaneously through the heart to and from the two blood systems of the body.

HEART MALFUNCTION

Any impairment in the original structure of the heart, any damage to the walls, or malfunction or obstruction of the valves, vessels, or signal system can cause cardiac disability. When oxygenated blood mixes with unoxygenated blood or is prevented from travelling properly through the system, metabolism of the entire body will be affected. When there is an extra load on the heart because of its malfunction, the heart will enlarge to compensate. Hence, an enlarged heart is both a sign and result of heart problems. It can be discovered through X-ray studies. Children with heart disease may have shortness of breath, limited tolerance for exercise, and may occasionally have a blue appearance of the skin due to poor oxygenation of the blood (cyanosis).

There are many sophisticated medical techniques for diagnosing heart damage. The change of rhythm of the beat, the intensity of heart sounds, the murmur of leakage through valves or walls, and enlargement of heart chambers can be detected. Cardiac surgery is also highly developed and often helpful with infants and older persons. Technical advances in artificial parts have contributed to successful medical treatments. Even young children are occasionally fitted with electronic pacemakers.

Defects that are not correctable, or only in part correctable, leave patients with some degree of disfunction and discomfort. Through the American Heart Association, a uniform system of classifying patients with diseases of the heart has been widely used:

Patients are identified in terms of a *therapeutic* classification, as follows:

Class A–Patients with a cardiac disease whose ordinary physical activity need not be restricted.

Class B–Patients with cardiac disease whose ordinary physical activity need not be restricted, but who should be advised against severe or competitive physical efforts.

Class C–Patients with cardiac disease whose ordinary physical activity should be moderately restricted, and whose more strenuous efforts should be discontinued.

Class D–Patients with cardiac disease whose ordinary physical activity should be markedly restricted.

Class E–Patients with cardiac disease who should be at complete rest, confined to bed or chair.

RHEUMATIC FEVER AND ITS TREATMENT

Rheumatic fever is a chronic disease with acute flare-ups, which involves the connective tissues of the body. Although it is a disease of the whole body, its main danger is in damage to the heart. It results in inflammation of the muscle, valves, and lining of the heart. Its inciting factor is a streptococcal infection, the same germ that causes severe sore throat and scarlet fever. The streptococcus triggers an autoimmune reaction of antibodies on the heart valves. However, usually streptococcal infection does *not* result in rheumatic fever. In fact, very few strep infections result in rheumatic fever.

Most first attacks occur in children from five to ten years old. Although deaths from acute rheumatic fever have been declining steadily in the past fifty years, the aftermath, rheumatic heart disease, still cripples many young persons and causes death in many young adults in the United States.

Rheumatic heart disease is the residual left from damage caused by rheumatic fever. It takes its final major toll in persons from twenty-five to forty-five just when most adults are functioning at their occupational peak. About one-third of those who have had rheumatic fever have residual heart damage. Most are still able to live relatively normal lives but will restrict themselves from strenuous physical exertion. Surgery is helpful in about half the cases where people have residual impairments. It may not be necessary until years after the original attack of the disease. Most who have had rheumatic heart disease can expect to be able to engage in sexual activity and to bear children.

The early signs of rheumatic fever are the same as those of several childhood diseases. Fever, pains in the joints, and a recent sore throat may signal its onset. An organic heart murmur may be the definitive medical sign. A definite diagnosis is difficult to make in some instances. The disease may be so mild that the person does not realize it was ever developed until heart damage is discovered some years later.

When the symptoms are severe and definite, the child is usually treated in the hospital. Medication will be given to relieve the joint inflammation, pain, and fever. After the acute symptoms have passed, laboratory signs may show that this persistent disease is still present, even though the child feels perfectly well again. Therefore, after a return to home, a prolonged convalescence of bed rest is necessary, because with the inflammation, any exertion might strain the heart and lead to permanent damage. At this stage, which may last typically from two to six weeks but may last many months, homebound instruction and school to home phone contact may be of great therapeutic as well as educational value.

The physician determines when the patient has recovered from the rheumatic fever. The child who recovers from rheumatic fever without heart damage can participate in all physical activities without harm. With medical approval, the recovered student can be treated as absolutely physically normal in terms of school activities.

Recurrent attacks of rheumatic fever are a threat–both in terms of a prolonged period of recuperation and the further danger of heart damage. A protective program involves taking penicillin or a sulpha drug routinely to keep the streptococcus from ever invading the body. These medicines may be taken up to the age of fifteen, or for a period of years after the last attack. Drugs may be taken whenever there is an unusual risk of strep infection, such as in the event of a definite exposure to someone with a strep infection or in a period of a known epidemic. These medications will be given before and after any heart surgery.

Predisposition to this disease does seem to run in families. Therefore, families at risk may be treated with preventative measures during times of exposure to streptococcus infections. When one child in a family has had rheumatic fever, parents are urged to be particularly careful to have the infections of all their children treated medically.

The school nurse and teachers may need to assist the young child who has had rheumatic fever or has a family history of the problem by monitoring the intake of the prophylactic medicines. Faithful drug compliance will prevent a recurrence of the problems, so is very important.

ADMINISTRATION OF MEDICATION

When medication must be administered during the school day, it is very important to establish, ahead of time, policies and procedures to be followed by school and health personnel.

Grotsky, Sabatino, and Ohrtman wrote the following guidelines, which were offered in the context of chemotherapy for behavior disorders, but these also apply well in other circumstances in which medication is needed:

> The procedure under which you may administer medication varies by school district. Check to see if there are established policies for your district. Adhere to these policies, if for no other reason than

your legal protection. The following guidelines will aid school systems in dealing with this situation:

a) Written orders are to be provided to the school from a physician, detailing the name of the drug, dosage, and the time interval in which the medication is to be taken. These orders are to be reviewed periodically.

b) A written request is to be received by the school district from the parent or guardian of the pupil, together with a letter from the physician indicating the necessity for the administering of the medication during the day, the type of disease or illness involved, the benefits of the medication, the side effects and an emergency number where he can be reached. Both letters should be placed in the pupil's file.

c) Medication must be brought to the school in a container appropriately labeled by the pharmacy or physician.

d) The initial dose at school must be administered by the school nurse. If a teacher is to give subsequent medication, the nurse should discuss the medication, including its side effects, with the teacher.

e) The school nurse shall prepare a written statement to the building administrator as to the side effects of the drug, if any, and a copy should be placed in the pupil's file.

f) A locked cabinet must be provided for the storage of the medication. Opportunities should be provided for communication with the pupil, parent, and physician regarding the efficacy of the medication administered during school hours.

g) With the parent's and physician's consent, medication of a short-term duration may be administered by a teacher.

h) The school district retains the discretion to reject requests for administration of medicine.

You will need some information in order to effectively understand and teach a child who is on medication. With written parental permission and through your school nurse, obtain the following information from the child's physician:

a) How does the medication work?

b) What change in the student's behavior can be expected?

c) What effect will the medication have on the child's attention span, memory, motor dexterity, personality, sleeping and eating habits?

d) Does the medication have undesirable side effects?

e) What behavioral and/or motoric reactions indicate that the dosage may be toxic or inadequate for the child's needs?

f) How long will the child have to take the medication?

g) Could the child become physically and/or psychologically addicted to the medication?[1]

THE HEART PATIENT AT SCHOOL AND BEYOND

The small amount of extra attention needed by the child with heart disease can usually be supplied in the regular class. It will first involve a collaboration between the medical team and the school to make realistic accommodations in terms of physical tolerances of the student and to allay any fears or overreactions to the disability.

It is a frequent experience that persons are overinclined to restrict and protect the child with a cardiac difficulty. Every effort should be made to give the student as much independence as possible so as not to create a psychological handicap that the disability does not warrant. While the student with continuing heart problems should not be pressed to the point of excessive fatigue, undue apprehension about participation in school activities should not be fostered.

While the child is having bed rest and is later physically limited with regard to physical activities, participation in many more sedentary occupations can be encouraged. Even homebound heart patients have enjoyed pen-pal clubs, participating in the student United Nations activities, stamp collecting, amateur radio building and operation, and caring for small pets. During sports activities at school, the physically limited pupil can be timekeeper or team manager.

Both girls and boys can be encouraged in skills of home science. Sewing by hand and machine, weaving, and other home crafts are self-fulfilling and might later be important skills for employment or housekeeping. Cooking skills can be developed without physical strain. They are enjoyable, creative, and may later be vital for independent living. While wood shop might conceivably pose over-energetic tasks for the fragile student, courses in electrical repair and other activities requiring fine-motor dexterity may be ideal

---

1. Grotsky, J., Sabatino, D., and Ohrtman, W. (Eds.): *The Concept of Main streaming; A Resource Guide for Regular Classroom Teachers.* King of Prussia, PA, Eastern Pennsylvania Regional Resources Center for Special Education, 1976, pp. 8-10.

In fact, there are so many interesting, exciting alternatives to more vigorous physical activities that resourceful teachers should easily be able to emphasize remaining abilities, rather than focus on disability.

It is very important for the student with a cardiac problem to have opportunity for vocational and career counselling early in the school experience. It is even realistic to consider career planning in the selection of junior high school classes. Sedentary classes leading to realistic future careers are available for students across a broad spectrum of academic ability and interest. Furthermore, modern technology has made many tasks physically easier than they once were. For example, an electric typewriter requires less exertion of energy for the clerk or secretary in training in vocational classes, or for the budding novelist in English class. The telephone or school intercom system replaces the running feet for the manager of the school paper or the student in the laboratory reporting to the teacher. The severely physically limited student may find tapes and records easier than writing and holding books. The Library of Congress, Division of the Blind and Physically Handicapped, may be an important resource for this student at school and at home.

More adult cardiac patients have been consigned to the role of the permanently disabled than their actual conditions warrant. Some employers are reluctant to hire a person with a known cardiac disorder because of the possibilities of industrial accident suits or higher workmans' compensation insurance premiums and group insurance rates.

Therefore, the student with a cardiac problem may need a great deal of help and support in making a successful transfer from school to the vocational world. The cardiac student is eligible for State Bureau of Vocational Rehabilitation services at age sixteen. This essentially positive and optimistic process can even be emotional therapy for a student who may have become discouraged by physical limitations or feared impotence and fragility in future life.

Whether in public school, in technical training, or in higher education, those in contact with the heart disabled student should attempt to communicate with the physicians managing the case rather than make inferences about necessary physical limitations. Obviously, with older students it is important not to go behind the back of the patient himself, either to the family or medical personnel. Student, physician, teacher, and parents can profitably communicate on the advisability of specific physical tasks and activities that might be undertaken at school and beyond.

Review Guide

After reading Chapter 15 the reader should be able to define the following terms:

congenital heart disease

pulmonary circulation

systemic circulation

pacemaker

rheumatic fever

rheumatic heart disease

After reading Chapter 15 the reader should be able to answer the following questions:

1. How many chambers does the heart have?
2. What are four general causes of heart damage?
3. Why does the heart sometimes enlarge?
4. What does the gradient of the therapeutic classification of heart patients measure?
5. What are 7 guidelines for the administration of medication in school?

Chapter 16

LUNG DISEASE

"There are," Hans Castorp once says, "two ways to life: one is the regular, direct and good way; the other is bad, it leads through death, and that is the way of genius." It is this notion of disease and death as a necessary route to knowledge, health and life that makes the Magic Mountain a novel of initiation.

Thomas Mann
The making of the Magic Mountain

RESPIRATORY CONDITIONS account for over half the acute illnesses of children under the age of fifteen. The nature of lung disease has changed markedly over the past twenty-five years. In the United States acute pneumonias and chronic progressive tuberculosis were prime killers of young and middle-aged adults prior to 1950, but these are no longer as serious threats in areas where the standard of living is adequate and the quality of health care good. A major problem now in primary lung disease is the damage to cells and tissues of the lungs from chemicals or as a result of pulmonary and cardiac arrest.

THE FUNCTIONS OF THE LUNG

The main function of the lung is to breathe clean air in and out, performing a gas exchange with the blood. Oxygen is taken into the blood and wastes are expelled. Air enters the lungs from the windpipe (trachea), which divides into the two main tubes (bronchi), one to each lung. The system can be envisioned as an inverted tree of which the windpipe is the trunk (Fig. 17). The two main tubes divide into smaller twigs (bronchioli) at the end of which are thin-walled air sacs (alveoli). Capillaries are the small blood vessels that are embedded in the walls of the air sacs.

211

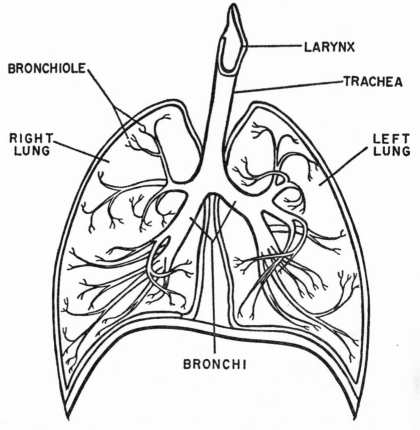

Figure 17. Diagram of the lung showing action of the diaphragm.

The capillaries exchange carbon dioxide from the blood and oxygen from the air through these small air sacs of the lung.

The strong wall of muscle that separates the chest cavity from the abdominal cavity is called the diaphragm. By moving downward, it creates suction to draw in air and expand the lungs.

The lung has an umbrella of defense to protect it against many environmental agents, such as infections and disease, allergic agents, air pollution, cigarette smoke, industrial material, and other subtle products. Two kinds of potentially injurious materials can enter the lung: tiny particles and toxic gases.

When tiny particles are breathed in, the larger ones are screened out by the nose. The medium ones continue on through the throat (pharynx), which collects incoming air from the nose and mouth to send downward to the windpipe (see Fig. 7). In a healthy lung, these particles drop out of the air stream onto the surface of the bronchial tubes as the air diverts into the branches. The particles are trapped in mucus (produced by goblet cells) and are removed by a mucociliary cleaning system. The mucus, holding the unwanted matter, is carried upward and out into the throat, where it is either coughed up or swallowed. Wandering cells (macrophage) are also present. They are white cells from the blood, which change their function so that they can gobble up bacteria and other particles in one small area in the lung.

The very smallest particles penetrate deeply into the lung all the way to the air sacs at the end of the tracheobronchial tree. Cells, called dust cells, ingest these particles.

The lung is still growing in children until about the age of eight. Therefore, the young lung is much more susceptible to permanent injury. Infections of childhood that go untreated can affect health in later years. An example is whooping cough, which before its control by vaccine in recent years led to lung scarring and consequent chronic coughing in adults.

AIR POLLUTION

As long as the air breathed is of normal composition of oxygen and nitrogen, it causes no problem to the lungs. The lung even has a tremendous absorptive capacity for toxic gases of contaminated air. A good portion of irritating gases is absorbed by the upper respiratory tract and never reaches the lower part of the lung.

Although much of the suspended dirt and dust that reaches the first portion of the lung is deposited there, irritating particles deposited at these locations can produce direct injury to lung tissue. Further, when irritating gases are inhaled with particles, they tag onto them, particularly in the presence of moisture. These gas-carried particles are then distributed to the depths of the lung where they would not ordinarily penetrate. The combination of particles, water, and toxic gases can be extremely harmful. This is what happens with cigarette smoke, air pollution, and some industrial exposures to make them so injurious.

Chemicals can directly damage the cells and tissues of the lungs. These harmful agents produce inflammation, scarring, hypersecretion, and dissolution of the lung tissue. The continuous and repeated exposure to such things as tobacco smoke, air pollution, and irritant dusts also damages the lung's defense mechanisms.

As a concomitant of urbanization and industrialization, all types of contamination have occurred with increasing repetitiveness. In larger urban areas the most obvious pollution has been that of air. Industrial pollutants have been most severe in the residential areas surrounding the sources of pollutants, such as steel mills. Automobile pollutants are a serious problem in areas with intense sunlight and atmospheric inversions, as are found in the coastal California cities. Materials from fossil fuel are widespread and have raised the level of carbon dioxide. Personal air pollution due to cigarette smoking may have more effect than the other various pollutants.

Small amounts of particulate matter are retained in everyone's lungs. Some is relatively harmless, such as the coal smoke and soot pigmentation in the lungs of all city dwellers; some is highly dangerous. It is recognized that occupational exposure to asbestos can lead to serious lung conditions. The miner's disease, silicosis, is due to inhalation of dust containing crystalline-free silica. It can cause lung damage and contribute to the development of active tuberculosis.

The effects of the numerous pollutants include irritation of the eyes and respiratory tract, decreased physical performance, and decreased peak respiratory air flow. Allergic reactions, discussed in the next section, are exacerbated. Increased rates of pulmonary disease, including lung cancer, are associated with the urban environment. Lung cancer has increased to the point where it now causes more deaths than tuberculosis. Some children have particular sensitivities to pollutants. If they live in areas of high concentration, they may die of lung damage at an early age.

TUBERCULOSIS

In underprivileged parts of the world, tuberculosis (TB) remains one of the largest causes of disease and death. In the United

States it is still prevalent among persons of low economic status, although it also occurs in affluent communities in the form of localized outbreaks. The precipitating cause of active tuberculosis may be lowered resistance, which is often associated with low socioeconomic status. Therefore, poor, rural, Indian, black, and Spanish populations are at risk for this disease because of poor nutrition and overcrowded conditions. Also, persons with diabetes are in danger of developing it. Tuberculosis is one of the few communicable diseases that still causes chronic problems in children.

TB is a bacterial infection whose bacilli may destroy parts of various organs in the body, particularly the lungs. Lumps are formed on or within the normally soft, spongy lung, and from these, tubercles are produced, whence the disease gets its name.

This rod-shaped bacillus can live for months outside living organisms in cool, dark places. Even without moisture, it can live for some time. It can ride the air on particles of dust. Light and heat kill it. It is transmitted from one person to another through the air when infected persons sneeze or cough. One strain of this bacillus, the bovine variety, used to be transmitted from infected cows through milk. With tuberculin testing of dairy herds and by pasteurization of milk, this infection is now extremely rare.

Infection with TB is not an active sickness, but it can become so. Having had the infection does not confer a dependable immunity. It spreads most easily through intimate contact with those who have the active form of disease. Contaminated articles also spread it.

When the bacillus is inhaled into the lungs, it becomes implanted in the best ventilated regions. In someone who has never been infected before, in other words, has a primary infection, these organisms multiply freely until the body develops an allergy, or hypersensitivity, to these foreign organisms.

The defense system of the body rallies to control the primary infection. The white cells of the blood surround and try to engulf the germs. Meanwhile, the invaders are surrounded with a wall of cells and fibres, the tubercles, characteristic of the disease.

The fact that the body now manufacturers antibodies, the special disease fighters against this bacillus, does protect it somewh₂ against further attack. The body has some immunity, therefor₁ to future infections.

Before the development of allergy and immunity, some bacil escape from the primary site of infection in the lungs into th lymph and blood systems. They may focus in other parts of th body, such as the tops of the lungs, the skin, kidneys, the ends ₀ the long bones, the spine, or the brain. Usually organisms at thes₁ secondary foci are also controlled by the developing antibodi₁ Even though the primary infection sites and seeding sites heal, th tubercle bacilli often remain alive.

A positive tuberculin skin test indicates the presence of livin₁ tubercle bacilli in the body at some time in a person's history. Th positive reaction will show as a slight swelling or thickening of th skin with distention of the blood vessels on the spot of skin whe₁ a protein from the tubercular bacillus was injected. By this tes₁ it is known that millions of Americans were infected with the t₁ berculosis bacillus, but it is usually in a latent phase. TB can l₁ dormant in old scars for many years, still alive and still able t erupt into active tuberculosis. Usually this primary infection is s₁ well controlled that it causes no illness and heals without being d₁ agnosed.

The vast majority of children contracting the infection g₁ through the primary phase, the initial infection, without any a₁ parent illness. The latent phase follows and usually lasts the re mainder of the child's life. Only if the infection is a heavy one an₁ of a virulent strain does it tend to be uninterruptedly progressiv₁ early in life. Although lung (pulmonary) tuberculosis is rare b₁ fore puberty, TB may become active in other parts of the child body, where there are bacilli foci, or it can be newly spread a₁ over the body (miliary tuberculosis). Among young adults it ma₁ also progress very rapidly and be very serious. For this reaso₁ preventative measures are especially important for these young ag₁ groups.

Reinfection tuberculosis, either from the old primary infectio₁ or a new transmission of disease, in rare cases, is a danger. Seriou₁ trouble may come from later attacks. Body resistance can be low ered due to fatigue, poor food, or other illness, to promote reinfection. Since the invaded tissues are now more highly sensitive, or allergic, to the invading germs, there may be a more violent reaction to a reinfection, and the destruction of tissues takes place faster than the walling up of tissues in the infected areas. When the walled up germs in the tubercles break out and start to spread and resistance fails completely, the disease may progress rapidly in the secondary foci, with the possibility of fatal consequences.

In the chronic disease there are repeated relapses, with a fluctuating battle between the resistance of the body and the virulent bacillus. Advances or spreads occur quickly, and recovery is slow. Each time, there is further scarring of tissue and consequent loss of functioning.

In an allergic individual, the defending cells may die. Then a soft, cheeselike tissue is discharged into an adjacent bronchus and a cavity is left in the lung. The formation of a cavity is a turning point for the patient and those around the patient. Astronomical numbers of virulent bacilli are released from the cavity daily and may be discharged for many years. Therefore, the threat of infection to others is severe. The bacilli can also go to other parts of the diseased person's lungs to increase infection.

In the final stages of the disease there are ulcerative complications and lowered body resistance in the larynx and intestine as well as in the lungs. Modern medicine has very much increased the percentage of recoveries and reduced the number of relapses in active tuberculosis. Also, it has increased the number of persons who are living with chronic lesions who would not have survived earlier.

Because of strain mutations, specific drugs may lose their effectiveness, but several have proven successful when taken in prescribed ways. Drugs have also increased the safety of surgery when it is required to remove diseased portions of the lung. The lung may also be surgically collapsed, allowing it to rest and heal.

Persons can have TB and not know it and thus transmit the disease unknowingly. By the time the classic symptoms appear, emaciation, a flush of the cheeks, and a persistent cough, the person has an advanced disease. When a person in a family is known to have the active disease, other members, frequently children and young adults, have often been found to have an active case also, or to be newly infected. Therefore, such contacts may be given preventative drug treatment.

Vaccination for TB is routinely administered in some parts of the world. It is generally not used in the United States but is given in some high risk populations. Teachers, student teachers, and other persons in contact with school children are obliged by law, in some regions, to have a tuberculin skin test. This regulation is apt to exist in large cities where pockets of poverty and very crowded living conditions are found, so populations are at high risk for the disease. The National Tuberculosis Association recommends the skin test for all groups, such as school employees, that are apt to infect children.

Generally, the size of the positive reaction to the skin test bears a direct relation to the likelihood of developing an active disease. However, the test is not foolproof in indicating infection or the severity of the infection.

When a person has a positive reaction to the skin test, an X-ray of the lungs is taken. Persons with abnormal X-rays are more likely than those with normal X-rays to develop active disease, so the former should be examined regularly. Most tuberculosis cases are discovered in a medical setting in the course of a physical examination, rather than through mass screening procedures. It is important to discover the disease as early as possible, both in order to prevent the spread of infection and to arrest the course of the disease through treatment.

RESPIRATORY EMERGENCIES

Accidents and injuries rank high as causes of death and crippling among children. For every child who dies in an accident many more are left permanently impaired. A sizeable number of lives are lost due to drowning. In drowning, water does not actually enter the lungs. Death comes from the deprivation of oxygen and accumulation of carbon dioxide and other acids in the body. Partial drowning describes the effects on a person who has suffered lack of oxygen (anoxia). Anoxia is the result of remaining underwater too long or of first aid efforts that were delayed or failed to start breathing and heart action promptly.

Asphyxiation can be due to choking on large food particles and is rather common at all ages. Allergic shock and heart attacks can cause pulmonary and cardiac arrest.

The brain is the organ most sensitive to lack of oxygen, and it will suffer destruction before the other organs of the body in its absence. Such irrevocable brain damage and dysfunction can lead to mental retardation, perceptual and learning deficits, sensory and motor problems, and seizures.

THE ROLE OF THE SCHOOL

The school, as the educator of future citizens, can take an active, informed stand on the subject of pollution reduction. Also, students can be apprised, in a nonmoralistic approach, of the dangers of excessive and prolonged smoking in the development of lung disease as adults.

There are several fictions about TB for teachers to keep in mind. The first is that this is surely a fatal disease. While that was true in living memory of some, it is not true today. Today, under good medical care, a person has a twenty to one chance in his favor of recovering from active disease without becoming chronically ill. The State Bureau of Vocational Rehabilitation agencies have been active in the rehabilitation and job placement of thousands of former tuberculosis patients. Another fiction is that anyone who has had the disease is still a danger to others. The physician will say when a person has recovered, and at that point the disease cannot be transmitted. Again, people can be reassured that TB is not inherited, although, as with many disorders, there may be a predisposition to develop it. If people live where they are repeatedly exposed, they may contract it. It was formerly believed that a special climate was of help in recovery from TB. Actually, climate does not seem to make much difference. Probably the healthy life of persons in the old TB sanatoria such as the one described in *Magic Mountain* was the most important factor in aiding recovery, rather than the sunny, dry atmosphere surrounding them.

In the case of cardiopulmonary arrest, prompt emergency procedures can save lives and prevent later complications. The American Trauma Society, the American Red Cross and other nonprofit organizations have as a goal the saving of lives of persons who are dying needlessly of trauma. Among their efforts is education of the public in emergency life saving techniques. School staff and students are urged to take advantage of these courses when they are available. Frequently a school can request the courses from these organizations or through local hospitals. These skills in artificial breathing techniques, heart massage, expellation of air by impact on the diaphragm, and other first aid procedures can be of lifetime service to students and staff alike. Already the dissemination of this knowledge has helped to prevent many needless deaths and maimings.

The various training courses will differ somewhat in specific techniques advocated. They will differ with children and adults. These courses are generally recommended for persons from about thirteen years and older.

A basic review of cardiopulmonary resuscitation in basic life support is provided below:

If Patient Is Not Breathing[1]

1. See that an emergency medical team is called.
2. If the person is unconscious, sweep the inside of the mouth with your finger to clear it out.
3. Put the victim on his back on a hard surface.
4. With one hand, lift up under the neck. Push the forehead back to open the airway.
5. If the person does not start to breathe, pinch his nose shut and begin artificial breathing. Take a deep breath, open your mouth wide and put your mouth wide over the victim's mouth to make a tight seal.
6. Blow to fill up the patient's lungs. Watch the chest rise. Listen for the air to come out. (With an infant it is not

---

1. Courtesy of the Emergency Medicine Service, 564 Forbes Avenue, Pittsburgh, Pennsylvania, 15219.

necessary to pinch the nose if your mouth covers both nose and mouth. Blow very gently every three seconds.)

7. Do these steps over and over once every five seconds until the victim starts breathing.

If Pulse Is Absent[2]

If the pulse is absent it is important to begin artificial circulation. If there is only one rescuer and the person is not breathing, two techniques must be carried on simultaneously.

1. Depress sternum (the flat narrow bone in the median line in front of the chest) 1½ to 2 inches. Do 15 compressions a little less than a second for each.
2. Give 2 quick breaths of artificial breathing.
3. If two rescuers can work together, one will administer the breathing and the other will administer 5 compressions (each taking a second) for every breath administered.

It should be mentioned that a young or small person will have difficulty administering artificial circulation to a very large person. Also, the techniques will vary depending on the age and size of a person.

It is highly recommended that school staff and students take a certified course in order to be fully prepared for emergencies.

To Stop Bleeding[3]

A person who is bleeding severely requires immediate first aid. Before medical aid arrives, do the following steps:

1. Keep the victim lying down.
2. Apply direct pressure to stop bleeding. Place a clear pad or your hand on the wound, and press firmly. If pad becomes soaked with blood, leave it on. Place another pad on top of first pad.
3. Raise the cut area above the level of the victim's heart, if it does not harm the patient.

---

2. Courtesy of the American Heart Association.
3. Courtesy of the Health Education Center, 200 Ross Street, Pittsburgh, Pennsylvania 15219.

4. After the bleeding is under control, bandage the wound.
5. Get the victim to medical personnel.

Choking[4]

Obstructions in the throat can lead to choking and even death without emergency treatment. Bits of food or small objec such as toys, coins, and jewelry may lodge in the throat of chi dren and adults alike. The emergency procedures to be used a listed below:

If the person with something caught in the throat is breathir easily, allow him to cough in any sitting or standing position th; is comfortable. Do not hit the choking person on the back.

If the breathing is hard, or has stopped, the following ste should be followed:

1. Have a call put in for an emergency vehicle.
2. Lay a choking child over your arm, face down, or an adu turned over on the side.
3. Apply several sharp blows with the flat of your hand b tween the victim's shoulder blades.
4. If this procedure proves unsuccessful in dislodging the ol struction, use the Heimlich maneuver described below:

Heimlich Maneuver:

1. Wrap your arms around the victim's waist from behind.
2. Make a fist with one hand and place it with your thum against the victim's abdomen between the naval and th rib cage.
3. Clasp your fist with your free hand and pull in with quick *upward* thrust.
4. Repeat this procedure several times if necessary.

It should be pointed out that a person might use this procedur on himself, using his own hands or a projection from a piece c padded furniture to cause the sudden upward pressure on th diaphragm necessary to dislodge the obstruction in the throat.

If breathing does not start immediately after the Heimlic: maneuver, you should give mouth to mouth resuscitation until th emergency team arrives.

---

4. Courtesy of the Health Education Center, 200 Ross Street, Pittsburgr Pennsylvania 15219.

Review Guide

After reading Chapter 16 the reader should be able to define the following terms:

windpipe (trachea)   tubercles
air sacs   skin test
capillaries   partial drowning
diaphragm   emergency procedures
tuberculosis   Heimlich maneuver

After reading Chapter 16 the reader should be able to answer the following questions:

1. What is the primary function of the lungs?
2. In what three ways are harmful particles trapped by the body?
3. What combination of substances can be particularly harmful to the lungs?
4. What are five causes of air pollution?
5. What organ of the body is most sensitive to oxygen deprivation?
6. What are three fictions about TB?
7. What resources can the school use to teach emergency procedures?

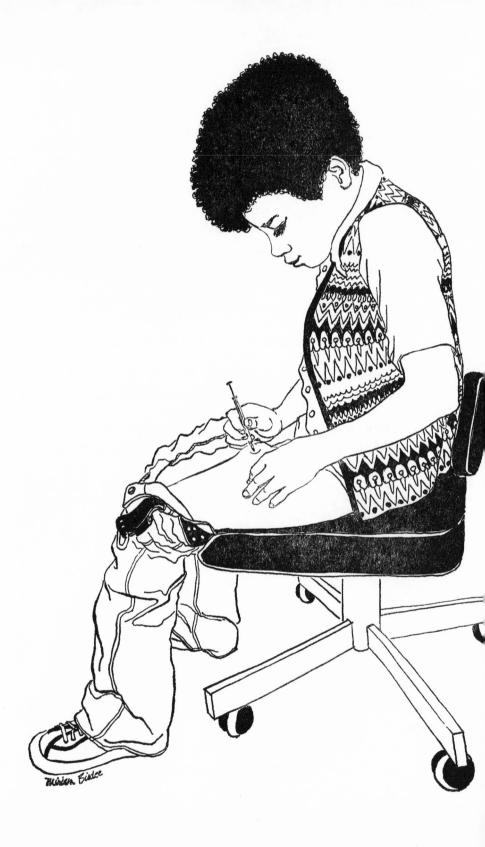

Chapter 17

DIABETES

"Was nicht umbringt, mach mich starker."
(What does not conquer me makes me stronger)
Nietzsche

Life is not a spectacle or a feast;
It is a predicament.
Santayana

D IABETES MELLITUS (Diabetes = syphon, Mellitus = honey) is the most common of the inborn errors of metabolism. It runs in families, but its exact transmission is open to controversy. Diabetes can become apparent any time from infancy to old age. An earlier onset or a long duration of the disease can result in a more serious condition.

In most cases the diabetes begins during one of three peak age periods. Juvenile diabetes starts between the ages of eight and twelve, with symptoms developing rapidly and unmistakably. About 10 percent of diabetics are children. A much larger number of cases occurs in the forty to fifty age group with the onset of the disease much slower. The third peak in onset is in the late seventies. In all, about 5 percent of the population in the United States can be expected at some time, sooner or later during their lifetimes, to develop diabetes.

NORMAL METABOLISM

In the discussion about life's beginnings, it was said that cells are the basic building blocks of the body. Cells differentiate into the tissues, organs, and systems that comprise the living being. In the human, the main energy source of the cells is a simple sugar known as glucose. Glucose is a component of carbohydrates,

225

found in the sugars and starches of food. Glucose is "burned" (metabolized) inside the cells of the body and converted into energy used to carry on the various functions of the body. For glucose to be able to penetrate the cell wall and enter the cell, a chemical called insulin is required. Insulin is a hormone made in the pancreas, which is an organ important in the entire digestive process. When the normal person begins to digest food, the amount of glucose in his blood rises. The rise signals the pancreas to release the hormone, insulin, into the bloodstream. The insulin and glucose are taken through the bloodstream to all the parts of the body to provide needed energy for its activities, growth, and development. When more food is taken in than the body needs for energy at the time, that is there is left over glucose, it is stored as fat. Then, if the person has not eaten for a time, the fat cells are broken down and released to the body in the form of fatty acids. Many tissues of the body can utilize fatty acids directly as an energy source, rather than glucose. (This is true of muscle tissue, including the heart.)

There are some important differences in the ways the body burns or metabolizes the two sources of energy, glucose and fatty acids. When glucose is the fuel source, it is burned very efficiently, leaving only carbon dioxide (which is breathed out) and water (which is excreted in the urine). When fatty acids are burned, the end products are organic compounds called ketone bodies. There are three types of ketone bodies formed from fat metabolism, one of which is acetone. An abnormally high ketone level in the body would create a dangerous condition, acidosis. The kidneys, therefore, excrete ketone bodies as waste in the urine in order to keep a healthy balance of chemicals in the body.

JUVENILE DIABETES

In juvenile diabetes the pancreas apparently becomes unable to make any insulin. Therefore, the sugar in the blood cannot be burned. Consequently, the amount of sugar in the blood rises. The kidneys regulate normal concentration of blood constituents by the excretion of water and waste substances as urine. Therefore, sugar is then taken out of the blood into the urine or "spills over" into the urine. As the kidneys try to eliminate the sugar, extra water is pulled from the body also, so that at the onset of diabetes there is a production of large amounts of urine. This leads to dehydration of the body, consequent great thirst, and drinking of large amounts of liquid. Further, since the sugars and starches of food cannot be burned as glucose in the cells, the body acts as if it were starving. Even though the child begins to eat large quantities of food, there is weight loss at the onset of diabetes. The child will also show fatigue and listlessness. Because the body cannot utilize the glucose of carbohydrates for energy without insulin, it begins to break down fats instead, both those stored in the body and those in the diet. The conversion of so much fat into energy produces a rising level of ketone bodies, which also spill over into the urine. As the level rises, if nothing is done about it, acidosis begins to occur and can lead to diabetic coma and eventually to death.

MEDICAL TREATMENT

Before 1921, the average life span for diabetic children was a little more than a year after the disease was diagnosed. Then a Canadian surgeon, F. G. Banting, and a graduate student, C. H. Best, discovered the protein hormone insulin, which is now extracted from the beef or pork pancreas and is administered daily from the time the disease is discovered.

The teacher, as a watchful observer, may be the first to detect signs of the onset of diabetes. The teacher would not make a tentative diagnosis, even if he were certain. Rather, the teacher would report symptoms to medical personnel at the school and to the parents. A physical examination should be encouraged.

While pills can be used in some forms of adult-onset diabetes, they are not helpful in the juvenile form. Insulin must be injected daily under the skin. Present practice is to teach self-management as early as possible. Children nine or ten years old and even younger will be expected to give themselves their own injections.

The physician will determine which type and strength of insulin is most effective for each patient. There are three main kinds of insulins; the fastest, short action insulin, has to be injected as often as four times a day.

Types of insulin are supplied in three strengths, each in a different colored bottle to avoid confusion. Syringes, which are made of plastic and disposable, have a scale so that the exact amount of insulin can be measured. Some children may use glass syringes with a carrying case. The approximate dosages of insulin will be decided for each individual on the basis of routine, diet, and amount of exercise.

Enough insulin is to be injected to control the levels of sugar and acetone in the blood. These levels are influenced by the child's diet, exercise, and general health. Therefore, the urine of the child must be tested three or four times a day to check the degree of spillover in the urine of sugar and of acetone. (Spillover indicates a buildup of sugar in the blood.) Children are taught to do their own urine testing as soon as possible. If parents are still helping the child, it is often possible to dispense with a prelunch testing so that the urine testing and injections will not have to be done in school. Other children may achieve better control with an injection an hour or so before lunch.

To test the urine, it is voided into a small vial (there are pocket sizes) that comes with strips of reagent for sugar and for acetone or with chemical tablets, which are dropped in the vial. The resulting color of the urine in each test is compared with a color spectrum on respective charts and recorded. The amount of glucose in the urine is an indirect measure of how much glucose is in the blood and reflects how well the insulin is acting. If acetone begins to appear in the urine, it indicates that fat is being broken down so insulin is not present in adequate amounts.

Regulation of diet is very important in the control of diabetes. The specific type of diet will depend on the individual child's needs and upon the philosophy of the physician in charge. The child may be on a free diet, that is food is not measured and only the intake of sweets is discouraged. The child could be on a weighed diet, where the kinds of food and amount are weighed at each meal. The most common diet recommended today, the Exchange or Substitution diet, was developed by the American Diabetes Association. There are lists of foods under headings "Milk, Vegetables, Fruit, Bread, Meat, and Fat." Any food on a given list can be substituted for any other on that list. This enables the diabetic to have some flexibility in eating patterns.

It is very important that diabetic children keep a regular schedule for eating, both in terms of times and amount. Usually they will eat five times a day, three meals and two snacks.

MANAGING DIABETES IN SCHOOL

A cooperative school staff can contribute to the diabetic child's health and also to the psychological comfort experienced in managing the diet. The school dietician, or the nurse or doctor, can help plan meals and snacks that are nutritious, tasteful, and allowed to the diabetic pupil. Actually, this diet is more healthy for everyone. Milk and fruit are better for all than carbonated drinks and candy bars, for example.

Exercise should be as regular as possible in terms of time of day and amount for best control of blood sugar level. Diabetic boys and girls will learn to eat a snack before and after a half-hour or so of vigorous exercise at recess or in gym sports and to carry candy.

Diabetic coma is a serious condition for which the teacher should watch. When discussing the onset of the disease, the symptoms of tiredness, weakness, weight loss with great appetite and thirst were mentioned. Initially, the development of these symptoms may take weeks. Later, when insulin has been taken but discontinued, the same symptoms would recur in the course of a few days. If for some reason the dosage of insulin is insufficient, either because of changes in growth, diet, exercise, or other illnesses, there is danger of diabetic coma. The teacher should be watchful of the diabetic child. Listlessness, which might be discounted in another child, will be an alert sign for the teacher with a diabetic student. The onset of coma is slow, so the teacher has time to call the school nurse, the doctor, or the parents about the situation.

Diabetic shock (insulin reaction) is a more common occurrence. While enough insulin must be given to allow cells to utilize sugar for energy, too much insulin, relative to blood sugar, is harmful. If an excessive dose is given, or a delayed meal or unusual amount of exercise has caused the body to use up blood sugar, the child will have a low blood sugar (hypoglycemic) reaction, which has a rapid onset, usually in minutes or a few hours. The reaction occurs because certain organs of the body, such as the brain, have absolute requirements for glucose as an energy source and cannot substitute fatty acids.

The onset of diabetic shock can be very variable for different persons depending to some extent on individual tolerance to go for shorter or longer periods with a low level of blood sugar. Thus, the reaction of some children might be rapid–they will sink rather quickly into unconsciousness. Others might have a protracted period when they seem nonattentive or sleepy. They might seem irritable, shaky, or even hyperactive. Some children might seem dazed or "spaced out." If they are changing classrooms or on the playground or in the swimming pool, this condition might prevent them from exercising normal safety precautions and could be dangerous. Therefore, the symptoms of faintness, headache, dizziness, blurred vision, personality change, or not being able to waken, should alert the teacher to the possibility of diabetic shock, which can usually be easily managed in the school environment.

Normally, some form of concentrated sugar will end the insulin reaction in several minutes. All diabetics will become sensitive to the onset of insulin reaction and will carry sugar or candy with them. Different physicians prefer different forms of sugar for these emergencies. The teacher should plan ahead with the parents or doctor and keep handy what is prescribed: fruit juice, or carbonated beverages with sugar, or sugar lumps.

Many students will wear a tag or ID bracelet containing the word *diabetic* (see Fig. 18). They also carry a card describing their condition, their physician's name and phone, and instructions on what to do if they should be unconscious from shock.

Physicians are very anxious to have self-management of the disease completed before adolescence. Patient education is begun in the hospital, at the time of initial medical care, and is often ongoing in pediatric clinics. The American Diabetes Association furthers this purpose. Summer camps are available where children can learn disease control with peers under happy conditions.

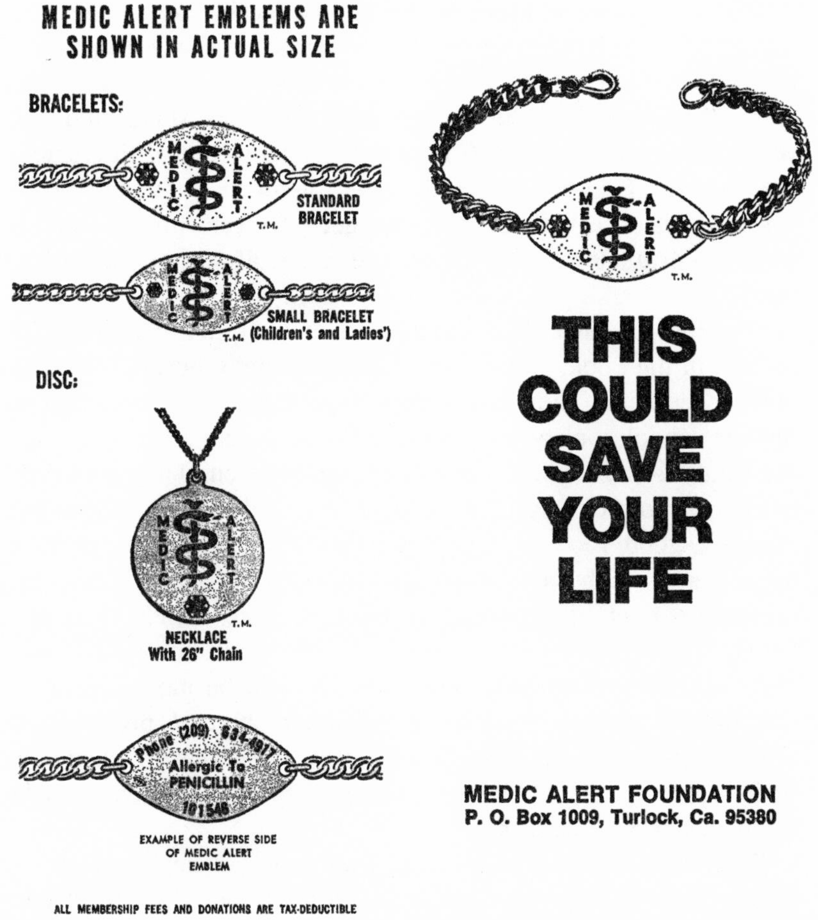

MEDIC ALERT EMBLEMS ARE SHOWN IN ACTUAL SIZE

BRACELETS:

STANDARD BRACELET
T.M.

SMALL BRACELET
T.M. (Children's and Ladies')

DISC:

NECKLACE
With 26" Chain
T.M.

THIS COULD SAVE YOUR LIFE

Phone (209) 634-4917
Allergic To
PENICILLIN
101546

EXAMPLE OF REVERSE SIDE
OF MEDIC ALERT
EMBLEM

MEDIC ALERT FOUNDATION
P. O. Box 1009, Turlock, Ca. 95380

ALL MEMBERSHIP FEES AND DONATIONS ARE TAX-DEDUCTIBLE

Figure 18. Medic Alert. Courtesy of the Medic Alert Foundation International, Turlock, California, 95380.

Adolescence, a difficult time physically and psychologically for most youngsters, can be extremely hard for those who must cope with diabetes. Overreactions of all kinds are hallmarks of the adolescent and must be expected. Social limitations, such as not being able to eat or stay with the gang, probably hurt more at that age, while older friends are resigned to the limitations. (They may just quietly eat a packed lunch alone to avoid the inappropriate diet in the usual lunch place, for example.)

While the teacher needs to be knowledgeable about the physical condition of the students for which he or she is responsible, that information should be, as far as possible, confidential. Students themselves should decide how much to share and with whom, as far as they can. It is in the teacher's control to create an atmosphere of acceptance and matter-of-course. It would be unwise to "get on a kid's back" over diet infringements or other activities. Fortunately, those things are not really the teacher's business!

Diabetic students, like those with many other conditions described in the book, can be treated as essentially normal. They are normal learners. They have every expectation of fitting into the regular school society and community with ease. However, they are what will be termed here susceptible children. They must learn to adhere more closely than others to the healthy life, with regular routines, good food, and rest. Parents and teachers need to be more vigilant with them in recognizing signs of trouble. When they are adults, they will continue to monitor more closely their phsical signs than other persons might do. They will continue to need close medical surveillance. Any infection will be more serious for the diabetic person. Pregnancy and birth, normal processes for most women, can be difficult and even dangerous for some diabetic women and their babies. Their offspring will have a higher frequency of birth defects.

Whereas diabetic persons often lead long and healthy lives, the disease may significantly reduce life expectancy. Their most common cause of death is diabetic kidney disease. Heart attacks are two and one-half times more frequent in diabetics than nondiabetics of the same age. Since there is a degeneration of blood vessels associated with the condition after a number of years, other disabilities may be acquired by middle or old age. Half of the blindness in the United States is caused by diabetes. Therapeutic amputations are frequently required in older diabetics because of disorders in circulation and consequent danger of gangrene. The fact that diabetes is a very serious condition should stimulate the teacher to a great effort of cooperation and support in giving the student with diabetes the very best send-off in school.

The Following Information Should Be Obtained from Parents When Conference Is Held at the Beginning of the School Term

Child's Name	Date	
Parent's Name	Address	Phone
Alternate person to call in emergency	Relationship	Phone
Physician's Name	Address	Phone

Signs and symptoms the child usually exhibits preceding insulin reaction:_____

_____

Time of day reaction most likely to occur:_____

Most effective treatment (sweets most readily accepted):_____

Kind of morning or afternoon snack:_____

_____

Suggested "treats" for in-school parties: _____

Substitute and/or Special Teachers Should Have Access to the Above Information
This material may be reprinted for the child's cumulative school record.
For additional information or copies of this card, contact:
American Diabetes Association, 600 Fifth Avenue, New York, New York 10020

Review Guide

After reading Chapter 17 the reader should be able to define the following terms:

glucose   fatty acid
pancreas   acidosis
insulin

After reading Chapter 17 the reader should be able to answer the following questions:

1. What are the two main thrusts of medical management of diabetes?
2. What two daily routine tasks will juvenile diabetics learn to do to control their disease?
3. What are three physical symptoms present at the onset of juvenile diabetes?
4. What is the treatment for diabetic shock?
5. What are the symptoms of onset of diabetic coma that the teacher might see in class?
6. What might be a cause of distress to diabetic adolescents?

Chapter 18

HEMOPHILIA

"Mishaps are like knives, that either serve us or cut us, as we grasp them by the blade or the handle."

Herman Melville
Cambridge Thirty Years Ago

HEMOPHILIA IS A BLEEDING disorder due to an inadequate amount of certain coagulation factors within the blood. The most common form (hemophilia A), is a hereditary deficiency of coagulation Factor VIII. In some cases, it is due to lack of coagulation Factor IX (hemophilia B or Christmas disease). A deficiency of these factors results in a poor quality clot, which can be easily dislodged. When the affected person suffers a small wound, either internal or on the body's surface, bleeding is prolonged, but it is no faster than in a nonhemophilic person.

Although hemophilia may be classified as severe, moderate, or mild based on the extent of factor deficiency, the actual frequency and severity of bleeding are unpredictable. Since the hemophilia is a genetic, sex-linked defect, it usually occurs in boys, and in about 1 in 10,000 births.

THE CLOTTING MECHANISM OF THE BLOOD

When skin or other membranes are injured so that the lining of a blood vessel is broken, three processes normally begin to allow the body to stop the bleeding. One process is *vascular reaction,* a contraction of the blood vessel itself. Whenever a blood vessel is broken, small smooth muscles surrounding the injured place in the vessel immediately contract the size of the vessel to decrease or stop the blood flow. This contraction is only temporary, to allow time for a blood clot to form.

Another process is the *platelet plug*. Platelets are light grey, round bodies that float in the blood along with the corpuscles. They do not cohere to the walls of the blood vessels but will stick to any other tissues of the body. Therefore, when the blood vessel is broken, the platelets converge on the margins of the broken blood vessel to plug the opening and stem the loss of blood. Platelets also release the chemicals that stimulated the muscles around the muscle to contract and attract other platelets to the injured area to enlarge the clot. Lastly, they release enzymes (organic catalysts) that assist in the formation of a firm clot.

Formation of a *firm fibrin clot* is the last stage in the clotting process. Fibrin is made of clotting factors that make up fibrous protein. This fibrous protein, in turn, forms in a network in which the blood corpuscles are enmeshed. When the clot is complete over the injured part of the blood vessel, bleeding stops.

There are thirteen different clotting factors (I-XIII) in the blood, which are essential to form the fibrous protein necessary to the clotting process. A deficiency in the amount of any of these can cause abnormal clotting. The most common cause of bleeding disorder is an insufficient amount of Factor VIII, the anti-hemophilic factor (AHF). Blood of hemophiliacs may have as little as 1 or 2 percent as much Factor VIII as normal individuals. In that case, they will be severely affected. The seriousness of the disorder will depend in part on the amount of clotting factor present. The person with only a small deficiency of Factor VIII might bruise more easily than normal, but he would probably not experience difficulty unless he had major surgery or a serious injury.

The seriousness of hemophilia, then, varies in each case. While a general description of symptoms will be given and guidelines for management offered, it is important to remember that each person's physical capabilities and limitations will have to be individually assessed. Furthermore, these may change as the child grows older.

MAJOR SYMPTOMS AND TREATMENT OF HEMOPHILIA

It may not be immediately evident at birth that a child is hemophilic. Usually, the disorder is recognized by the second or third year of life. The first symptom may be that he bruises easily. The first real problem noticed by the parents might be the profuse bleeding of a very small cut. The majority of bleeding episodes occur in "stress points" such as elbows, knees, and ankles. The pressures and strain of ordinary walking and exercise can cause little bleeding points within the joint, which normally clot and heal. Because of the inadequate coagulation associated with hemophilia, this bleeding can continue, making the joint swell and causing pain. With repeated joint bleeds, the joint lining (synovium) becomes thick and brittle. Therefore, the joint lining bleeds more easily. The recurrent bleeding causes destruction of the smooth lining of the surfaces of the touching (articular) surfaces of the bone at the joints (cartilage). As a consequence, joint deterioration (degenerative arthritis) may cause permanent crippling. Splints, braces, and casts are sometimes used to ease these problems.

Blood may ooze around baby (deciduous) teeth. Dental treatment is a source of concern with hemophiliacs. A tooth extraction may be a medical crisis. Even minor dental work or routine examination may result in swellings from bleeding into the gums and cheeks.

Often, internal bleeding can result with no apparent injury at all. Or, bleeding can occur hours, or even days, after the initial injury. Bruises and bleeding may occur during sleep. Bleeding into the brain may cause headaches, mental confusion, and even death. The kidneys may hemorrhage in children with hemophilia. If the child urinates red or dark brown urine, therefore, he should get immediate medical treatment.

Most hemophiliacs learn by age six or seven to discriminate the first symptoms of a hemorrhage long before objective signs appear. Prompt attention to the symptoms is necessary. Subjective symptoms, such as pain or tenderness at rest or with movement, and feelings of pressure or stiffness must be noted. If the child has delayed seeking therapy and visible signs of bleeding are present, measurements of swelling or changes in joint mobility are obtained.

Until recently hemophilia was usually a life threatening disease, and most of its victims died before adulthood. Up to the last decade, the only known replacement therapy was with whole blood or plasma, which contains only small amounts of the clotting factors. The large volumes necessary to achieve therapeutic levels sometimes resulted in circulatory overload. This complication and the frequent occurrence of idiosyncratic side effects and transfusion reactions usually necessitated hospitalization.

The development of highly purified and easily administered clotting-factor concentrates in the mid-1960s radically changed the medical care of hemophiliacs. Today, the increased availability and relative safety and effectiveness of these concentrates permit easy treatment of acute bleeding in an emergency room, outpatient department, or even at home.

Therapy depends on the site of bleeding. Bleeding from minor lacerations generally can be controlled by a simple pressure dressing, ice packs, and oral medications. Bed rest may be necessary. More serious bleeding, such as hemarthrosis, bleeding into a joint, usually requires replacement of the deficient clotting factor.

Some hemophiliacs receive prophylactic infusions to prevent hemorrhages or decrease their severity, and many patients successfully undergo such procedures as open heart and rehabilitative orthopedic surgery.

The philosophy of therapy has changed from "wait and see" to "when in doubt, infuse early."[1] It is not the actual injury, but the delay in treatment that contributes significantly to morbidity. Early treatment, before swelling and limitation of joint mobility occur, decreases pain, injury to the site, and recuperation time. This change in treatment enables many hemophiliacs to enjoy increased freedom, including regular attendance at school and work. Their lives no longer revolve around hospitalizations, and indeed, many learn to self-administer the factor wherever they happen to be.

One of the major concerns is the danger of idiosyncratic reactions to the factor concentrate. Children have had such allergic reactions as wheezing, itching, flushing, and hives–all relieved by injections of medications such as Benadryl®. A major medical

---

1. Michele Boutaugh, Phyllis C. Patterson. "Summer Camp for Hemophiliacs," *American Journal of Nursing,* August, 1977.

problem still facing hemophiliacs is the development of inhibitors (antibody). About 5 to 20 percent of hemophiliacs develop an inhibitor to the factor and, in effect, destroy the infused factors. The major bleeding episodes of these individuals are difficult to manage. Fortunately, clinical experimentation with new types of therapy for individuals with inhibitors is underway.

The newest concentrates for both Factor VIII and IX have been separated out of plasma and can be injected into the vein by hypodermic needle. Children learn to mix their own medication, learn the technique of venipuncture (a more complicated procedure than the subcutaneous injection that diabetic children apply), and learn to estimate their own dosage requirements.

Children may attend a special summer camp, where they learn these procedures in a happy atmosphere.[2] Experience has confirmed that placing hemophiliacs together creates a homogeneous environment that helps to minimize a sense of difference. "Having a bleeding problem" ceases to be an isolating issue, and campers begin to recognize their capabilities within a unique peer group.

The new clotting factor preparations can be safely stored at home, and patients can be taught home administration of the concentrates. However, at the time of this writing, even with an effort of blood banks in the United States to produce the clotting concentrate, there is not enough medication available for those who could benefit from it. Moreover, it is also very expensive. The medication can cost in the hundreds of dollars a year for one person. Medical research must continue to alleviate these problems.

THE TRANSMISSION OF HEMOPHILIA

Hemophilia was known to the ancient Egyptians and was recognized as hereditary. Now it is known that it is due to a defective gene on the X chromosome, so is a sex-linked gene (see Fig. 5). The mother who is a carrier does not have the disease but has a 50-50 chance at each pregnancy of transmitting that trait to an offspring. If she transmits the trait to a girl (who has received a normal X chromosome from her father) the girl will be a carrier like her mother. If the mother transmits the trait to a boy, he will

---

2. Op. cit.

have hemophilia, since the Y chromosome, given by the father, does not carry genes. Therefore, the mother that carries the trait for hemophilia has a 50 percent chance of transmitting the defect to her sons. Since hemophilic men can have children, they can give the defective gene on their X chromosome to girl children. If the mother were a carrier and gave her defective gene also, a girl, with the trait on both X chromosomes, would have hemophilia.

At present there is no reliable test to identify carriers of hemophilia. Family history of the disease can indicate the probabilities of being a carrier. Of course, if one son has been produced with the disease, the mother knows she is probably a carrier. Parents at risk always have the options of not producing offspring. Another option available today is the extraction and examination of amniotic fluid (amniocentesis) at the end of the third month of pregnancy to determine the sex of the unborn child. If the amniotic fluid withdrawn from the mother's womb shows that the child is a boy, an abortion might be performed, since the boy would have a 50 percent chance of having the disease.

It is estimated that about a third of the cases of hemophilia are sporadic, that is they are due to a mutation. In these cases there has been no family history of the disease, and it is assumed that a new mutation developed in the cells producing egg cells of the mother or recent ancestor. This was apparently the situation with Queen Victoria of England, in whose family there was no evidence of the disease. As a result of the recent mutation she produced one son with hemophilia and two daughters who were carriers. The daughters transmitted the disease to six of the Queen's grandsons, whose royal unions thereby spread the disease to the royal families of Spain and Russia in three generations. The disease had its most dramatic impact on the history of modern Europe when it was manifest in the only male heir of the Russian royal family.*

THE STUDENT WITH HEMOPHILIA

A hemophiliac's physical condition, general sense of well-being, and exposure to stress, as well as the level of his factor deficiency,

---

* This is chronicled by Robert Massie (whose own son is afflicted with the disease) in *Nicholas and Alexandra*, Atheneum Publishers, New York, 1967.

can affect his bleeding history. Clinical manifestations of the disorder range from spontaneous bleeding without known injury to bleeding only after significant trauma. He may require close surveillance and some special school management.

Aside from the debilitating effects of pain and possible school absences, children with hemophilia should be as able learners as their peers. In the areas of transportation, mobility, recess, and gym, however, there may be need for special arrangements or curtailments, depending on the severity of symptoms.

A braced, physically fragile child might find the regular school bus unsatisfactory, for example. Whether or not the student is allowed sports such as tennis and baseball will be a decision of the physician. Body contact sports, strenuous competitive games, and diving may well be interdicted. However, children with hemophilia seem to have fewer episodes of bleeding if they are active than with inactivity. Exercise improves joint function and muscle tone. Therefore, sports such as golf, swimming, calisthenics, tennis, and hiking, for example, may be strongly encouraged for some.

Adaptations of sports can be made in the regular P.E. program. Whiffleball, using soft plastic bats and balls, can be substituted for baseball. If a child cannot navigate the bases, a substitute can run for him or the umpire can determine how many bases the hitter could walk.

Injuries and hemorrhages may happen at school. The teacher should be alert to signs of bleeding, such as limping, guarding a limb, or a large discoloration of the skin. Any danger signs should be discussed with the child, nurse, parent, physical therapist, or physician. The school staff will have planned ahead how to report and treat such an episode. Many hemophiliacs have learned from experience the doses of factor concentrate necessary to control their own bleeding episodes. The particular situation will vary, depending on the severity of the disease, the availability of medication, and other factors.

PARENT COUNSELING

It has been observed by some parents of hemophiliac children themselves and by school personnel that parents, and particularly mothers, seem to react to their sons with this handicap in certain characteristic ways. First, there seems to be an inordinate amount of guilt on the part of the mother over having transmitted the defect to her child. Secondly, perhaps in response to these feelings, there is a tendency toward over solicitousness, even to the point of martyrdom, with the health handicapped son. An outcome of this seems to be an overprotectiveness that results in either excessive dependency or extreme, perhaps self-destructive, rebelliousness on the part of the youngster. Either of these final consequences is poor, particularly for a student who will be expected to achieve in school and go on to be a fully contributing member of society as an adult.

The teacher may be able to understand the student's plight better than the mother's. It cannot be imagined by those who have not lived through it how excruciating it must be for parents to watch helplessly as their children suffer pain, and more so perhaps when they see themselves as direct agents of that suffering.

Further, the caretakers of the young hemophilic child may have had to give most of their time and effort to that child at an early period, so that by necessity outside pleasures and activities were dropped. If the child no longer needs that encompassing care, the parent may be left without anything left to do but to now invent need where it does not exist.

By being very understanding, but neither falling in the trap of overidentifying with the mother nor becoming angry on behalf of the child, the teacher may begin to ease the situation. A dispassionate appraisal of what seem to be the child's tolerances and capabilities in school can be described. The teacher can be encouraging about the student's successes and vocational possibilities. The helpful services of the National Hemophilia Foundation and, for the older youth, the State Bureau of Vocational Rehabilitation can be suggested. The parents can be encouraged to participate in school affairs where they can see their child in the perspective of the whole school society. The student may learn from the teacher some objectivity and sympathy for his parents and see them as fallible but loving beings as well.

We must be cautious in anticipating reactions of parents to their

handicapped children. Too often observations about how so*
parents do respond get translated into principles dictating how
parents should behave. Furthermore, everything the parent d(
in the way of overprotecting, fostering dependence, complaini*
etc., may be seen in relation to the handicap, even though pare*
of normal children occasionally do exactly the same things. Last
if certain behaviors are expected, those might be the ones that *
noticed, even though they are not those that are the most rep*
sentative of the person observed. The teacher will want to *
spond to and reinforce the positive, healthy responses the pare*
show toward their child, rather than dwell on the more negati*
aspects to prove a suspected unhealthy attitude.

Review Guide

After reading Chapter 18 the reader should be able to defi*
the following terms:

clotting factors	venipuncture
stress points	sex-linked factor
internal bleeding	

After reading Chapter 18 the reader should be able to answ*
the following questions:

1. What are the three processes contributing to cessation
   bleeding in a wound in the body.
2. What is the most common cause of bleeding disorder?
3. What medical advance has radically changed the outlook f*
   the future of hemophiliacs?
4. What is an important economic factor in the treatment
   hemophilia?
5. What three early danger signs might indicate an attack of i*
   ternal bleeding?
6. In what ways can a teacher help the parents of a stude*
   with hemophilia to a positive approach toward their child?

STRESS RELATED DISORDERS

Certainly there is a consent between the body and the mind; and where nature erreth in one, she ventureth in the other."

Bacon

Physical disposition is always influenced by a *predisposition* or tendency relating to physiological type and function, whether due to heredity, environment, or both. It is often evident that critical physiological or psychological stresses can act as *precipitating* factors that can contribute to pushing the vulnerable person into a state of illness. Such an illness may be perpetuated after the precipitating stress, such as an infection, a school examination, or family tension, has lessened. This is because there may be secondary gains to the illness, which act as *perpetuating factors.* Such factors might be extra attention, relief from responsibility, or the sick person's discovery that other persons can be controlled through the illness.

The school environment may be a source of stress that contributes to the onset of an illness. On the other hand, the school environment may be the healing environment in which stresses are reduced and where students are not rewarded for perpetuating their symptoms.

The following two chapters are concerned with disorders that are generally conceded to have a very high psychologic or psychosomatic component. It must be emphasized that the mental component does not make the physical disability any less real or painful than any other physical problems. Nor is the alleviation of symptoms under the voluntary control of the sufferer.

243

Chapter 19

ALLERGIC REACTIONS

*I got used to everything pretty quickly. Even to the asthma. It's
remarkable how easy it is to get used to other people's asthma. After
2 or 3 experiences I was taking Henry's attacks as calmly as the rest
of them. One moment he'd be strangling; the next he was good as
new and talking nineteen to the dozen about quantum mechanics.*

Aldous Huxley
The Genius and The Goddess

IN 1909 AN AUSTRIAN pediatrician, von Pirquet, proposed the
word *allergy,* derived from two Greek words meaning "altered
response." Allergic reactions are explosive reactions on the part
of a body that is hypersensitive to substances that are benign to
most persons. These can take place in various parts of the body,
such as the eyes, nose, skin, and lungs. Allergies tend to run in
families, so it can be assumed that some persons have a predisposition to them.

MECHANISM OF THE RESPONSE

Antibodies are part of the body's defense system against substances interpreted as foreign invaders (antigens). These foreign
invaders may actually stimulate the production of antibodies.
When the offending substance comes in contact with the antibody,
the release by the cells of various chemicals occurs to destroy the
invader or neutralize it. This process is usually protective to the
body.

In infectious diseases, such as measles, this process often leads
to permanent immunity from further attacks. The smallpox vaccination makes use of the fact that an injection of a very mild contagious disease, cow pox, builds up antibodies in the human being,
which then confer immunity to the related, very serious disease.

245

The poliomyelitis vaccine is prepared from killed microorganisms that again cause the body to build an active immunity through the production of antibodies to the dead and live microorganism. In Chapter 6, we saw the effects of an autoimmune reaction involving antibodies to the joint's own abnormal substances, the rheumatoid factor, which led to arthritis.

It is thought that the allergic individual has an overabundance of antibodies to antigens such as pollen or house dust (inhalants), certain foods or drugs (ingestants), poison ivy or feathers (contactants), and wasp stings or penicillin (injectants). Antigens involved in the allergic reaction are called allergens. Allergies are not a simple intolerance of the body to a substance, because they always involve an abnormal reaction of the defense mechanism so that the body produces what are called allergic antibodies. Allergic antibodies are not protective. When they react with the offending substances, injurious chemical compounds are released. Among these is histamine, which comes from the cells in the connective tissue and directly causes swelling of the mucous membranes found through the body. The stuffy nose associated with hay fever is a result of this reaction. Antihistamine medications are sometimes helpful to relieve this condition. Another compound (bradykinin) can contract the smooth muscles such as those in the small tubes of the lungs. The resulting breathing difficulties are the symptoms of asthma.

Antibodies are formed during the initial reaction with an offending substance. This first contact, however, is unlikely to result in any clear symptom of a developing allergy. Often it is only after considerable exposure to an allergen that enough antibodies are formed to cause symptoms. Sensitization to a particular substance can last for many years.

Allergic reactions may begin at any time of life. They may get better or progressively worse. They can be very mild, such as itching or a few momentary hives, or catastrophic, resulting in shock or other severe symptoms. A person may have spontaneous remissions from allergies.

SKIN ALLERGIES

A number of skin disorders have their origin in hypersensitivity of a person to specific substances that are eaten or are contacted by the skin. Among the most common forms of skin allergies are hives. In hives, the skin erupts in lesions, or wheals, which may be as small as a pin head or as large as the palm of a hand. The hives may burn or itch. The eruptions are usually of short duration and clear up spontaneously.

Another skin allergy is an inflammatory response of the skin to irritants that the skin directly contacts (contact dermatitis). Poison ivy is a common contact irritant. Some persons are allergic to substances in soaps, or face creams and makeup. These sensitivities usually can be managed easily, by wearing nonallergic makeup, for example.

Eczema is a skin condition most common in infants, but it may also be suffered by school-aged children and adults. It is a noncontagious inflammation of the skin, which is most frequent in the creases of the elbows, the back of the knees, and on the neck, but it can be widespread over the body. In the mildest form the skin is reddened and slightly swollen. It can progress to thickened exuding skin and even warty outgrowths. It is characterized by intense itching, and scratching the affected areas only exacerbates the condition. Therefore, gloves may be put on little children to keep them from further irritating the skin. Eczema is known to be aggravated by contact with offending substances, lack of cleanliness of the skin, and stressful situations. Oral medications and ointments are helpful in its control.

Some individuals seem to have an inherited tendency to become easily sensitized to very small amounts of offending substances. Some very allergic children who start out with eczema may end up with an allergic triad including hay fever and asthma.

HAY FEVER (ALLERGIC RHINITIS)

Many hay fever sufferers have a family history of this allergy. Usually airbourne substances such as pollen, animal dander or house dust inflame mucous membranes in the nose of the person with hay fever. Specific sensitivities can often be determined by skin tests, if it is not readily apparent which substances are offending. If the sensitivity is to a seasonal inhalant, such as pollen from ragweed, the complaint will disappear after the seed production is over.

Antihistamines and related drugs are used to control symptoms. Sometimes injections are given periodically to lessen the attacks in a desensitization procedure. Desensitization is used primarily for inhalant allergens. It is of little value for injectant allergens, which can be avoided. Densensitization may take a great deal of time and money. Care must be taken to see that the injections themselves do not cause serious reactions.

ASTHMA

Bronchial asthma is one of the most common chronic disorders of childhood. Over 2½ percent of children in the United States have asthma. It is characterized by laboured breathing or wheezing due to excessive constriction of the small air passages in the lungs (bronchioli) causing a decrease in airway diameter of the lungs and an overinflation. As air passes through the passages, the asthmatic wheeze results. There may be shortness of breath and coughing. The disease can be very serious but is amenable to treatment.

Some children with asthma will wheeze in a mild, almost inaudible way all during the day. Others will have acute attacks, with laboured breathing as the sufferer attempts to get enough air. In severe attacks, hospitalization may be necessary, since the disorder can be fatal. A severely involved child may develop a barrel-shaped chest as overinflated air sacs in the lungs push down on the diaphragm. Usually this condition is reversible, and the chest will return to normal with the asthma under control. Medical treatment of asthma is advised very early. During an acute attack, drugs are given to relax the muscles of the bronchial tree. These are usually given by mouth, but they may be given rectally, or controversially, by aerosol spray. (If children are using the latter in school, the teacher should be very sure what the directions are for the frequency and duration of use.) Mechanical drainage of excess mucus may be taught to parents.

Medical management may involve some control of diet. Common foods such as eggs and wheat may be curtailed. The physician may prescribe various medications, possibly including injections. Since physical stresses such as infections play a role in precipitating or worsening allergic symptoms, the child's general health is carefully watched. Offending substances such as house dust may be decreased by the use of air filters and removal of dust-catching rugs and drapes. Feather or kapok pillows and wool blankets can be replaced by synthetic materials such as plastic covers and foam rubber. Smoking is to be discouraged.

PSYCHOLOGICAL FACTORS

The psychological aspects of allergic reactions are important to consider. Whether symptoms are skin allergies, hay fever, or asthma, it is thought that multiple variables contribute to producing those illnesses. Allergic persons are said to have an "allergic threshold," meaning the level of the body's resistance to allergic disease. This threshold fluctuates, depending on many factors—presence or absence of infection, emotional state, overexertion, changes in weather and temperature, and so on.

Most people today feel that there is a physiologic or organic predisposition plus some psychological predisposition, which, when given a triggering event or precipitating factor, produces the manifest illness. For instance, a child with the allergic predisposition who has been infantalized and made overly dependent might have his asthmatic attack at the time he learns his parents are going away on a vacation.

MANAGING ALLERGIES IN SCHOOL

Emotional stresses in a family sometimes tend to precipitate the asthmatic condition. Therefore, psychotherapy or a residential school away from home has greatly improved some children.

With all disabling conditions there can be a tendency on the part of the impaired individual to use the condition to control others. A little child cannot fail to enjoy the extra attention and solicitousness that his asthma attack involves. He can learn that mommy and daddy can be stopped from leaving the house if they hear a wheeze. This situation can carry over to school if the teacher only pays attention to and, therefore, reinforces the sick behavior and ignores the student in a period of relative health. If all meals, parties, or trips are planned around the needs of the allergic child, there has to be some satisfaction in being so much the center of attention. Therefore, the environment can actually be a perpetuating factor by encouraging the illness.

It is very important to allow an afflicted student every bit of autonomy and encouragement possible in areas of ability while minimizing as much as possible the disability. Otherwise he is forced into a social behavior pattern that is ultimately unsatisfying for the handicapped person and unpleasant for others. Neurotic behavior problems are more likely to develop in the home, where relationships are more intense; where guilt feelings, anxieties, and normal tensions between generations are apt to involve all family members, and particularly those with the added stress of impaired children. The school can present a disinterested alternative environment where healthy interactions are fostered and disabilities are tolerated.

If a student is sensitive to animal dander, the family and teacher can be sure not to have pets, or pets of the particular offending species, in class or in the home. Allergies to contactants may present a real problem in school if a student is allergic to chemicals that are inseparable from certain activities, such as photographic chemicals in the darkroom or varnishes in the shop.

Aside from being a nuisance to the student and perhaps to others around, hay fever should not usually interfere with school activities. The teacher should be understanding when a student avoids proximity to substances that are known to precipitate an irritating reaction, such as chalk dust.

The physical symptoms of an allergic condition can add to stress. For example, persons who have marked eczema may be very embarrassed about their appearance. A particular problem with stress related disorders is that if the disorder itself leads to more stress, a downward spiral of adverse action and reaction is possible. The teacher's role in creating an accepting social climate is very important. The afflicted student can feel fairly confident that eczema will improve and that the blemishes are temporary. Schoolmates can be assured of this also and that the eczema is not catching.

A fact about asthma most relevant to the school is that it is the single chronic condition causing the highest number of days of school absence. While these absences may be often the result of legitimate physical incapacity, educators should be skeptical about unusual amounts of school absence. If the school environment is causing the psychological stress that precipitates an allergic response, it is tempting to remove the student from the situation. This avoidance behavior should be discouraged, while coping skills are taught and encouraged in school. Otherwise, the student will fall farther and farther behind in ability to adjust to the normal environment. Homebound instruction for the allergic student should be a last resort and used only in very unusual situations.

The inability to breathe during an asthma attack is very frightening. Further, laboured breathing causes fatigue and distress. These physical and psychological stresses can play a role in triggering further asthma attacks. Therefore, the disease itself and the medical management of the disease can create anxieties that then worsen the condition. The treatment of asthma may lead to some problems, as in the event of a restricted diet. This may be a burden to children who want to eat with the gang, or who must give up ice cream and cake at birthday parties.

The child whose general resistance is low because of the debilitating effects of a chronic condition is frequently at the brink of some secondary respiratory infection. Subjecting him to the marked temperature change involved in such activities as running around the track in shorts on a very cold day or taking a cold shower and then going outdoors with wet hair might well trigger a secondary respiratory infection as well as an attack of asthma.

There are side effects of some of the drugs commonly used for asthma. One is a drug in the adrenalin family, which can stimulate a child who is already overstimulated because of his asthma. This may be evidenced by nervousness, talkativeness, or generally hyperactive behavior. Another, used to open up or dilate the bronchial tubes, may cause a side effect of nausea. Barbiturates used in combination with one or more of the above drugs may have a sedative effect, or even a stimulating effect. Antihistamines, which can be used for accompanying upper respiratory allergies, frequently cause some drowsiness. A teacher who feels that a child appears to have any of these side effects from medication should inform the parents so that the drugs may be adjusted to the proper dose or another medication prescribed.

The teacher can be alert to physical factors affecting the allergic student's well-being that are in the control of the school. Because asthma attacks can be triggered in school, the teacher may be the first to realize that a child has asthma. The parents should be advised that the teacher has observed these episodes of coughing and wheezing. If parents are aware of the condition but not of the severity of attacks that occur in the classroom, the situation should be brought to their attention. If an asthmatic child is not receiving medical treatment, parents should be advised to consult a physician.

If a child has had asthma several times after being at the chalkboard, working in the woodworking shop, or wrestling on a dusty mat, he should transfer to another activity. If a child wishes to have another try at an activity that apparently has made him ill, he should be allowed to do so after a wait of from three to four weeks. Should attacks recur, then the activity should be omitted for some months with advice from the physician.

It is important to treat the allergic child as normally as possible. The physical education program should be continued as much as is feasible, although sports requiring great endurance and exertion are not recommended for any students at high risk for physical complications. The wise teacher will take into account the more obvious factors in deciding whether an asthmatic child should run around the track on the day in question or stay in the gym and play basketball, for example.

The Allergy Foundation of America is one of the many organizations to endorse the Medic Alert Foundation (Fig. 18), a nonprofit, charitable organization. The applicant provides medical information for a confidential file, which will only be released in time of emergency. Further, he or she is issued, at cost, a bracelet or necklace in child or adult size that has the Medic Alert Symbol on one side and vital information, such as "Allergic to Penicillin" and an identification number on the back. The user also has a card with more detailed information for pocket or purse. Teachers can alert students and their families to this service.

Of the fourteen most common problems of users of Medic Alert, five are specific allergies and another is asthma. Among the fourteen are a number that have been discussed in this book: diabetes, heart condition, epilepsy, glaucoma, and contact lens wearers. The list concludes with the problems of taking anticoagulant medication, an implanted pacemaker, and a neck breather (laryngectomee).

Review Guide

After reading Chapter 19 the reader should be able to define the following terms:

allergy	asthma
antibody	allergic threshold
allergic antibody	predisposition
hives	precipitating factor
eczema	perpetuating factor
hayfever	

After reading Chapter 19 the reader should be able to answer the following questions:

1. What are four different ways through which substances may react with the body to produce allergic reaction?
2. What reactions are common as a result of the release of histamine and bradykinin in the body?
3. How can health rather than allergic illness be encouraged in the school? Give at least four ways.
4. What service does Medic Alert provide?

Chapter 20

ULCERS AND COLITIS

An ulcer,
gentlemen, is an unkissed
imagination taking its
revenge for having been
jilted. It is an unwritten
poem, a neglected music, an
unpainted water color, an
undanced dance. It is a
declaration from the mankind
of the man that a clear
spring of joy has not
been tapped, and that
it must break
through, muddily,
on its own.

John Ciardi

MUSCLE FUNCTIONING can be influenced by anxiety and tension. The voluntary muscles may react by tense posture, spasm, or twitching. Hypertension of the smooth, involuntary muscles of the heart and vascular system may cause elevated heart rate and high blood pressure. Children with a predisposition to high stomach acidity or a tense colon seem to be particularly disposed to several disorders of the gastrointestinal system, known as peptic ulcers and ulcerative colitis. These conditions are increasing in incidence, apparently as the result of the enormous anxieties and tensions in modern society.

THE DIGESTIVE SYSTEM

The organs of the digestive system are chiefly located in the belly (abdomen) (Fig. 19). The belly is the large interior cavity of

254

the trunk, which extends from the diaphragm down to the brim of the pelvis. It is protected by the lower ribs and by the abdominal muscles.

The abdominal cavity is lined with a membrane called the peritoneum. When the lining of the cavity (peritoneum) becomes inflamed due to irritation or infection, there is pain, vomiting, and constipation.

The digestion of food begins in the mouth. A salivary enzyme works on the breakdown of starches, and the work continues by the same enzyme in the stomach. Food is moved from the mouth

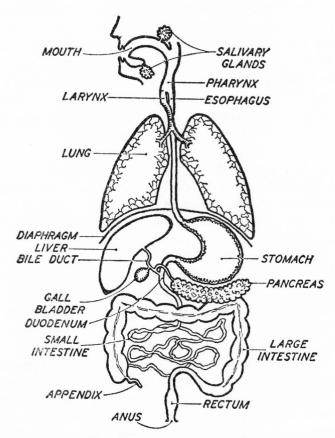

Figure 19. The organs and glands of the digestive tract. (Part of the respiratory system is also shown.)

to the digestive tube (pharynx) in back of the mouth, nose, and larynx. This tube becomes continuous with the gullet (esophagus), a nine-inch tube that joins to the stomach. The stomach is lined with a mucous membrane. Digestive juices are secreted by the glandular layer of the stomach. The enzyme pepsin is useful in the digestion of proteins. Hydrochloric acid is important in the conversion of starch into glucose, a sugar.

Down the entire length of the gastrointestinal tract there is a wormlike movement of the smooth muscles, which moves the food all the way from the pharynx, through the stomach, small intestine, and large intestine to the anal opening.

The stomach has an opening (the pylorus), which connects to the first part of the small intestine, 10 inches long (duodenum). This part has the openings of ducts from the pancreas and the liver, which carry digestive juices from those organs. The second division of the small intestine (jejunum) measures about 8 feet in length. The lower part of the small intestine (ileum) is about 11 feet in length and connects to the large intestine. A valve in the ileum is constructed in such a way that fecal matter is kept in the large intestine. The appendix is a wormlike tube at the place the small intestine opens to the large intestine. The appendix is an important organ for some animals in the digestion of raw plants, but it does not seem to serve a purpose in humans.

Most of the digestion of carbohydrates is carried out in the small intestine. The enzymes from the pancreas perform this function. Enzymes from the liver and the pancreas break down fats and oils. The final step in the conversion of proteins to amino acids, the building blocks of the protein molecule, also takes place in the small intestine. The converted food is absorbed through the mucous membrane of the small intestine into the lymph and blood systems.

The large intestine is about 5 feet in length. It runs up and down the lower abdominal cavity. The major work of the large intestine is to absorb water and electrolytes from the food contents that have undergone digestion. The contents become progressively less watery and eventually become the semisolid material of feces, which is made up of food residues, bacteria, and intestinal secretions.

The colon is the first part of the large intestine. It extends to a bend or fold (sigmoid flexure) where the colon connects with the rectum, the lower part of the large intestine. It terminates in the anal channel through which elimination of the bowels takes place. The discharge of feces is initiated by passage of the feces into the rectum. Sensory impulses are relayed to the spinal cord, and muscle contractions are stimulated. At the same time, the anal sphincter is relaxed to aid passage through the anal opening.

PEPTIC ULCERS

Ulcers that pertain to digestion occur in the stomach and on the first portion of small intestine (duodenum). There is a hypersecretion of gastric juice that causes a hyperacidity in the stomach and erodes the mucous membrane in these organs. The signs and symptoms of ulcers include pain, nausea, weight loss, diarrhea, and anemia. Sometimes eating lessens the pain; sometimes it increases it.

Children may have rather urgent diarrhea and have to be excused frequently and quickly to go to the bathroom. Grave complications are perforation, massive hemorrhage, or an obstruction of the outlet to the stomach. Ulcers have been known to occur and even cause death in neonates, though rarely.

While peptic ulcers can develop at any time, when children develop them, it is most commonly in the age range from five to twelve years old. When ulcers are suspected, children will be given a barium meal, a tasteless powder that will serve to heighten X-ray contrast in pictures taken of the stomach. Medical treatment centers on suppressing the hyperacidity and gastric activity. Since emotional tension is clearly involved, mental and physical rest are prescribed. If these measures fail, surgery is considered.

Most ulcers in childhood will respond well to medical management. A combination of a bland diet and antacid medication is often beneficial. Children may need to eat frequent bland snacks. Even when surgery is indicated, it is usually very successful.

COLITIS

The term *colitis* applies to inflammatory diseases of the colon. The disease may be caused by an organism (as in amebic or bacillary colitis). Ulcerative colitis is noninfectious and related to reaction to stress. The colon, rectum, and the sigmoid flexure are typically involved. In some cases, the ileum may also be affected.

In colitis, in addition to the inflammation of the mucous membrane, there is an excessive accumulation of fluids in the tissue spaces (edema). Ulcers develop and membrane tissues die. Peritonitis may also develop. Death may be caused if the wall becomes pierced or perforated and if hemorrhaging occurs. The incidence of cancer of the rectum and the colon among people with colitis is about ten times the rest of the population.

The average age of onset of colitis in children is around eight years old. There is no specific treatment for colitis. Rest for the bowel and supportive therapy are prescribed. When these measures fail, surgery is recommended. Around one-third of those who require hospitalization may have elective surgery to relieve the symptoms and reduce the risk of cancer. The operation consists of a removal of the colon and an ileostomy or colostomy.

In an ileostomy, an artificial opening (stoma) is made in the abdominal wall and connected to part of the small intestine, the ileum. The opening will be protected by a ring of material glued on the skin and fastened to a plastic bag, through which the still-watery contents of the upper intestine constantly drain. Special care must be paid to the opening, because the expelled contents still have strong digestive juices, which can literally digest the skin surrounding it. An ileostomy is distinguished from a colostomy by the intestinal site of the diversion. In the colostomy, a small portion of the large bowel will remain. This lower opening is not such a risk, because the digestive juices are not present. The person with a colostomy may not have to wear a sac. The bowel is irrigated with enema-like equipment.

It has been found that even very young children can adjust well to an ostomy if they are of normal intelligence. They can learn how to use the equipment and dressings, skin care, and diet control. Therefore, bowel management should not be a problem in the school. These students should be allowed to keep information about this problem private if they wish.

Groups of ostomees or ostomates have clubs throughout the country. Such self-help groups are also formed by persons who have the organ of speech, the larynx, removed in a laryngectomy, or had a breast removed in a mastectomy. In such groups (listed in the Appendix), people learn from each other, sharing information about equipment, common problems, and their successes in achieving happy and productive lives.

PSYCHOLOGICAL CONCERNS

There is a hereditary tendency that predisposes people to ulcers. Psychological stress is also known to play an important role. When ulcers and colitis are diagnosed, the psychological concerns are much the same as those about allergic or asthmatic children. Because minds are incorporated in the brain and the brain is connected to the body, there is an interaction between all of them. Therefore, teachers and doctors should feel comfortable considering psychological and social factors affecting the physical development and well-being of children. Professionals may find a need for investigation of family interaction and the need to understand the child's past history of growth and development of a psychological and social nature.

Teachers can be encouraged to consult with physicians as to what they, as teachers, might do for children in the school situation. And, of course, the converse is true that physicians should have involvement with the schools and teachers of children for whom they are caring.

An irony in stress related conditions is that the symptoms and treatments for the disorder can in themselves cause further stress and further exacerbate the condition. Therefore, teachers want to make students as relaxed and unashamed as possible over special problems or regimens that are required. On the other hand, the illness should not become a classroom focus or spectacle. There is a fine line to be tread between solicitousness and ignoring symptoms.

Review Guide

After reading Chapter 20 the reader should be able to define the following terms:

belly (abdomen)	peptic ulcers
peritoneum	colitis
small intestine	ileostomy
large intestine	colostomy

After reading Chapter 20 the reader should be able to answer the following questions:

1. What are two main factors causing the development of peptic ulcers or colitis?
2. What are the three thrusts of treatment for these problems?
3. Which treatment thrust is of most concern to the teacher?

Section VI
LIFE THREATENING DISEASES

There's something about dying that separates you from all other people. Nobody can come to terms with death. Nobody can walk into death and walk back out the same person. Everybody else, no matter who they are, whether they are a poet, a man of power, a frightened little child, whoever it is, they are afraid of the limitless possibilities of their own nature. Once you have nothing, you can be anything, and that's a feeling of freedom.

But it turns out that you can live a lifetime in a day; you can live a lifetime in a moment; you can live a lifetime in a year—so that to the extent they can prolong your life, dying is not a lie. It's something that's beautiful.

I don't think people are afraid of death. What they are afraid of is the incompleteness of their life. I think what society does is strip you of your self-confidence from the moment you are born; strip you of the sense that what you are is all you're ever going to be.

Ted Rosenthal
How Could I Not Be Among You?

All sufferers of serious physical problems are more at risk and likely, on the average, to have a lower length of life expectancy than more healthy persons. However, advances in medical and health knowledge and care continue to increase chances for a good life.

Until the past fifty years, fatal illnesses in children were common events. Modern medicine has reduced the threat of some chronic diseases such as hemophilia and diabetes so that they are problems children live with, rather than die from. Even the diseases mentioned in this section have a more favorable course now than previously. Advances in research can give further hope to youngsters with these problems within their lifetime.

The following diseases are very different in their symptoms and courses. The overriding characteristic that they have in common is their irrevocability.

261

Chapter 21

CANCER

"Help them to face fear and show them that through strength and sharing we can overcome even the fear of dying, then they will be better prepared to face any kind of crisis . . . including the ultimate reality, death."[1]

ASIDE FROM ACCIDENTS, cancer is the number one cause of death among children from one to fifteen years old, occurring in about 1 in 3,000, usually white, children. More than half of these deaths are due to leukemia or cancers related to leukemia. Malignant tumours comprise another large component of childhood cancer. Hodgkin's disease, which involves the lymph glands, spleen, and liver, also occurs in children.

LEUKEMIA

Leukemia (a Greek word for "white blood") is second only to lung cancer as the most rapidly increasing lethal disease of modern times. Most adults contact one form (acute myelogenous), and about 85 percent of children have another kind (acute lymphocytic).

Medical progress has been made in the treatment of this disease so that its fatal outcome can sometimes be delayed for years. The causes of leukemia are usually unknown. Leukemia rarely strikes more than one child in a family, except in the case of identical twins, where both might be affected. It is conclusively associated with increases in radiation. The incidence of leukemia among victims of the atomic bomb blasts in Hiroshima and Naga-

---

1. Elizabeth Kubler-Ross. "Facing Up to Death," *Today's Education, LXI (1):* 80-82, 1972.

saki is proportional to the distance people were from the epicenter, and how much radiation they consequently received.

Leukemia is a disease involving the blood-forming organs, the bone marrow. Red blood cells are manufactured in the bone marrow. Platelets, the blood cells that aid in blood coagulation when blood vessels are injured, are also formed in the bone marrow. Some white blood cells are formed in the bone marrow, while others are developed in the lymph system and the spleen. The role of the white blood cells is to protect body tissue from strange or foreign chemical substances (antigens), whether living (viruses and bacteria) or inert (such as ragweed, pollen, or poison).

Leukemia is characterized by a massive abnormal increase in the production of white cells, which eventually become very numerous in the leukemic blood. In extreme cases they may reach 100 times or more the normal number. There is a concomitant decrease in the production of red blood cells and platelets so that every aspect of blood function is disrupted. Red cells may be destroyed by antibodies. Their life span falls far short of the normal 120 days, and anemia is the result. Very often there is a deficiency of the blood protein, gamma globulin, which is shaped into antibodies. Consequently, patients show a disastrous susceptibility to infections. Numerous other changes in the blood may accompany leukemia. There may be a reversion to a primitive method of producing blood, normally only seen in the prenatal state. There is a loss of a factor that destroys leukemic cells. Proteins required for normal clotting of blood are diminished. Hence, there may be small or massive hemorrhaging.

A child who is developing leukemia may show symptoms such as pallor, fatigue, fever, weight loss, joint pains, and excessive bruising. Since these symptoms also occur in other illnesses, very thorough medical tests must be done before the diagnosis is confirmed. Bone marrow analysis is a definitive test.

Treatment of acute leukemia has increased the interval of survival from less than six months to as much as an average of five years or more. Length of survival is related to the initial level of elevation of white blood cells and to the age at which the child contracted the disease. The younger children are less likely to have a favorable progress than older children. In rare cases, spontaneous remissions are reported.

The child with leukemia has initial treatment in the hospital with the goal of getting the disease into remission of symptoms. Various medicines may be injected and taken by mouth. These medicines may cause side effects of swelling, pain, and great appetite, but these symptoms are transient and will disappear when the medicines are discontinued.

After the patient has gone into remission, a series of radiations to the skull will be done because chemotherapy does not protect the central nervous system. This causes a loss of hair, but it will grow back when the treatment is over. Spinal puncture may be done to introduce medication into the central nervous system. In a successful remission, there may be a complete disappearance of signs and symptoms of the disease so that the child is perfectly healthy and able to resume normal school activities. The remission may last for months or years before the disease reappears. Some children may have to undergo repeated hospitalizations. Others may attend school without many absences. The course of the disease will vary in different individuals.

OTHER CANCERS

Tumours are excessive cell growth that may occur in any organ of the body. A *benign* tumour is usually not endangering to health or life. A *malignant* tumour has such virulent, uncontrolled cell growth that it is life threatening. Around 40 percent of cancer in children is due to tumours. Some are brain tumours; tumours of the kidney and bone are also common.

Some tumours can be removed by surgery, possibly necessitating the removal of an eye or a limb, and others can be shrunk or controlled by radiation and chemotherapy (medication).

If, as a result of tumours, children have had some incapacitating surgery, they may now fall into another category of exceptionality, and must be helped with this new problem. They and their parents may have uncertainties about their life expectancies or may face the probability of an eventually fatal disease. Some children can be expected to return to school after a contention with cancer, and some will lead completely normal lives thereafter.

Medicines for the treatment of Hodgkin's disease, involving the lymph system, have been developed in recent years. Therefore, it is possible to be far more optimistic than in the past about the possibility of recovery from this disease.

FAMILY ADJUSTMENT

The physical needs of the child with cancer will have an effect on the entire family unit. The medications, hospitalizations, repeated transportation for treatment, and extended care at home will be a drain on family finances and physical resources. Lower income families will have access to disability funds from social security. Funding may be available from other sources as well. Centers are increasingly available where families and patients may stay at little cost on an outpatient basis when they have had to travel long distances to cancer centers for treatment. Nevertheless, there may well be financial and physical strains on family members. A mother might have to give up a job, for example.

When a child, particularly a young, very sick child, is hospitalized, continual parent presence is very important. Brothers and sisters become jealous, guilty, and afraid as they experience parental absence and see attention of parents and friends centered on the ill sibling. It seems helpful to have brothers and sisters visit the hospital often and be exposed to some degree to the kinds of hospital procedures the sick child must endure.

In recent years the process of grief and mourning has been studied. The pioneer work was done by Elizabeth Kubler-Ross[2] with adult patients who were hospitalized with fatal illnesses.

These processes also seem to operate in those around the critically ill and in those who have suffered a major loss, such as eyesight or a limb, as well. The stages of mourning are seen as necessary psychological coping mechanisms that gradually help persons to adjust to their impass or loss.

The first of the five stages is *denial*. At this stage adults may "doctor shop," or make implausible rationalizations about the implications or correctness of the diagnosis. Even after the fact of

2. Elizabeth Kubler-Ross. *On Death and Dying* (New York, Macmillan, 1969).

illness is finally acknowledged, the person will go back to a stage of denial or partial denial from time to time. Denial allows the mourner to mobilize inner forces and recover from the initial shock.

The mourner, when prepared, may then be able to fully receive the news of the illness and take the next steps in living. However, a constant confrontation with the fact of dying might paralyze people to the point of not being able to make use of the time that still exists. People must be allowed the time necessary to break down the defenses that isolate them from the harsh realities. It is then, however, that the second stage of mourning begins.

The second stage is the *anger* that is felt when a person finally allows the information of his condition to reach him. It is sometimes so powerful or so unacceptable to the person that it becomes misplaced. Questions of "why me?" continually haunt, and the person becomes furious at the unfairness of the whole situation. When this anger is understood by others who are sympathetic and willing to listen, this stage of mourning can be worked through.

The next stage is that of *bargaining*. This is connected with a great amount of guilt, and the illness is seen as punishment. Even very young children will say that the reason they are sick and hospitalized is that they have been bad. In exchange for a certain amount of time, the bargainer may agree to "devote his life to God," "make up for all his sins . . . " in short, to be good. In effect, what the bargainer is saying is that the illness is seen as a punishment. In this stage, as in all the others, the feelings of the patient must give others the cue as to his or her psychological needs.

A next stage is *depression*. There are two types of depression identified: reactive and preparatory. It is important to recognize the differences between these. Reactive depression occurs when the patient or the family realizes the eventual loss is near and cannot or may not accept the possibility for a variety of reasons. Statements such as "look on the bright side of things" and "cheer up" may be said because the speaker, not the sufferer, needs the reassurances and cannot tolerate the sadness of the situation. This type of encouragement might be beneficial–if it is given with the idea that the speaker is prepared to help with some of the burdens. For example, if the patient has children, it would be helpful to know that an arrangement has been made to care for them while the spouse visits. The depression of the patient might be caused by just such worries, and it is important that he/she be able to express these fears and have something done about them.

The second type of depression is used to prepare for the final loss of all "love objects." The words of encouragement and reassurances are not as meaningful because the mourning individual is actually beginning to contemplate exactly what his death or loss will mean. In contrast to reactive depression, this is a time for silence on the part of understanding friends. It is the time when those around the patient must also prepare and accept the impending death. A cheery disposition, urged by relatives and friends, is inappropriate. Crowds of visitors may be inappropriate also. The patient may need the quiet and comfort of his own thoughts, although knowing that someone is there when needed to give comfort.

Kubler-Ross defines the final stage of *acceptance.* The mourner will have been able to express the previous feelings: the envy for the living and the healthy, the anger at those who do not have to face their end or a loss so soon, the futility of bargaining, and depression.

These stages may be overgeneralizations, for each person must approach death in an individual way, depending on the particular circumstances of a unique life. However, a lesson learned from study of Kubler-Ross was that the dehumanization process that begins once the patient is diagnosed as "terminally ill" need not occur if those involved continually remind themselves that in most cases it is the body and not the mind that has been diagnosed as "ill." The patient has a right and a need to be heard. Also of importance is the need for hope throughout the dying–or what might possibly be–the dying process. People do have remissions, and there is always hope of an unconventional course of illness.

Children with life threatening illnesses will have varying perceptions about what is happening, depending to some extent on their age. Preschool children fear hospitalization as an abandonment. If little children are surrounded by their loved ones and have reassurances that they have these important persons as long as they live, they can live happily from day to day. When a little hospitalized one asks one doctor, "Am I going to die," he says "Yes, but not today," which seems to satisfy the child. The statement is both honest and hopeful. It is said that children under nine do not understand the irreversibility of death. They are probably in the company of many adults.

Older children have strong feelings of isolation at a stage when it is normal to be establishing strong bonds with a peer group. They and adolescents will also react to the constant assault on their bodies necessitated by hospital treatment.

Adolescents may be most upset by physical losses, such as their hair, which are a constant reminder of the greater loss yet to be endured. In adolescents, who are normally striking out for independence, the feeling of powerlessness can be overwhelming. Dying is seen as a loss of control over one's body. They may express their need for autonomy until the very last minutes of life by insisting on doing for themselves those things they can still accomplish, even if it is just pouring their own water in a glass.

Since remissions and illness are periodic, particularly with leukemia, with outcome of each always uncertain, families must over and over make a psychological preparation for death. This is an emotionally exhausting process and may in a few cases even lead to a wish to get it all over with.

How often people say, "I couldn't live with that problem; I couldn't cope with such an affliction." Then, when the time comes and misfortune must be endured, people find unexpected strengths and resources, and even new joys and appreciation along with the sorrows. It is typical for the family of the dying child to become a stronger coping unit. Communication becomes more open between family members.

The ill child seems to mature psychologically at an enormous rate, as if to pack a lifetime into the few remaining years. As one leukemic patient put it, "I went from thirteen to thirty-one overnight." Actually, the patient may be the source of strength for the rest of the family in many ways.

These children may develop a strong priority list, which reflects those things they personally think are the really important things to do. Thus they can experience the completeness of their lives as did thirty-one-year-old Ted Rosenthal, as the opening quotation of this section suggests.

FACING DEATH OF A CLASSMATE

The teacher with a student who has a life threatening illness is confronted with some major psychological challenges. The student's reaction to the dilemma will depend on the coping dynamics of the family unit, professional intervention, and also on the psychological environment created by understanding teachers.

Reentry into school is a difficult time for the student whose cancer is in remission. He may still be pale, tired, and susceptible to infection. It is hard to explain to classmates why there is a lack of energy and enthusiasm for the activities of the school.

When a remission is successful, the student may want to put the illness as completely out of mind as possible and just go normally about the business of living. While this coping behavior certainly has aspects of denial in it, it should be respected as the good solution to the problem. It may lessen the unhappy feeling of isolation the ill student is inclined to feel. On the other hand, if he wants to talk about aspects of the illness, either in class or alone with classmates or teachers, this wish should also be respected. In other words, others should take the cue from the child on the appropriate approach to the illness.

The same advice applies to the relationship to the parents. Teachers would be taking an inappropriate role to act as counsellors. However, the parent might need a sympathetic listener to whom to vent feelings of frustration and helplessness.

If persons have strong religious convictions these may be a great solace. Even if the teacher does not share the beliefs, they should be respected and can be referred to as a source of comfort.

It would be completely gratuitous for the school staff to indulge in overwhelming reaction to the catastrophies of students or parents. The latter are hard pressed enough without having to bear the added burden of expressed impotence and dispair of disinterested others. Furthermore, a catastrophic pose is certainly not a good example to other young persons who are presumably being educated to the exigencies of life in the school. The teacher needs to look squarely at the certainty of death and the universality of suffering, while coming to a personal reconciliation with these grievous facts of life.

A kind, calm, and positive approach to the suffering child and parents can be a bulwark of strength for them and a necessary example for dismayed classmates. Professionals are in a stronger position then, not being quite so personally bound up in the tragic situation. They can be more dispassionate than the principle actors and ascertain more realistically what restitutive processes are going on.

The teacher's own ability to put the probable fact of early death of the student in a perspective will enhance rather than depress the quality of life at school. Even experienced teachers find that handling the class around the death of a classmate is a terribly difficult experience. Children have the same emotions of frustration, helplessness, and loss as adults, and they deserve the same honesty and respect for their feelings. If their classmate had been hospitalized, they may already have sent cards and made visits. Some teachers have found that group discussion around class participation in funeral arrangements is beneficial. For example, a letter composed by the class and signed by everyone might be sent to the family; or, a member of the class might be delegated to pick out a sympathy card that all sign. Contributions might be collected to send flowers or to contribute to an appropriate charity. The fact that the students are able to do something makes their feelings more manageable. Further, it is far easier to focus on the mundane logistics of how, what, and when to send something to the family than to focus on the imponderable questions concerning the death of children.

Review Guide

After reading Chapter 21, the reader should be able to define the following terms:

leukemia	remission
red blood cells	benign tumor
white blood cells	malignant tumor

After reading Chapter 21, the reader should be able to answer the following questions:

1. What are the blood-making organs of the body?
2. What cause of leukemia has been conclusively demonstrated?
3. How lasting are the side effects of medication and radiation of the leukemic child?
4. What is a common positive effect on a family as a result of having a child with cancer?
5. What are the five main stages of mourning?
6. Name three ways a teacher can interact with the class over the death of a classmate.

Chapter 22

ANEMIAS

*The Enlightened One
because he saw mankind drowning in the great
sea of birth, death and sorrow, longed to
save them; for this he was moved to pity.*
Upasaka Sila Sutra
"Buddha's Pity"

If I were to choose between pain and nothing, I would chose pain.
William Faulkner
"Wild Palms"

SEVERAL ANEMIC DISORDERS of the blood are life threatening diseases. Two of the most common are sickle cell anemia and Cooley's anemia (thalessemia). These disorders are each transmitted through a specific codominant gene. The gene for sickle cell anemia is found primarily in black people but is found in some frequency in Arab and other Mediterranean populations. The gene for Cooley's anemia is also sometimes found in black populations. Therefore, it is possible for people to have a mixture of the traits.

There are other abnormal genes for hemoglobin (C and D), which may also combine with a gene for sickle cell causing other sickle cell diseases with varying degrees of severity. Besides causing anemia, these diseases cause other serious health problems as well.

NORMAL RED BLOOD CELLS

In order to understand the symptomatology of the anemic disorders, we will first examine the normally functioning blood sys-

273

tem: The blood consists of a liquid (plasma) in which are foun(*platelets* (important for blood coagulation), *white cells* (protec tive cells), and *red blood cells*. The function of red blood cells i₁ to transport oxygen from the lungs to all the organs of the body that is from an area of high oxygen concentration to areas of lo₩ oxygen concentration. Oxygen is needed by all cells for food synthesis and the production of energy. The red cells comprise abou¹ 45 percent of a normal person's blood volume. Normal red blooc cells are round and flat and are very flexible. They can bend anc twist into the smallest capillaries, which are the minute blood ves sels connecting the smallest arteries and veins. Once pressure i₁ removed they will resume their normal shape. The red blood cel¹ has an outer cell wall or membrane (like all cells). Inside the normal cell, over 80 percent of the contents is a protein, *hemoglobin* which is the molecule binding the oxygen that is carried by the cell through the arteries to all parts of the body. The chemical abilit₹ of hemoglobin to hold onto oxygen is related to the presence o₦ iron. Normal hemoglobin remains in a semifluid state whether o₨ not oxygen is on the iron molecule.

Red blood cells are constantly manufactured in red bone marrow. A normal blood cell lives for about 120 days, after which i₦ is broken down by the body. The iron cells are saved, but the chemical structure that surrounded the iron cell is broken dow₦ by the liver into a yellow pigment (bilirubin), which is excreted through the bile ducts into the intestines. New blood cells are constantly formed in the bone marrow to replace those that were destroyed.

SICKLE CELL ANEMIA

The term *sickle cell* was coined to describe the changes in shape of red blood cells from the flat, round disc of the normal blood cell to a long, thin, angular red cell that resembles the shape of a sickle used to cut grasses.

In the sickle cell condition, the DNA in the abnormal gene carries incorrect instructions for the production of hemoglobin. A displaced amino acid in one of the hemoglobin chains leads to an abnormal hemoglobin chain. This in turn causes the chain to make an abnormal chemical bonding within the hemoglobin cell when oxygen is *not* being carried. The abnormal bonding clumps the molecules inside to make the cell rigid, and the cells tend to achieve a sickled appearance (the *sickling phenomenon*). There is a tendency for the sickle cells to stick or mass together when they have become sickle shaped. This will not often happen if there are also normal blood cells in the body, but when all the cells are the abnormal cells, it is very likely. The clump of rigid sickle cells will now be unable to progress through very small blood vessels and will therefore cause an obstruction or "log jam" (occlusion). Now the surrounding tissue is deprived of proper blood flow, and the amount of oxygen in that part of the body is lowered. Therefore, more blood cells will give up their oxygen and produce sickling. Hence, a vicious cycle of more obstruction, less oxygen, and more sickling occurs, leading to damage or death of local areas of tissue.

How serious are the problems created depends on where in the body the obstructions occurred and how prolonged they happened to be. For example, the obstruction may cause a settling of blood in the liver, spleen or kidneys, causing swelling and pain.

Besides the vascular occlusion caused by the disease, there is accompanying anemia. Sickle red cells are rapidly removed and destroyed as the body responds to their abnormality. Instead of living the normal 120 days, they have a shortened life span of only 15 to 25 days. The rapid destruction of hemoglobin and consequent rise of bilirubin in the body will cause a yellowish discoloration in the eyes (jaundice) in about half of persons with the disease. To compensate for the high rate of destruction of blood cells, large numbers of new red cells are formed by the bone marrow. However, the body's capacity is limited, so most persons with sickle cell disease will have only one-half or one-third as many red blood cells as a normal person. Enlargement of the heart muscle, attempting to compensate for the anemia, may result. Lack of sufficient oxygen (carried in hemoglobin) to the joints causes tissue deterioration and pain. Skin ulcers may also be a constant problem. It is not uncommon to have the manufacture of blood cells stop, or to have blood breakdown accelerate. This is a very serious crisis.

There are no physical characteristics "typical" of sickle cell anemia. Rather, the findings are similar to those found in anyone with chronic anemia in childhood, such as stunted growth, pale skin, jaundice, susceptability to infection, and intolerance for exercise. Infections, particularly respiratory infections, are also more serious for children with the disease and often lead to pneumonia. Infants do not have sickle cell crisis because fetal hemoglobin inhibits sickling even though they have abnormal blood cells.

Often the first symptom of sickle cell disease in a small child is a swelling of fingers or toes. Then, between the ages of two and six, the affected youngster will experience severe bouts of pain (sickle cell crisis) in the abdomen, joints, muscles, and bones. The obstruction can occur in any of the organs of the body, such as the liver or the lungs. When it occurs in the brain, it will cause brain damage, which can, of course, severely affect the cognitive abilities of the child and cause paralysis.

Up to the age of ten it is common for children to have from eight to ten crises a year. The number of crises diminishes into adulthood, if persons have survived the disease, and between the ages of twenty to thirty they will have an average of one or two crises a year. Persons in crisis may have a fever, fast and shallow breathing, and a dry tongue (due to decreased fluid intake), tender joints, and increased blood pressure. Patients' complaints are of excruciating pain. Typically, patients describe pain as "gnawing me down," "cutting me to pieces," or "like a toothache."

Many agents are presently being used on an experimental basis to control or prevent sickle cell crisis, but none are yet proven. There is no specific therapy for sickle cell anemia at present. Treatment is supportive and aimed at reduction of symptoms.

Medicine will be given to relieve pain and to reduce infection, if it is present. Fluids will be administered to correct dehydration. Possible acidosis will be treated. In a prolonged crisis, blood transfusions may be of value. However, transfusion reactions and the danger of hepatitis make this a last resort procedure.

Until rather recently, there was not adequate medical understanding of sickle cell diseases. Physicians were inclined to diagnose the secondary consequences of the disease, such as liver disease or hemiplegia, or to misdiagnose the problem, for example, as arthritis. Further, the largest group affected, black Americans, were (and are), in general, poor and frequently did not have access to adequate health services. There were very few black doctors, who might have had a special interest in the problem. Now there is far more awareness and understanding of the problem, which has resulted in more prompt and appropriate medical treatment.

In many hospitals it is now routine to check young black patients for sickle cell. The test is a very simple one, requiring a small amount of blood taken as in any routine blood test. In the past, half the persons with sickle cell disease died before they were twenty and few lived longer than forty. Some improvement in their prognosis is probably due to earlier diagnosis, prompt treatment of infection, stressing good nutrition, and better patient and physician education about the disease.

In order to have sickle cell disease, the individual must have two genes for that condition. In other words, all of the red cells of the body must be programmed genetically to sickle. If a person has only one gene for sickle cells and one gene for normal cells, that person will have half normal blood cells and half sickle cells. This person is said to have *trait* for sickle cell. The blood of persons with trait is far less prone to the sickling phenomenon because there are enough normal cells to prevent the stack-up of the sickle cells. These persons are essentially normal, although they are sometimes admonished to avoid high altitudes, swimming underwater, or other activities that might severely deplete their oxygen. If they have some reaction, they may be advised not to fly in airplanes without pressurized cabins.

The problem that the person with trait faces is the possibility that he or she will produce a child who has sickle cell disease, if the partner also has sickle cell trait. If people come to understand some of the hereditary principles and mechanisms relative to this problem, they will be in a strong, knowledgeable position to exercise their options, rather than being victims of misconceptions, myths, and ignorance.

Sickle cell hemoglobin is due to a codominant gene with the

normal gene for hemoglobin. Therefore, if a person has two normal genes (homozygous for normal) for hemoglobin, he will have normal hemoglobin. If a person has one normal gene and one gene for sickle cell (heterozygous), he will have in the bloodstream half normal cells and half abnormal cells. This person is said to have sickle cell trait and is, therefore, a carrier of the sickle cell gene. If a person has two genes for sickle cell (homozygous for the disease) he will have all abnormal hemoglobin cells in his body and show the illness.

If two parents are carriers of the trait, for each pregnancy they will have a 50 percent chance of producing children who are carriers (have trait), a 25 percent chance of producing a child who has the illness, and a 25 percent chance of having a normal child (see Figs. 4 and 20).

The percentage of the abnormal sickle cell trait is very high in the gene pools of some groups of people. In certain tribes along the central coast of West Africa there is an estimated 40 percent incidence of the trait in the gene population. Because the ancestors of many black Americans came from West Africa, the gene is now prevalent in the United States. It is estimated that from 8 to 10

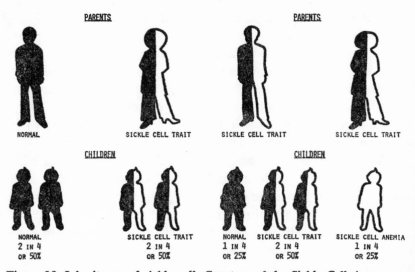

Figure 20. Inheritance of sickle cell. Courtesy of the Sickle Cell Awareness Group of Greater Cincinnati, 3595 Washington Avenue, Cincinnati, Ohio, 45229, and the Cincinnati Health Department.

percent of black Americans carry the trait. Approximately one in 400 black children in the United States has sickle cell disease.

The trait is also found in gene pools of populations living in areas of southern Italy, Turkey, and India where malaria is endemic. One hundred and fifty miles north of Athens, in the Greek village of Archomenos, 23 percent of the residents carry the sickle cell trait. This is the highest concentration in any group of nonblacks and, of course, is higher than the prevalence in the black American population.

The trait for sickle cell became so prevalent because it offered an evolutionary advantage to the populations living in malaria-infested regions. This process highlights the benefits derived from nature's experimentation. Even relatively small environmental alterations can alter the preferred balance of genetic characteristics for a group.

The explanation for the propagation of the trait seems to be as follows: Malaria is an infectious chronic disease, which is still one of the world's greatest killers in technically undeveloped areas of the world. It is transmitted by the *Anopheles* mosquito to the human bloodstream, where it enters normal hemoglobin molecules, causing anemia, weakness, and high fever. In subsistence economies where food is limited and the level of health care is not high, it is frequently fatal. Malaria does not enter sickle cell hemoglobin. Therefore, a person with trait (one sickle cell gene and half sickle cell red cells in his body) has a better chance to survive a bout of malaria than a person with all normal red cells in his body.

What about the babies born with two genes for sickle cell–the children with the disease who are of main concern in this discussion? Sickle cell anemia has been known for centuries in Africa. Some victims may have lived until their teens and may have reproduced by then. In the relatively primitive farming communities of Africa, the Mediterranean region, and India, child mortality was formerly high, and medical care for sick and fragile children, rare. Therefore, children who had sickle cell anemia have had less chance for survival than normal children.

With improved public health and medicine in these areas of the world, the disease is now prevalent in modern cities in Africa, for example. As malaria is eradicated, the presence of the trait will no longer be of benefit to persons having it. In fact, it will be of some disadvantage. This is the situation in the United States today.

COOLEY'S ANEMIA

This anemia, also known as thalassemia major and Mediterranean anemia, is not a single disease, but refers to four or more separate types of mutations of genes controlling hemoglobin production. The person with the disease has an insufficient amount of hemoglobin to carry enough oxygen to the body's tissues to permit normal functions, growth, and development. The severe anemia results in decreased function of the vital organs and, finally, death.

The treatment of the disease is regular blood transfusions. Children receiving this treatment can be relatively active and live a fairly normal life for many years. However, regular blood transfusions over a long period of time may result in other medical complications.

The person who has one normal gene for hemoglobin production and one for the trait does not become ill because the normal gene allows the body to produce enough hemoglobin for normal life. This condition is sometimes called thalassemia minor.

Again, the carrier of this trait has the possibility of transmitting the defect to offspring. If two carriers reproduce, for each pregnancy they have a 25 percent chance of producing a child with the disease.

Cooley's anemia is found primarily in the population surrounding the Mediterranean Sea, such as Italian, Greek, and Arab populations. It has been known in Greece since the time of Alexander the Great, five thousand years ago. It is estimated that 15 to 20 percent of all Greek Americans carry the trait.

There has been popular confusion about the difference between sickle disease and Cooley's anemia. They are similar in that both are inherited disorders causing anemia. While sickle cell is due to a genetic point mutation coding for a specific amino acid in one of the hemoglobin chains, Cooley's anemia is due to a mutation of a gene controlling the *rate* of hemoglobin chain production. A reduced amount of a normal hemoglobin chain is the result. In sickle cell, there is a qualitative defect; in Cooley's anemia, there is a quantitative defect. It was mentioned before that it is possible for people to have a mixture of the traits. One physician reported several black patients and one white patient who each had genes for each trait.

CLASSROOM MANAGEMENT

The student with a serious anemic disorder is a susceptible child who requires more than ordinary good health care and watchfulness. An anemic person, by definition, has a lower number of red blood cells than is normal. Therefore, the anemic individual will appear pale, tire easily, and have less energy. These signs of anemia will appear in children with the disease. Children with sickle cell disease are physically fragile children. They should not be involved in vigorous exercise because the increased utilization of oxygen from the blood predisposes them to a crisis.

A crisis will require prompt medical attention to the symptoms. A disease crisis can come on slowly, in which case the teacher might have observed listlessness in the student. The child might have complained of pain or evidenced some joint swelling. These symptoms should be reported to the school nurse, parents, or hospital. The channels of communication will have been worked out in advance between the family and medical personnel. If a crisis comes on quickly, this is a medical emergency that requires immediate hospitalization, possibly by ambulance. Prompt transfusions or blood thinners may be necessitated in order to prevent tissue damage. Pain relievers may be essential to the sufferer's comfort.

The teacher can help to lower physical and psychological stress for children with sickle cell disease and for their parents as well. The school staff should be watchful of physical signs of crisis and be understanding of the child without much energy, who must endure frequent pain and hospitalizations. We can be hopeful with the child with a life threatening disease because the chances are improving for this boy or girl to have a more normal life.

PREVENTION SERVICES

Both sickle cell anemia and sickle cell trait can be readily identified by routine blood tests. Populations at risk, that is populations where there is a high prevalence of the gene in their gene pool, can be screened to identify carriers of the trait.

If people with these hereditary anemic diseases and carriers of these diseases want to prevent the birth of defective offspring, they have a number of options. Two carriers might decide not to produce offspring together because they have a 25 percent chance of having a defective child for each pregnancy. A person with the disease might choose to only produce offspring with someone who is not a carrier and not diseased (childbirth is more risky for women with sickle cell disease and Cooley's anemia). This option might be difficult given the fact that the number of available sexual partners is not always multiple. If persons who are carriers or manifest these diseases want substantially to reduce the percentage of the trait in the gene pools of their groups, they should not produce offspring at all, or else they will be perpetuating the trait.

In Pittsburgh, Pennsylvania, a sickle cell society was founded by Nathaniel Murray who was, as far as he knew, at fifty-three the oldest survivor of sickle cell disease in the United States. Services of this founding group included setting up a blood bank for families who need blood transfusions, dissemination of information and the establishment of free blood-screening programs in high schools of the city. It was very soon found that counselling and education services were needed to accompany the screening programs.

Mr. Murray and his medical advisor gave freely of their time to speak to various groups and agencies about sickle cell disease. In a quiet, dignified, and understated manner, he would describe the vicissitudes of his disease: the crises, pain, hospitalizations, and open sores. While obviously a person who had fulfilled himself deeply in this life, he was convincing in his belief that sickle cell disease was too excrutiating to be risked in offspring. (Mr. Murray died the night he was to have spoken to one of the writer's classes.)

Recently, Americans of Greek and Italian extraction have become concerned about the prevalence of abnormal trait in their populations and have formed the Cooley's Anemia Blood and Research Foundation for Children, Inc. Information about the disease is being disseminated to young persons through church publications, walk-a-thons, etc.

When information about heredity is disseminated to youth, it must be very carefully done. When blood tests are available, the screening is voluntary and confidential. Young persons are told the facts about their inheritance, such as their probabilities of transmitting the trait and producing diseased offspring, objectively and without further coercion and follow-up. Nevertheless, knowledge about heredity has created some unexpected social problems, both in the United States and in programs in Greece.

One problem is simply misinterpretation of the facts. Young persons (and probably their elders) sometimes confused the carrier state with the disease state, which seems to result in despondency or fear on the part of an identified carrier. Another problem is that persons may begin to avoid carriers as if they had a "bad seed" and were different from others. Yet, as the reader knows by now, the fact should be stressed with all young persons that *everybody* carries defective genes, and they will show sooner or later by chance. With some defective genes, we are lucky enough to be able to identify them and reduce our probabilities of transmitting them to offspring. It must be emphasized, again, that the decision whether to have offspring should be made by the parents and should be respected.

Review Guide

After reading Chapter 22 the reader should be able to define the following terms:

red blood cells	sickle cell anemia
hemoglobin	malaria
sickle cells	Cooley's anemia
sickle cell trait	thalassemia minor

After reading Chapter 22 the reader should be able to answer the following questions:
1. Why does a person with sickle cell trait seem essentially healthy?
2. Why is a person with only sickle cells anemic?

3. What is the difference between sickle cell and Cooley's anemia with regard to blood formation?

4. What are at least five symptoms a student with sickle cell may show?

5. What are the chances in each pregnancy for a couple who both have trait to produce a child with sickle cell or Cooley's anemia?

6. Why did the trait for sickle cell proliferate?

7. What should the teacher do with regard to a crisis of a student with sickle cell?

8. What are the options open to carriers of sickle cell or Cooley's anemia trait?

9. What are two common hazards associated with screening problems of youth in populations at high risk for sickle cell and Cooley's anemia?

Chapter 23

CYSTIC FIBROSIS

He, being made perfect
in a short time,
Fulfilled a long time,
For his soul pleased the Lord
Epitaph for one
dying young
St. Pauls Cathedral,
Melbourne, Australia.

CYSTIC FIBROSIS (CF) is the most common of the life threatening genetic disorders in the United States and Canada and occurs in one in every 1,500 births. Most is seen in white children. Cystic fibrosis is a chronic, noncontagious, hereditary disorder of the *exocrine* glands; these are glands that secrete to their outer surface rather than inward to the bloodstream or lymph (as endocrine glands do). The mucus, saliva, and sweat produced by the exocrine glands are chemically abnormal in cystic fibrosis.

SYMPTOMS OF CYSTIC FIBROSIS

Most of the symptoms and complications of CF are associated with the unusually thick and sticky mucus, which interferes with the functioning of the lungs and digestive system. The underlying cause of the disorder is not understood.

There is great variation in the severity of this disease, so it may not be recognized until children are older, or even in adulthood. It is important to diagnose CF as early in life as possible so that treatment can prevent or postpone lung damage and retarded growth. Later changes become irreversible, but progressive infection and damage may be controlled.

When cystic fibrosis is suspected, a test of the salt content of the

285

sweat is analyzed. Even though sweat tests are commonly used, the disease often goes undetected in young children for well over a year after the first symptoms are shown.

Cystic fibrosis is a great masquerader. It is often diagnosed as pneumonia, chronic bronchitis, asthma, celiac disease, or malnutrition. If a child is being treated for one of these conditions but also has a dry, hacking cough, unusual appetite, and small stature, a check should be made for CF. In some children with CF the lung problems cause the most distress and require the most medical attention, while in others, digestive symptoms appear first and are the most troublesome.

The normal lung can be thought of as a large tree with the windpipe (trachea) being the trunk and the branches the bronchial tubes (bronchi and smaller bronchioles) that extend into each lung. When we inhale, the lungs and bronchial tubes increase in size. When we exhale, they decrease in size, having expelled the air. The cells lining the bronchial tubes secrete mucous, which is carried out of the lungs on fine hairs (cilia) that line the walls of the bronchial tubes and wind pipe. It is constantly carried away from the lungs to trap inhaled particles, thereby keeping the lungs clear. The mucous is swallowed or spat out in sputum.

Cystic fibrosis is the most common cause of chronic lung disease in children. In the lung affected by CF, a thick, sticky mucus is exuded, which does not move effectively. Therefore, it accumulates in the small branches of the bronchial tubes, causing blocking or trapping of air (overinflation) and small areas of lung collapse (atelectasis).

Without treatment, sufferers will develop increasing areas of overinflation, lung collapse, and infections such as bronchitis (inflammation of the mucous membrane) and pneumonia (inflammation of the lungs). Later symptoms include shortness of breath, fatigue, a barrel-shaped chest, and frequent coughing with sputum. There may be clubbing of the fingers and toes and a decreased appetite. Because of the breathing difficulties, heart complications may arise. Generally, it is the severity of the lung disease that determines how long a child with CF will survive. When CF was first identified, most children having it apparently died in infancy of lung infection.

Cystic fibrosis was not described until 1936, when it was first identified as involving the pancreas, an organ important for digestion of foods. It was observed that infants who had died of lung disease also had cysts and scarring in the pancreas, and from this the disease gets its name. Now it is known that other organs can also be involved. Abnormal mucous is also secreted into the salivary glands, the walls of the stomach, the intestine, and the liver.

Small glands in the pancreas secrete digestive juices into channels that unite into larger and larger ducts and empty into the small intestine. When blockage occurs because of thick, sticky mucous, the glands continue to secrete, swell up, and become cysts with scarred fibrous tissue surrounding them. Less and less digestive secretion reaches the intestine, so symptoms become worse.

When pancreatic juices do not reach the intestines, the stomach and the intestines are full of partially digested food, causing the child to have a round abdomen. The stools are full of undigested food particles and are frequently fatty, bulky, and foul smelling. Children fail to gain weight despite a voracious appetite.

Diabetes is associated with a pancreas that does not make insulin, important for digestion. More persons with CF develop diabetes than in a random population. Some have small or large involvement of the liver.

The earliest gastrointestinal indications of the disorder may be present at birth. In from 5 to 15 percent of affected infants, the intestinal tract becomes blocked by a long plug of meconium, the substance found in a newborn's intestines and eliminated naturally. When the cystic fibrosis is severe enough to prevent pancreatic juices from reaching the intestines, the meconium becomes too hard to expel (meconium ileus). The infant must have surgery, which will save the life in about half the cases.

Young children with CF may have feeding problems and diarrhea. They may fail to gain weight. When the child gets a cold, it may be difficult to shake off. Coughing, wheezing, and a running nose may develop and persist. Dehydration in warm weather is possible because of excessive salt loss in sweat.

Cystic fibrosis is usually fatal to children or young adults. However, with the development of antibiotics in the 1940s and 1950s, the average age of death has risen. During the 1960s more effective means of clearing the lungs and diet control were developed, thereby increasing life expectancy. Furthermore, physicians have become more aware of the disease, contributing to earlier diagnosis and treatment. At present the average age of death is around fourteen years, but an increasing number of children can hope to reach adulthood and live relatively normal lives. A woman with CF can have children. Men with CF are almost always sterile because semen is not emitted, but the sexual function is not usually impaired.

TRANSMISSION OF CYSTIC FIBROSIS

The hereditary transmission of CF is understood, so parents who have had a child with it can predict their chances of having another affected child. This disease is known to be an inborn error of metabolism due to the lack of an enzyme essential to the normal functioning of the body. It is caused by a defect in a single recessive gene located on one of the twenty-two pairs of autosomal chromosomes (Fig. 4). It is recessive, so the child with CF must have inherited a defective gene from each of his or her parents, although they did not show any symptoms. It is estimated that one white person out of twenty in the United Sates carries this gene. Medical researchers have made some progress in identifying a basis for carrier identification. Of course, if a couple has produced one child, boy or girl, with CF, they know their chances are one in four of producing a child with the disease in each subsequent pregnancy.

HOME TREATMENT

The treatment of CF is empirical, that is, it is guided by practical experience. It will depend on the child's symptoms and to some extent on the biases of the particular physician or medical clinic. In most cases it will involve a rigorous home program, eventuating in self-care for the older patient.

The main treatment is directed to keeping the lungs as clear of mucous and free from infection as possible. At home this will be accomplished by postural drainage, the positioning of the body at several different angles so that gravity helps the lungs to discharge the mucous, while that portion of the chest is clapped vigorously as one would bang a catsup bottle. Medical vibrators are used for self-drainage. The use of postural drainage two to four times a day greatly aids in breathing. Some children sleep in a mist tent at night in which a pump fills the air they breathe with extra moisture in order to thin the mucous. Sometimes an aerosol treatment, with the child breathing aerosolized medicine through a mouthpiece, is recommended before postural drainage, or as a method of taking antibiotics.

SCHOOL MANAGEMENT

The teacher cannot help but be sympathetic to parents and their children who must engage in the arduous procedures and costly treatments that this disease entails. Very few management problems will be encountered in school, however.

Physical activity is an important aid in preventing secretions from blocking the lungs. Therefore, the regular recess and gym activities of running, swimming, and active play should definitely be encouraged. However, diving should be prohibited. High altitudes may have a bad effect on the person with CF, precluding such activities as mountain climbing and high skiing. A child with CF may experience fatigue and limitations on physical energy and may be small for his age.

The student may have to cough very frequently. He or she needs to cough to clear the lungs so should be made comfortable about it in the class or in leaving the room. Peers can be assured that the cough is not contagious. Youth with CF are strongly advised not to smoke.

The use of antibiotics is essential to keep down infections. The student may need to take medications during the school day. These may be changed every two or three months because individuals build up a resistance to particular antibiotics with frequent use. In hot weather, particularly when playing hard, the student might need to take salt pills.

Because of the problems surrounding the digestive system, the child may have a modified diet with a limited fat intake and some control of starches. It does not have to be strictly enforced in school, however. To make up for the pancreatic juices that do not reach the intestine, a powdered enzyme preparation is sprinkled on the food eaten by people with CF all of their lives. Most children dislike the additive intensely.

Even with the special diet and added enzymes, many children with the disease must eat at least twice as much as normal youngsters to maintain near normal weight and growth. The affected student may take seconds and thirds in the lunchroom. This appetite should be taken as a matter of course rather than discussed. Because the stools are bulky, they may need to be eliminated more frequently during class hours. The stools will have a characteristic odor.

A child with CF may be subject to many colds and even pneumonia because of lung involvement. In consequence, he or she may have frequent absences from school, particularly in bad weather. Still, these children can be expected to be normal learners. In fact, they have sometimes been noted to be exceptionally studious, possibly in response to curtailment of more athletic school activities.

The teacher should maintain a hopeful attitude with children with cystic fibrosis. When considering many of the life threatening illnesses, one can point to advances in medical research and treatment that have changed the course of the diseases within one's lifetime. That hope can be extended with great encouragement in the case of cystic fibrosis. In a few years it has gone from a usually fatal disease of early childhood to a manageable disease of childhood and even adulthood.

Discussion in some sections of this book has emphasized the important role that the State Bureau of Vocational Rehabilitation can play in the education and vocational planning and placement of handicapped youth over sixteen years old. Vocational rehabilitation services are only available to persons with the potential of becoming economically productive. When planning for youth with life threatening illnesses, the physicians' referral and assessment are often crucial in getting a client accepted into a Vocational Rehabilitation Program. They may be called upon to intercede on behalf of their patients when difficulties arise. The teacher may give valuable input to the rehabilitation team in developing a reasonable educational and vocational future for the student with CF.

Review Guide

After reading Chapter 23 the reader should be able to define the following terms:

exocrine glands   postural drainage
cystic fibrosis   autosomal recessive trait

After reading Chapter 23 the reader should be able to answer the following questions:

1. How is the lung involved when a child has cystic fibrosis?
2. If parents have had one child with CF, what are their chances of producing another?
3. What are the three main digestive symptoms of cystic fibrosis?
4. What three medicines might the student with CF take in school?
5. Why does the child with CF cough often?
6. Why might the student with CF have frequent absences?
7. What is a stipulation made by the Bureau of Vocational Rehabilitation with regard to funding handicapped persons?

Chapter 24

MUSCULAR DYSTROPHY

He who has a "why" to live for can bear almost any "how."
Nietzsche

TYPES OF DYSTROPHIES

MUSCULAR DYSTROPHY (MD) refers to several disorders grouped together because they all involve progressive weakening of the muscles supporting the skeleton. Most of the dystrophies are known to be due to a genetically determined metabolic error. Two types, which do not usually occur in childhood, are classified on the basis of the muscle group affected (limb-girdle muscular dystrophy and facioscapulohumeral muscular dystrophy). The symptoms of muscle weakness in these forms may begin as early as between the ages of twelve and twenty. The pitch of the voice will lower in males and females, and walking will gradually become difficult, as the disease progresses. While these diseases are debilitating, adults may live successfully a long time with them, being able to walk twenty-five to thirty years after the onset.

Several inherited diseases (classified as spinal muscular atrophy of childhood) are characterized by progressive degeneration of motor nerve cells of the spinal column. The degeneration may progress to the motor nerves in the brain stem, causing death. Traditionally the term Werdnig-Hoffmann disease has described a serious, rapid progression, which begins in infancy and results in death before school age. A more benign form (Kugelberg-Welander disease) can cause muscle weakness and symptoms similar to those of muscular dystrophy. However, the outcome of this disease is much more variable than Duchenne muscular dystrophy.

293

The most common form of muscular dystrophy, Duchenne type muscular dystrophy, is a childhood form. In this disease there is a progressive diffuse weakness of all muscle groups characterized by a degeneration of muscle cells and their replacement by fat and fibrous tissue. It occurs in one in 5,000 births and seems to occur equally among races. Boys are mainly affected, but a few girls will have the disease.

SYMPTOMS OF MUSCULAR DYSTROPHY, DUCHENNE TYPE

Typically, the symptoms begin during the first years of life with enlargement of the muscles of the calves of the legs and in those surrounding the pelvis. At this stage the child may seem awkward and clumsy. Tiptoeing may be an early sign of weakness in the muscles of the foot. When getting up from the floor the child may use his hands and arms to "climb up himself." The disability progresses rapidly to involve the muscles of the trunk. At this stage the child may show poor posture with a protruding abdomen and a swayback (lordosis). More slowly, the disability progresses to the muscles in the arms, legs, and face. As the muscles become infiltrated with fat and fibrous tissue, the body becomes increasingly deformed. Eventually the child loses the ability to walk, to use upper limbs, and, in some cases, to speak.

The progression is more rapid the earlier the first symptoms were first experienced. When the condition begins in later childhood, it progresses more slowly. With onset in early childhood, children have to use wheelchairs by about nine to twelve years old. Death can be expected within ten to fifteen years after the first symptoms. Most sufferers are dead by twenty years old. Death usually occurs in the preteens, frequently from respiratory complications or an acute infection that the weakened youngster cannot overcome. Because of the progressive nature of the disease, it is sometimes called progressive muscular dystrophy.

Sometimes the affected child will look very muscular because of a false enlargement, which is due to the replacement of muscle with fat. Enlargement in the calf of the leg is most common. For this reason, the disease is sometimes called pseudohypertrophic (false enlargement) muscular dystrophy. Both obesity and underweight condition can be associated with the disorder. There is no existing treatment or therapy that will influence the course of the disease in any but a slight degree. There are supportive medical and rehabilitative services that can reduce the side effects of the crippling process and make life for the child more comfortable at school and at home.

HEREDITY OF MUSCULAR DYSTROPHY

It is important to understand the hereditary mechanism of muscular dystrophy because there are options open to people regarding its propagation. It has been estimated that up to one-third of all cases of muscular dystrophy are sporadic; that is, they are due to a mutation. If there is no history of muscular dystrophy in a family, this situation may be the case. Once mutation occurs in the genes, however, it will be transmitted in the future.

The typical mode of inheritance is a sex-linked, recessive gene (Fig. 5). Therefore, it is transmitted by a mother, who is a carrier of the gene on one of her X chromosomes, to her boys. For each pregnancy she has a 50 percent chance of giving that gene to male children, who will then show the disease, since the Y chromosome of the male does not have corresponding genes to mask the recessive. On the other hand, a father will always have a normal gene on his X chromosome, which he will always contribute to all female children. The mother will have a 50-50 chance of giving either of her X chromosomes to her daughters. The daughters will not show the disease, but half of them will be carriers. Mothers who have produced one son with muscular dystrophy know that they have the same probabilities of producing another, without intervention.

If the mother wants to be sure not to have more children with this disease, there are two options available: one is, of course, to produce no more children. This can be assured through abstinence, contraception, or sterilization. Secondly, she can take a more drastic measure. She can decide to risk pregnancy, have a test *in utero* (aminocentesis) to determine the sex of her child, and have an abortion of all boys. If she takes this option, she has a 50 percent chance of having aborted a normal boy.

Sisters of brothers with muscular dystrophy know that they have a 50 percent chance of being a carrier of the defect. Usually their blood will have an elevation of a particular muscle enzyme CPK (creatine phoskinase) before their maturity. Testing can be arranged through the Muscular Dystrophy Association or genetic clinics to see if they are carriers. When girls have muscular dystrophy, it seems to be transmitted as an autosomal recessive gene.

REHABILITATION—SELF-CARE TECHNIQUES

A self-care and rehabilitation program should attempt to help the child approximate as normal a psychosocial development as possible in congruence with an attempt to delay the progressive physical deterioration of the disease. The progressiveness of muscular dystrophy requires that those involved with the care of the afflicted child be flexible and adaptable in their expectations of the child and in care techniques. Many of the care techniques will be discovered through trial and error and are, therefore, highly individualized.

To assure independence and mobility for the greatest length of time, leg braces and a standing table are necessary for those who can no longer support themselves standing. The bracing prevents the development of joint deformities and severe contractures in the weight-bearing joints. Long leg braces allow the children to be more independent when performing such duties as using the toilet or getting a glass of water.

For the child who is still able to walk, a high stool or chair suited to his particular height will enable him to arise without assistance. Placing the child in a standing table prevents urinary complications and maintains the child's sense of standing balance. These preventative measures along with the self-care program are the foundation of treatment for children with muscular dystrophy.

Physical aids are used to allow for a maximum amount of independence in performing the activities of daily living at various stages in the progress of the disease. When assistance from another person is not required, it should not be given, although the task will be less efficiently performed. It is important for the child to experience a feeling of complete independence in performing some or most tasks. The child may wear oversized clothing and wide pants so that dressing will be easier, for example.

A wheelchair with such features as adjustable, swing-out foot-rests, extended leg rests, removable step-down arms, a zipper back, and good brakes should be acquired when the child is no longer walking, but not sooner. Confining the child to a wheelchair prematurely is to his detriment. A motorized wheelchair may eventually be used. The Muscular Dystrophy Association of America can provide information about financial aid toward the purchase of a wheelchair.

A smooth, sturdy board that bridges the wheelchair and seat at an even level will enable the child to move independently from car to wheelchair or vice versa. The child's inch-by-inch progress will be slow, but this task can be performed without any assistance.

A toilet seat can be raised to be level with the wheelchair by purchasing a commercial attachment or placing a few wooden blocks on the underside of the seat. This again allows for complete independence in that the child is able to maneuver himself from wheelchair to toilet and back again without being lifted. The child with MD remains continent, so bowel and bladder control are not a problem. A male urinal can be used if the child is difficult to transfer to the toilet.

When eating, an MD child should always be allowed to place his elbows on the table since they serve as a pivot for lifting his spoon, fork, or glass. An arm sling suspended from the wheelchair will raise the child's arm to a position where he can perform activities and will greatly assist the child who has difficulty in raising his arm to the table. A long-handled teaspoon requires less strength to grip and therefore makes eating easier. A child can pick up things on the floor or above his head with a commercial reacher that contracts in an accordian fashion or is made like tongs.

THE CHILD WITH MUSCULAR DYSTROPHY AT SCHOOL

The teacher may have been the first to recognize early signs of the disease. The child may have stumbled or had trouble mounting the stairs or getting up from the floor. Again it is stressed that the teacher should not make the medical diagnosis, but rather recommend a medical examination when students seem to be acting abnormally. Unfortunately, there are reports of educators labeling early muscular dystrophy as "learning disability" or "educational handicap" or "minimal cerebral dysfunction," to the detriment of the children and their families.

Physicians have observed that muscular dystrophied children made much better medical progress while in school than confined to their homes. Being away from home for an entire day, or part of a day, has proven helpful, since it alleviates the effects of understimulation and isolation for the child and gives a measure of freedom to the parent.

Of course this very fragile, vulnerable child will require very close and ongoing medical management. Particular attention will be paid to upper respiratory infections and sickness, which could keep him bedridden for some time. It is much more difficult for the child with MD to bounce back after an illness that would be rather routine for a normal child. Therefore, this student may have more frequent, prolonged absences than his peers.

As a rule, these children are very cooperative and cheerful in the classroom. It is far better whenever possible to keep them in the environment of their regular schools with ongoing accommodations for their management than to remove them to a special school. Once transportation is made available, the dystrophic child becomes easily absorbed in the special or regular class. It is helpful if the school building has special equipment such as ramps, handrails, mechanical lifts, wide hallways and doors, adjustable desks, and accessible bathrooms.

Some studies have been reported in medical journals that have associated low average or borderline intelligence with muscular dystrophy. It seems to be the experience of teachers, however, that these children run the gamut of academic ability, and some are superior learners. Certainly they are often the best learners in special classes for physically handicapped students.

It is quite understandable that these children might show depressed IQ scores, particularly in timed tests, tests requiring writing, or tests that take a relatively long time to complete. Further, they may very well lack the motivation to do their best at a psychometric task that seems so irrelevant to their situation. On the other hand, they are usually eager to accomplish the educational tasks in the classroom where they are part of the school society.

It would be a great disservice to the student in class to lower expectations below what can reasonably be fostered, given the disability. It would also be a mistake to abandon all future aspirations, because some MD children *do* live into adulthood and have become successful college students, mathematicians, artists, etc. In any given case, the diagnosis *could* be wrong, or the disease atypical when it runs its course. These things do happen and lend some hope to children who, as a group, have such a limited prognosis.

When a student has probably a shorter life expectation, the teacher may pay a little more attention to the quality of his life each day. If he hates mathematics and loves reading, it might be better to encourage a literature course instead of calculus. Enrichment courses can be used to stimulate new interests such as music appreciation, creative writing, arts and crafts, and skills such as playing a musical instrument, balancing a budget, repairing household gadgets, typewriting, sewing, and weaving. The development of these skills and interests helps the child to utilize constructively the large amount of leisure time at his disposal rather than spend an excessive amount of time watching television, which many homebound children do.

The Library of Congress is eager to extend the talking book program to all eligible patients afflicted with muscular dystrophy and related neuromuscular diseases, many of whom may not know of its existence. Students suffering from muscular dystrophy and related neuromuscular disorders can have enormous intellectual and emotional satisfaction that comes from "reading" even when their disabilities prevent them from handling printed books. As a result of legislation enacted in 1966, such physically handicapped persons can now enjoy the talking books formerly available only to the blind. The range of materials extends from Shakespeare through popular current works to the best in children's literature.

In addition, over twenty different magazines are available on records, including *Newsweek* and *Sports Illustrated* and, for younger readers, *Jack and Jill* and *Ranger Rick's Nature Magazine*. To be eligible, a person must have any physical limitation preventing him from reading regular print books. These limitations include inability to turn pages, inability to hold a book, or extreme weakness or excessive fatigue.

Talking books are free on loan to anyone whose doctor, nurse, teacher, or librarian testifies to his eligibility. He can receive without charge a talking book phonograph, which is his for as long as he needs it. Once the person has received the machine, he can order free talking books–best sellers, mysteries, magazines, and others–which are circulated from regional libraries across the United States. Also, he will receive, again at no cost, a regular subscription to *Talking Book Topics,* a bimonthly magazine of new titles available on talking books.

Application for the service can be made through any local affiliate of MDAA. If there is no local affiliate, the eligible patient should have his disability certified by a physician, social worker, nurse, or therapist and apply directly to the Division for the Blind and Physically Handicapped, Library of Congress, Washington, D.C. 20542.

When a student has a fatal disease, the teacher must be very cautious in supplying even correct specific information about it. For example, it would be most unwise to give a Fact Sheet on Muscular Dystrophy to a child with that condition. Furthermore, it is the province of the physician, rather than the teacher, to give it to the parents of the child. Specific medical issues should be handled by a medical expert. When in doubt, the teacher should not hesitate to consult other school personnel and any members of the rehabilitation team before using any resources (such as those listed in the Appendix) or knowledge from them for other than his or her own information. In this area, it is better to do nothing than risk doing the wrong thing!

In some ways MD is one of the cruelest diseases. While other children are growing physically in a positive direction, the child with MD is going downhill. He cannot do this month what he could do last month. He suffers complications of bones and muscles. He cannot have ambitious hopes for the future. On the positive side, the condition is painless, so the child escapes the suffering that accompanies some other life threatening conditions. There is no degeneration of mental or sensory faculties. Therefore, this child really can enjoy each day for most of his brief years. Naturally, there are going to be moments of great despondency, anger, and fear in the child who faces early death. This may be doubly true if the child has watched siblings die of the disease already.

The attitude of the teacher and peers should not be an added burden, but rather a help to the handicapped student. The teacher's philosophy of life will depend on many things: his or her experiences, age, religion, and temperament. The attitude will ultimately reflect how the teacher views his own, most certain, death. Each individual has to come to grips with life's ultimate realities in his own way. It is important for teachers of these very vulnerable children to "get themselves together," so that they can give strength and calm to the stricken pupil and others in the school.

Review Guide

After reading Chapter 24 the reader should be able to define the following terms:

pseudohypertrophic muscular dystrophy

Duchenne muscular dystrophy

After reading Chapter 24 the reader should be able to answer the following questions:

1. What are the main symptoms of childhood muscular dystrophy?
2. How long can the disease be expected to last?
3. Is muscular dystrophy associated with mental retardation?
4. How much physical pain is associated with muscular dystrophy?
5. Why might a child with average intelligence show depressed IQ performance after contracting muscular dystrophy?
6. What is the preferred type of educational placement after a child has been diagnosed as having muscular dystrophy?

7. What cautions should a teacher exercise about sharing information about fatal diseases?
8. What organization is helpful to children who have muscular dystrophy and their parents?

SENSORY IMPAIRMENTS

Silence is painful; but in silence things take form, and we must wait and watch. In us, in our secret depth, lies the knowing element which sees and hears that which we do not see and hear.

Kahlil Gibran

The two senses most important for human learning are sight and hearing. Impairment in one or both of the sensory systems of the eye and ear is of great significance for education. For this reason, management and educational strategies and materials have been highly developed in the areas of education of the visually or hearing impaired student and of the deaf or blind student. The teacher who is not a specialist in these areas can expect much co-operation from special teachers and relevant agencies when a student with sensory impairment is a member of the class.

Chapter 25

VISUAL DISORDERS

"Listening to a tale told in the dark is one of the most ancient of man's entertainments."

Moss Hart
Act One

I have walked with people
Whose eyes are full of light
But who see nothing in sea or sky,
Nothing in city streets,
Nothing in books.

It were far better to sail forever
In the night of blindness
Than to be content
With the mere act of seeing.

The only lightless dark
In the night of darkness
Is ignorance and insensibility.

Helen Keller

THE VISUAL SYSTEM consists of the eyeballs, through which light is focused and converted through photochemical means to electrical activity, which is then transmitted by the optic nerves and tracts to the brain, where visual perception or "seeing" takes place. In addition, numerous accessory structures are present, such as the tear glands, the muscles that move the eyes, and the eyelids. Disorders in parts of any of these structures can result in some degree and type of visual defect. It is estimated that one-fourth of all

305

school children have or will develop visual problems. Total lack of vision is rare. Children who are considered legally blind constitute the low incidence of 10 percent of the blind population. An estimated one child in 500 is significantly visually impaired.

Among visually impaired young children there is a significant proportion of children with multiple handicaps. This group, estimated to be as high as 40 percent of visually impaired children, will have problems associated with other categories of the physically and cognitively disabled as well as visual disability.

School-aged children have about 85,000 eye mishaps a year. These occur for the most part in unsupervised play with balls, sticks, stones, knives, air rifles, and firecrackers. For some unknown reason, damage to one eye will sometimes be followed by a gradual diminution of vision in the other eye.

One-half of the blindness found in the United States today is found among people sixty-five or older and is primarily associated with late effects of diabetes. As with the multiply handicapped youngster, the older person with multiple disabilities has many more difficulties to contend with than the person who is normal except for a visual problem.

IMPAIRMENTS OF THE EYE

The eyeball is an extremely complex organ, which developed embryonically as an outcropping of brain tissue. It is spherical in shape and composed of three layers (Fig. 21).

The Outer Layer of the Eyeball

The outer layer of the eyeball has firm fibrous tissue, the *sclera,* which is continuous with the sheath of the optic nerve and also continuous with the outer, transparent portion of the eyeball, the *cornea.* The sclera is the white of the eye. The cornea is the clear, shiny window of the eye. Most of the refraction of light rays occurs at the front surface of the cornea. The light rays are bent to enter the interior of the eyeball.

Gonorrhea is a very common venereal disease, which can be passed on to the infant during its passage through the birth canal. In former times in the United States this bacterial infection might lead to severe corneal scarring and perforations, which caused

Schematic Section of the Human Eye

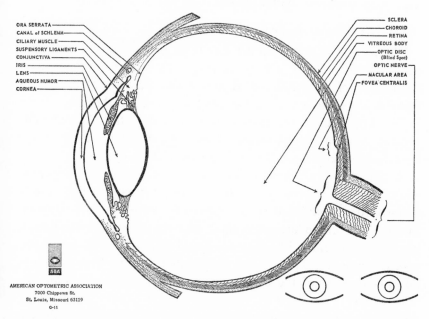

ORA SERRATA
CANAL of SCHLEMM
CILIARY MUSCLE
SUSPENSORY LIGAMENTS
CONJUNCTIVA
IRIS
LENS
AQUEOUS HUMOR
CORNEA

SCLERA
CHOROID
RETINA
VITREOUS BODY
OPTIC DISC
(Blind Spot)
OPTIC NERVE
MACULAR AREA
FOVEA CENTRALIS

AMERICAN OPTOMETRIC ASSOCIATION
7000 Chippewa St.
St. Louis, Missouri 63119
G-11

Figure 21. Schematic section of the human eye. Courtesy of the American Optometric Association.

blindness in the child. In some parts of the world this is still the case. However, in the United States there are nationwide laws mandating an application of silver nitrate or penicillin to the neonate's eyes in order to prevent development of this infection. Therefore, blindness caused by gonorrhea is virtually nonexistent today in America.

The most common cause of blindness in the world, though not in the United States, is a viral infection called trachoma, which effects the cornea and lid of the eye. Symptoms are redness and swelling, tearing, pain, and fear of light. In a late stage, scars and corneal thickening cause blindness. Trachoma can be successfully treated with sulpha drugs.

The cornea is one tissue of the body that can be successfully transplanted from person to person. Therefore, persons with corneal vision problems can sometimes be enormously improved by this surgery. Persons can will their corneas to tissue banks upon their death to enable another to see.

The Middle Layer of the Eye

The middle layer of the eye has three parts. There are a number of diseases of the eye, some temporary, which involve an inflammation of these different tissues. Some are associated with infections, some with other illnesses such as juvenile arthritis.

The first part of the middle layer is called the choroid. The choroid is a nourishing vascular tissue lying between the sclera and the retina, which is a part of the inner layer of the eyeball.

A complication involving choroid tissue occurs in congenital toxoplasmosis. Toxoplasmosis is a parasitic organism that infects many bird and animals. It is commonly transmitted to humans through raw or undercooked meat and the feces of cats. Infants who have congenital infection are found to have defects in 20 percent of the cases. The visual impairment they may have is due to an inflammation of the choroid tissue. They may have brain defects and epilepsy as well. Toxoplasmosis is usually a very mild disease after infancy. One woman in three or four has antibodies indicating that she has had the disease and is therefore immune. A blood test is available that can determine if a person is in risk of infection and needs to be extra cautious during pregnancy. Teachers of adolescents can alert their students to these facts.

The choroid is continuous with the ciliary body behind the iris, which in turn is continuous with the iris. The iris is the colored part of the eye, which is perforated in the center with the small opening or pupil through which light enters from the clear cornea. The iris acts as a diaphragm of a camera. The pupil size gets larger with decreasing light and smaller with increasing light. Thereby, the iris regulates the amount of light reaching the interior of the eye.

There is a rare condition, usually inherited, which consists of mild to severe partial absence of the iris of both eyes and other associated visual abnormalities. There is a consequent decreased vision with this condition. Vision can sometimes be improved by the use of contact lenses, which often will have an iris painted on them to make the eyes appear more normal.

There is an autosomal recessive hereditary condition called albinism in which skin and hair pigments are reduced or absent. Albinism can occur even among races whose members usually have very dark skin. In albinism, pigment is also absent in the iris, so pinkish colored eyes result. Vision may be impaired to the point of legal blindness with concomitant involuntary oscillations of the eye called nystagmus. Most people with albinism have some useful vision. The albino is very bothered by bright light and needs to wear dark glasses in its presence.

Between the clear cornea and the iris is a transparent fluid, which is produced by the ciliary body. This fluid is responsible for the pressure within the eye. The watery substance is produced continually, and it exits from the eye through the structures of the anterior chamber angle between the iris and the cornea.

When the liquid is prevented from exiting by abnormalities, pressure within the eyeball builds up, progressively deteriorating the tissues of the eye in the condition called glaucoma. This condition usually develops in adults and rather gradually. Without medical intervention, glaucoma will cause blindness.

There are several rare types of glaucoma that affect children. In little children, the cornea will greatly enlarge with pressure, and eyes will bulge. Early diagnosis and treatment of this condition by eye drops, pills, and possible surgery can prevent or lessen the damage. Unfortunately, the glaucoma is too often discovered only after irreversible damage has occurred in both children and adults. The necessity for routine eye examinations and need for careful attention to small symptoms are highlighted by the case of glaucoma.

The ciliary body is also attached to an important internal structure of the eye, the lens. The lens is a resilient, transparent, biconvex structure that aids in the selective focusing of the light rays (first bent by the cornea) on to the light-sensitive membrane of the inner layer of the eye, the retina. In *near vision,* changes in the ciliary muscle cause the lens to change the shape or increase the refraction of the lens. This process is called accommodation. At the same time, contraction of the pupil and convergence of the two eyes occur reflexively. The *near point of vision* is the closest point upon which the eyes can focus clearly.

In older persons the crystalline lens becomes less elastic and the near point of distinct vision is removed farther from the eye, so they have increasing difficulty focusing on close objects. This condition is presbyopia (presby =old, opia =defect of the eye). That is why most persons need glasses or stronger corrections in their glasses as they grow older. In *far vision* the lens is flattened to focus on more distant objects, with the muscles around the lens relaxed.

A *cataract* is a clouding of the crystalline lens. Cataracts can occur congenitally because of maternal infections such as rubella or by maternally transmitted syphilis. Half of congenital cataracts are associated with other ocular anomalies as well. Many children who have Down's syndrome develop cataracts in childhood.

Treatment of cataracts in children is not uniformly successful. Sometimes with children cataracts may be treated by medical irradication of the clouded area. In older persons, cataracts that interfere too much with vision require lens removal; this is often necessary with children also. After the removal of the lens, the person is infinitely farsighted. The rays of light are bent by the cornea, but the lens is no longer present to make accommodation for near vision. Therefore, after a cataract operation, the person wears thick corrective lenses and, in some cases, contact lenses. Peripheral vision and depth perception are reduced. There may be some problems if only one lens was removed so there is an imbalance in vision. The important point for the teacher to remember is that a successful cataract operation does not mean the restoration of perfect vision.

A partial or complete dislocation of the lens is associated with an autosomal dominant condition called Marfan's syndrome. In children with this condition, the tissues of the ciliary body that normally hold the lens in place do not work effectively. This condition is often correctable with high power glasses. In this syndrome, there may be other physical abnormalities as well, such as associated hearing loss or heart disease. Persons with this syndrome have a gaunt, bony appearance with long, spindly fingers. It is speculated that Abraham Lincoln and some of his children had the syndrome.

The Inner Layer of the Eyeball

In the interior of the eyeball, the rounded space between the lens and the inner layer is filled with a transparent, gelatinelike substance that occupies two-thirds of the volume of the back of the eyeball. Diseases of this substance may lead to retinal detachment. Also, congenital or acquired diseases can cause the substance to lose its transparency. Fortunately, this opacity can often be surgically corrected.

The inner layer of the eyeball is a neural layer of transparent membrane called the retina, which is light sensitive. Light waves bent and focused onto the retina cause a photochemical conversion on the photo receptors of the retina. Electric signals thus produced are transmitted to the optic nerve (the second cranial nerve) at a position on the retina where there are no light receptors. That place is the blind spot.

The light-sensitive cells are of two kinds, called the rods and cones. The slender rods are more sensitive in dim light and report the black and white world of night vision. These 120 million receptors are on the periphery of the retina. The thicker cones, comprising the center of the retina, need the stronger stimulation of bright light and can distinguish color. There are 7 million cones on each retina. Some persons are born with some degree of color blindness. Those in which it is complete only see the visual world in black, white, and gray as we see it on a black and white television screen.

The teacher might assume that color blindness would be a very significant handicap in certain school situations, such as the art class. Again, limitations should not be assumed beforehand. Color-blind persons have much ingenuity in adapting to their situations. For example, the writer knows a totally color-blind man who has become an expert on metallurgical engravings throughout the world. He also has an important collection of black and white etchings. His knowledge and appreciation of art are surely far above those of the average, color-seeing person.

Most of the cones (that register color) are concentrated in one area of the retina called the macula. The center of this area is called the fovea. It is responsible for the most distinct vision. The fovea is the small portion of the retina used for fine point discrimination tasks. The reception of light outside the area of distinct vision broadens the field of vision, which can then be scanned by the eye for new distinct focus.

Three common refractive errors are associated with inability to focus the light rays on the fovea of the retina (Fig. 22). In nearsightedness (myopia), the light rays focus in front of the retina, because the eyeball is too long. Sometimes this is a progressive condition in children due to the normal increasing growth of the eyeball during childhood. Glasses are almost always required by these children. In farsightedness (hyperopia), the light rays focus

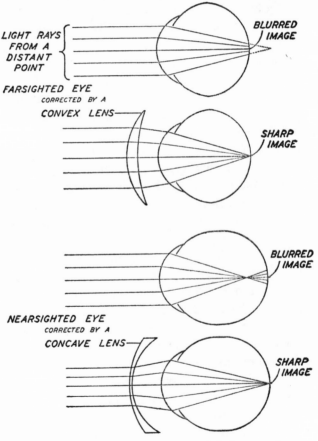

Figure 22. Errors of refraction and their correction.

behind the retina, because the eyeball is too short. To some extent one can accommodate for this through the accommodative mechanism of the eye, but this might lead to eye strain. In astigmatism, the curvature of the cornea is irregular on one or more of the refractive surfaces, so that some light rays are focused in front and some behind the retina. Astigmatism can be accommodated for to some extent, but eye strain might develop unless glasses are prescribed.

Since the cornea, lens, and contents of the eye are transparent, the retina can be seen clearly with a magnifying instrument that shines a light in the eye and magnifies the retinal image. Retinal changes and abnormalities are often specific for various vascular diseases and give evidence for differential diagnoses: the retinal degeneration associated with diabetes is characteristic and easily observable, for example. The ophthalmologist may therefore be the first to recognize some medical problems.

Damage to the macula, the central area of the retina, can severely reduce central vision. Persons with this problem can see objects on the edge of vision, but these become obscured when an effort is made to focus. Some hereditary generative diseases cause progressive degeneration of the retina. Histoplasmosis is a life threatening fungal infection of the macula, which is thought to be transmitted through the fecal matter of chickens.

On the other hand, the peripheral area of the retina can be destroyed to the point that vision is contracted to a very small visual field, as if one were looking down a tube. This is referred to as tunnel vision. A person with this problem might happen to see a doorknob perfectly, for example, but have to do a painstaking visual sweep to find out where the rest of the door was. This person is left with no figure-ground discrimination because only the figure, or part of a figure, or part of a ground can be seen. For this person, reading and other close work are easier than activity that takes place in larger space.

In the early stages of some hereditary retinal degenerative diseases, there is progressive degeneration until the peripheral vision is virtually nonexistent. Retinitis pigmentosa is the most common of these diseases. In this condition, all the layers of the retina are involved in a progressive proliferation of connective tissue and pigment cells of the membrane, with a wasting of the nerve elements. The first sign will be a difficulty in night vision or difficulty seeing in the dark. This is gradually followed by the child's losing peripheral vision. Eventually, central vision is lost at various ages, depending on the hereditary pattern of the disease.

Since the retina is a delicate membrane, it can become detached in a disease process or as a result of severe physical impact to the head. Usually the condition is found in older persons. It can also occur as a result of trauma in children. It is tragically observed in infants and children who were blinded as a result of batterings. These children frequently have other physical problems resulting from the brutality and, understandably, many emotional difficulties.

In 1950 approximately half the blindness of preschool children was caused by a problem of the retina, retrolental fibroplasia (RLF). This condition is associated with too high a content of oxygen being administered to premature babies. In the neonate, a concentration of oxygen over 40 percent in the air stimulates the still-forming retina to grow opaque tissue on the surface, which subsequently hemorrhages and detaches. This caused blindness in many babies. In 1954 the dangers of high concentrations of oxygen were realized. Since then, monitoring devices that regulate carefully the amount given to premature babies have lessened the frequency of RLF. However, there are times when the baby can only be saved if overoxygenation is risked, as in the case of the newborn with cardiac difficulties. Those students who are visually impaired from RLF are usually normal learners, healthy and attractive. They are very easy to assimilate in a regular class and later into adult society.

Malignant tumors can occur in the eyes of children. The most common tumor (or group of tumors) on the retina is treated with radiation therapy in the affected eye or eyes. Surgical removal of the eye or eyes is occasionally necessitated. If treatment is prompt, most children can be cured but will be left with visual impairment. A very rare malignant tumor grows very rapidly in the orbit of the eye and pushes the eye out. It requires removal of the eye, irradiation, and chemotherapy. The treatment is successful in saving life in somewhat less than half of the cases with this problem.

When the entire globe of the eye must be removed, the empty orbit or orbits are fitted with artificial eyes of plastic or glass. These do not help the child to see, but they are of cosmetic benefit.

Retinal problems can arise as a complication of other diseases. A viral infection transmitted from the mother in utero can lead to congenital scarring of the retina. Diseases of the central nervous system often affect the eye, since the optic nerve and retina are a segment of the brain. In multiple sclerosis, vision may be affected but usually returns to normal. Children with leukemia may suffer decreasing vision in one and occasionally both eyes.

Optic Nerve

The base of the skull has two openings for the optic nerve to enter the brain. After the optic nerve leaves each eye at the back of the eyeball, it branches out for the brain's two hemispheres (Fig. 23). To enable us to have stereoscopic vision, part from each eye goes to the right side of the brain and part to the left side of the brain, where they enter the occipital cortex of the brain. Thus, one is not right-eyed, or left-eyed in the sense that one is right- or left-handed or footed. In the latter case, the right hand or foot is regulated from the left side of the brain and vice versa, but each side of the brain "sees" in each eye.

The beginning of visual perception is handled by the neurons on the retina. The forms of things we see can ultimately be reduced to a series of minute lines at angles to each other. Most visual information is concerned with edges, contours, and corners. Some cells of the retina only fire when the image of a line is at a certain angle and some neurons in the brain will only receive information about such a line at one particular place and one precise angle. Farther back in the visual pathway to the brain are still other cells that respond to more specific patterns such as curves or corners. All of these basic sets of cells can be thought of as the building blocks of perception.

It is postulated that there must be a net of neurons that makes

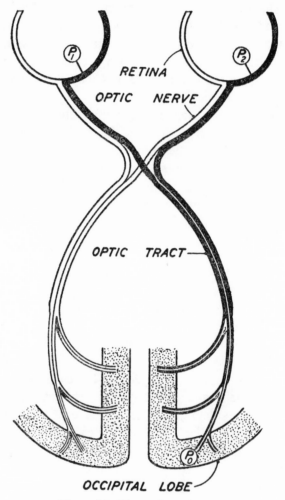

Figure 23. The optic pathways.

up pattern detectors or feature filters in the brain. These give neural models for basic shapes such as a triangle or the letter *E*, which will be instantly recognized whether large or small, moving, in color, or half scuffed out. It also seems that patterns of eye movements and the moving of the rest of our bodies comprise an interaction with patterns of sensing that are necessary for visual perception. Thus, the act of visual perception begins in the retina through the selective responses of the nerve endings to simple stimuli, such as horizontal, vertical, or angular movements. More complex patterns and regulation of binocular eye movements seem to occur in ascending segments of the optic nerve.

The Brain

Visual perception is completed in the visual cortex of the occipital lobes of the brain, which lie in the large area at the back of each cerebral hemisphere. Fully one-tenth of the cerebral cortex is required to interpret visual data. A person can be blind because of a severe insult to the optic nerve or cortex, occurring as a result of a bullet wound or partial drowning, for example. This is a case of cortical blindness, because the ocular structures are normal but the brain is damaged.

Extraocular Structures

Each eye has six muscles that focus it on interesting objects. Because of the peculiar chemical requirements of the rods and cones, an image disappears if it stabilizes on the retina. Therefore, the muscles keep the eye quivering to prevent a stabilized image. These are usually very rapid and undetectable. The muscles are regulated through various cranial nerves.

Exaggerated involuntary eye movements are called nystagmus. These may be observed in blind persons, or those who have had a disease affecting the brain, such as meningitis. It may be congenital or even acquired by persons who work in cramped quarters with insufficient illumination, such as miners might experience.

Binocular vision exists when the images of a particular object are projected on the respective maculae of the retina of the two eyes and are subsequently perceived as a single visual image. The slight discrepancy of the images gives depth perception. This process, called fusion, depends on both eyes being straight and also upon the coordinated voluntary movements of the muscles of the eyes.

When the eyes are not straight, the person is said to have a squint or strabismus. This is one of the most frequent and serious ocular disorders of children, affecting between 1 and 2 percent. A minority of children will have an eye that turns or wanders out, but most will have an eye that turns in, commonly known as cross-eyes. Some crossed eyes can be treated with glasses alone, although patients may be left with some lack of depth perception. Surgery is frequently successful.

Because of strabismis or any condition that may have obstructed light from entering through an eye, a condition may develop that is known as lazy eye (amblyopia). It is associated with the brain's habit of suppressing or ignoring one image, thus avoiding double vision or visual confusion. If it is allowed to persist, this repression becomes a permanent dimming of vision. It may begin as early as three months of age or as late as nine years of age, but it is most usual in children under five who have one turned in eye.

The only effective treatment of a lazy eye is to stimulate it with normal visual images. Usually this is accomplished by patching the good eye or using blurring drops in it to force use of the weaker eye. The younger the child treated, the more significant the improvement. Treatment is not effective in children over seven. Again the importance of early and routine medical checkups is emphasized.

The treatment for a lazy eye will present only a minor and temporary inconvenience in the classroom. Naturally the child with an eye patch should be made to feel comfortable about it. The other children in the classroom might need to be assured that the child wearing the patch is not in pain and will soon not need a patch at all.

A final minor impairment of the eye involves muscle weakness in the muscle of the eye located within the upper lid that serves to elevate it. If this muscle is weak or partially paralyzed, the lid or lids droop—a condition called ptosis. This can be a congenital disorder. It is sometimes observed in children with other neurological dysfunction.

The impairments of the eye, which have been discussed so far, are essentially medical in their treatment and management. However, it is useful for the teacher to have some understanding of these impairments for several reasons. The disabilities and consequent classroom management problems discussed below will make more sense and seem less frightening if their basis is understood.

Furthermore, the teacher can be a very able diagnostician, not of eye pathology, of course, but of abnormal behaviors that might indicate visual problems. The teacher may be the first person to detect signs of possible eye problems in children. Any health problems such as red, swollen, or watery eyes, nausea, or dizziness might be signs of visual problems. Crossed eyes have been mentioned. The child just beginning to do desk work might squint, blink, or hold work too close or at awkward angles, indicating an impairment. Activities requiring fine focus might not occur as often at home, so that parents missed these signs that are more evident in school. The teacher may notice that the child cannot see distant things clearly. It must be emphasized that even the older student may not be aware of his own visual problem. One does not necessarily know that others can see so much farther or more clearly.

Lastly, the school staff can also be influential in creating a safe environment and educating students for the prevention of damage to the eyes. The National Society for the Prevention of Blindness circulates information through national media to help prevent children's eye injuries and to lessen eye damage through industrial accidents. From preschool up, students can learn valuable safety rules and procedures.

VISUAL PROBLEMS

Visual acuity is routinely measured by the Snellen eye chart. This test only measures distance vision and should be considered a screening test rather than a thorough eye examination. The chart is placed at a distance of 20 feet. Standard symbols, either letters for literate persons or *E*s in various positions for little children, are scaled in diminishing size in each line down the chart. These subtend uniform visual angles corresponding to levels of accuracy achieved by "normal" eyes. Thus the person with normal vision sees the series of letters on the 20/20 line at a distance of 20 feet. If a person sees no lower than the 20/70 line he sees at 20 feet what the average person sees at 70 feet and would be termed partially sighted.

Partially sighted children used to be put in "sight saving"

classes, with the idea that they needed to rest their eyes or face further deterioration of vision. Actually, it is now known that, unlike the ear, the eye does not fatigue or deteriorate with use. The surrounding muscles can certainly suffer strain, and the brain can suffer from overstimulation, but the organ of the eye does not require sight saving. The partially sighted student *can* be subject to a severe and total body fatigue from the extra effort that he or she must make to utilize residual vision.

If a person sees at 20 feet what the average person sees at 200 feet, on the 20/200 line, he would be labeled "legally blind," or blind for administrative or legal purposes. The definition of blindness is an arbitrary one. The legal definition was established by the federal government for purposes of providing services to blind persons. Legal blindness is defined as a central acuity of 20/200 or less in the better eye after correction, or a restriction in the visual field in the better eye after correction to a maximal angle of 20 degrees or less. It will be noted that this is a definition of far vision rather than of near vision.

There are glasses available to the person with normal vision, which simulate the vision of persons with different levels of acuity. When these are tried, it is surprising to most people how much usable vision is present, even with 20/200 vision or less.

The legal definition includes consideration of restriction of visual field, or peripheral vision. Medical problems can cause highly restricted peripheral vision. Peripheral vision also differs greatly among normal individuals. The reader can roughly determine his own angle of vision by looking ahead while moving the arms horizontally from the shoulders from a forward position around toward a sideward or spread eagle position. The angle at which both arms can last be seen peripherally will describe the maximum angle of peripheral vision. A person with the restricted angle of visual field of 20 degrees or less will see as if looking down a long tube to one small area.

Classification of visual performance for purposes of health statistics has traditionally been on a simple dichotomy between "legally seeing" and "legally blind." This dichotomy, made to determine eligibility for benefits, ignores the very real and unique problems of individuals with low vision, that is, of those who have a definite visual handicap but still have a considerable amount of useful vision.

A 1966 study by the World Health Organization found 65 different definitions of blindness used for statistical reporting in various countries. In view of this confusion, a Study Group on the Prevention of Blindness convened by WHO in 1972 proposed guidelines for a uniform definition of blindness and standard categories for the reporting of visual acuity for statistical studies. The 9th revision of the International Classification of Diseases (effective 1978) will introduce the term Low Vision in addition to Blindness. This revision will also contain a supplementary classification of Impairments, Disabilities and Handicaps. . . . Tentative definitions have been drafted to provide more clarity and uniformity in the use of terms relating to visual performance. . . . To replace the two categories "legally seeing" and "legally blind," the total scale of visual performance has been divided into three segments: NORMAL, LOW VISION and BLINDNESS. . . . The modifiers *moderate* blindness and *severe* blindness stress the fact that blindness, when used in this connection, is not an absolute term but includes individuals with varying degrees of residual vision.

The terms blindness and low vision describe quantitative levels of performance. The terms visual impairment, visual disability and visual handicap describe qualitatively different dimensions of visual performance:

Visual impairment indicates a limitation of one or more of the basic functions of the eye and visual system.

Visual disability indicates a limitation of an individual's potential to perform certain visual tasks. The most commonly considered visual tasks are reading and writing (detailed vision) and orientation and mobility (largely gross vision).

Visual handicap indicates the disadvantage an individual actually experiences due to his visual impairment or visual disability. The disadvantage must be considered in relation to societal and individual expectations and actual environmental demands.[1]

In progressive diseases, eventual serious visual impairment results at various ages, depending on the pattern of the condition. If the child has had vision and learned a visual scheme, perceptual orientation will be far different from that of the child who has not had that advantage. In the example of a person with tunnel vision

1. Spivey, Bruce E. and Colenbrander, August: American Academy of Ophthalmology and Otolaryngology, Committee on Terminology, International Council of Ophthalmology, Committee on Information, *Classification of Visual Performance*, Tentative Definitions, Draft, January 1976.

seeing a doorknob, it is a different experience to perceive only a doorknob when you know how doorknobs usually relate to doors through former visual experience, than to need to learn that relationship nonvisually through other means.

Some blind persons who cannot utilize their eyes for fine discrimination such as that required for reading still have enough vision for light-dark discrimination, and some have enough to identify objects such as windows, buildings, cars, or shapes of persons. The amount and type of light reception available to the person do not give sufficient information to predict how well any given individual will utilize the information. One person with relatively little actual visual information available to him may make extremely good use of it in terms of visual discrimination and interpretation. Another person with considerably more visual acuity may not use the remaining vision so efficiently.

For purposes of the school it is better to look at the individual child than at categories and define the visual defect in terms of educational implications and actual functioning.

A child would be totally blind in the case that no sensation of light was transmitted from the ocular mechanism. This is a rather rare situation in children or adults but is the case when the child was born without eyes at all, when surgical removal of the eyes was necessitated, or in the situation of the degeneration of the optic nerve.

A child can be considered *educationally blind* if vision cannot be used as a channel for academic learning. Such a child would have to substitute the tactile and auditory modes for reading, for example.

ORGANIZATION FOR INSTRUCTION

Residential schools for the blind are the oldest special schools in the United States. The present trend is away from placement of normally learning, visually impaired children in such segregated settings, although they are sometimes necessary for children from remote areas who could not otherwise receive special services. The present trend is for residential schools and special classes in day schools for the blind to serve children who are multiply handicapped and who need a number of specialized long-term services.

Multiply handicapped children often comprise nearly half of the residential school's population. Children handicapped by maternal rubella fall in this category. Such children are often too difficult for parents to handle at home. They may have sensory impairments of vision and hearing as well as other physical problems. If the visual problem seems to predominate, they may be assigned to a school for blind children. They make up the bulk of the population of deaf-blind children. The intellectual and emotional disabilities compound the problems of managing and educating these very complex children. A few of the residential schools for the blind have special departments for the education of deaf-blind children.

Educators of the blind have pioneered in arrangements for early intervention with blind children. Without guidance, parents of blind children are inclined to overprotect and understimulate blind preschoolers. They cannot be expected to know the special techniques for encouraging and stimulating blind babies to develop normally physically and psychosocially unless they are instructed systematically. The American Foundation for the Blind has excellent pamphlets and books for parents on raising blind children. Home visits and home teaching are available in the larger cities.

With the support services of child development specialists, through home visits, in child care centers, or hospital clinic settings, blind babies can be expected to achieve their full motoric and intellectual potential, and the visual handicap will not be compounded by the effects of understimulation and sensory deprivation in nonvisual sensory avenues. Visually handicapped children can learn speech and language in the normal manner. While their concepts may be different or slower to develop with regard to some visual and spacial realities, the teacher will find otherwise normal blind children very easy to integrate into the society of the classroom.

Preschool educational experiences are usually more strongly recommended for handicapped children than nonhandicapped children. One reason for this is that handicapped children may not pick up important information and concepts that normal children get from incidental learning. When situations are structured and learning goals explicit for that content, it is learned satisfactorily.

(In fact, with some sighted children labeled "learning disabled," this inability in incidental learning may be their *only* disability. With systematic instruction, they become normal learners.)

When a blind child is integrated in a regular nursery school, the other children can become the "eyes" for that child. They can verbally locate objects by saying, "Its over here," or "turn around," or "keep going." Their verbalizations can teach the emotional tone of communications that are more difficult for blind children to assess because they do not have facial clues to guide them. Little children are very matter of fact about people's differences and can easily be encouraged to be helpful to handicapped schoolmates. Self-stimulating repetitive motions, called blindisms, may not develop as often or may be eliminated in children with this type of preschool experience.

Special classes for visually impaired students may be organized according to any of the following basic patterns, or combinations of these:

1. Self-contained units, in which instruction is conducted by specially qualified teachers throughout the school day.
2. Cooperative units, in which students are registered with the special teacher, and the cooperative unit serves as a homeroom and special study room for them. They attend regular classes for a sizable portion of each day.
3. Resource rooms, in which students are registered with regular teachers who assume the major responsibility for their education. They utilize the provisions of the resource room and its teacher as the need arises.

Special classes for multihandicapped persons may be housed in special education centers or diagnostic centers, as well as in a regular school building, with special regard for such acoustical treatment and for architectural modifications as may be required by the students.

It is surprising to some, but acknowledged by teachers with experience, that blind children are the most easily integrated into an academic setting of any children with serious disabilities. One reason for this is the blind child's successful language acquisition, which forms the basis for academic learning. Another reason is the highly developed network of support services and equipment available to the blind student and classroom teacher. There is a growing trend toward the use of itinerant teachers and consultants to community schools, since the blind group is of low incidence and children are apt to be widely scattered through the community. Itinerant services may be organized as general visually handicapped instruction services or orientation and mobility services, or a combination of these.

Itinerant general instruction services, when provided on an individual basis, might be conducted within the schools utilizing conference rooms, offices, classrooms, or other suitable school settings. Itinerant general instruction services also may be conducted outside the school for those visually handicapped students who are homebound, hospitalized, or in detention, or who are assigned to instruction in the home programs.

Special curriculum for blind students emphasizes instruction in the Braille systems for reading, writing, arithmetic, and music notation, electronic print reading systems, tactual discrimination, auditory training and/or listening skills development, basic orientation and mobility techniques, typewriting, opticon, techniques of daily living, sexuality, and career education. Low vision utilization is stressed for those students with any residual vision. The special teacher may transcribe materials on a tape recorder or check Braille homework.

Orientation and mobility services may be conducted within the school, in the student's home, or in the community. Special curriculum for orientation and mobility services includes body awareness, concept formation, development of appropriate gait and posture, identification and familiarization with environmental clues and specific environments, safety precautions, techniques for travel with sighted guides, cane travel techniques, use of public transportation, and information pertaining to electronic travel aids and guide dogs.

Guide dogs are only used by totally blind persons. Children do not have enough maturity and strength to handle the animals, but an older student may acquire one. Dogs are more often used by younger, active persons than sedentary or routinized people, both because the animals require vigorous physical exercise and because they must constantly use their guiding skills or they will forget them. The training courses are available in a number of places. For those who might benefit from a dog it is often a matter of personal preference and life-style whether a guide dog is satisfactory.

Some persons prefer to rely on cane travel, usually using the long cane with prescribed techniques taught by trained orientation and mobility instructors. The blind person learns to sweep the cane across the path being traversed to be sure it is free, and to use the cane to pick up other tactile cues, such as the presence of stairs or curbs.

Special curriculum for partially seeing students emphasizes vision stimulation activities, sight utilization training, auditory training, basic orientation and mobility techniques, typewriting, activities of daily living, and career goals education. Not the least of the special teacher's duties is to facilitate the successful integration of the blind or partially sighted student into the regular classroom and school society. The itinerant teacher is a vital support to the blind student who is integrated with a regular class. The itinerant teacher will teach Braille reading and writing to the blind student. Ideally there will be close cooperation between the regular teachers and the specialists with regard to proper seating, use of instructional aids, modifications for physical education activities and vocational classes.

Many visually handicapped students will proceed through to postsecondary education and full participation in the adult community. They will have acquired relevant skills and techniques to accommodate to their disabilities but will be made more comfortable in settings where there has been a little attention paid to their special needs.

About half the blind persons in the United States are receiving public assistance either as blind or aged persons. Veterans blinded in service receive benefits and services. Additional income tax exemptions are permitted to blind persons. Some blind persons who are homebound contract with agencies for sale of handmade products and for telephone sales jobs. Sheltered workshops have long served the blind where small contract work is performed. A livelihood is provided by the vending stand program, based on federal legislation, authorizing eligible blind persons to operate stands on federal property and other buildings.

For many visually handicapped youths, however, the possibilities for adult employment should be almost as many as for normal people. The local office of the state Bureau for the Visually Handicapped (BVH) is an invaluable source for the visually handicapped adolescent. Too often parents and students do not know about the financial aid to which disabled youths are entitled to help them prepare for the world of work, or of the counseling and placement services that BVH provides. Teachers should be sure to indicate this resource to any student with a visual handicap who has the potential for competitive employment.

Unfortunately, persons with visual impairments have often been more handicapped by denied opportunities for employment than by their own disabilities. Some school systems have denied employment to blind teachers, even though blind teachers are performing successfully all over the country. Such discrimination can be taken to the courts, of course. Some blind persons cannot get work only because they cannot get to the place of work. However, federal guidelines and legislation with regard to the hiring of handicapped and new interest on the part of citizens augur a better future for our visually handicapped students.

MANAGEMENT TECHNIQUES

There are many specific techniques that the teacher can use to accommodate the educationally blind student in a regular classroom. Motivation and opportunities for training seem to be important factors in utilization of low vision. Of importance to the teacher is the fact that utilization of any degree of vision can be encouraged and facilitated in school. Unfortunately, the converse has been shown to be true–children can be taught not to attend to visual cues. Earlier a person was mentioned who did not know until he was a teenager that he had sufficient vision to read book print. He was not educationally blind, but it was assumed that he was on the basis of a diagnosis of legal blindness. The blind person with traveling vision can get from place to place using visual cues. This is of enormous advantage to the visually impaired student and adult.

Some totally blind persons become very adept at sensing the distances of solid objects such as walls by sound reflection, using a sort of radar system similar to the highly developed sensory system of the bat. The skill of attending to nonvisual cues can become highly developed and is the substance of what has mistakenly been taken for a "sixth sense."

New cues can be a factor in spacial disorientation, however. There is the case of a very young blind child who was perfectly oriented to his home in the winter months, but greatly confused in the summer when open windows gave changed sound reflections and air pressures. New carpeting or switches in furniture can cause confusion.

Sighted students may be taught how to and how not to function as a sighted guide. Unfortunately, the plight of the proverbial blind person being wisked repeatedly back and forth across a street by overzealous dogooders is not all fancy. Blind persons have many stories about the mistakes of the well-meaning misinformed; about guides who thrust them ahead to stumble on curbs and stairs; those who, thinking a blind person cannot hear, talk loudly to the sighted companion as to the blind person's wishes; or those sighted persons who cross the street to avoid an encounter because of embarrassment or disinterest.

For ease and safety of movement, the child should grasp the guide's upper arm, just above the elbow (a younger child walking with an adult may hold the adult's wrist) so that the thumb is on the outside and the fingers are on the inside of the guide's arm. Both the visually handicapped child and the guide hold their upper arms close to their own bodies. This should automatically position the child one-half step behind his guide.

For negotiating narrow passageways, the guide can either press his arm close to his body or place his arm behind his body so that the blind child knows he must stand directly behind him. Verbal cues are also important: the guide should inform the student whether stairways and curbs are ascending or descending. As the student and guide become more familiar with each other, a full pause with feet together by the guide may be sufficient to indicate an approaching change in level. The guide will ascend or descend the first step and the student will follow one step behind. The resource or itinerant teacher or specialists in orientation and mobility will demonstrate these techniques.

For the safety of the visually handicapped person as well as for others, doors and cupboards should be all the way open or all the way shut. The visually handicapped student should also be told of any changes in the position of classroom furniture.*

The resource or itinerant teacher will have familiarized a totally blind or severely visually handicapped child with the classroom and surrounding areas and will also teach the student how to get to and from the classroom independently. The classroom teacher should encourage the visually handicapped student to move about the classroom to obtain his materials or visual information. He will know his own needs, and his method of compensating will soon become part of classroom routine. The student should feel free to walk up to or move his chair closer to the chalkboard; help him to position himself so as not to block the view of other students.

When the chalkboard is located in the front of the classroom, the front row center is usually a good seat for a visually handicapped child. If demonstrations are given during class, the location of the demonstrations should be taken into consideration when assigning permanent seats. Because glare may cause discomfort or inability to read, some children prefer seats away from the window.

Partially sighted and low vision children have very specific needs with regard to the manner in which they can best utilize their remaining vision. These must be determined for each child. Some will be trial and error on the student's part, but the teacher

---

* The author is indebted for much of the material on management to the pamphlet, *When You Have a Visually Handicapped Child in Your Classroom: Suggestions for Teachers*, by Anne Lesley Corn and Iris Martinez, published by the American Foundation for the Blind, 1977.

can be of great help, particularly with young children. One child might need to sit in a dark place with a bright tensor light on reading material. Dim light will not harm the eyes. As a result of some eye conditions (cataracts, albinism), a child may require dim lighting in order to see more comfortably.

For children with field defects or with special lighting needs, a consultation with the resource or itinerant teacher will be helpful. A sun visor, other shield, and tinted glasses are helpful to light-sensitive persons to block out glare. A child might have great difficulty reading the conventional light blue on white ditto sheets. Still another might be hampered by the glare of white paper or the bright light near the window.

For children who find it difficult to see the lines on regular writing paper, bold lines are available in various formats, e.g. graph paper, large print staves for music notation. Acetate, usually preferred in yellow though available in various colors, placed over the printed page will tend to darken the print itself as well as heighten the contrast of the background paper.

Some children may need to hold their materials very close or at an odd angle. Holding a book close to the eyes will not harm vision. This is often done by visually handicapped children to help compensate for the size of the print. When these children are taking notes, they will probably use black felt tip pens. These are available in varying widths and produce a bold letter or diagram. Using different colored markers will often help a student emphasize sections of notes when scanning would otherwise be quite difficult. Some visually limited children find their own handwriting difficult for themselves and others to read and the task of writing fatiguing or, with blind children, nonproductive. Typing provides an alternative means of doing written assignments.

A problem for partially sighted children can be that they can rely on their vision in one setting but be essentially blind in another. The child with albinism might function very well in the relatively dimmed light of the classroom, using visual clues for spacial orientation as well as for seat work. When that same child encounters the bright sunlight of the playground, the effect might be to render him blind. On the other hand, some diseases affect the

:entral vision rather than the peripheral area of the retina. A child with this problem might manage quite well on the playground, or n walking or biking with buddies, but be treated as educationally ɔlind in the classroom. It is very difficult for partially sighted :hildren to integrate such perceptual and social shifts. The world :an seem very arbitrary and confusing for them. In this way, :herefore, the low vision child may be far more handicapped and ınhappy than the totally blind child, who can make a consistent, nonvisual perceptual schema of the world, on which he or she can ılways rely.

When presenting demonstrations, the teacher should try not to stand with his or her back to the window. Glare and light will silhouette the demonstration, and eye fatigue may occur. (Cutting down on glare will benefit not only the visually handicapped child but the entire class.) Allow the visually handicapped child to stand next to or to the side of the demonstration, and allow the child to assist in doing the demonstration or to handle the materials before or after the observation period. Closed circuit television (if available) may be useful and permit magnification of the demonstration. If the television is functioning properly, sitting close to the set will not harm the eyes.

With older students, the teacher can assign a classmate (or permit the visually handicapped student to choose his own) to make carbon copies of his notes, lend them to the visually handicapped student, and speak the notes aloud as he is copying them (in a low voice). All teachers can lend visually handicapped students a copy of the notes to be put on the board or the book from which they are taken. Notes can be lent in advance to the resource or itinerant teacher to enlarge, darken, or Braille. This is especially helpful in a math class, where following step-by-step instructions is necessary.

Social encounters are more difficult for blind than sighted persons. Blind persons cannot easily initiate encounters. The nonverbal communications of facial expressions and posture are lost to the blind person. The special teacher may serve as a highly prized confidant of the visually impaired student who is, though integrated in society, always a different and exceptional person.

These students can be very lonely, as unseen classmates pass by without a word of greeting or casually turn away, leaving the blind student unsure of where everybody is.

People often avoid encounters with handicapped persons only because they are unsure how to act around them. Sighted classmates may have to be reassured that it is okay to ask a visually handicapped person if assistance is desired, and that it is equally okay to be refused or ask instructions on how to be of help.

It is important to substitute for unseen visual cues during instruction and social times. Always say hello and possibly identify yourself in a meeting to orient the blind student. Teachers can say aloud what they are writing on the blackboard or describe in words what they are doing in a chemistry experiment. They can describe someone's new coat that they have just admired, when the blind student is present. Fellow students can learn to go over the menu in the cafeteria with the blind classmate. Touch is also more important in encounters with a blind student. With this student one might always shake hands, when a smile might have sufficed with a visually intact student.

The teacher, in consultation with the specialist, is a logical person to help a visually impaired student correct a habit that is socially offensive. This should, however, be done in private and in a nonthreatening way. For example, a student might be inclined to rock, pick his nose, or pull hair while sitting in class, unaware that others are not doing this and that these behaviors do not add to peer acceptance. The teacher can most calmly and kindly help students with these subtleties in socialization.

As a result of getting to know their classmate with a visual handicap, students may become interested in topics related to vision and visual impairment. These can be incorporated into class lessons: in science, light and optics may be a topic for discussion; in health, attitudes toward disabilities; social studies lessons may include information about service agencies in the community. There is a current effort to induce textbook publishers to include more of this kind of material in future publications. When this happens, the job of the teacher in this regard will be easier.

Our language is replete with visual referents and figures of speech. People may worry about using color words and visually oriented communication with their blind compatriots. It is virtually impossible to irradicate the host of visually related words from a conversation, so even blind persons become comfortable using expressions such as, "See you soon," or "From my point of view."

Persons who recover their vision for the first time in adulthood may find restored vision meaningless or an encumbrance. Part of the reason is that their whole conceptual framework and way of operating were organized without reference to visual perception.

When visual perception has occurred, one maintains an internalized schema of perception upon which concepts can be based even when eyes are closed or vision is lost. However, persons who have never had any sight have formed all of their concepts using nonvisual cues and, hence, have a different basis for cognitive development than persons who have sight. There is some evidence that even a brief period of sight in the first year of life can effect the individual's process of subsequent concept formation. Educational methodology, therefore (not covered in this book), may be much influenced by the age of onset of the visual problem.

Since congenitally blind children grow up with a consistent nonvisual world view, they seldom see anything remarkable in their adjustment to their condition, because it is the only mind set they have ever known. Adventitiously blinded persons, on the other hand, must reckon with a termination of themselves as sighted persons with a world view of the sighted. The stages of mourning described earlier seem to be experienced by these persons as they proceed from a denial through a reconciliation to their new identity as blind persons. There are a host of good books written by blind persons, chronicling their adjustment to blindness. Most of the authors were adventitiously blinded. Probably the very act of writing the narrative was cathartic to them.

ADAPTIVE AIDS AND SERVICES

Some visually impaired children who are not included in the legal definition of blindness still have serious visual disabilities, which may require some modifications in classroom management. The partially sighted child would use sight for the purposes of reading and writing but might need specialized procedures and materials in order to do so.

Most partially sighted children and those with lesser refractive errors or muscular imbalance will wear glasses or contact lenses. It is important for the teacher to realize that glasses do not necessarily restore normal vision. The correction for myopia or nearsightedness, for example, reduces the size of the visual field.

There are a number of helpful educational optical aids for the utilization of low vision. These include various magnifying glasses, some mounted and lighted, and prism glasses that bend rays to a convenient angle for persons who must read flat on their backs in bed. These can be obtained from companies listed with organizations for the blind, some of which have low vision aid clinics. Closed circuit TV and microfiche readers are also being used because the type can be blown up and contrast is good. Either hand held or in spectacles, magnifiers increase the size of the image reaching the eye. (It should be remembered that for some eye disorders, magnification can hinder rather than assist visual abilities.) Telescopic aids, small telescopes, are hand held or placed in spectacle frames to view the chalkboard and class demonstrations.

Bookstands help to reduce postural fatigue by bringing the work closer to the reader's eyes. When a bookstand is not available, one may be improvised by placing other books beneath the book that is to be read.

Lamps with variable intensities and positioning can provide the additional or dimmed illumination that a visually handicapped child may require.

Some visually handicapped students will rely on tactual aids. A Braillewriter is a manually operated, six-key machine which, as its name indicates, types Braille. The slate and stylus, used to take notes, is easily carried in a pocket or on a clipboard. The slate is a metal frame with openings through which Braille dots are embossed with the aid of a pointed stylus.

A raised line drawing board is a rubber covered board on which the blind child can draw or write on acetate with a pen or similarly pointed object, and feel the lines "raise up" as they are made. The geometric shapes, script letters, or other line diagrams thus reproduced are generally simple in form for tactual understanding.

The cubarithm slate is an aid to enable the blind child to do mathematics using standard Braille characters. Cubes with raised Braille notation fit into square recesses in a wafflelike frame.

When the visually handicapped student brings adaptive aids into the classroom, the teacher should encourage use of the aids as needed and answer any questions that others have about the aids as they arise. Additional work, desk, or locker space may be needed to accommodate special materials (bulky Braille or large print books, reading stands, etc.).

The services of the Division for the Blind and Physically Handicapped, a part of the Library of Congress, are an invaluable resource for the visually impaired student. Originally these services were restricted to the visually handicapped, but since 1966 the total program of the Division has been available by law to all those persons who are unable to read conventional printed materials because of physical limitations, as well as to the legally blind. These services are helpful to students with low vision or those who have difficulty holding a book steadily or to turn pages. Persons who are flat in bed also find listening to records and tapes much easier than visual reading, for example.

The need for these services must be certified by a competent authority such as medical staff, heads of agencies, and educators. Thus the classroom teacher can obtain services for a student, both for school and home use. Many persons do not know they are eligible for services and can be assisted by school personnel to make contacts.

After the Library of Congress had confirmed the eligibility of the recommended person, the applicant will be sent, if desired, post free and free of charge, a talking book machine. He will be entitled to borrow, post free of charge, talking books, books on tapes, and Braille books. These persons will be served either through one of the fifty-four lending agencies and thirty-eight regional libraries or directly from the Library of Congress, Division of the Blind and Physically Handicapped listed in the Appendix.

Talking books refer to books and magazines recorded on unbreakable microgroove records, which are supplied by the Division, with machines on which to play them. The chief publishers of talking books are found in the Appendix. Playback tape recorders are also available. A variety of publications such as talking book topics in Braille Book Review are distributed to library users. A problem with talking books is that they take much longer to read than visual reading. The reading rate can be adapted by using recorders equipped for increasing or decreasing speed.

Page markers and reading windows may be especially helpful to a child who finds it difficult to focus on a word or line of print. Through the Division for Blind and Physically Handicapped and some publishers listed in the appendix, *large type* books can be obtained for classroom and home use. Type size refers to size of the type face of the individual characters of the alphabet and other characters used in the letterpress printing process using foundry or hard set type. Besides size, each character will have definite design characteristics. Type size is measured in points, defined as $\frac{1}{72}$ of an inch. This book is printed in eleven point type. Since the human eye does not fully mature until a child is eight or over, normal primary-aged children usually read school books in large type, from eighteen to twenty-four point.

While there is no definitive research and no complete standardization of type and design, partially sighted students seem to benefit from a continuation of large type reading after primary years. Many older persons also can benefit from large type books. It may be that some normally sighted children with reading or perceptual problems also profit from large type books and periodicals. The type size in such books is twenty-four point.

There is some research evidence to show that those children who can see to read smaller print might read large type somewhat more slowly. The effects are negligible, so probably the comfort and preference of the student should be the first consideration, when large type materials are available. Large type books are considerably more expensive and more bulky than ordinary books. The periodicals are not costly, however.

For those who cannot read visually, Braille materials are used. An estimated half or more of legally blind children rely on Braille. The Braille system is comprised of signs formed by the use of possible combinations of six raised dots numbered and arranged in cells three dots high in two columns. These are embossed on heavy paper (Fig. 24). The Nemeth code is the variation of Braille used for mathematical symbols. The abacus will be an important aid for teaching arithmetic skills and performing calculations. Talking calculators and Braille calculators are also avail-

BRAILLE ALPHABET AND NUMERALS

The six dots of the Braille cell are arranged and numbered thus:

	a	b	c	d	e	f	g	h	i	j

The capital sign, dot 6, placed before a letter makes it a capital. The number sign, dots 3, 4, 5, 6, placed before a character, makes it a figure and not a letter.

	k	l	m	n	o	p	q	r	s	t

	u	v	w	x	y	z	Capital Sign	Number Sign	Period	Comma

In addition to the braille symbols on this card, the braille system contains equivalents for all the other punctuation marks and special symbols, such as the italic sign and the general accent sign. There are a total of 189 contractions and short-form words.

One type of contraction consists of a single letter, which, when standing alone, represents a common word, such as "b" for "but", "h" for "have". Other whole-word contractions consist of dot combinations not used in forming the letters, such as "and" ( ) or of a letter or contraction preceded by dots from the right-hand portion of the preceding cell, such as dot 5 before a "d" for "day". ( )

Commonly recurring letter combinations, such as "gh" "ou" are represented by other dot combinations. Short-form words are abbreviations for common words, such as "alm" for "almost" ( ), "ei" for "either" ( ). An expert braillist must know and apply a great many technical rules.

Figure 24. Braille alphabet and numbers used by the blind. Courtesy of the Division for the Blind and Physically Handicapped, The Library of Congress, Washington, D.C.

able. Blind readers use a form of Braille in which words are shortened and contractions are made that speed up the reading and writing of Braille. At best, the reading rate for Braille is much slower than visual reading and the math symbols cumbersome.

Children who are blind begin to learn Braille in kindergarten by manipulating peg boards and other materials to develop pre-reading skills. In first grade they learn to use Braille writers, which are similar to a typewriter, but with just six keys to emboss the Braille character. They will also learn to use the regular typewriter in order to write for sighted persons. Older children will use a stylus and Braille form to take notes in class.

Persons over sixty-five, who comprise half of the blind population, often do not learn Braille. Insensitivity in their finger tips, particularly if they are diabetic, may make tactile discrimination difficult.

The transcription and publishing of Braille materials is, of course, limited, so that the Braille reader does not have the same access to literature or news as sighted persons. However, with the help of the special teacher and the supportive volunteer and professional agencies serving the blind, the blind student can be well maintained in class.

Textbooks and educational materials are chiefly supplied to schools and classes by the American Printing House for the Blind or by local volunteers who transcribe books into Braille.

There are many special aids with Braille markings. Braille playing cards have standard pictures for sighted persons so they can be used by all, for example. Braille markings in elevators and office doors are easily added and are becoming more common.

An interesting device using the Braille symbol system and used to communicate with deaf-blind individuals, is called the *teletouch*. The sighted speaker uses an ordinary typewriter, in which the letters are converted to Braille letters which appear as pins raised on a small plastic disc and read by the deaf-blind listener's index finger.

A promising new electronic device to allow tactile reading of visual symbols is the *optacon*. Reading is done by the index finger. Shapes of letters, numbers, and patterns are formed by 144 pins, which can be raised on a small surface. The blind person scans the visual material by means of a small camera about the size of a large fountain pen. It has been very successfully used by some blind persons, who have for the first time been able to read their own personal letters, the daily newspaper, or job application.

Review Guide

After reading Chapter 25 the reader should be able to define the following terms:

outer layer of the eye	rods
sclera	cones
cornea	color blindness
trachoma	macula
middle layer of the eye	fovea
choroid	nearsightedness

congenital toxoplasmosis
ciliary body
iris
pupil
partial absence of iris
albinism
nystagmus
fluid pressure
glaucoma
lens
retina
near vision
accommodation
near point of vision
presbyopia
cataract
Marfan's syndrome
inner layer of the eye
retina
retinal detachment
optic nerve
blind spot

hyperopia
astigmatism
histoplasmosis
tunnel vision
retinitis pigmentosa
RLF
cortical blindness
fusion
amblyopia
lazy eye
ptosis
Snellen chart
legal blindness
blindisms
low vision
totally blind
educationally blind
Braille
Braille writer
opticon
BVH

After completing Chapter 25 the reader should be able to answer the following questions:

1. What are the three main components of the visual system?
2. Why is an application of medication to a neonate's eyes mandated by law?
3. What is a rather unique characteristic of corneal tissue?
4. What is one of the most frequent and serious ocular disorders of children?
5. Give three reasons teachers should know about impairments of the visual system.
6. Why is the environment sometimes more confusing for a partially sighted person than for a blind person?
7. What are the main kinds of administrative arrangements made for visually impaired students?

8. Why is early childhood intervention important for visually impaired children?
9. What curriculum does the special teacher teach blind students?
10. When the resource room or itinerant teacher provides special services, who has prime responsibility for the education of the blind student?
11. What is the relationship between the itinerant and regular teacher?
12. What is an orientation and mobility specialist?
13. Who can profit from a guide dog?
14. What are five aids helpful to totally blind children in the classroom?
15. What are five aids helpful to low vision children in the classroom?

Chapter 26

DISORDERS OF THE EAR AND HEARING

In silent study, I have learned to tell each secret shade of meaning,
and to hear, a magic harmony, at once sincere, that somehow notes
the tinkle of a bell, the cooing of a dove, the swish of leaves, the
raindrops pitter-patter on the eaves, the lover's sigh, a thrumming
of guitar—and, if I choose, the rustle of a star!

Robert Panara
"On His Deafness"

MOST DISORDERS OF THE EAR result in some degree of hearing defect. The type of hearing loss a person experiences is a function of where in the auditory mechanism the impairment is present and also the precise nature of the impairment.

A hearing loss may be mild enough so that the hearing impaired student is still able to use the auditory avenue for learning. In this case, for educational purposes, the student is considered more or less hard of hearing. This student may need some special aids and some help from the teachers and classmates, but his problems should not be difficult to solve.

On the other hand, the hearing impairment may be so severe that the auditory avenue is not available for academic learning. The student with this degree of hearing loss can be called deaf from an educational point of view. The learning needs and problems of this student are very specialized and of great educational consequence.

A major variable in the cognitive development of the deaf child is the age at which the impairment was experienced. If the child was congenitally (at birth) deaf or deafened before the development of language (prelingually deaf), the learning problems will be of greater severity than deafness acquired later.

341

EAR IMPAIRMENTS

Impairments can occur in any of the auditory mechanisms and cause disabilities or handicapping conditions (Fig. 25). One or both of the outer ears may be impaired. The outer ear consists of the sound-collecting shell, which is the external projection, and the auditory canal, which leads to the eardrum of the middle ear.

In some animals, the external ear projection can be moved in the direction of sound, but only the vestiges of that ability are left in humans, in those who can "wiggle" their ears. The ear projections of most persons lie rather flat against the head, but in a few, they stick out. Mothers have mistakenly thought they could change the angle of the ear projection by taping babies ears back, but the resilient cartilage of the outer ear springs back when pressure is released. Even though there may be some advantage to protruding ears, which give the effect of cupping the ears, some persons consider them a blemish. Cosmetic surgery is an operation primarily performed to beautify a part of the body. Cosmetic surgery to flatten the ears is very simple and frequently performed.

A congenital condition is not infrequent where one or both of the external ear projections are missing, and the auditory canal may be covered with a module of skin. Hearing is often not impaired, in which case the problem is purely a cosmetic one. Many persons have done nothing about this relatively minor blemish. Some wear an artificial shell, which can be well fitted and is not too distinguishable from a normal ear. Others undergo a rather complicated plastic surgery in which skin grafts are painstakingly formed to resemble a normal external ear. Some of these operations are cosmetically very satisfying.

Earwax is secreted in the outer ear canal to help trap particles that might be harmful. Earwax may become hard and tenacious in some cases. Accumulated wax can dampen hearing acuity so that a person becomes functionally hard of hearing. This wax can be removed by a medical professional.

The function of the whole middle ear mechanism is to magnify the vibrations of air, which will eventually be interpreted by the listener as sound.

Plate XIV

ear

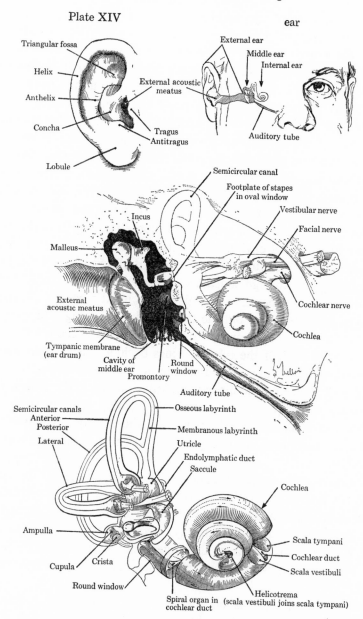

EXTERNAL AND INTERNAL STRUCTURES OF EAR

Figure 25. Ear structures and relationships. From *Dorland's Illustrated Medical Dictionary,* 23rd ed., 1957. Courtesy of the W. B. Saunders Company, Philadelphia, Pennsylvania.

The first part of the middle ear is a thin membrane of skin called the eardrum. The vibrations of air that traveled through the ear canal cause the eardrum membrane to vibrate. The eardrum is attached to the first of three small bones, the smallest bones in the body, which extend across the middle ear to attach to the oval window of the inner ear. These small bones are named for their shape with Latin names: the malleus (hammer), incus (anvil), and stapes (stirrup). These bones move in a lever action, increasing the effective vibration from the eardrum to the oval window about fourteen times. In other words, the loudness of the sounds is increased. The middle ear is normally filled with air, in which the movement of the bones can proceed smoothly and rapidly.

The Eustachian tube is a 1½ inch tube extending from the middle ear to the nasal cavity. Its opening in the nasal cavity is lined with sphincter-ring muscles, which keep it closed most of the time to guard against foreign substances encroaching on the middle ear. The Eustachian tube vents the air of the middle ear. It alleviates changes in air pressure outside the head by "popping" the ears. It also acts as a drainage conduit for fluid collected in the middle ear, as in a head cold. If the tube becomes occluded, a vacuum builds up, causing pain from the membrane and possibly stimulating secretions of fluid into the air cavity. Any disorder in the middle ear can cause a temporary or permanent hearing loss, because the loudness of sounds is not increased. If the disorder is caused by infections, there may also be pain and sickness as well as hearing disability.

Children have frequent middle ear problems. They are more likely to have these than adults for two reasons: first, children have more swollen adenoids, which can obstruct the opening of the tube opening to the nasal cavity; second, in the young head, the tube is almost horizontal, so drainage is not as facilitated by gravity. In the adult, whose head has elongated, the tube has more slant.

Middle ear infections or allergies are common ear problems. The infection itself, either chronic or acute, is damaging to a child's health, and it can result in permanent hearing loss. When the middle ear is infected, the air, normally in the middle ear, is replaced by fluids that may contain bacteria. While this condition is active, hearing is temporarily impaired to some degree and can be variable. Therefore, learning problems are apt to develop. The teacher may suspect a hearing problem if a child is responding variably or not responding to sounds and if the child seems run-down or listless. The teacher may be the first to recognize these subtle symptoms and should feel justified in consulting any medical personnel at school or bringing the suspicion of a hearing problem to the attention of parents.

With medical attention, middle ear problems will probably not be serious. Frequently, a ventilating tube, or ear shunt, will be inserted. This will drain the fluid from the drumhead of the middle ear out to the ear canal. The tube might fall out into the canal, but this will only be discovered in periodic visits to the physician. When an ear shunt is in place, there is an opening from the ear canal to the middle ear, so water can easily pass in and cause infection. Therefore, the child must be very careful to keep ears dry, and swimming is forbidden. The drainage of the ear should make the child hear better and feel better, so school performance will improve.

Otosclerosis is another problem of the middle ear, which is more common in adults than children. It may be due to heredity or associated with diseases such as osteogenesis imperfecta. It is a pathological process of the laying down of new bone around the oval window, so that the bones of the middle ear cannot transmit sound properly. Therefore, a hearing loss results. This condition is twice as common in women as in men and afflicts white persons almost exclusively in the United States. A very sophisticated surgical technique has been developed, which is sometimes successful in restoring hearing. Adults usually have operations on respective ears a year apart, but teenagers and very young adults wait several years. The hearing loss experienced by persons with otosclerosis will become progressively worse. The high school or college teacher may be very conscious of this progression in a student and may need to give a great deal of support as the condition worsens.

Hearing losses that are due to impairments of the outer or middle ear are called *conductive hearing loss.* The essential problem is that the sound vibrations are not being successfully transmitted to the inner ear. Increasing the intensity of the vibration, either to travel through the ear channel or through the bone conduction, is helpful. The person with a conductive loss is helped if we talk louder, or into a hearing trumpet. Conductive hearing losses are often very satisfactorily reduced by amplification by a hearing aid, because a hearing aid increases the loudness of sounds, just as the middle ear does.

The function of the inner ear is to transform the intensified sound vibrations or physical information arriving at the oval window of the cochlea into electrical activity, which will then be relayed to the brain, where it is interpreted as sound. The cochlea is the cavity of the inner ear that resembles a small shell, for which it is named. The opening of the cochlea is sealed by the membrane of the oval window. Fluid fills the channels of the cochlea. The shell-like cochlea makes two and one-half turns around a central pillar in a tight spiral. The inside membrane of the cochlea is lined with 25,000 receptors, each of which has sensory hair cells rising from it. These are attached to a jellylike shelf above the membrane. The nerves from the receptors join together and exit from the center of the spiral as the auditory nerve (which is the eighth cranial nerve).

The cochlea is a hydromechanical system. The footplate of the last bone (the stapes) of the chain in the middle ear vibrates the membrane of the oval window, causing change in fluid pressure and a wave pattern that travels through the cochlea. When vibrations pass through the cochlea, the hairs are alternately stretched and compressed, and the receptors translate this motion into electrochemical pulses. The resonance of the traveling wave is a function of the original sound frequencies hitting the ear, and it differentially displaces the hair cells. Various hair cells translate the mechanical vibrations into specific electrochemical responses, which in turn generate nerve impulses through the auditory nerve to the brain. The auditory nerve also sends nerve impulses from the brain to the cochlea. The entire structure of the inner ear is less than a cubic centimetre in size, but it is remarkably complex.

Sense of balance is a function of another part of the inner ear.

Attached to the cochlea, this system consists of two units operating on simple mechanical principles. One unit consists of four sets of receptor cells, which directly measure the effects of gravity. The second unit signals the body's attitude in space.

Hearing losses due to impairments in the outer and middle ears are conductive losses affecting loudness of the sounds received. Hearing losses due to impairments in the inner ear are called *sensorineural hearing loss.* Of course, there can be more than one impairment in the ear so a person might have a "mixed" hearing loss.

A congenital hearing loss is an impairment with which the baby is born. About 40 percent of congenital hearing loss is due to genetic factors. Rubella contracted by a mother in the first trimester of pregnancy accounts for a third to a half of congenitally deaf populations in some areas. Infections such as meningitis also cause sensorineural damage. Most children with congenital hearing loss have a sensorineural loss, but they usually have some residual hearing. One in 2,000, however, will have a profound loss and be prelingually deaf. Sensorineural loss may also be acquired at any time of life. It is estimated that about 20 percent of overall deafness is hereditary. Some is developed as a secondary symptom of another hereditary disorder.

An interesting disorder in point is Waardenburg's syndrome. Persons with this condition always have an outward displacement of the inner angles of the junction of the eyelids. They may have a median white forelock of hair and premature greying. Their eyebrows converge over the nose bridge, and they may have different colored eyes. Twenty percent of persons with this condition will have a severe hearing loss, and they may have some equilibrium problems due to involvement of the structures affecting balance. This syndrome is inherited as a dominant trait.

Environmental conditions can contribute to sensorineural hearing loss. Loud sounds can snap the sensory hairs of the cochlea or even damage the receptor cells, resulting in partial deafness. During the course of the day, the ear, usually barraged by sound, fatigues and is less efficient. If the ear has surcease from sound and if the sound was not of a level to cause nerve damage, the ear will recover. However, continual exposure to loud sounds will eventually result in some hearing impairment. Thus, with age, or in certain sound-filled occupations such as a traffic policeman or pneumatic drill operator, hearing impairment is common. Amplified music is said to be causing hearing loss in present day teenagers.

Head injuries can also cause inner ear damage. Thomas Edison became hard of hearing as a result of a "boxing" of his ears. Children should never be punished by blows to the head.

A serious aspect of sensorineural loss is that there is usually more nerve damage to the nerve endings that pick up the sound frequencies used in human speech than to those picking up very high or very low frequencies. If amplification is attempted, high and low frequency noise will sound louder, but the person with the sensorineural loss will still not pick up speech sounds on the damaged nerve hairs. Unlike cases of conductive hearing loss, it does not help to talk more loudly to persons with sensorineural loss. These persons only pick up the increased loudness of the noise around them rather than meaningful sound when they have sound amplified. However, some children with considerable sensorineural hearing loss will wear hearing aids. The aids will give them an increased awareness of sound and may help them to hear some noises that are important, such as the roar of car motors.

The last stage of the transmission of sound is from the inner ear to the brain. Auditory information, in the form of electrical activity, is relayed from the ear mechanism to the brain by way of the eighth cranial nerve, the auditory nerve. This cranial nerve exits from the cochlea and relays auditory information through the brain stem to the cortex, where it is interpreted. This nerve is subject to nerve damage also. Nerve degeneration and tumors can cause deafness.

In the cerebral cortex of the brain, auditory information, both symbolic, such as speech, and noise, enters the first auditory storage system, the short-term memory storage. The function of this storage system is to maintain an accurate sensory image of everything that arrives from the sensory organ, the ear, for a long enough period of time (one to one and a half seconds) to permit the higher processes to decide which of the received information is relevant. This period of storage allows the central processes to accept information that is judged as relevant and reject that which is irrelevant. This selective filtering is a first crucial step in auditory perception upon which all successful processing of auditory information depends.

Any interference with sound transmission from the brain stem to and including the auditory cortex is described as a *central hearing loss*. This is brain damage, whether congenital or acquired. Central hearing loss cannot be lessened by amplification. It is a form of central language disorder and may be called receptive aphasia. Education of children with significant central hearing loss will require highly specialized techniques and cooperation of the neurologist and speech pathologist. Also, treatment of older persons with acquired central hearing loss, frequently due to strokes, entails arduous and painstaking reeducation and relearning.

HEARING LOSS

When hearing loss is suspected, the patient has an otologic hearing examination by a physician to determine the type of impairment and its amenability to medical treatment. In addition, there will be an audiologic examination made by an audiologist. The audiologist will give a battery of audiometric tests that will indicate whether a hearing loss exists and what kind of disability is present.

By using audiometric tests, developed in part from the basic principles of the tuning fork, the examiner can determine whether a conductive loss is present and if a bone conduction loss exists. The audiologist can estimate the amount of conductive loss at different sound frequencies. A series of tuning forks are used that range in frequency of vibrations of sounds from very low sound (256 hertz) to very high sound (4,096 hertz) by octaves.

The threshold of hearing is also measured by an audiometer. This is the loudness a sound needs to have to evoke a sensation—to be heard. In audiometry, the threshold is recorded as the intensity of a tone to which the listener responds 50 percent of the time. Hearing thresholds are reported in decibels (dB) in exponential progression. A zero dB threshold level, or hearing loss, is the average hearing level of normal young adults. A hearing loss less than 27 dB is considered inconsequential.

The pure-tone audiogram is obtained by testing air and bone conduction at several frequencies of sound and at varying loudness (thresholds). These scores are recorded on a form (Fig. 26). Human speech occurs generally in a frequency range of 1,000 to 3,000 hertz. Hearing in this range, then, is socially more important than the ability to hear in higher or lower frequency ranges. Therefore, hearing loss is usually given in decibels in the speech range and is generally quoted in levels accepted by the International Standards Organization.

A hearing loss above 30 or 40 dB in both ears (bilateral) in the speech range is considered serious in its impact on communication and language because it is sufficient to hamper the acquisition of language or speech in most children. Such a loss in one ear (unilateral) will not interfere with speech and language development. Children with mild hearing loss, from 30 to around 50 dB, can greatly profit from a hearing aid, which thus reduces their loss to a level where they can hear speech and language fairly satisfactorily. It is obvious that such hearing losses should be de-

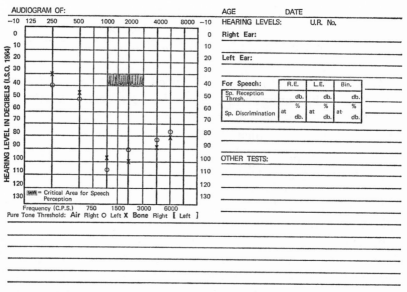

Figure 26. Pure tone audiogram of a child with bilateral sensorineural hearing loss, which is more severe in the speech frequency range.

tected early and remediated during the early years when speech and language are normally acquired (Fig. 27). Language acquisition will not only be influenced by the amount of hearing loss, but also by other individual factors such as intelligence, motivation, and some very specific abilities such as innate skill in speech reading.

On the other hand, a child with a hearing loss of 50 to 70 dB, a moderate deafness, may not improve speech detection to a level below 40 to 50 dB with a hearing aid. The amplification is an im-

Age	
	Birth Cry
1 month	Differential crying for discomfort, pain, and hunger.
2 months	Random vocalization, definite reaction to different voices.
2-6 months	Coos as response, coos or crows to express pleasure.
5-6 months	Babbling; experimenting with sound.
7-9 months	Reduplicated monosyllables; "ma-ma" and "da-da."
12 months	Imitation of words with "circular reflex reaction pattern" (by making sounds, stimulates self to make more sounds). Normal echolalia; imitation with "blind repetitious parroting."
13-15 months	Expressive jargon; imitation of speech with inflection and fidelity.
11-17 months	Obeys simple commands and prohibitions: Pivotal speech, "Ma Ma Go."
15-17 months	Recognizes names of common objects and parts of his body.
17-24 months	Combines words; Short sentences.
24-30 months	Expressive vocabulary of at least 50 words. Uses pronouns; I, me, you. Understands two prepositions; up and on. Greater use of verblike words, possessive forms, and prepositions to make comparisons, define boundaries, and express feelings of ownership.
36 months	Simple sentences with subject, verb, and object "Egocentric Communications" (Piaget)
42 months	Mastery of b, m, p, h, and w sounds.
48 months	Names all primary colors accurately.
54 Months	Mastery of y, k, g, (f), and d sounds.
60 months	Uses speech as social tool and for social communication.
66 months	Mastery of f, (s and z only temporarily) sounds.
78 months	Mastery of v, zh, sh, th, and i sounds.
96 months	Mastery of r, z, and s sounds.
7-8 years	Conceptualization processes underway.

Figure 27. Normal language pattern.

provement for language acquisition, since cadence and inflection of speech may be detected, but specialized language instruction will also be necessary. For children with a severe loss, from 70 to 90 dB, or a profound hearing loss, that is 90 dB or above, the hearing aid may only indicate to them that there is presence of sounds of speech. The hearing aid on the severely and profoundly deaf child does not imply, then, that the child can interpret sounds. The aid may improve awareness of sounds and their associated sources, particularly low frequency sounds. Therefore, the deaf child may be able to detect an airplane overhead, or an automobile, but it does not follow that the deaf child can hear what is said, even loudly, in class.

It is important to diagnose hearing problems very early, because intervention is necessary in the critical years when speech and language are acquired, that is between the ages of one and five. It is very difficult, however, to test very young children. A differential diagnosis between hearing impairment, infantile autism, or retardation is often very tentative. The careful observations of parents and preschool teachers may be crucial in reaching a correct conclusion.

ORGANIZATION FOR INSTRUCTION

Some knowledge about the various administrative arrangements for deaf education will be helpful in planning for a hearing-impaired student. Residential schools for the deaf are among the oldest special schools in the United States. It has been mentioned that children from low population areas might have to go to a residential school in order to receive any special services. Increasingly, residential deaf students are spending part or all of their day in surrounding community schools. Community children are even joining deaf students in residential facilities for preschool and school activities.

Special classes within community schools can allow both for needed special instruction and for integration in regular classes whenever feasible. Special day schools, found in very large population areas, will provide for special instruction but allow little integration with normal children.

Gallaudet College, founded in 1864, is the only college in the world funded for a disability group. It is primarily a liberal arts college, which serves a very select group of high school graduates.

Postsecondary programs have been made available to deaf students in vocational technical institutions since 1968 by government funding. These programs have provided supportive services including tutoring, counseling, notetaking and interpreting, while students participate in the regular classes. Of course, other deaf students go individually to educational postsecondary programs. Successful graduates are reversing the trend of nonemployment and underemployment of deaf individuals. There are a number of organizations listed in the Appendix whose members are specifically involved with deaf persons in various capacities.

MANAGEMENT OF THE HEARING AID

The prescription of amplification for hearing-impaired and deaf children may follow the diagnosis of deafness. Even very young children are fitted for hearing aids. The audiologist, speech pathologist, and parents and children who have been instructed know some very specific techniques for care and efficient use of the hearing aid. These can be issued to the teacher who is in a position of sharing this responsibility. There are also some rather general principles that have more to do with classroom management of the aid.

Children frequently wear the unit containing the microphone, amplifier, volume control, and battery for the hearing aid on a light cloth harness that holds the apparatus safely in place at chest height. For some very young or disruptive children the microphone may be harnessed on the child's back, at least until the child is in a position to be closely supervised.

An individually moulded earpiece fits into one ear, in a monaural hearing aid, or in both ears in the binaural device. Wires connect the earpieces with the microphone, which picks up sound.

The hearing aid is a marvelous piece of equipment. If the hearing-impaired student can be induced to demonstrate it and allow classmates to try it, they will be more inclined to see it in a positive light. The teacher is cautioned to closely moniter any handling of the aid by other students because its parts can be rather easily cracked or broken.

Hearing aids on little children do present the teacher with some need for management strategies. One of the problems with an amplifying system is that while the signal, such as speech, is amplified, noise is also. The reader can demonstrate this by trying on the earpiece of the hearing aid and turning up the volume. The teacher should listen to the aid through the earpiece to see that amplification is satisfactory and that the batteries are not dead.

Extraneous classroom noise should be minimized. Noise that is generally tuned out by normally hearing children, such as the rattle of paper, scuffle of feet, or clatter of pencils, can be disturbingly loud through an aid. A child has to have very good figure-ground discrimination to be able to select meaningful sound from all extraneous noise of the typical classroom. It may be necessary to arrange a very quiet place for the student to receive important directions or instruction.

It was mentioned that loud sounds can damage hearing. Amplification of sound by a hearing aid, then, can actually cause nerve damage and increase hearing loss. It is very important for the young child to be reminded to turn down or off the hearing aid in situations where there is a great deal of noise. The older child will be able to do this for himself, but the little one can too easily learn to tune out the loud bangs of the hammer or screams in the playground, to his eventual detriment.

Parents sometimes dress young children with their clothing over the aid. They and older children might like to hide the device from view. The problem is that the rubbing of shirts and dresses is picked up by the aid and adds to extraneous noise. It is far better if children are made to feel comfortable about displaying the hearing aid, at least until they themselves are old enough to make judgments about efficient use of the aid.

Children who can hear speech by proper use of the hearing aid, the hard of hearing or mildly deaf, will quickly learn to adjust their devices for the best reception. They come to value the aid because it opens a new world to them.

A management problem, which plagues teachers of young children who use hearing aids, is the breakage of the earpiece. Earpieces are expensive, and furthermore, replacement takes time. Also the situations that precipitate breakage may be undesirable.

On the playground or in gym, a child with a hearing aid can be hit on the side of the head, and this is painful. Some small children will deliberately clout a child on the aid because the action gets such a response. The earpiece is likely to fall out and crack on something when a child is very active. In class, breakage may occur if the child fiddles with the earpiece, to clean it or adjust it. The aid may be broken at home, where activity may be less supervised. The child may forget the aid when coming to school.

Solutions to these problems may be discussed with parents, a speech pathologist, or the medical management team. It is possible that the hearing aid should be left in school, and perhaps left in the classroom, to be available for structured, academic learning. On the other hand, some children are very upset if they cannot use the aid in most waking situations. A duplicate earpiece, as well as replacement batteries, may be the best solution. If the hearing aid is to be removed in class, the teacher and student should make sure it is stored in a safe place. If the aid does not have a box, one can be appropriated and lined with cotton for safety's sake.

COMMUNICATION AND SOCIALIZATION

In the various culture groups are spoken over 250 natural or native languages, that is languages that have evolved naturally in population groups. These native languages are judged by linguists to be equally serviceable vehicles for the expression of human thought, whether they are the languages of stone-age culture people, or those of technically sophisticated groups. That is not to say that all languages are equal in the efficiency with which they symbolize specific ideas and descriptions. The Eskimos have over a dozen words precisely designating particular kinds of ice, taking into account age, temperature, composition, and so on. In English an elaborative paragraph may be necessary in lieu of one Eskimo word for ice. The vocabularies differ in size from one language to another. English has more words than French, for example, although one speaker would not know them all. However, all natural languages have universal serviceability. Natural languages have components of sound, or phonics; structure or syntax; and meaning.

Natural languages are to be distinguished from other symbol

systems that have more limited areas of expression and creation. Mathematics is a case in point. Mathematical symbols and operations are far more efficient than the corresponding verbal descriptions, which we have to use when teaching the system initially. However, mathematics can only apply to logical thinking, as opposed to expression of emotions. It cannot, therefore, be a vehicle for the expression of all human thought and is not a natural language. Each of the various natural languages seems to be learned at approximately the same rate and in the same sequence of stages by all the world's normal children (Fig. 27). Of course, more than one language can be learned by a child or adult. However, there is some evidence to suggest that one's first language is learned differently and more efficiently than any subsequent languages. Further, there is a critical period during which language learning takes place most efficiently: from the first to fifth year of life, by which time most of the sounds and structure of language are mastered. Recent research by linguists is focused on illuminating how children learn their native language and how adults teach it.

Gestural signs have long been used by differing language groups as a common mode of communication. Nomadic groups such as American Indians and Australian aborigines communicated in this way. Meaningful gestures are natural to very young children.

Language acquisition is very difficult for the prelingually deaf child because the auditory channel through which it is normally learned is blocked. There are many philosophies and methods suggested for treatment and education of the young deaf child. All stress early intervention during the critical period for language development. Some children seem to respond better to one approach, others to another. The teacher who is not specifically a teacher of the hearing impaired, will, in the case of an individual deaf child, take as given the particular therapies and education that are being advocated by experts. The teacher may work closely with the teacher of the deaf, speech pathologist, and audiologist to make the classroom experience congruent with the special supportive services.

A major goal of educators of the deaf is the development of the native language symbol system. Speaking the language is of course an important goal, but some deaf persons who never acquire very intelligible speech will achieve skill in written communication. Some few will become so adept at speech reading and speech that the listener may forget the disability and turn away when speaking, or try to call a deaf friend on the phone.

Some deaf persons will never achieve much skill in their native language and will instead use a variation of manual communication (Fig. 28), which is a system that has been used all over the world and for hundreds of years. Deaf persons will also learn some finger spelling of the native language. Some deaf and hearing persons, too, will be proficient in both language systems; that of the native language (including finger spelling) and sign language.

Various manual sign systems have been codified for use by deaf people. The one most commonly used by deaf people in the United States today is the American Sign Language (ASL). It is not known whether this system would qualify as a natural lan-

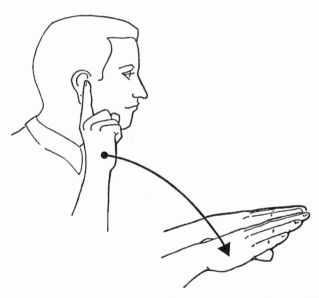

Figure 28. The sign for "deaf." This sign is made up of two other signs, "hearing" and "closed."

guage. It has several thousand signs and a non-English syntax. Other systems such as Manual English attempt to render signs in an English syntax.

Schools that have some deaf students can obtain instructional materials that are essentially a dictionary of signs that can be used by hearing and deaf alike from Caption Films for the Deaf (see Appendix).

Some educators of the deaf are violently opposed to the use of signs with young deaf children. If the first learned language is the most effective one, they feel that that language should be the child's native language. Others argue that a great majority of deaf people will eventually use Sign, so it should be taught properly concomitantly with English language instruction. Some argue for Total Communication, which is embraced in the philosophy that any and all means of communication should be utilized to aid the deaf child to internalize language and develop socially.

It should be mentioned that increasingly children are prone to multiple handicaps, so that a deaf child may also have a visual, mental, or motor impairment as well. It is very difficult for a cerebral palsied child, for example, to master the precise fine-motor movements necessary for signing. On the other hand, a child who lacks much academic potential may learn signing with relatively greater proficiency than learning a native language. Indeed some children without hearing handicaps have learned to communicate in sign. Usually students with so many problems will require a special environment for the major part of their education and possibly for all of their lives. While this book is not focused on the management of students with such complex problems, it is recognized that any teachers may encounter them and should be alert to the benefits normal and disabled students accrue when they can be integrated for school and social experiences.

Persons who are to any extent auditorily impaired learn to use visual cues to supplement the auditory information they receive and, in the case of deafness, perhaps to supplant auditory input.

Efficient speech (or lip) reading presupposes that the person has an internalized language system. Without the language, the speech reading would be no more useful than when a reader looks at the printed page of an unknown language. The symbols are there, but they are meaningless. With young deaf children, speech reading and language are taught simultaneously. Persons who are hard of hearing or have acquired deafness also may find instruction in speech reading of great benefit.

Lip cues are often important aids for the hearing-impaired student in understanding speech. Hard-of-hearing children do not receive all the auditory information in speech that is available to the normally hearing. Vowel sounds come through, but consonant sounds are likely to drop out. Therefore, the hard-of-hearing person will need to get visual cues from the speakers mouth to supplement the defective auditory input. Lipreading, or speech reading, can be successfully mastered even by some profoundly deaf individuals. People differ greatly on their ability to acquire this particular skill, which does not seem to be related to general intelligence. Visual cues from the face of the speaker can also help the hard of hearing or deaf listening understand the affective tone of the communication. Emphasis, emotion, and questions can be inferred from facial expression.

Whether or not the student is strictly a speech reader, some guidelines for the teacher can facilitate the hearing-impaired student's understanding. Attention should be paid to seating so that the faces of speakers in the class can be easily seen. Therefore, there should not be a glare behind the speaker. The speaker should remember to face the student, rather than turn away in midsentence to write on the board, for example. This will probably take a little practice. In most cases, speaking excessively loudly or unnaturally will only distort speech, but speakers are admonished to speak clearly, rather than mumble in a beard or behind a hand.

With older hard-of-hearing students, it is helpful to prepare written notes on the blackboard or mimeograph. These students can profit from sitting next to a good note taker or sharing classmates' notes after class. If written material is to be elaborated in class, the deaf student might want to go over it before class, as well as after class.

Deaf students may not know what proportion of an oral presentation they have missed. Therefore, it is not always useful to ask if the material was understood. Also, deaf persons are sometimes in the habit of saying yes to most questions–partly to be agreeable and partly to avoid repetition of communicative exchanges that are unsatisfactory or embarrassing.

Finger spelling refers to communication in which words are spelled out, using manual symbols to represent the letters and numbers (Fig. 29). It would be cumbersome but possible to communicate completely in this system, just as it is possible to communicate entirely through writing. In both these cases, however, subtle communications indicated by voice, tone, rhythm, and stress are lost. The receiver of manual communication can see the facial expression of the speaker, so picks up more than what can be communicated on the written page.

In the Rochester Method of teaching language to deaf children, oral speech and finger spelling are presented simultaneously. In Russia, success in teaching language has been claimed by the method of introducing the infant to finger spelling and using it always as a method of communication with the child until reading and writing are taught.

Deaf-blind persons cannot use the visual channel or the auditory channel for communication. A number of tactile methods have been developed based on the principle of finger spelling. The various fingers or parts of the hand and manual pressure are utilized to represent the various letters of the alphabet. Deaf-blind persons cannot, of course, utilize visual cues from the face. They can become remarkably adept, however, in speech reading by tactile contact with the speaker's face. Deaf-blind persons will only use this method selectively, because it may not be acceptable socially in many instances.

The area of the deaf is fraught with professional controversy, so any stand taken on important issues will undoubtedly be disputed in good faith by some experts. The author feels it is important to state some convictions that are congruent with the general philosophical framework offered in the beginning. These are personal opinions to be considered when the reader formulates his or her own view.

First, surely there is no one right method in teaching or treat-

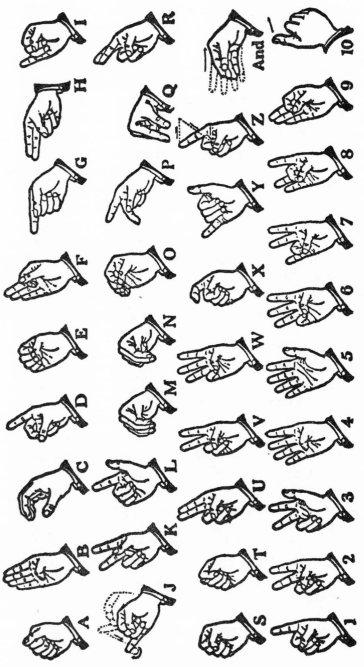

Figure 29. Manual alphabet (visible English).

ing hearing-impaired persons, any more than there is one right method of teaching reading. The capabilities and circumstances of the child and family are as important determinants of treatment as any methods. Deaf parents may use sign, for example.

Second, the end-all of education and management of deaf children is not correct speech and total integration, which are, after all, goals not achieved by the great majority of deaf adults. The important goals have to do with providing opportunities and choices relative to finding a happy and productive place in the human community. A deaf student may be completely competitive in wrestling or computer class, but be segregated in composition class. The deaf student may talk with hearing friends, and sign in deaf groups. The purpose of education is to increase options for individual choices, not deny them. A deaf student should not be made to think there is anything less than good about communicating with others in sign, any more than in communicating in Spanish or in a dialect; yet this has been done in all these instances.

It has been observed that successful integration of deaf students in regular school is best accomplished when everyone in the school learns some sign language and finger spelling. Young people are very facile at picking up manual communication and enjoy it. In so doing, they also have broadened their skills and increased their options for knowing their schoolmates.

Deaf persons have been traditionally underemployed and relegated to certain types of jobs such as shoe repair and print setting. Furthermore, they have faced legal and social discrimination. However, on the bright side, the deaf community has been notably cohesive and protective of its members, asking for no special favors or exemptions. Deaf communities tend to cluster around schools for the deaf in larger cities. They have many social and religious organizations and groups and even a national theatre for the deaf. Many deaf persons will always retain a close association with deaf groups even when they are also able to assimilate in hearing society.

A number of deaf professionals are in the special education and rehabilitation fields. When professional meetings or talks are given in the area of the deaf, interpreters are usually provided, and in informal conversations, sign will often be observed.

After reading Chapter 26 the reader should be able to define the following terms:

hard of hearing	central language disorder
educationally deaf	receptive aphasia
prelingual deafness	otologic examination
outer ear	audiologic examination
cosmetic surgery	audiologist
middle ear	decibels (dB)
eardrum	bilateral hearing loss
malleus	mild hearing loss
incus	moderate deafness
stapes	severe deafness
eustachian tube	profound deafness
otosclerosis	Gallaudet College
conductive hearing loss	natural language
sensorineural hearing loss	gestural language
inner ear	critical period of language
oval window	learning
cochlea	sign language
mixed hearing loss	finger spelling
congenital hearing loss	threshold of hearing
Waardenburg's syndrome	speech reading (lipreading)
auditory nerve	deaf-blind
auditory perception	Rochester Method
central hearing loss	total communication

After reading Chapter 26 the reader should be able to answer the following questions:

1. What technique can be used to induce the other students to see the hearing aid in a positive way?
2. Name three techniques to maximize the usefulness of the hearing aid.
3. Name three hazards in the care of the hearing aid with young children.
4. What is the function of a hearing aid for a child with severe or profound deafness?

5. What is the function of a hearing aid for a child with a mild hearing loss?
6. Give four specific practices that will aid a deaf student in speech reading.
7. How can a deaf student obtain visual information to help him understand verbal classroom presentations? Name three means.
8. What are the arguments for and against teaching young deaf children to sign?

WHERE TO TURN

An effort made to help another lifts one above himself.
Voltaire

The preceding text has discussed many helpful organizations, services, and materials that are available to disabled persons and their families, and to teachers who may be the crucial link between those who have special needs and those who might answer them. It is astonishing how often people, including professionals, lack this information. Below, information is given in categories which might suggest its particular usefulness.

RESOURCES

You glance at a thin, flat object made from a tree, as you are doing at this moment, and the voice of the author begins to speak inside your head. (Hello!)

Carl Sagan
Dragons of Eden

THE GENERAL REFERENCES in the first section below are valuable in their own right and have excellent bibliographies for those readers who wish to learn more about normal development, different disabling conditions, and implications for education.

References for parents in the second section may also be of interest to teachers in training and to school staff. Some are highly scholarly and others are written in a less sophisticated style. In addition, many pamphlets and folders are available from the asterisked (*) organizations in the *organization* section, which are of special interest to parents.

The next section deals with architectural modifications and accessibility. The final section lists specific adaptive materials, devices, and services. It should be of interest to anyone needing a starting place for specific practical help with the management of physical problems in school, home, and community.

"A true university is a collection of books."
Thomas Carlyle

GENERAL PROFESSIONAL REFERENCES

Barsch, Ray: *The Parents of the Handicapped Child.* Springfield, Thomas, 1968.

Best, Gary A.: *Individuals with Physical Disabilities: An Introduction for Educators.* St. Louis, Mosby, 1978.

Bigge, June L. and O'Donnell, Patrick A.: *Teaching Individuals with Physical and Multiple Disabilities.* Columbus, Merrill, 1977.

Bleck, Eugene E. and Nagel, Donald A.: *Physically Handicapped Children: A Medical Atlas for Teachers.* New York, Grune, 1975.

366

Brooks, Stewart M.: *Basic Science and the Human Body*. St. Louis, Mosby, 1975.

Cobb, Beatrix A. (Ed.): *Medical and Psychological Aspects of Disability*. Springfield, Thomas, 1973.

Conner, Frances, Wald, Joan, and Cohen, M. (Eds.): *Professional Preparation for Education of Crippled Children*. Report of a Special Study Inst., Teacher's College, Columbia University.

Cutler, Donald R. (Ed.): *Updating Life and Death, Essays in Ethics and Medicine*. Boston, Beacon Pr, 1968.

Davis, Malcolm D.: *Exceptional Children in Regular Classrooms*. A publication of the Leadership Training Institute/Special Education, sponsored by the Bureau for Educational Personnel Development, U.S. Office of Education, 1976.

Edgington, D.: *The Physically Handicapped Child in Your Classroom: A Handbook for Teachers*. Springfield, Thomas, 1976.

Garret, James F. and Levine, Edna S. (Eds.): *Psychological Practices with the Physically Disabled*. Columbia U Pr, 1967.

Gearheart, B. R. and Weishahn, M. W.: *The Handicapped Child in the Regular Classroom*. St. Louis, Mosby, 1976.

Goffman, Irving: *Stigma, Notes on the Management of a Spoiled Identity*. Englewood Cliffs, P-H, 1963.

Gordon, Sol: *Living Fully: A Guide for Young People with a Handicap, Their Parents, Their Teachers and Professionals*. New York, John Day, 1975.

Haring, Norris G.: *Behavior of Exceptional Children: An Introduction to Special Education*. Columbus, Merrill, 1974.

Haslam, Robert H. A. and Valletutti, Peter J. (Eds.): *Medical Problems in the Classroom: The Teacher's Role in Diagnosis and Management*. Baltimore, Univ Park, 1975.

Hobbs, Nicholas: *Issues in the Classification of Children*. Vols. 1 and 2. Washington, Jossey-Bass, 1975.

Love, H. and Walthall, J.: *A Handbook of Medical, Educational and Psychological Information for Teachers of Physically Handicapped Children*. Springfield, Thomas, 1977.

McDaniel, James W.: *Physical Disability and Human Behavior*. Elmsford, Pergamon, 1969.

Public Affairs Pamphlets. 22 E. 28th, New York, 16. (These deal with specific disabilities.)

Reynolds, Maynard C. and Birch, Jack W.: *Teaching Exceptional Children in All America's Schools*. Reston, Va., The Council for Exceptional Children, 1977.

Rusalem, Herbert: *Guiding the Physically Handicapped College Student*. New York, Columbia U Pr, 1962.

Rusk, H.: *Rehabilitation Medicine*, 2nd ed. St. Louis, Mosby, 1964.

Travis, Georgia: *Chronic Illness in Children: Its Impact on Families.* Stanford U Pr, 1976.

Wisconsin Vocational Studies Center: *It's About Time Physical Disabilities Came Out in the Open.* Madison, U of Wis Pr, 1976.

Wright, Beatrice A.: *Physical Disability—A Psychological Approach.* New York, Har-Row, 1960.

REFERENCES FOR PARENTS

Children begin by loving their parents;
As they grow older they judge them;
Sometimes they forgive them.

Oscar Wilde

American Annals. Comprehensive Directory of Programs and Services for the Deaf in U.S., Yearly Publication of the Deaf. Convention of American Instructors of the Deaf and Conference of Executives of American Schools for the Deaf, Pub.

Apgar, Virginia and Beck, Joan: *Is My Baby All Right?* New York, Trident, 1973 and New York, Pocket Books, 1974.

Ayrault, Evelyn West: *You Can Raise Your Handicapped Child.* New York, Putnam, 1964 (318 pp.).

Barbara, Dominick A.: *Questions and Answers on Stuttering.* Springfield, Thomas, 1965 (102 pp.).

Bleiberg, Aaron H. and Leubling, Harry E. B.: *Parent's Guide to Cleft Palate Habilitation: The Team Approach.* Hicksville, N.Y., Exposition, 1971.

Bloom, Freddy: *Our Deaf Children,* Washington, Alexander Graham Bell Association for the Deaf, Inc., 1965.

Blumenfeld, Jane, Thompson, Pearl E., and Vogel, Beverly S.: *Help Them Grow!* (A Pictorial Handbook for Parents of Handicapped Children.) Nashville, Abingdon, 1971. This handbook provides parents of young educable and trainable retarded children with suggestions for teaching basic skills and developing individual potential (64 pp.).

Caniff, Charles E.: *Directory of Rehabilitation Facilities.* Published by the Association of Rehabilitation Centers; available from publisher, lists 400 facilities, including ARC institutional members with data on available services, bed capacities, and other pertinent information (113 pp.).

Cantoni, Louis and Cantoni, Lucille: *Counseling Your Friends.* New York, William-Frederick Press, 1961. Common sense approach to the layman in giving information about the facts of disability, but turning emotional problems over to those equipped to diagnose and treat them objectively (150 pp., paperbound).

Directory of Workshops for the Handicapped. Washington, U.S. Govt. Print. Office, 1962. 631 workshops listed by state, giving disabilities, number of clients served, and services.

Egg, Maria: *The Different Child Grows Up.* New York, John Day, 1969. This book deals with the mentally retarded child and suggests how the adult should deal with him.

Egg, Maria: *When a Child Is Different* (A Basic Guide for Parents of Mentally Retarded Children). New York, John Day, 1964 (155 pp.).

Finnie, Nancie R.: *Handling the Young Cerebral Palsied Child at Home* (illustrated). New York, Dutton, 1970. In this complete manual for parents, methods of handling the very young CP child are illustrated in sketches (224 pp.).

French, Edward L. and Scott, Clifford L.: *Child in the Shadows.* Philadelphia, Lippincott, 1967. A manual for parents, this publication tells how to help a retarded child (190 pp.).

Hart, Verna: *Beginning with the Handicapped.* Springfield, Thomas, 1974.

Heisler, Verda: *A Handicapped Child in the Family.* New York, Grune, 1972. The author, herself handicapped, developed this book from experiences with parents of handicapped children (56 pp.).

Helsel, E. D.: *Avenues of Action.* The book discusses long-term care, variety of noninstitutional programs, financing, guardianship, and includes a reference list. United Cerebral Palsy (no date).

Helsel, E. D. and Graham, Earl C. (Eds.): *Tomorrow Is Today.* United Cerebral Palsy Association, free booklet. Planning ahead for long-term care, legally and financially. For parents of CP children who will not be able to live independently.

Hewett, Sheila: *The Family and the Handicapped Child.* Chicago, Aldine, 1970. A study of cerebral palsied children in their homes (240 pp.).

Jerman, Betty: *Do Something.* London, Garnstone Press, 1970. This book is a guide to self-help organizations. It reflects the frustrations of parents with mentally retarded children (224 pp.).

Joyce, M. (Ed.): *Rights of the Physically Handicapped: A Layman's Guide to the Law.* Marshall, Minnesota, Southwest State University, 1976 (179 pp.).

Kromm, Elizabeth R.: *Families of Mongoloid Children.* Washington, U.S. Govt. Print. Office, 1963. (Available from: Superintendent of Documents, Children's Bureau). Families of children with Down's syndrome will benefit from this book in understanding their own reactions and feelings, as well as those of their children.

Kubler-Ross, Elizabeth: *On Death and Dying.* New York, Macmillan, 1969.

Kvaraceus, William C. and Hayes, Nelson E. (Eds.): *If Your Child Is Handicapped.* Boston, Sargent, 1969. This book, a collection of 50 case histories of different handicaps, contains personal reactions of parents to these children (413 pp.).

Lacey, Phyllis R.: *Life with the Mentally Sick Child: The Daily Care of Mentally Sick Children in Hospitals and at Home.* Elmsford, Pergamon, 1969 (77 pp.).

Lowenfeld, Berthold: *Our Blind Children: Growing and Learning With Them.* Springfield, Thomas, 1971. This book is applicable to blind children of all age groups and to multihandicapped blind children (280 pp.).

Messner, Sherwood A.: *Cerebral Palsy.* Voluntary and Tax Supported Services in the U.S.A. Free from the United Cerebral Palsy Association. A good guide to resources for services available in various parts of the country.

McMullen, Margery D.: *How to Help the Shut-In Child.* New York, Dutton, 1954.

Spock, Benjamin and Lerrigo, M. O.: *Caring for Your Disabled Child.* New York, Macmillan, 1965. The authors offer suggestions and advice for the care of the disabled child and discuss needs of parents and children (373 pp.).

Snyder, G. B.: *Your Cleft Lip and Palate Child.* Florida Cleft Palate Association and Meade-Johnson Laboratories.

Stern, Edith and Castendyck, Elsa: *The Handicapped Child: A Guide for Parents.* New York, A. A. Wyn, 1950 (179 pp.).

Swinyard, Chester: *The Child with Spina Bifida.* Available from Publications Department Rehabilitation Medicine, New York University Medical Center, 400 East 34th Street, New York, 10016.

Watson, D. P. and Burlingame, A. W.: *Therapy Through Horticulture.* New York, Macmillan, 1976.

ADAPTIVE DEVICES, MATERIALS, AND SERVICES

Life is not meant to be easy, my child;
but take courage: it can be delightful.
He-Ancient in George
Bernard Shaw's *Back*
to Methuselah

The list below is not complete. The organizations cited as publishers and additional organizations on the list of Organizations are often helpful in suggesting special resources. Also, the reference librarian in the public library can search out sources that cater to specific needs.

*Accent on Information and Accent on Living. P.O. Box 700, Gillum Road and High Drive, Bloomington, Illinois 61701, periodical by the disabled, Information Research Service on Products and Service.

American Automobile Association. *Vehicle Controls for Disabled Persons.* Published by the American Automobile Association; available from Traffic Engineering and Safety Department, AAA, 1712 G Street, N.W., Washington, D.C. 20006.

*American Diabetic Association. *A Cookbook for Diabetics: Meal Planning with Exchange Lists.* A basic instruction booklet, which explains how to use food exchanges to vary the diet. It gives the exchange lists and is illustrated.

*American Heart Association. *Do It Yourself Again, Self-Help Devices for the Stroke Patient,* 1965.

American Printing House for the Blind, P.O. Box 6085, Louisville, Kentucky, 40206. Supplies books and educational materials to schools and classes. Manufactures Talking Books of school texts.

Ames Company, Div. Miles Laboratories Inc., Elkhart, Ind. 46514. "Diabetes in the News," *A Guide Book for the Diabetic.* Free digest.

Ames Company. Two booklets available, *Care of the Child with Diabetes, A Guide Book for the Diabetic.* Free Digest "Diabetes in the News," Div. Miles Laboratories, Inc., Elkhart, Ind., 46514.

Ampersand Group for Medical Engineering, Highland View Hospital, 3901 Ireland Drive, Cleveland, Ohio, 44122.

Amputee Service Association, 520 North Michigan, Suite 1504, Chicago, Illinois, 60611.

Automatic Toilet. Inquire from United Cerebral Palsy* for information. An automatic toilet imported from Switzerland is especially well suited for use by the multiply handicapped.

Avis and Hertz® Rental Car Agencies. Information on cars with hand controls is available in local city offices.

B.O.K. Sales Company. Box 32, Brookfield, Illinois, 60513. Catalogue of items to adapt devices for eating and drinking, such as curved spoons and scoop dishes.

*Bare, C., Boettke, E., and Waggoner, N.: *Self-help Clothing for Handicapped Children,* Chicago, National Society for Crippled Children and Adults, 1962.

Bell Telephone Company. (Supplies: school to home telephone service, electric larynx, volume control for amplification on the telephone, bone conduction telephone receivers, watchcase receivers for the deaf, light and amplified telephone rings.)

Biomedical Engineering Program Team Research Center, Room 227, Texas A & M University, College Station, Texas, 77843.

Book of the Month Club. Recorded Book Society offers members new titles each year.

Bowar, Miriam: *Clothing for the Handicapped.* Over 30 fashions are illustrated along with hints on fittings, alterations, and fabrics. Sister Kenny Institute, Publications Department #265, Chicago Avenue at 27th Street, Minneapolis, Minnesota, 55407.

Braille books (American Foundation for the Blind*)

---

* See Organizations list.

Braille Magazine. Contains articles on education, science, culture, and communications. The *Braille Review,* published in English, French, and Spanish contracted Braille. Visitors Information Center, Information Division, UNESCO, 7 Place de Fontenoy, 75700 Paris, France.

Braille Tales: A book club for Braille Readers. Braille, Inc., 184 Seapit Road, East Falmouth, Massachusetts, 02536.

Braille World Book Encyclopedia, World Book, Inc.

Campbell's Cookbook. *Easy Ways to Delicious Meals.* A free cookbook available in Braille and large-print editions. Volunteer Services for the Blind, 919 Walnut Street, Philadelphia, Pennsylvania, 19107.

Canadian Paraplegic Association, *G.U. SERIES:* Central Western Division; available from publisher at 825 Sherbrook Street, Winnipeg 2, Manitoba, Canada. A highly practical booklet on G.U. care with illustrations of gadgets and adaptive devices (17 pp.).

Caption Films for the Deaf. Programs for the Handicapped, Room 338D South Portal Building, 200 Independence Avenue, SW, Washington, D.C., 20201.

Cerebral Palsy Communication Group, University of Wisconsin, 2554 Electrical Engineering Building, Madison, Wisconsin, 53706.

*Cleft Palate Research Center, Salk Hall, University of Pittsburgh, Pittsburgh, Pennsylvania, 15208. Film "Everything You Always Wanted to Know about Clefts—But Was Afraid to Ask," made by teen group at the center.

Cloth Research Development Foundation, One Rockefeller Plaza, Suite 1912, New York, New York, 10020. Information about Levi's® jeans adapted for handicapped and sources of other adapted clothes.

Clovernook Printing House for the Blind, Cincinnati, Ohio. Braille press books.

Communication Outlook is a quarterly newsletter addressed to individuals interested in application of technology to needs of persons who experience communication handicaps due to neurological and neuromuscular disabilities. Artificial Language Laboratory, Computer Sciences Department, Michigan State University, East Lansing, Michigan 48824.

Copeland, Keith (Ed.): *Aids for the Severely Handicapped.* London, Sector Publishing Ltd., 1974.

Cybernetics Research Institute, 2233 Wisconsin Avenue, NW, Washington, D.C., 20007. Communication devices have been developed for the severely involved child and adult.

Danzig, A. L.: *Handbook for One Handers.* New York, Federation of the Handicapped, 1957 (pamphlet).

Easter Seal Society.* Airline information for the handicapped.

---

* See Organizations list.

Elkomi 2®. A portable electronic device developed in the Netherlands permits vocally handicapped persons to communicate by pressing keys. For further information contact the Netherlands Consulate General, Commercial Division 533, One Rockefeller Plaza, New York, New York, 10018.

Encyclopedia of Associations (see local library). List has many organizations for those with special needs (such as Nat'l Odd Shoe Exchange).

Evergreen Travel Service (Wings on Wheels). 19429 44th Street, West, Lynnwood, Washington, 98036.

Fashion Able, Rocky Hill, New Jersey, 08553. Source of self-help items for independent living and easy-on, easy-off clothing.

Feldman, Rubin: National Odd Shoe Exchange, 1415 Ocean Front, Santa Monica, California, 90401. Matches people with complementary special shoe needs (such as one-legged people).

Fischer, Alfred E. and Horstmann, Dorothea L.: *A Handbook for Diabetic Children*, 3rd ed. Intercontinental Medical Book Corporation, 381 Park Avenue, S., New York, New York, 10016, 1965.

Gallagher, Anna May: "Typewriter Town." A method for teaching typing to retarded children. 106 Pennfield Place, Pittsburgh, Pennsylvania, 15208.

Gifford, L.: *If You Can't STAND to Cook*. Easy-to-fix recipes for the handicapped homemaker. Grand Rapids, Zondervan, 1973.

Givens Company, Downers Grove, Illinois. Catalogue of eating devices such as two-handled mugs.

Hamilton, S.: *My child has an ostomy*. Los Angeles, United Ostomy Association, 1974.*

Haycraft, Howard: *Books for the Blind and Physically Handicapped*. Division for the Blind and Physically Handicapped, Library of Congress, Washington, D.C., 20542.

Hodgeman, Karen and Warpeha, Eleanor: *Adaptation and Techniques for the Disabled*. Homemaker, Publication 710. A/V Publication Office, Sister Kenny Inst., 1800 Chicago Avenue, Minneapolis, Minnesota, 55404, 1973.

Howe Press, Perkins School for the Blind, Watertown, Massachusetts, Braille press.

International ITI Percussor Therapeutics, Inc., P.O. Box 36022, Dallas, Texas, 75235. Produces a hand-held mechanical vibrator helpful in lung clearance.

J.A. Preston Corporation. *Self-help Devices for Rehabilitation*. 71 Fifth Avenue, New York, New York, 10003. Catalogue of adaptive devices for eating, such as suction cup bases and build-ups for cutlery.

---

* See Organizations list.

Jennison, Keith: Books (A division of Franklin Watts Inc., specializing in large type books), 575 Lexington Avenue, New York, New York, 10022.

John Tracy Clinic, 807 W. Adams Boulevard, Los Angeles, California, 90007. (Home program for oral education of young deaf children.)

Joseph, F. and Mullins, J.: *Total Communication.* A workbook for beginning writing, reading, and concept development in a simplified script to supplant cursive writing or printing for physically or perceptually handicapped children. Available from Mafex Associates, Inc., 90 Cherry Way, Johnstown, Pennsylvania, 15902.

Kamenetz, H. L.: *The Wheelchair Book.* Springfield, Thomas, 1969. This book gives complete descriptions of all wheelchairs made, plus many other kinds of equipment and transfer techniques.

Knights of Pythias. Provide adjustable postural draining tables for persons with cystic fibrosis.

Krusen Center for Research and Engineering, Moss Rehabilitation Hospital, 12th Street and Tabor Road, Philadelphia, Pennsylvania, 19141.

Large Type books (see Organizations) for the blind and physically handicapped and different publishers.

Laurie, G. and Laurie, J.: *Housing and Home Services for the Disabled.* New York, Har-Row, 1976. Mail order: USA P.O. Box 19083, Washington, D.C., 20036.

Lee Communications, Inc. Telephone holder device and intercom, 486 Park Avenue, S., New York, New York.

Library of Congress, Division for the Blind and Physically Handicapped, Taylor Street, NW, Washington, D.C., 20542. Includes Talking Books, Braille books, Playback machines, tapes. Publishes selected reading lists (also on large type).

Lowman, E., and Klinger, J. L.: *Aids to Independent Living: Self-help for the Handicapped.* New York, McGraw, 1969. This book gives many illustrations of adapted equipment.

Marx, Orrin: *Physical Activities for Handicapped Children in the Home.* University of Iowa, 1972.

May, E. E., Waggoner, N. R., and Boethke, E. M.: *Homemaking for the Handicapped.* New York, Dodd, 1966.

May, E. E., Waggoner, N. R. and Hotte, E. B.: *Independent Living for the Handicapped and Elderly.* Houghton Mifflin Co., Boston, 1974, pp. 271. Many techniques and resources for activities of daily living are compiled.

Mealtime Manual for the Aged and Handicapped. Institute of Rehabilitation Medicine, New York University Medical Center.

Medic Alert Foundation International, Turlock, California, 95380. At cost—bracelet with identifying medication information, emergency answering service—call collect from anywhere in the world, 24 hours a day, (209) 634-4917.

Resources 375

Medicon Inc., Box 325, Holbrook, Massachusetts. Information about bottle straws, "Sit and Sip."

Mullins, June and Wolfe, Susanne: *Special People Behind the Eight Ball: An Annotated Bibliography of Literature Classified by Handicapping Conditions.* Mafex Associates Inc., Johnstown, Pennsylvania, 1975.

Muscular Dystrophy Associations of America,* Inc. *Around the Clock Aids for the Child with Muscular Dystrophy.*

National Braille Association Inc., Thousands of volunteer transcribers transcribe Braille Books, coordinated by the Division for the Blind and Physically Handicapped.

National Foundation for Happy Horsemanship for the Handicapped, Inc. Contact Mon Ami le Cheval, Box 462, Malvern, Pennsylvania, 19355.

National Institute for Rehabilitation Engineering, Pompton Lakes, New Jersey, 07442.

New York Times, P.O. Box 2570, Boulder, Colorado, 80302. Weekly large type editions.

New York Times Cookbook (large type cookbook).

Opticon and other electronic aids. Telesensory Systems Inc., 3408 Hillview Avenue, Palo Alto, California, 94304. Instruments for the blind to read book print, play games, etc.

Oster® Vibrator, Jr. Model. Oster Company, a hand-held vibrator helpful in lung clearance.

Patient Engineering Service, Rancho Los Amigos Hospital, 7601 East Imperial Highway, Downey, California, 90242.

"Premie Nipples" (Curity®), Kendall Company, 304 W. Jackson B., Chicago, Illinois.

Prosthetic and Sensory Aids Service, Department of Medicine and Surgery, 810 Vermont Avenue, NW, Washington, D.C., 20420.

Rambling Towns, Inc. P.O. Box 1304, Hallandale, Florida. Or, Handi-Cap Horizons, Inc., 3250 E. Loretta Drive, Indianapolis, Indiana, 46227, Travel Agencies.

Readers Digest Fund for the Blind, Inc. Pleasantville, New York, 10570. Reader's Digest in large print.

*Recreational Research Institute, 258 Broadway, New York, New York. Free pamphlet: *Active Games for the Handicapped.* Free reprints about the handicapped from Recreation Magazine.

Recording for the Blind, Inc., 215 E. 58th Street, New York, New York 10022.

Rehabilitation Gazette. 4502 Maryland Avenue, St. Louis, Missouri, 63108. International Journal and Information services for the disabled.

Responaut, 62 Priory Road, Newbury, Berkshire, England. Margaret Haines, treasurer, will send free copies of the quarterly publication,

---

* See Organizations list.

Responaut. The editor and writers are quadriplegics dependent upon respirators or other gadgets because of respiratory polio or other disabilities.

Robinault, Isabel P.: *Functional Aids for the Multiple Handicapped.* Har- Row, 1973.

Rosenberg, C.: *Assistive Devices for the Handicapped.* Minneapolis, Minnesota: American Rehabilitation Foundation, 1968. This book gives descriptions and instructions on adapting objects for the disabled.

Rosenthal, Joseph and Rosenthal, Helen: *Diabetic Care in Pictures,* 4th ed., 1968. Publisher: J. B. Lippincott Company, East Washington Square, Philadelphia, Pennsylvania, 19105.

Rusk, H. and Taylor, E.: *Living With a Disability.* Garden City, Blakiston, 1953.

Saville, Shirley: Barkley Avenue, Argyle, New York, 12809. "The Able Disabled," *Instructional Material Kit.*

Seeing Eye, Inc., P.O. Box, Morristown, New Jersey, 07960.

Sensory Aids Foundation, 399 Sherman Avenue, Suite 4, Palo Alto, California, 94306, (415) 329-0430.

Stanwix House, Inc., Pittsburgh, Pennsylvania. Publishers of large type books.

Steed, F.: *A Special Picture Cookbook.* Lawrence, Kansas, H & H Enterprises, 1974.

Talking Books, Lioraphone Inc., 15 E. 48th Street, New York, New York (see American Printing House for the Blind, Library of Congress).*

Talon Velcro Consumer Education and Velcro Corporation. *Convenience Clothing and Closures.* 41 East 51 Street, New York, New York, 10022. A free book of clothing adaptations for the handicapped (illustrated).

Texas Institute for Rehabilitation Research, Texas Medical Center, 1333 Moursund Avenue, Houston, Texas, 77025.

Ulverscroft Large Print Books, F. A. Thorpe Ltd., American representative, 1749 Grand Concourse, Bronx, New York, 10453.

United Cerebral Palsy Association, Inc.* Cerebral Palsy Equipment and Accessories patterns are available for making large size diapers, support vests, safety helmets, and improvised thigh or waist cuffs.

United Cerebral Palsy Research and Educational Foundation. *Non-vocal Communication Resource Book,* University Park, Baltimore, 1978, 228 pp. Book lists hundreds of devices ranging from simple word boards to sophisticated electronic instruments which produce synthesized speech.

Vannier, Maryhelen. *Physical Activities for the Handicapped,* Prentice-Hall, Englewood Cliffs, New Jersey, 1977. Includes list of sources of equipment and supplies.

Vocational Education Resource Materials Collection, Center for Studies in

---

* See Organizations list.

Vocational and Technical Education, 321 Old Education Building, Box 49, University of Wisconsin, Madison, Wisconsin, 53706, "Classroom Organization to Teach the Physically Handicapped," S-1632 Filmstrip.

Washam, V.: *The One-hander's Book: A Basic Guide to Activities of Daily Living.* New York, John Day, 1973.

Zimmerman, Muriel E.: *Self Help Devices for Rehabilitation, Parts I & II.* Published by William C. Brown Company; available from publisher at 135 Locust Street, Dubuque, Iowa; hundreds of self-help devices, gadgets, ideas, etc. for handicapped people. Part I 428 pp., Part II, 228 pp., illustrated.

Zylon Products, Post Office Box 158, West Lafayette, Ohio. Adaptive devices.

ARCHITECTURAL STANDARDS AND ACCESSIBILITY

American Association for the Advancement of Science (AAAS) Project on the Handicapped in Science, *Barrier Free Meetings: A Guide for Professional Associations.*

American Institute of Architects *AIA Journal,* "Buildings for All to Use," Reprinted by the National Easter Seal Society, March, 1969, for Crippled Children and Adults.

American Library Association. Standards for Library Services for the Blind and Physically Handicapped, 50 East Huron Street, Chicago, Illinois 60611, 1967.

American National Standards Institution, Inc., 1430 Broadway, New York, New York, 10018. *American National Standard, Specifications for Making Buildings and Facilities Accessible to, and Usable by, the Physically Handicapped.*

Annand, Douglas R. (Ed.)—Publisher. *Wheelchair Traveler.* A book containing lists of accessible motels throughout the United States. Ball Hill Road, Milford, New Hampshire, 03055.

Architectural and Transportation Barriers Compliance Board (an agency of the Department of Health, Education and Welfare), Washington, D.C. 20201, or the Airport Operators' Council International, 1700 K Street, NW, Washington, D.C. 20006. The guide, entitled *Access Travel: A Guide to Accessibility of Airport Terminals,* covers 118 airports in U.S., Canada, England, Germany, Switzerland, New Zealand, and Australia. It lists 71 different airport features, such as reserved parking areas, wheelchair ramps, etc.

Birch, Jack and Johnstone, Kenneth: *Designing Schools and Schooling for the Handicapped.* Springfield, Thomas, 1975.

Committee on Employment of the Handicapped, Washington, D.C., 20210. *Architectural Checklist, Making Colleges and Universities Accessible to Handicapped Students.*

Easter Seal Society. *Wisconsin's Capitol with Ease, Guidebook for the Physically Handicapped, Disabled Veterans, Senior Citizens.* MOBIL and Dane County Easter Seal Society, no date.

Edgington, Eugene S.: Colleges and Universities with Special Provisions for Wheelchair Students, *J Rehabil,* official publication of the National Rehabilitation Association, May-June, 1963, Vol. XXIX, No. 3, pp. 14-15; available from the National Paraplegia Foundation, 333 N. Michigan Avenue, Chicago, Illinois, 60601.

Gentil, Eric A.: *A Layperson's Guide on Building Evaluation.* Lansing, Michigan. Office of Special Programs, Environmental Studies, Michigan State University, 1975.

Goldsmith, Selwyn: *Designing for the Disabled,* 2nd ed. New York, McGraw, 1967.

Gutman, Ernest M.: *Wheelchair to Independence.* Springfield, Thomas, 1968.

Institute of Physical Medicine and Rehabilitation, 400 E. 34th Street, New York, New York, 10016. "A Severely Handicapped Homemaker Goes Back to Work in Her Own Kitchen."

Kira, A.: *The Bathroom: Criteria for Design.* Ithaca, New York: Center for Housing and Environmental Studies, Cornell University, 1966. This book gives many floor plans and ideas for convenient bathrooms for the disabled.

Laus, Michael D.: *Travel Instruction for the Handicapped.* Springfield, Thomas, 1977.

McCullough, Helen E. and Farnham, Mary B.: *Kitchens for Women in Wheelchairs.* University of Illinois Bulletin, Circular 841, Volume 70, No. 24, September 29, 1972.

Michelle Morgan of Interface, Box 5688, Raleigh, North Carolina 27607. Monograph on "Design Criteria for People with Deafness."

National Endowment for the Arts, 850 Third Avenue, New York, New York 10022. *Arts and the Handicapped: An Issue of Access.* Excellent guide for all types of disability to accessible theaters, museums, colleges, special schools, community service centers, etc.

National Park Service, U.S. Department of the Interior, *National Park Guide for the Handicapped,* U.S. Govt. Print. Office, Washington, D.C., 20402, #2405 0286 (79 pp.).

Olson, Sharon C. and Meredith, Diane K.: *Wheelchair Interiors,* National Easter Seal Society for Crippled Children and Adults, 1973.

Paralyzed Veterans of America, Inc., 7315 Wisconsin Avenue, Suite 301-W, Washington, D.C., 20014. Pamphlet: *Motels with Wheelchair Units,* 1971.

President's Committee on Employment of the Handicapped, Washington, D. C. 20210, 1975 (free). *First Ponder, Then Dare.* Illustrated brochure of 14 accessible colleges and universities.

President's Committee on Employment of the Handicapped, Washington, D.C., 20210, no date. *People are asking about displaying the symbol of access.*

Recreation Resource Center. *Design Standards to Accommodate People with Physical Disabilities in Park and Open Space Planning,* Ries, Michael. Recreation Resources Center, University of Wisconsin-Extension, 1973.

Sawyer, Ernest M.: *Where Turning Wheels Stop,* published by Paralyzed Veterans of America, available from publisher at 3636 16th Street, NW, Washington, D.C. 20010; list of hotels, motels, and restaurants accessible to wheelchair users plus travelling tips (60 pp.).

Schoenbohm, W.: *Planning and Operating Facilities for Crippled Children.* Springfield, Thomas, 1962.

State University Construction Fund, 194 Washington Avenue, Albany, New York, 12210, January, 1974. *Making Facilities Accessible to the Physically Handicapped.*

The Travel Information Center, Moss Rehabilitation Hospital, 12th Street and Tabor Road, Philadelphia, Pennsylvania, 19141 (will send about any area of the country that will be visited).

United Cerebral Palsy. *Design and Planning of an Elementary School for Handicapped and Normal Children,* B. Rowles. Reprint: Considerations of site, entrance, rails, equipment, toilets, fountains, lounges.

Vocational Education Resource Materials Collection Center for Studies in Vocational and Technical Education, 321 Old Education Building, Box 49, University of Wisconsin, Madison, Wisconsin, 53706. Filmstrip: "Making Vocational Education Accessible to the Physically Handicapped."

Wheelchair Traveler, 1975, Ball Hill Road, Milford, New Hampshire, 03055.

Wheeler, Virginia Hart: *Planning Kitchens for Handicapped Homemakers,* Rehabilitation Monograph XXVII, the Institute of Physical Medicine and Rehabilitation, no date.

Yuker, Harold E., Revenson, Joyce and Fracchia, John F.: *The Modification of Educational Equipment and Curriculum for Maximum Utilization by Physically Disabled Persons, Design of a School for Physically Disabled Students,* Human Resources Center, Albertson, New York, 11507, 1968.

ORGANIZATIONS

"We are all so much together, but we are all dying of loneliness."
Albert Schweitzer

"A thousand times everyday I remind myself that my inner and outer life depends on the labors of other men, living and dead, and that I must exert myself in order to give in the same measure I have received and still am receiving."
Albert Einstein

THE ORGANIZATIONS listed below should be of interest to physically handicapped persons, parents of exceptional children, and teachers. Those with asterisks (*) have an extensive list of helpful publications, often free or at cost, suitable for teachers, students, and parents. Some provide extensive services to their clientele. The author is indebted to many of these groups and agencies for information included in the book.

Often, states, cities, and towns will have community affiliates of these groups, which can be of great help to local residents. Offices can often be contacted through the local education department, universities, the Community Chest, Departments of Health, hospitals in an area, or from the telephone directory. The reference departments in public libraries may also be helpful.

Parents, teachers, and others do not have to go it alone when confronted by disabilities and health problems. The teacher may have to pay attention to the organizational professional hierarchies mentioned earlier when linking the appropriate agency to the individuals in need of help. On the other hand, it cannot be assumed that other professionals, such as social workers or physicians, actually know or will communicate what resources are available, what benefits are due to disability groups, and what information is available, even though these may relate closely to their professional interests. Therefore, the teacher is urged to be a tactful but aggressive advocate of handicapped children and their families,

380

and of adults also, who often do not know where to turn for assistance.

GENERAL ORGANIZATIONS

Academy of Dentistry for the Handicapped, 10518 Wellworth, Westwood, California 96137.

*Alexander Graham Bell Association for the Deaf Affiliates are: International Parents Organization, Oral Deaf Adults Sector, American Organization for the Education of the Hearing Impaired, The Volta Bureau for the Deaf, 3417 Volta PC, NW, Washington, D.C. 20007.

*Allergy Foundation of America, 801 Second Avenue, New York, New York 10017.

American Academy of Allergy, Insect Committee; 756 Milwaukee Street, Milwaukee, Indiana 53202.

American Academy of Pediatrics, 1801 Hinman Avenue, Evanston, Illinois 60204.

American Association for Health, Physical Education and Recreation, 1201 16th Street, Washington, D.C. 20036. Information and Research Utilization Center in Physical Education and Recreation for the Handicapped (IRUC).

American Association for Maternal and Child Health, 116 S. Michigan Avenue, Chicago, Illinois 60603.

*American Association of Mental Deficiency, 5201 Connecticut Avenue, NW, Washington, D.C. 20015. This organization publishes a scholarly journal.

*American Cancer Society, 219 East 42nd Street, New York, New York 10017. (Lost Chord Clubs for laryngectomees). Many pamphlets, services, and lists are supplied by the branches and affiliates of this large organization.

*American Cleft Palate Association, 331 Salk Hall, University of Pittsburgh, Pittsburgh, Pennsylvania 15261. *Cleft Palate Journal* is their professional publication.

American Coalition of Citizens with Disabilities (ACCD), 346 Connecticut Avenue, NW, Washington, D.C. 20036.

American College of Obstetricians and Gynecologists, 79 W. Monroe Street, Chicago, Illinois 60603.

American Council of the Blind, 818 18th Street, NW, Suite 700, Washington, D.C. 20006.

*American Foundation for Blind, 15 West 16th Street, New York, New York, 10011. Reference and circulating library of pamphlets and books relating to blindness. Manufacturers of Talking Books.

American Medical Association, 535 N. Dearborn Street, Chicago, Illinois 60610.

*American Diabetes Association, 18 East 48th Street, New York, New York 10017. Many pamphlets, bibliographies, resources are available. List of summer camps for diabetic children.

*American Heart Association, 7320 Greenville Avenue, Dallas, Texas 75231 (Information on Mended Hearts Clubs). Life Saving Courses are sponsored.

*American Lung Association (formerly the National Tuberculosis and Respiratory Disease Association, Christmas Seal League of Southwest Pennsylvania), 2851 Bedford Avenue, Pittsburgh, Pennsylvania 15219.

American Recreation Society, Hospital Recreation Section, 1404 New York Avenue, NW, Washington, D.C.

*American Red Cross National Headquarters, 17th and D Streets, NW, Washington, D.C. 20006. Recreation service for the handicapped. First aid and safety courses, literature, transportation for the handicapped and other services are offered through local affiliates.

*American Speech and Hearing Association, 9030 Old Georgetown Road, Washington, D.C. 20014.

*American Trauma Society (concerned with accidental death and disability, and life saving), Arlington and Detroit Avenues, Toledo, Ohio 46615.

Amyotrophic Lateral Sclerosis Foundation, Inc., 2840 Adams Avenue, San Diego, California 92116.

Architectural and Transportation Barriers Compliance Board, Switzer Building, Washington, D.C. 20201.

Arthogryposis Association, 106 Herkimer Street, North Bellmore, New York 11710.

*Arthritis Foundation, 1212 Avenue of the Americas, New York, New York 10036.

*Association for Children with Learning Disabilities, 2200 Brownsville Road, Pittsburgh, Pennsylvania 15210.

*Association for Education of the Visually Handicapped, 1604 Spruce Street, Philadelphia, Pennsylvania 19103.

*Association for the Aid of Crippled Children, 345 E. 46th Street, New York, New York 10617.

Association for the Visually Handicapped, 1839 Frankfort Avenue, Louisville, Kentucky 40306.

Association of Rehabilitation Centers, 828 Davis Street, Evanston, Illinois.

Boy Scouts of America, North Brunswick, New Jersey 08902. Scouting information for boys with handicaps.

Camp Fire Girls, Inc., 1740 Broadway, New York, New York 10019.

Cancer Patients Anonymous, 48 Cedar Valley Lane, Huntington, New York 11743.

Center for Sickle Cell Anemia, College of Medicine, Howard University, 520 W Street, NW, Washington, D.C. 20001.

The Center on Human Policy, 216 Ostrom Avenue, Syracuse, New York 13210. An advocacy organization for people with special needs. The Human Policy Press publishes and distributes information concerning the needs and rights of the handicapped.

Center for Independent Living, 2539 Telegraph Avenue, Berkeley, California 94704.

Children's Defense Fund, 1520 New Hampshire Avenue, NW, Washington, D.C. 20036, "Your Rights Under the Education for All Handicapped Children Act."

*CLOSER LOOK, The Special Education Information Center, Box 1492, Washington, D.C. 20013. Specializes in helping parents and others find services for children with mental, physical, emotional and learning handicaps.

Comeback, Inc., 16 West 46th Street, New York, New York.

Committee for the Handicapped, People-to-People Program, 1028 Connecticut Avenue, Washington, D. C. 20036, (202) 223-4450.

Committee on the Treatment of Intractable Pain, Suite 302, 2001 S Street, NW, Washington, D.C. 20009.

Committee to Combat Huntington's Disease, 250 West 57th Street, New York, New York 10019.

Compassionate Friends, P.O. Box 1347, Oakbrook, Illinois 60521. A self help group for parents who have lost children.

*Conference of American Instructors of the Deaf, an organization of teachers of the hearing impaired. Jointly publishes the *American Annals of the Deaf.*

Cooley's Anemia Blood and Research Foundation for Children, Inc., Hyde Park, New York.

Coordinating Council for Handicapped Children, 407 South Dearborn, Chicago, Illinois 60605, (312) 939-3513. A non-profit coalition of parents and professional groups, whose purpose to improve services to all handicapped children. It offers information and referral services to parents; conducts workshops; and publishes a variety of booklets and guides.

*Council for Exceptional Children, 1920 Association Drive, Reston, Virginia 22091. Free phone—800-336-3728. A department of the National Education Association; publishes journals, books about all exceptionalities. CEC offers a Professional Liability Protection Plan (PLPP) to CEC members. This policy provides liability protection coverage for three distinct areas when your actions cause: bodily injury to another; damage to property of another; and personal injury (libel, slander, etc.) to another.

Deaf Blind Regional Centers, 10 centers operate under the auspices of the Bureau of Education for the Handicapped, Washington, D.C.

Developmentally Disabled (Polling Magazine), 122 East 23rd Street, New York, New York 10010.

Epilepsy Foundation of America, 729 F Street, NW, Washington, D.C. 20005.

*Epilepsy Information Center, 73 Tremont Street, Boston, Massachusetts 02108. Free films, speakers, and pamphlets are available.

*Epilepsy Information Center, Inc., Room 204, 73 Tremont Street, Boston, Massachusetts 02108.

*Family Service Association of America, 44 East 23rd Street, New York, New York, 1964.

*Foundation for Research and Education in Sickle Cell Disease, 421-431 West 120th Street, New York, New York 10027.

Friedreich's Ataxia Group in America, Inc., Box 11116, Oakland, California 94611.

Goodwill Industries of America, Inc., 9200 Wisconsin Avenue, Washington, D.C., 20014. Training, work evaluation, placement and employment of handicapped adults in many regions of the country.

Handicapped Aid Program (HAP), which was formed in 1972 to help disabled persons in the hobby of shortwave listening (SWL). Lawrence I. Cotarin, 8041 North Hamlin, Skokie, Illinois 60076.

Human Growth, Inc., 1900 McElderry Street, Baltimore, Maryland 21205. A parent's group under the auspices of NPA, National Pituitary Agency, sponsored by National Institute of Health and College of American Pathologists.

Institute for the Crippled and Disabled, 400 1st Avenue, New York, New York.

*Institute of Rehabilitation Medicine, New York University Medical Center, 400 East 34th Street, New York, New York 10016.

*International Association of Laryngectomees, 219 East 42nd Street, New York, New York 10017, sponsored by the National Cancer Society.

Joint Commission on Accreditation of Hospitals, 875 North Michigan Avenue, Chicago, Illinois 60611.

Kennedy, Joseph P., Jr. Foundation (for mental retardation), Suite 205, 1701 K Street, NW, Washington, D.C.

The Lighthouse New York Association for the Blind, P.O. Box 126, Owatonna, Minnesota 55060. Sponsors a broad program of recreation. Lighthouse Music Schools trains amateurs and professionals.

Little People of America, Inc., (Pres.) Gerald Rasa, P.O. Box 97, Greenville, Pennsylvania 16125.

Lupus Foundation of America, Inc., 11675 Holly Springs Drive, St. Louis, Missouri 63141.

*Muscular Dystrophy Associations of America, Inc., 1790 Broadway, New York, New York 10019. Much information and service is offered by this organization.

National Aid to the Visually Handicapped, 3201 Balboa Street, San Francisco, California 94121. A volunteer organization concentrating on large type materials for the school age.

*National Association for Retarded Children, 2709 Avenue E, East Arlington, Texas 76011. Legal services, preschools, workshops and political activities are offered in regional branches.

*National Association for the Retarded, New York, New York.

National Association for Practical Nurses Education and Service, 654 Madison Avenue, New York, New York 10021. 800 homemaker health aide programs provide an aide in families with chronically ill or disabled members.

National Association of Councils of Stutterers, Speech and Hearing Clinic, Catholic University of America, Washington, D.C. 20064.

National Association of Hearing and Speech Agencies, 919 18th Street, NW, Washington, D.C. 20006.

*National Association of Sheltered Workshops and Homebound Programs, 1522 K Street, NW, Washington, D.C. 20005.

*National Association of Social Workers, 2 Park Avenue, New York, New York 10016.

National Association of the Deaf, run solely by and for the deaf; publications: *Deaf American, NAD Newsletter, Junior Deaf American,* 814 Thayer Avenue, Silver Spring, Maryland 20910.

National Center for a Barrier Free Environment, 8401 Connecticut Avenue, Washington, D.C. 20015.

National Center for Law and the Handicapped, 1235 N. Eddy Street, South Bend, Indiana 46617. *Amicus* is a bimonthly publication.

National Center for Deaf-Blind Youth and Adults, Hyde Park, New York.

National Committee for Prevention of Child Abuse, Box 2866, Chicago, Illinois 60690.

*National Council for Home-maker Health Aide Services, Inc., 1740 Broadway, New York, New York 10019.

*National Cystic Fibrosis Research Foundation, 521 Fifth Avenue, New York, New York 10017.

National Disabled Law Officers Association, Inc., 75 New Street, Nutley, New Jersey 07110.

*National Easter Seal Society for Crippled Children and Adults, 2023 West Ogden Avenue, Chicago, Illinois 60612.

National Environmental Health Association, 1600 Pennsylvania Avenue, Denver, Colorado 80203.

*The National Foundation-March of Dimes, 800 Second Avenue, New York, New York 10017. A list of the location of many genetic counseling services can be obtained, as well as bulletins, pamphlets.

National Federation of the Blind, 218 Randolph Hotel Building, Des Moines, Iowa 50309.

*National Health Council, Inc., 1740 Broadway, New York, New York 10019. Career information in the health fields.

*National Hemophilia Foundation, 25 West 39th Street, New York, New York 10018.

The National Institute for Rehabilitation Engineering, Pompton Lakes, New Jersey.

*National Kidney Foundation, 116 E. 27th Street, New York, New York 10016.

*National Multiple Sclerosis Society, 257 Park Avenue, South, New York, New York 10010.

*National Paraplegia Foundation, 333 N. Michigan Avenue, Chicago, Illinois 60601. Film: "No Man Walks Alone."

National Pituitary Agency, Suite 503-7, 210 W. Fayette Street, Baltimore, Maryland 21201.

*National Society for Prevention of Blindness, Inc., 79 Madison Avenue, New York, New York 10016.

National Poison Center Network, 125 De Soto Street, Pittsburgh, Pennsylvania 15213; 412-681-7423. Information and standardization of treatment on poisons.

National Recreation Association, Consulting Service on Recreation for the Ill and Handicapped, 8 West 8th Street, New York, New York 10011. Publishes books and bibliographies; 11 district offices.

National Tuberculosis and Respiratory Disease Association (see American Lung Association).

*National Rehabilitation Association, 1522 K Street, NW, Suite 1120, Washington, D.C. 20005.

National Safety Council, 425 N. Michigan Avenue, Chicago, Illinois.

National Self-Help Clearing House, 184 5th Avenue, New York, New York 10010. Lists self-help organizations.

National Tay-Sachs and Allied Diseases Association, Inc., 200 Park Avenue, South, New York, New York 10003.

Office of Independent Living for the Disabled, Office of Housing-HUD, Washington, D.C.

Office of the Assistant to the Secretary of HUD, Programs for the Elderly and Handicapped, Washington, D.C. 20410.

*Osteogenesis Imperfecta, Inc., 1231 May Court, Burlington, North Carolina 27215.

Our Way, 4304 Bradley Lane, Chevy Chase, Maryland 20015. A non-profit group concerned with the problems of disabled in general and specifically with those who may be single-handed.

Paralyzed Veterans of America, 7315 Wisconsin Avenue, Suite 301-W, Washington, D.C. 20014.

Parent Network, 1211 Chestnut Street, Philadelphia, Pennsylvania 19107, (215) M19-9292. This volunteer organization is comprised of parents of handicapped children who assist and support others who have a newly diagnosed handicapped child.

Public Health Service, Office of Public Inquiries, Bethesda, Maryland 20034. Information on birth defects.

Programs for the Handicapped, Office for Handicapped Individuals, Washington, D.C. 20201.

*Planned Parenthood—World Population, 810 7th Avenue, New York, New York 10019. Services for the handicapped are included in many regional agencies. These may include counseling, fertility, contraceptive, sterilization, abortion information, and service.

*President's Committee on Employment of the Handicapped, Washington, D.C. 20210.

Registry of Interpretors for the Deaf. These are certified interpreters. The council maintains membership directory.

Registry of Medical Rehabilitation Therapists and Specialists, 4975 Judy Lynn, Memphis, Tennessee 38118.

Rehabilitation Engineering, Office of Research and Demonstrations, Social and Rehabilitation Service, Room 5320, South HEW Building, Washington, D.C. 20201.

Rehabilitation International, 432 Park Avenue, South, New York, New York 10013.

Rehabilitation Services Administration, Office of Human Development, Department of Health, Education, and Welfare, Washington, D.C. 20201.

*Sickle Cell Society, Inc. of Pittsburgh and Southwestern Pennsylvania, Medical Center East, Suite 742, 211 Whitfield Street, Pittsburgh, Pennsylvania 15206.

Small Business Administration: Handicapped Assistance Loans, The Washington District Office, 1080 15th Street, NW, Washington, D.C. 20417.

Spina Bifida Association of America, 104 Festone Avenue, New Castle, Delaware.

State Bureaus of Vocational Rehabilitation Services under the Office of Vocational Rehabilitation in the Department of Health, Education and Welfare. Provides education and services to persons 16 and over to prepare for employment. This agency should be contacted by most handicapped teenagers when making vocational decisions.

Stroke Clubs of America, 805 12th Street, Galveston, Texas 77550. Ellis Williamson, President.

Telephone Pioneers of America, a volunteer organization of senior telephone industry employees who repair and restore talking book machines and transcribe Braille in chapters in nearly all 50 states.

Totally Disabled Helpers Association, 217 Hullett Street, No. 3, Long Beach, California 90805.

The Troubleshooters, Northwest Center for the Retarded, 1600 West Armory Way, Seattle, Washington 98119. Consumer/civil rights group working on behalf of all handicapped citizens. The Troubleshooters communicates through a monthly newsletter *The Inside Scoop*.

*United Cerebral Palsy Association, Inc., 321 West 44th Street, New York, New York 10036. Sheltered workshops, preschools, research and publications are sponsored by regional affiliates of this group.

United Ostomy Association, Inc., 1111 Wilshire Boulevard, Los Angeles, California 90017. *Ostomy Quarterly*.

*United States Children's Bureau, Washington, D.C. 20013, National Center on Child Abuse and Neglect.

*U.S. Government Printing Office, Washington, D.C.

*U.S. Office of Education, Department of Health, Education, and Welfare, Bureau of Education for the Handicapped, Washington, D.C. 20201.

Veterans Administration Central Office, Spinal Cord Injury Service, 810 Vermont Avenue, NW, Washington, DC 20420.

Veterans Administration Prosthetics Center, Bioengineering Research Service, 252 Seventh Avenue, New York, New York 10001.

*Vocational Rehabilitation Administration, Washington, D.C. 20201. Magazine: The Rehabilitation Record.

WHEELCHAIR ORGANIZATIONS

American Wheelchair Bowling Association, 2635 NE 19th Street, Pompano Beach, Florida 33062 (Bowling).

National Wheelchair Athletic Association, 40-24 62nd Street, Woodside, New York 11377.

National Wheelchair Basketball Association, 110 Seaton Building, University of Kentucky, Lexington, Kentucky 40506 (Basketball).

Rehabilitation-Education Center, University of Illinois, Oak Street at Stadium Drive, Champaign, Illinois 61820 (Football).

National Wheelchair Athletic Association, 40-24 62nd Street, Woodside, New York 11377 (Table Tennis, Weight Lifting, Swimming).

The National Archery Association, Ronks, Pennsylvania 17572.

Committee for the Promotion of Camping for the Handicapped, 2056 South Bluff Road, Traverse City, Michigan 49684 (Camping).

North American Recreation, P.O. Box 758, Bridgeport, Connecticut 06601 (Sporting Equipment for Handicapped).

Bill Blackwood, 1117 Rising Hill, Escondido, California 92025 (Flying Controls).

Arizona Wheelchair Pilots Association, 7008 Willetta, Scottsdale, Arizona 85257 (Flying Clubs).

Southern California Wheelchair Aviators, 671 North Dexford, La Habra, California 90631 (Flying).

Wheelchair Pilots Association, 11018 102nd Avenue, N., Largo, Florida 33540 (Flying).

National Amputation Foundation, 12-45 180th Street, Whitestone, New York 11357 (212) 767-0596.

National Information Center for the Handicapped, Box 1492, Washington, D.C. 20013.
American Wheelchair Bowling Association, 2635 NE 19th Street, Pompano Beach, Florida 33062.
Boy Scouts of America, Scouting for the Handicapped, North Brunswick, New Jersey 08902.
Boy Scouts of America, Scouting for the Handicapped, Allegheny Trails Council, Flag Plaza, Pittsburgh, Pennsylvania 15219.
Girl Scouts of the USA, Scouting for the Handicapped, 830 Third Avenue, New York, New York 10022.
National Association of the Physically Handicapped, 6473 Granville Avenue, Detroit, Michigan 48228.
National Inconvenienced Sportmen's Association, 3728 Walnut Avenue, Carmichael, California 95608.
National Wheelchair Basketball Association, Box 100, Rehabitation and Education Center, Oak Street and Stadium Drive, Champaign, Illinois 61820.

Magazines for Wheelchair Users

Accent on Living. Quarterly. 802 Reinthaler, Bloomington, Illinois 61701. Free subscription for handicapped available.
COPH Bulletin. Quarterly of the National Congress of Organizations of the Physically Handicapped, Inc. 1405 Yale Place, Minneapolis, Minnesota 55403.
Courage. Bimonthly of the Fraternity of the Wooden Leg, Inc. 600 South Oak Street, Sapulpa, Oklahoma 74066. Free to all newly amputated persons.
DAV Magazine. Monthly of Disabled American Veterans. 1425 East McMillan Street, Cincinnati, Ohio 45206.
NAPH National Newsletter. Quarterly of the National Association of the Physically Handicapped. Editor Mary Ellen Howard, 405 Colonial Avenue, Portage, Michigan 49081.
National Hookup. Monthly newspaper of the Indoor Sports Club, Inc. 1255 Val Vista, Pomona, California 91766.
New Horizons. Quarterly of New Horizons, Inc. 2150 Corbin Avenue, New Britain, Connecticut 06053.
The Open Window. Monthly of the National Shut-In Society, Inc. 102 N. 34th Avenue, Longport, New Jersey 08403.
Paraplegia News. Monthly of the Paralyzed Veterans of America and the National Paraplegia Foundation, founded 1947. 935 Coastline Drive, Seal Beach, California 90740.
Toomey j Gazette. Semi-annually by, for, and about respiratory polios. Box 149, Chagrin Falls, Ohio 44022.

INDEX

391